Computerized Accounting with
QuickBooks® 2015
2017-2018 Update

GAYLE WILLIAMS
Sacramento City College

Cambridge
BUSINESS PUBLISHERS

Editor-in-Chief: George Werthman
Vice President, Brand Management: Marnee Fieldman
Digital Marketing Manager: Dana Vinyard
Managing Editor: Katie Jones-Aiello
Development Editor: Jocelyn Mousel
Product Developer: Jill Sternard
Compositor: T&D Graphics
Designer: Michael Warrell, Design Solutions

COMPUTERIZED ACCOUNTING WITH QUICKBOOKS 2015, 2017-2018 Update, by Gayle Williams

ISBN 978-1-61853-249-7

Bookstores & Faculty: to order this book, contact the company via email **customerservice@cambridgepub.com** or call 800-619-6473.

Students: to order this book, please visit the book's Website and order directly online.

Printed in the United States of America.

10 9 8 7 6 5 4 3 2

About the Author

 **Gayle Williams** is a Professor of Accounting at Sacramento City College, where she teaches computerized accounting. She received a BA in Comparative Literature and an MBA with a concentration in Accounting from the University of Washington. Professor Williams holds a CPA certification from the states of Washington and California and has worked in public accounting, with Voldal Wartelle & Co, P.S and Moss Adams LLP, and in private industry.

Preface

Welcome to *Computerized Accounting with QuickBooks 2015*. I wrote this book to give students an introduction to QuickBooks that focuses not only on the software mechanics, but also on the basic accounting concepts that underlie all accounting systems.

This book is not meant to be a user manual. It is meant to teach students how they can work with a computerized accounting system. It is my intention that students will come away from this book with an understanding that it is knowledge of the principles of accounting, not data-entry skills, that are needed to be successful in business.

TARGET AUDIENCE

This book is primarily intended for use in undergraduate accounting programs, although it could be used in business or computer information programs as well. It is expected that students taking this course have already successfully completed a course in financial accounting and have a firm understanding of the principles as well as the mechanics of accounting.

ACCESS TO 140-DAY TRIAL OF QUICKBOOKS 2015

Each new copy of this book includes access to a 140-day trial of the QuickBooks 2015 Pro software. Students should refer to the insert at the front of the book which contains the code and instructions on downloading access to the complimentary software.

OUTSTANDING FEATURES OF THIS BOOK

Structure

The book is designed in such a way that the accounting concepts, as well as the software mechanics, get more complex with each section. Other books focus primarily on software data entry. This book allows the students to see why events are recorded the way they are in a computerized accounting system while refreshing students' knowledge of accounting concepts and reinforcing the accounting and journal entries behind transactions.

Furthermore, rather than treating all company types in one chapter (as most computerized accounting books do), service, merchandising, and project-based companies are broken out separately. This approach helps students learn how the software applications would be implemented in a business environment, so they can practice computerized accounting as they would in the real world.

- *Section One—Introduction*
  - The first chapter introduces students to the basic structure of Quick-Books 2015.
    - File types
    - Lists
    - Navigational tools
    - Preferences

- *Section Two—Service Companies*
  - The next three chapters (Chapters 2, 3, and 4) cover the sales, purchase, and end-of-month cycles in a service company.
  - Students are introduced to accounting for basic accounting transactions in a computerized environment.
    - Sales on account and cash sales
    - Purchases on account and cash purchases
    - Customer collections and vendor payments
    - Bank reconciliations
    - Standard end-of-month adjusting entries
    - Financial statement reporting

- *Section Three—Merchandising Companies*
  - The section introduction includes a description of internal controls in QuickBooks.
  - Chapters 5, 6, and 7 cover the sales, purchase, and end-of-month cycles in a merchandising company.
  - Students are introduced to accounting for more complex transactions in a computerized environment.
    - Purchase and sale of inventory
    - Sales tax
    - Sales and purchase discounts
    - Inventory tracking, adjustment, and valuation
    - Sales of equipment
    - Bad debts and bounced checks

- *Section Four—Payroll, Project Costing, and Billing for Time*
  - Chapter 8 covers basic payroll functions that would be used in all types of companies (service, merchandising, and manufacturing).
    - Compensation (salaried and hourly)
    - Paycheck creation
    - Payroll taxes (withholding and remittance)
  - Chapter 9 covers job costing and billing for time.
    - Tracking time
    - Billing for time and expense
    - Tracking and reporting profitability by project

- *Section Five—Beyond the Basics*
  - Chapter 10 covers budgeting and segment reporting.
    - Creating budgets
    - Budget variance reports
    - Use class tracking to report on business segments
  - Chapter 11 covers a number of special tools in QuickBooks.
    - Memorizing reports and transactions
    - Customization of forms
    - Custom reporting
    - Exporting reports to Excel.
    - Creating reversing entries
  - Chapter 12 covers the initial set up of companies in QuickBooks and the conversion of existing companies to QuickBooks.
  - Chapter 13 provides an overview of QuickBooks Online.

Clear Writing

The author's focus on clarity and readability is a cornerstone of the text, and review feedback has been overwhelmingly positive about the quality of the writing and student comprehension. The book is written clearly to aid student understanding of difficult concepts. Clear explanations of why certain procedures are used in QuickBooks are supported by relevant examples and relatable end-of-chapter assignments, serving to bridge the gap between computerized accounting concepts and real-world application.

Real-World Scenarios

Most computerized accounting textbooks on the market approach the teaching of QuickBooks in a prescriptive manner, going through the procedures of the software while overlooking how an accountant would actually utilize the software in the real world. Williams's *Computerized Accounting* takes a practical approach and shows the student how the software is used in a business environment. In addition to the standard financial reports, students are exposed to job (project) costing, segment, and variance reports.

Unique Pedagogy

The book's four-color format facilitates student understanding and draws attention to the key concepts and pedagogy. Ample screenshots provide students realistic snapshots of what they will see when working in the software. A host of pedagogical elements serve as helpful illustrations, providing additional context and further concept reinforcement.

HINT Boxes

HINT boxes appear throughout to provide helpful quick tips and tricks for how to work in Quickbooks.

 HINT: To see the release currently installed on your computer, press the F2 key on your keyboard. (You must be in QuickBooks.) The release is identified after the product name. The screenshots in this textbook are from R10P.

WARNING Boxes

WARNING boxes highlight common pitfalls to avoid.

WARNING: You can only reorder accounts that are located within the same account type.

BEHIND THE SCENES Boxes

BEHIND THE SCENES boxes provide additional context in support of the accounting that is going on inside the computer.

BEHIND THE SCENES The journal entries related to transactions are automatically created by QuickBooks and posted to the general ledger when the "form" is completed (saved). Subsidiary ledgers, trial balances, and financial statements are also automatically updated every time a transaction is entered.

QuickChecks

> "QuickChecks are beneficial to students, as they…allow the student to relate the concept to what they learned in their accounting principles course."
>
> **Amy Chataginer**
> *Mississippi Gulf Coast Community College*

When students are learning accounting application software, it's natural for them to focus on the software mechanics and forget that they're taking an accounting course. To help put some of their focus back on accounting, students are periodically asked a question related to material covered in the chapter. The questions are intended to remind them, either directly or indirectly, of underlying accounting concepts. The answers are included at the end of each chapter.

QuickCheck 1-2 Why aren't purchase orders, sales orders, and estimates considered accounting transactions? (Answer at end of chapter.)

Key Terms

Appearing in red, bold font in the first instance, key terms are defined for the student in the margins of the text for a quick refresher. A comprehensive glossary is included in the back of the book.

Other Lists in Quickbooks

There are a number of other lists used in QuickBooks.

Inventory Goods purchased or produced for sale to customers.

The **item list** contains information about every product sold or service provided by the organization. **Items** are used when billing customers and when purchasing **inventory** in QuickBooks. The **payroll item list** contains information about every type of compensation and every employer and employee payroll tax specific to the organization. **Payroll items** are used when entering timesheets and when creating paychecks in QuickBooks.

Some lists represent options that might be used. For example, there is a list of customer

Practice Exercises

Practice Exercises are included at the end of every section in the first ten chapters. The exercises provide students an immediate opportunity to practice the material they just learned and prepare them for completing the chapter assignments. The exercises use a fictional but realistic company that provides accounting services to small business clients.

The Practice Exercises can be done in class, with the instructor, as part of the lecture component of the course or can be done by the students, on their own, as part of the lab component of the course. Check figures are included with the exercises to reassure students that they are recording the transactions accurately.

Customize QuickBooks for Sac City Accounting.
(Sac City wants to reduce some of the pop-up warnings.)

1. Change a **Preference**.
   a. Click **Edit**.
   b. Click **Preferences**.
   c. Click **Accounting** (on left bar of screen).
   d. Click **Company Preferences** tab.
   e. For both date warnings, click **Warn if transactions are** and enter "180" for the number of days.
   f. Click **OK**.

PRACTICE EXERCISE

End-of-Chapter Material

End-of-chapter review material includes:

- Chapter shortcuts.

- Chapter review with **matching of terms** to definitions and **multiple choice questions** that are a combination of accounting concepts and QuickBooks application questions.

- End-of-chapter assignments featuring realistic companies. Two sets of assignments are included per chapter, allowing the instructor the ability to change the material assigned to various course sections.

		Industry	Entity
Assignments for Chapters 1–4	Dancing with Dogs	Service	Sole proprietorship
	At Your Service	Service	Sole proprietorship
Assignments for Chapters 5–8	Software to Go	Retail	Corporation
	The Abacus Shop	Retail	Corporation
Assignments for Chapters 9–11	Champion Law	Project costing (service)	Corporation
	Constructed with Style	Project costing (service)	Corporation
Assignments for Chapter 12	Bella Beagles	Service & Retail	Sole proprietorship
	Chewy's Catering	Service	Sole proprietorship

The assignments include check numbers for students. This allows them to focus on the process and reduces student frustration.

End-of-Book Assignment

An optional assignment is provided at the end of the book that instructors can assign as an extra credit assignment. It includes two separate assignments requiring students to identify and correct errors in realistic sets of company files.

> "Using this book with the author's homework assignments gives students a chance to understand accounting concepts better."
>
> **Anne Diamond**
> *Sierra College*

Appendices

There are a number of additional topics that are helpful to students as they master QuickBooks, and these have been included as end-of-chapter and end-of-book appendices. Instructors may wish to cover these topics in class or have students go over on their own time. End-of-chapter appendices on special topics include:

Chapter Appendix	Topic	Description
Appendix 1A	Multi-User Mode	Brief coverage of using QuickBooks in multi-user mode.
Appendix 4A	Getting It Right	Suggestions to help students find errors in their month-end financial statements, mirroring what accountants in industry might look at before publishing financial statements.
Appendix 7A	Optional Year-End Closing Process	Covers an optional year-end closing process for companies that want to reduce the amount of data maintained in QuickBooks at the end of a fiscal year.
Appendix 8A	Tracking Employee Sick and Vacation Time	Covers tracking paid time off in QuickBooks.
Appendix 11A	Using Custom Fields	Creating custom fields in QuickBooks.
Appendix 11B	Using the Report Center	Covers accessing and using the additional features in the Report Center.

Students often have a difficult time seeing any similarities between computerized accounting systems and the more manual systems they saw in their introductory financial accounting classes (the journal entries, T-accounts, and general ledgers). To help students connect the two, **Appendix A (Is Computerized Accounting Really the Same as Manual Accounting?)** is an accounting refresher that compares manual and computerized accounting and provides examples of how journal entries, journals, T-accounts, and trial balances show up in QuickBooks. It also covers cash versus accrual accounting. Other end-of-book appendices review accounting principles and mechanics, including:

Appendix	Title	Description
Appendix B	How Do I?	A summary of shortcuts (also broken out by chapter and included as Chapter Shortcuts at the end of each chapter).
Appendix C	Account and Transaction "Types" Used in QuickBooks Pro	A summary of account types and transaction types in QuickBooks.
Appendix D	Common Options Available on Various *Form* Toolbars	Common options available on various toolbars in QuickBooks.
Appendix E	Additional Features	Outlines some of the more common features not covered in the book.
Appendix F	What if I Have a Mac at Home?	Options for using QuickBooks with a Mac.

Certiport Mapped

The book has been reviewed by Certiport and maps to the 10 domains that comprise the exam objectives for the QuickBooks Certified User Exam.

What Is the QuickBooks Certified User Exam?

The Intuit® QuickBooks Certification exam is an online exam that is proctored at Certiport Authorized Testing Centers. The certification program validates QuickBooks accounting skills while providing students with credentials that demonstrate real-world abilities to prospective employers. Once passed, test takers receive an official digital certificate representing their skills in QuickBooks.

The author has prepared a map correlating the chapter content to the Certiport domains. The following map will help students focus their review for the QuickBooks User Certification exam so they can streamline their exam preparation:

Mapping of Certiport QuickBooks 2015 Certification Objectives			
Domains		**Objectives a student should know:**	***Computerized Accounting with QuickBooks 2015***
1.0		**QuickBooks Setup**	
	1.1	What information is required before they set up a QuickBooks file	434-467
	1.2	How to start a new company data file in QuickBooks (Easy Step Interview)	New Company: 437–442; Converting existing company: 442–462
	1.3	How to keep the lists and preferences from an old file while removing old transactions	265–269
	1.4	How to customize the home page	18–20; 39–40
	1.5	How to set up lists (customers, vendors, items, etc.). This includes understanding which names and items should appear on which lists.	Chart of accounts list: 25–28; Items: 30–32; 64–67; Customers: 60–64; Vendors: 92–95; Payroll: 279–288; Employees: 290–295; Classes: 373–374; Terms: 102–104; Jobs: 326–329
2.0		**QuickBooks Utilities and General Product Knowledge**	
	2.1	How to navigate or move around QuickBooks (use home page, menus, icon bar, etc.)	17–22
	2.2	How to back up and restore a data file	12–16
	2.3	How to determine the release number and how to update QuickBooks	7
	2.4	How to use QuickBooks in single-user and multi-user mode	52–55
	2.5	What versions and editions of QuickBooks are available for a specific year (desktop versions)	Desktop: 4; Online: 470
	2.6	How to password protect QuickBooks	150–153
	2.7	How and why to use preferences	38-39; 95–98; 218; 278; 330; 343; 371-373; 441
3.0		**List Management**	
	3.1	How to manage lists (customers, vendors, items, etc.). List management includes:	
		3.1.1 Adding new entries	Chart of accounts list: 25–29; Items: 30–32; 64–67; Customers: 60–64; Vendors: 92–95; Payroll: 279–287; Employees: 290–296; Classes: 373–374; Terms: 102–104; Jobs: 326–329
		3.1.2 Deleting entries	Chart of accounts list: 28; Item list: 66; Customers: 60–64; Vendors: 98
		3.1.3 Editing entries	Chart of accounts list: 27; Item list: 66; Customers: 60–64; Vendors: 98; Payroll: 287–288; Employees: 295–296
		3.1.4 Merging entries	249–251

continued

	Domains		Objectives a student should know:	Computerized Accounting with QuickBooks 2015
4.0			**Items**	
	4.1		How QuickBooks uses items to perform the necessary accounting entries	31-33; 64–72; 158–159; 162–165; 166–168
	4.2		The different types of items and when to use each type	64; 158–159; 161–162; 166–168
	4.3		How to use items for different types of scenarios. These include companies that sell:	
		4.3.1	Products for a specified price	162–165
		4.3.2	Services for a specified price	64–65
		4.3.3	Unique products or services that have different prices for each sale	31–33; 64–65
		4.3.4	One service or product	162–165
5.0			**Sales**	
	5.1		Who should be listed in the Customer Center	61–62
	5.2		How to navigate and use the Customer Center	61–63
	5.3		How to complete the workflow (from the sale to making the deposit) for:	
		5.3.1	Invoicing (A/R)	68–70
		5.3.2	Sales Receipts (no A/R)	70–71
	5.4		How QuickBooks uses the Undeposited Funds, Accounts Receivable, and checking accounts in the invoicing cycle.	75–80
	5.5		How and why to record a customer credit	72–74
	5.6		How and why to create statements	183–185
	5.7		How to handle bounced (NSF) checks	175–179
6.0			**Purchases**	
	6.1		Who should be listed in the Vendor Center	92
	6.2		How to navigate and use the Vendor Center	92–98
	6.3		The different workflows for making purchases	
		6.3.1	Entering and paying bills (A/P)	100–110; 109–112
		6.3.2	Writing checks	104–105; 202
		6.3.3	Using a Credit Card	107–108
		6.3.4	Using a Debit Card	104–105
	6.4		How to record the transactions in the purchase workflows	100–112; 206–223
	6.5		How and why to record a Vendor credit	216–219
	6.6		How to complete the inventory workflow (PO to payment)	206–223
	6.7		How to set up, collect, and pay sales tax	156–159
	6.8		Bank reconciliation	123–126
7.0			**Payroll**	
	7.1		The differences between the Payroll Services available from QuickBooks	275
	7.2		How to set up Payroll (including employees, Federal and State taxes, and basic Payroll deductions) using the Payroll Setup Wizard.	446–458

continued

Mapping of Certiport QuickBooks 2015 Certification Objectives			
Domains		Objectives a student should know:	*Computerized Accounting with QuickBooks 2015*
		7.2.1	How to set up an employee's earnings and sick or vacation time	294; 318–324
		7.2.2	How to track sick or vacation time (accruing hours and using "banked" hours)	322–324
	7.3		How and why to setup Payroll Schedules	291
	7.4		How to run Payroll	298–306
	7.5		How and why to pay Payroll Liabilities	272; 306–309
	7.6		How to prepare payroll forms (941, W2) in QuickBooks	309
	7.7		Track time and use it for payroll or for invoicing customers	329–340; 341–345
8.0			**Reports**	
	8.1		Why and how to use the Report Center	430–432
	8.2		How to customize reports (report modifications, collapsing subaccounts, etc.)	35–39
	8.3		The basic question that each report answers (basic understanding of each report)	80–81; 125; 155; 182; 204–205; 223; 237; 241–242; 309–311; 323–324; 336–338; 345–346; 378–380; 386–388; 482–489
	8.4		How and why to process multiple reports	409–411
	8.5		How and why to send reports to Excel (understand and use the basic and advanced tab)	419–421
	8.6		How and why to process multiple reports	same as 8.4
	8.7		How to memorize reports	406–407
9.0			**Basic Accounting**	
	9.1		What the basic financial statements are and a basic understanding of what they mean	480
	9.2		The difference between cash and accrual reports	482–483
	9.3		How and why to set a closing date	132–135
	9.4		How to enter a Journal Entry if asked to do so by an accountant (they do not need to fully understand what accounts to debit or credit)	129–132
10.0			**Customization/Saving Time and Shortcuts**	
	10.1		How and why to memorize transactions (automatically enter)	406–407
	10.2		How to set up multiple users and what level of access can be granted or denied	149–154
	10.3		How and why to create custom fields (customer, vendors, and employees)	426–430
	10.4		How to customize an invoice	411–419

Supplement Package

For Instructors

- **Solutions Manual** files prepared by the author contain solutions to all the assignment material.
- QuickBooks **backup files** for each assignment are available.
- **PowerPoint** presentations illustrate chapter concepts and outline key elements with corresponding screenshots for each chapter.
- For Chapters 8 and 9, **additional check figures** related to payroll are available for instructors who choose to provide them to students.

- **Test Bank** questions written by the author includes true/false and multiple-choice questions for each chapter.
- Two **Midterm and Two Final Exams** prepared by the author are provided and are designed to test students' understanding of the fundamentals of accounting and the mechanics of computerized accounting in a small service business. The midterm exam covers the material included in Chapters 1 through 4. One of the final exams covers the material included in Chapters 1 through 8. The other final exam covers the material included in Chapters 1 through 10. The exams are to be completed using QuickBooks and can be completed in a two-hour class session.
- ^{my}BusinessCourse: A web-based learning and assessment program intended to complement your textbook and classroom instruction. This easy-to-use course management system includes question banks comprised of practice exercises, test bank questions, and assignment questions related to the end of chapter content that can be graded automatically. eLecture videos created and narrated by the author are also available (see below for list). myBusiness Course provides students with additional help when you are not available. In addition, detailed diagnostic tools assess class and individual performance. myBusinessCourse is ideal for online courses or traditional face-to-face courses for which you want to offer students more resources to succeed.
- **Website:** All instructor materials are accessible via the book's website (password protected) along with other useful links and marketing information. www.cambridgepub.com.

For Students

- Access to 140-day trial of QuickBooks 2015 Pro software with purchase of each new copy of the book.
- ^{my}BusinessCourse: A web-based learning and assessment program intended to complement your textbook and faculty instruction. This easy-to-use program grades assignments automatically and provides you with additional help when your instructor is not available. Access is free with new copies of this textbook (look for the page containing the access code towards the front of the book).
- **eLecture Presentations** created and narrated by the author and available in myBusinessCourse cover essential topics and procedures in QuickBooks, including:
  - Creating, opening, and backing up files.
  - Setting up accounts
  - Setting up customers
  - Setting up vendors
  - Setting up employees
  - Setting up payroll items
  - Setting up *items* (one for service, one for product)
  - Paying bills
  - Setting up 1099 vendor tracking
  - Reconciling bank and credit card accounts
  - Preferences in QuickBooks
  - Financial statement presentation hints
  - Customizing reports
- QuickBooks **Student data files** (as .QBB files) are available for download from the book's website.
- **Check Figures** are included for assignments, allowing students to focus on the process and reduce frustration.
- **Website:** Additional useful links are available to students on the book's website.

ACKNOWLEDGMENTS

I would like to thank the following people for their assistance and support. In particular, Anne Diamond and Melani Dovalina. I can't thank Anne and Melani enough. Without them, this book would not exist.

I would also like to thank the following computer accounting faculty from across the country who provided review feedback on the manuscript chapters:

Dave Alldredge, *Salt Lake Community College*

Rick Andrews, *Sinclair Community College*

Felicia Baldwin, *Richard J. Daley College*

Patricia Ball, *Massasoit Community College*

Sara Barritt, *Northeast Community College*

Marilyn Brooks-Lewis, *Warren County Community College*

Amy Chataginer, *Mississippi Gulf Coast Community College*

Dana Cummings, *Lower Columbia College*

Patricia Davis, *Keystone College*

Susan Davis, *Green River College*

Suryakant Desai, *Cedar Valley College*

Anne Diamond, *Sierra College*

Doris Donovan, *Dodge City Community College*

Carol Dutchover, *Eastern New Mexico University, Roswell*

Pennie Eddy, *Lanier Technical College*

Jen Emerson, *Cincinnati State*

Keith Engler, *Richland College*

Rena Galloway, *State Fair Community College*

Patricia Goedl, *University of Cincinnati*

Becky Hancock, *El Paso Community College*

Pat Hartley, *Chaffey College*

Janet Hosmer, *Blue Ridge Community College*

Merrily Hoffman, *San Jacinto College*

Bill Jefferson, *Metropolitan Community College*

Angela Kirkendall, *South Puget Sound Community College*

Becky Knickel, *Brookhaven College*

Christopher Kwak, *De Anza College*

Miriam Lefkowitz, *Brooklyn College*

John Long, *Jackson College*

Heather Lynch, *Northeast Iowa Community College*

Molly McFadden-May, *Tulsa Community College*

Allen Montgomery, *Bridge Valley Community & Technical College*

Sheila Muller, *Northern Essex Community College*

Carolyn Nelson, *Coffeyville Community College*

Jeffrey Niccum, *Spokane Falls Community College*

Lisa Novak, *Mott Community College*

Joanne Orabone, *Community College of Rhode Island*

Margaret Pond, *Front Range Community College*

Mark Quinlan, *Madison College*

Kristen Quinn, *Northern Essex Community College*

Robin Reilly, *American River College*

Cecile Roberti, *Community College of Rhode Island*

Perry Sellers, *Lone Star College*

Chrysta Singleton, *Sacramento City College*

Sherrie Slom, *Hillsborough Community College*

Stephanie Swaim, *North Lake College*

Melissa Youngman, *National Technical Institute for the Deaf*

Vasseliki Vervilos, *American River College*

Additionally, I would like to thank the following students who provided feedback on the text:

Mei Ern Cheng, *University of California–Davis*

Bethany Harman, *Sacramento City College*

Chrysta Singleton, *Sacramento City College*

Special thanks to my son, Marcus Williams, who has inspired me and encouraged me and remains my biggest fan.

I would also like to thank George Werthman, Katie Jones-Aiello, Jocelyn Mousel, Marnee Fieldman, Jill Sternard, Dana Vinyard, Debbie McQuade, Terry McQuade, and everyone at Cambridge Business Publishers for their encouragement, guidance, and dedication to this book.

Finally, thank you to the instructors and students using this book.

Gayle Williams

April 2016

Brief Table of Contents

Contents

7 End-of-Period Procedures (Merchandising Company)   *235*

Section Four

Payroll, Project Costing, and Billing for Time   *271*

8 Paying Employees   *273*

9 Project Costing and Billing for Time and Expenses   *325*

Section Five

Beyond the Basics   *367*

10 Management Tools   *369*

QuickBooks

SECTION ONE

Introduction

WHAT IS "COMPUTERIZED ACCOUNTING"?

Years ago, a client asked me to help him hire a full-charge bookkeeper. [A full-charge bookkeeper is someone who is responsible for all the basic accounting functions in a (usually) small business.] I had reviewed all the applications and had invited some of the applicants to come in for an interview. As part of the interview process, I asked them to take a short, 30-minute test covering basic accounting concepts. One of the applicants handed the test back to me after ten minutes and explained that she wasn't able to complete it. I was a bit surprised and asked her if there was something on the test that she didn't understand. Her reply was: "No, that's not it. It's just that I don't do this kind of accounting." Now I was even more surprised and I asked her what she meant by "this type of accounting." She said, "I don't do 'textbook' accounting, I do 'computerized accounting.'" Hopefully, that story made you, as an accounting student, smile. However, the story really illustrates the good news and the bad news about computerized accounting systems. On the one hand, accounting software systems eliminate much of the tedium of bookkeeping and allow us to produce "instant" and very detailed reports. They allow small business owners with no accounting background to keep a pretty good set of records. They allow small businesses to hire data-entry clerks with little accounting knowledge to do routine accounting tasks. Those are all real benefits.

On the other hand, accounting is more than data entry. The principles you've learned in financial accounting are there for a reason—to ensure that the financial statements give a clear and accurate picture (to internal and external users) of the financial operations and financial condition of the organization. A computer software system, no matter how sophisticated, can't analyze transactions and can't make the judgments necessary to determine how and where to record those transactions.

I'll tell you one last story to illustrate my point. My firm was asked by a new client to take a look at its financial statements. The company had a wonderful product, which was

1

selling quite well, and it was making a small profit. It had a full-charge bookkeeper and was using a well-respected accounting software program. The owner was concerned though because the company always seemed to be strapped for cash. One of the first things we noticed was that there were only a few payables recorded in the balance sheet. When we asked the bookkeeper about that, she said that she never entered vendor bills unless they had the cash to pay them. She kept them filed in her desk until the day she was prepared to cut the checks—not quite the practice imagined under the matching (expense recognition) principle! Once we recorded all the bills (in the proper accounting period), the company showed, not the small profit expected by the owner, but an overall loss. For someone who had been working very hard to develop his business, this was NOT good news. Once he recovered from the shock, though, he was able to use this new information, and some financial analysis tools we were able to develop for him, to make better decisions. He soon realized that his selling price was not covering the cost to make the product, so selling more products wasn't going to be the answer. Fortunately, as his product was very unique, he was able to increase the selling price without losing his client base. About five years later, he was able to sell his company for a significant profit.

So, to sum this up, "computerized accounting" is NOT a new kind of accounting. Underlying every accounting system (manual or computerized) is the same foundational base you learned in the first few chapters of your first financial accounting course:

- Assets must ALWAYS equal liabilities plus equity.

- Debits are on the left and credits are on the right!

It's the accountant, not the software, who ultimately controls the accuracy of the financial system. Accounting software just makes the whole process a lot faster with less tedium.

SECTION OVERVIEW

Chapter 1 covers the following topics:
- Getting in and out of QuickBooks Pro.
- The general organization of QuickBooks Pro.
- Customizing and navigating QuickBooks Pro.
- Reporting using QuickBooks Pro.

Introduction to QuickBooks Pro

After completing Chapter 1, you should be able to:

1. Install your trial version of QuickBooks Pro.

2. Open and close QuickBooks Pro.

3. Create working files from backup files.

4. Make and restore backups of your company files.

5. Open various transactions forms.

6. Use the Find function to locate transactions.

7. Demonstrate an understanding of the various lists in QuickBooks Pro.

8. Recognize various account types used in QuickBooks Pro.

9. Create, edit, and delete accounts in the Chart of Accounts.

10. Create and modify reports.

11. Customize the features and look of QuickBooks.

3

QUICKBOOKS PRO

There are many, many different accounting software applications available for purchase. They range in price from a few hundred dollars to a few million dollars. In this book, we're going to look at Intuit's QuickBooks Pro 2015. Intuit created the first version of Quicken (a personal finance management software program) in 1983. Shortly after that, Intuit came out with accounting software for small businesses (QuickBooks). In early 2002, the first version of QuickBooks Pro was released. Currently, Intuit has more than 90 percent of the small-business market (based on retail sales of standalone accounting software systems).

Intuit offers four desktop versions of QuickBooks.

QuickBooks Pro	Basic version used by many small businesses.
QuickBooks Premier	Includes all the basics, PLUS sales orders, ability to track assembled inventory (light manufacturing), and industry-specific reports. Accommodates up to 5 users working simultaneously in the same QuickBooks file.
QuickBooks Enterprise	Includes all features in Premier, PLUS the ability to handle much larger data files, inventory in multiple warehouses, bar coding, and FIFO costing. Accommodates up to 30 users working simultaneously in the same QuickBooks file.
QuickBooks Mac Desktop	Similar in functionality to QuickBooks Pro. Accommodates up to 3 users working simultaneously in the same QuickBooks file.

 HINT: This textbook uses the screenshots and features available in Quick-Books Accountant 2015. This is the version that is included with your textbook. The version installed on the computers in your school computer labs **may** be the Premier version of QuickBooks 2015. Don't worry. QuickBooks Accountant is actually an edition of QuickBooks Premier so the files you create in this class can be read by (accessed by) the QuickBooks program you install on your home computer. Any small differences will not hinder you in completing the assignments.

In this textbook, the terms "QuickBooks" and "QuickBooks Pro" are used interchangeably to refer to your trial version of the software. If you want more information about other QuickBooks products, go to www.intuit.com.

QuickBooks Pro is a **powerful** tool for small businesses.

- It is flexible (can be used by most small businesses).
- It is intuitive (easy to understand).
- It has great report writing capability.
- It has a great search function.
- It is relatively inexpensive.

These are some of the things that QuickBooks Pro automatically knows:

✓ Behind every transaction is a journal entry and that each journal entry must balance.

✓ Asset, liability, and equity accounts appear on the balance sheet, and revenue and expense accounts appear on the profit and loss statement (QuickBooks's name for the income statement).

These are some of the things that QuickBooks Pro **doesn't** automatically know (so make sure you **do** know):

✓ It doesn't know whether the account you just set up as an asset really does represent a resource owned or controlled by the company that is expected to provide future benefit.

✓ It doesn't know whether the amounts on the invoice you just created represent income the company has already earned or income that will be earned in the future.

✓ It doesn't know whether there are salaries that employees have earned but haven't been paid for.

✓ Etc., etc.

BEFORE WE GO ANY FURTHER

Although QuickBooks is a very intuitive program, there are a lot of "places to go and things to see"—and that can be intimidating. It's easy to forget what was covered in a previous chapter. Most of the time, you'll be able to find the answer by using the index for this book. If you can't, here are some options:

- Use the Help feature in QuickBooks. It's really pretty good.

- You can ask for help from your instructor, from a student assistant (if there is one), or from your fellow students (if they're willing and you're not taking a test!).

- As an additional resource, Appendix B ("How Do I?") contains abbreviated step-by-step instructions for the various transactions and procedures. These instructions are also included at the end of each chapter under **Chapter Shortcuts**.

INSTALLING AND UPDATING QUICKBOOKS PRO

If you're taking this class in a classroom setting, a QuickBooks Pro program will already be installed on each computer in your classroom lab. (It is not installed on a server, so you're each working with a separate application program.) QuickBooks Pro may also be installed on other computers at your school that you can use. Check with your instructor for additional availability.

If you're taking the class online or want to work on assignments away from school, you will need to install the program on your laptop or home computer. To install the software on your home computer, go to http://quickbooks.com/download and select the Premier 2015 version of QuickBooks.

A Setup.QuickBooksPremier2015.exe file will automatically be downloaded to your computer. Open the downloaded file and follow the online instructions.

As part of the installation process, you will be asked to enter your license number. Your license and product numbers are included inside your textbook. You will also be required to register the software. You must do this within the time frame given or you'll lose access to the application. Registration doesn't cost anything and it doesn't obligate you to future purchases.

 HINT: As part of the registration process, you will be asked a number of questions about your "business." QuickBooks is assuming, of course, that you're using the software in a business setting. Your answers to these questions will not affect the company files you work on in this class, so you are free to choose your own answers. As a suggestion, you might choose "accounting" as your industry and answer "no" to the questions related to credit cards, employees, etc.

The first time QuickBooks is **ever** opened on a specific computer, a window will appear titled *Welcome to QuickBooks Accountant Edition 2015*. You'll see four choices: **Overview Tutorial**, **Explore QuickBooks**, **Create a new company file**, or **Open an existing company file**. Feel free to try the tutorial or go exploring, but eventually, you'll need to create your own files.

If QuickBooks was previously used on the computer, you'll see a screen that looks similar to this when you open QuickBooks:

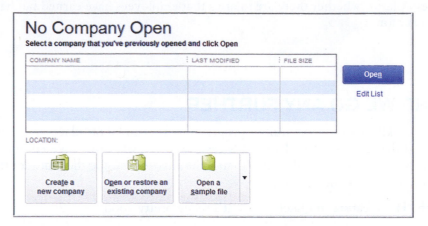

Updating The Program

When you download the application from the Internet, you will be downloading the most recent release. During the class term, QuickBooks may issue updates to the program (new releases). Unless instructed otherwise by your instructor, make sure the automatic update feature is turned **off**. Here's the reason: School lab computers usually can't be updated by anyone other than the administrator (and that's not any of us). Unless there is a major issue in QuickBooks during the term, the programs will probably NOT be updated at your school. If you update your personal version, you may not be able to share files between your personal computer and the school's computers.

To turn off the automatic update feature, click on the **Help** dropdown menu at the top of the screen and select **Update QuickBooks**.

The screen should look something like this:

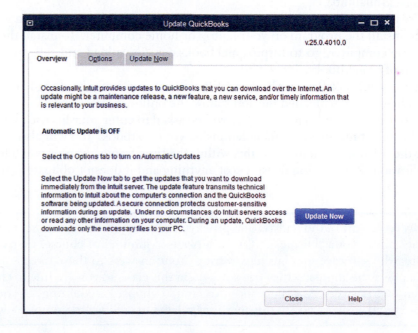

Click on the **Options** tab. Click **No** next to **Automatic Update** to turn the feature off. The screen should look something like this:

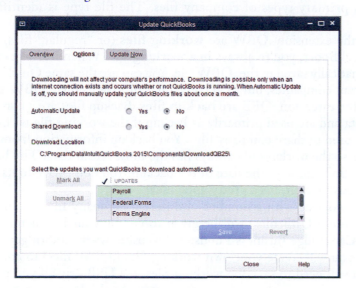

Click **Save** and then click **Close** to exit the window.

 HINT: To see the release currently installed on your computer, press the F2 key on your keyboard. (You must be in QuickBooks.) The release is identified after the product name. The screenshots in this textbook are from R10P.

WARNING: Updating company files is <u>not</u> the same thing as updating the program. You <u>will</u> need to update the company files if prompted by QuickBooks. The prompt to update a company file will look like this:

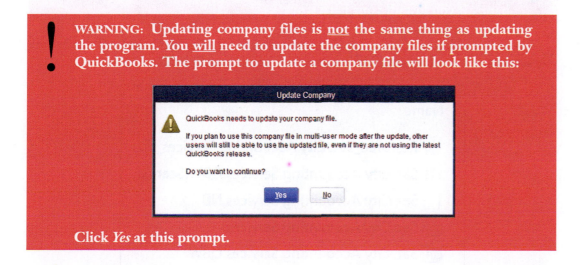

Click *Yes* at this prompt.

PRACTICE

Throughout this textbook, you will practice the steps necessary to record transactions and use the various tools available in QuickBooks using an imaginary company called Sac City Accounting Services (Sac City Accounting). Sac City Accounting Services is a partnership that provides accounting services for small businesses.

The Practice Exercises are located at the end of each section. Read through each section **before** you attempt the exercises. The explanations and screenshots provided in each section are meant to help you complete the Practice Exercises and your assignments.

WORKING WITH COMPANY FILES

There are two **primary** types of company files. The file type is identified by the file extensions.

Files with the extension .QBW are **working files** (or "regular" files). When you're working in QuickBooks, you're always in a **working file**. Whenever you enter a transaction, it is automatically saved in the .QBW file. You can use the same QuickBooks program for many different companies, but each company will have its own .QBW file.

Files with the extension .QBB are **backup files**. Backup files are a condensed version of company data and are used primarily as backup if the working file is corrupted or lost but can also be used to share company files. You back up information **from** a working file **to** a backup file so the working file always has the most recent data. The backup file only contains transactions through the date of the backup. You don't have to have backup files but, as we'll discuss in a bit, it's a pretty good idea!

You will be working with a number of different company files in this class. Backup copies of these files (.QBB files) will be given to you by your instructor. They can also be accessed at Cambridge Business Publishers' website (www.cambridgepub.com). Using these backups, you will create your own working files (.QBW files) to complete your assignments. You will need to save the working files to a USB drive if you plan to work on your assignments on more than one computer (a school lab computer and your home computer, for instance). Some students use two USB drives (one for the working files and one for the backup files), but that's up to you.

 WARNING: ASK YOUR INSTRUCTOR before saving company files (.QBW or .QBB) to lab computers. Any files saved to the hard drives of school computers are normally deleted every night. You would not be happy if you lost all your hard work!

There are additional files and folders created automatically by QuickBooks each time you set up a new working file. The list may look something like this:

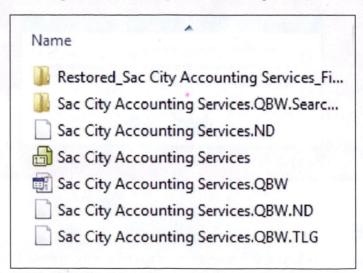

Name

📁 Restored_Sac City Accounting Services_Fi...
📁 Sac City Accounting Services.QBW.Searc...
📄 Sac City Accounting Services.ND
📗 Sac City Accounting Services
📘 Sac City Accounting Services.QBW
📄 Sac City Accounting Services.QBW.ND
📄 Sac City Accounting Services.QBW.TLG

The sheer number of files can be intimidating but you don't need to be concerned. You will only be working directly with .QBW and .QBB files. The other files are created for purposes primarily related to processing. For example the qbw.tlg file contains a log of transactions entered since a file backup.

Creating and Opening Working Files

Instructions for Creating a Working File (.QBW File) From a Backup File (.QBB File)

Click on the **File** dropdown menu at the top left of the screen. Click **Open or restore company**.

This screen will appear:

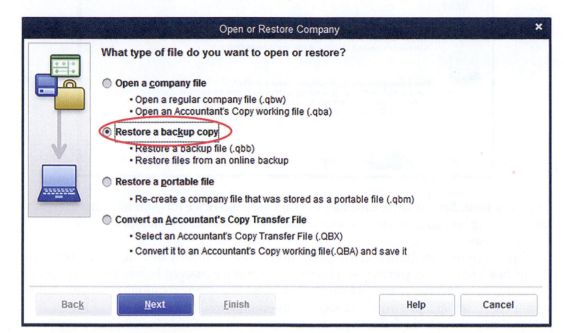

Click **Restore a backup copy** and then click **Next**.
You'll see this screen:

Click **Local backup** and then click **Next**.

Find the .QBB file you are using to create a working file. In this class, the first working file you create will be for Sac City Accounting Services. The .QBB file for Sac City is downloadable to your computer from the Cambridge Business Publishers website at www. cambridgepub.com.

Double-click the file or highlight the file and click **Open**.

You'll see this window:

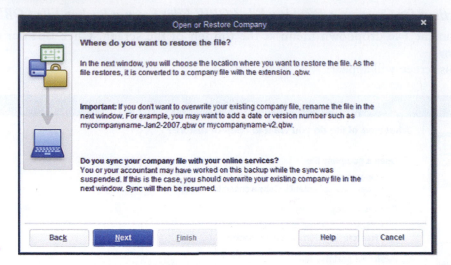

Click **Next**. Browse to find the location on your USB drive (or your hard drive if you're only working on assignments at home) where you want to save your working file.

Click **Save**.

Intuit requires an Administrator password for each company file. Since you're restoring from a back up file, you may be prompted to enter a password before you can proceed. If so, use 4Cambridge as the password. If a password is not required here, you will be prompted to set up a password and security question later.

You may also get the following message:

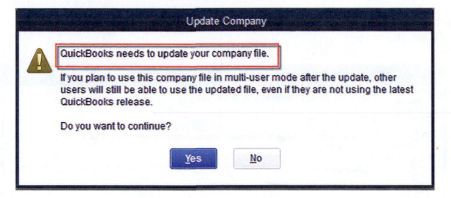

Click **Yes** if you get the prompt. QuickBooks will then update your data to work with the current release installed on your machine.

If you were not prompted to enter a password earlier, you will need to set up your password and security question in the next window.

HINT: Occasionally, QuickBooks will not prompt you to add a password when creating a working file from a backup. This will not cause problems when completing the assignments. If you're not prompted but do want to add security to your company file, select **Set Up Users and Passwords** on the **Company** dropdown menu on the main menu bar. Select **Change Your Password** and follow the instructions on the screen.

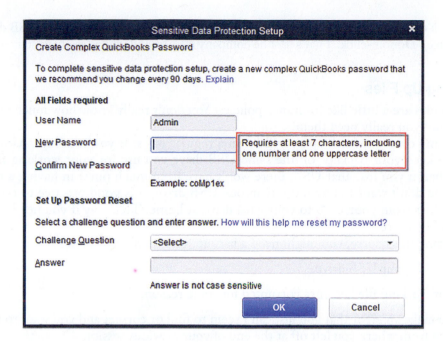

Passwords must be 7 characters long and include at least one number and one upper-case letter. The **User Name** (Admin) cannot be changed.

Selecting a **Challenge Question** will allow you to reset your password if you forget the original.

You will need to log in as the Administrator with your password each time you open your working file. After 90 days, you will be prompted to change your password.

Click OK. After a minute or so, you'll get a message that your file has been successfully restored. You have just created your first .QBW file. Congratulations! Once you have created your company file (.QBW file), you will be working only in that file.

Instructions for Opening Working Files Already Installed on Your USB Drive (or Hard Drive)

When you open QuickBooks, click **Open or restore an existing company** in the window in the middle of the screen. The following screen will appear:

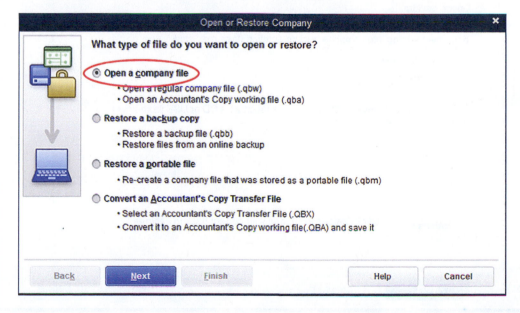

Click **Open a company file**. Locate your working file (.QBW file) on your USB drive (or hard drive). Double-click. That's it! The company is open and you're ready to start working.

Backing Up Files

Backup files are a little like insurance policies. You don't really know how much you need them until you really need them!

It's important to back up your data on a regular basis. If you're using a USB drive, you can keep your backups on the same USB drive you use for your working files but remember, if you lose that USB, there won't have been much point in having a backup! So, if you don't want to buy more than one USB drive, it is good practice to copy your backup files from your USB to your hard drive at home. That way if you need the files, they will be there.

During this course, you might need a backup for a number of reasons:

- You lose your USB drive.

- Your working file becomes corrupted for some reason.

- You make an error that you just can't seem to find or correct and you want to start fresh from where you left off at the end of your previous session.

Hopefully none of those things will happen, but, if they do, here's how to make that backup.

Instructions for Creating Backup Files (.QBB Files)

Click **File** (top left of screen). Click **Back Up Company** and choose **Create Local Backup**. The following screen will show:

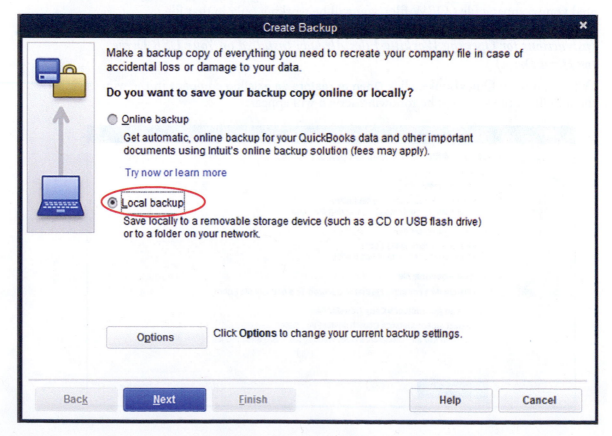

Select **Local backup** and then click **Next**.
The screen should look like this:

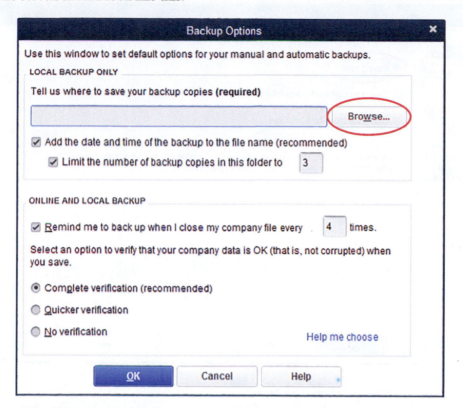

 HINT: If this is the first time you've used your QuickBooks program, you will
need to click **Options** first and then the above screen will appear.

Use the **Browse** link to locate your USB drive (or hard drive) and the folder where
you want your backup saved. (Using folders to organize your company files is highly
recommended.)

You are offered several options. The **Add date & time of the backup** and backup reminder options can be helpful but aren't necessary. The **Complete verification** option is
highly recommended. If selected, QuickBooks verifies that the file you're trying to save
isn't corrupt.

Click **OK**. If you're saving the backup to the same location that contains your working
file, you will most likely see a message similar to this:

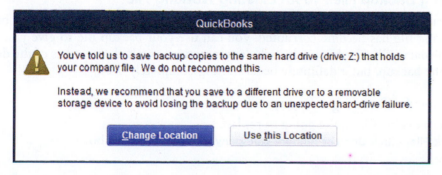

Click **Use this Location**. This screen will appear:

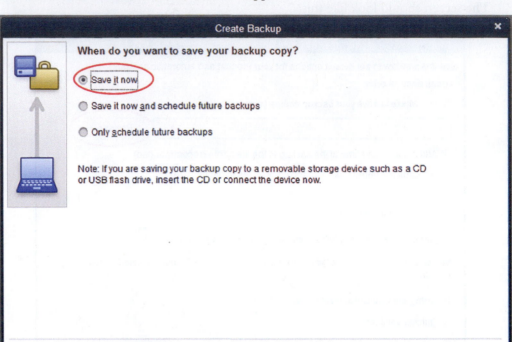

Select **Save it now** and then click **Next**.

Verify that the name and location of your backup are correct. You can change them here if you need to.

> **HINT:** It can be very useful to add information to the file name when you're saving the backup. For example, if you're in the middle of a chapter, you might include the page number or task last completed in the file name. Using the name of the company in the assignment, a backup of a completed Chapter 1 homework assignment might be labeled "Company Name-Ch 1-Completed."

Click **Finish**. The verification process starts after you've clicked **Finish**. It will generally take a few minutes. When the process is complete, you will receive a message that the backup has been successful.

Restoring Backup Files To An Existing Working File

When errors are made in the working file that are simply too difficult to correct or when the working file has become corrupted, you can use your backup file to give you a fresh start. The data will, of course, only include transactions you had entered as of the date and time of the backup, but it definitely beats starting completely over.

Instructions for Restoring a Backup File

Open the working file you're going to replace.

Click **File**. Click **Open or Restore Company**. This screen will show:

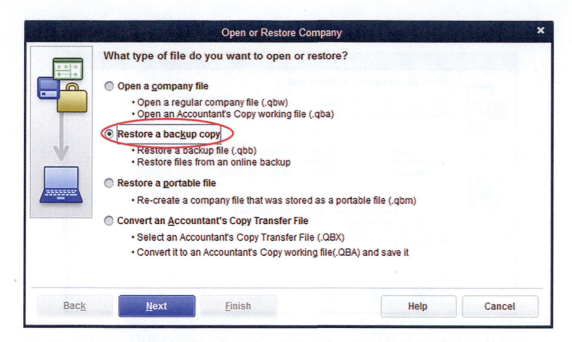

Select **Restore a backup copy** and then click **Next**. This screen will show:

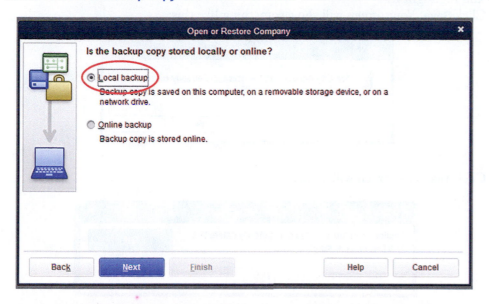

> **!** **WARNING:** You may get a message that the working file is "read only" and the backup can't be restored. You have two options here. You can change the properties of the working file by deselecting Read Only (or changing access to Read and Write) in the file properties or by creating a new working file (make a slight change to the name).

Click **Local backup** and then click **Next**.

Browse for the location of the backup file you'll be using. Double-click or highlight the company file and click **Open**.

This screen will show:

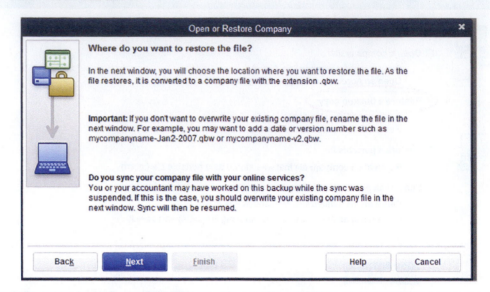

Click **Next**. Browse for the location of your working file (the .QBW file you are replacing) and highlight it.

Click **Save**. Your screen will show something like this:

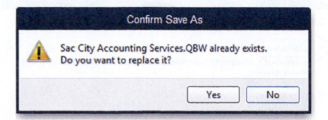

Click **Yes**. The screen will show:

Type "YES" in the open field and then click **OK**. When the backup is completed, you will get the following message:

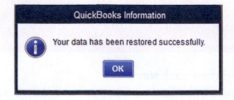

Create a working file for Sac City Accounting from a backup.
(Summary of preceding steps.)

The working file you are about to create from a backup given to you by your instructor (or accessed through the publisher's website) includes a chart of accounts, some customers and vendors, and all the transactions for Sac City Accounting through November 30, 2017. You will be making changes to the company and entering additional transactions for the company through the Practice Exercises included in each chapter.

1. Open **QuickBooks**.

2. Click **Open or Restore Company**.

3. Click **Restore a backup copy**.

4. Click **Next**.

5. Browse for the location where the backup for Sac City Accounting is stored. (Your instructor will let you know the location.)

6. Click **Open**.

7. Click **Next**.

8. Browse for the location on your USB drive (or hard drive) where you want to store the working file.

9. Click **Save**.

10. If prompted to enter a password, use 4Cambridge.

11. If prompted, click **Update Now** to update the company file. Click **Yes** to confirm.

12. If prompted to create a new password, follow the instruction on the screen.

13. Click **OK**.

PRACTICE EXERCISE

> **!** **WARNING: Remember, once you have created your own Sac City Accounting working file (.QBW file), you will be opening that file each time you complete the Practice Exercises in this book. Do not continue to create new working files.**

MOVING AROUND IN QUICKBOOKS PRO

Accessing Tools

You can access lists, forms, reports, and anything else you might need from a variety of sources.

Main Menu Bar

The main menu bar is located at the top of the screen right under the title bar. The main menu bar looks like this:

File   Edit   View   Lists   Favorites   Accountant   Company   Customers   Vendors   Employees   Banking   Reports   Window   Help

The main menu bar has all the options for entering and editing transactions, preparing reports, and setting up QuickBooks.

There are dropdown lists for each item on the main menu bar. The dropdown menu available under **Customers** would look something like this:

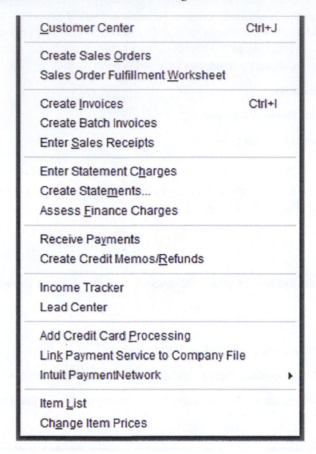

The options included in the dropdown lists on the main menu bar will change depending on:

- The type of transaction you're currently working on.
- The choices made in setting up and customizing the company file.

Icon Bar

In the default setup, the icon bar is located at the far left of the screen.

An abbreviated version of the lower section of the icon bar looks like this:

The **My Shortcuts** tab on the icon bar looks like this:

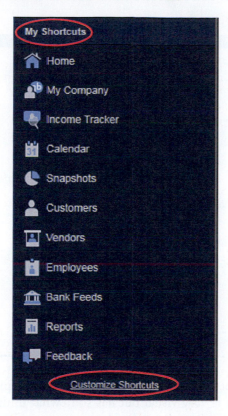

This tab includes links to information about customers, vendors, and employees. There are also links to a calendar and links to information about the company (**Snapshots** and **Income Tracker**). Clicking **Customize Shortcuts** at the bottom of the **My Shortcuts** tab can modify the links included.

The **View Balances** tab on the icon bar lists current cash and receivable and payable balances.

The **Open Windows** tab on the icon bar shows you the windows currently open in QuickBooks. (You can have multiple windows open at the same time.)

The icon bar can be minimized by clicking **<** at the top of the icon bar.

Home Page

The Home page can be accessed through the icon bar. (The icon is at the top of the **My Shortcuts** tab.)

The appearance of the Home page will vary depending on which QuickBooks features a particular company file is using. (The more features, the more icons!)

A Home page would look something like this for a merchandising company with employees:

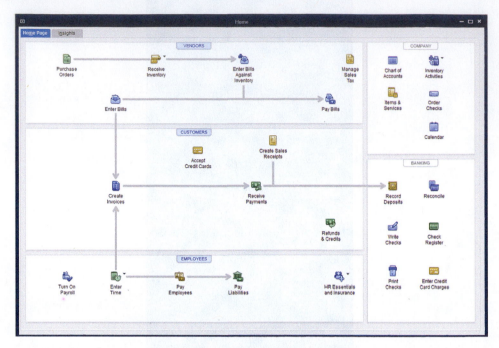

The Home page is set up in the form of a flowchart of typical vendor, customer, and employee transactions. It is very visual but has somewhat limited options. For common transactions, it's probably easiest to use the Home page to access forms.

The **Insights** tab on the Home page (top left corner) gives selected information for the company to date.

Accountant Center

The Accountant Center automatically appears when a company file is opened in the QuickBooks Accountant edition. You can turn that feature off by unchecking the box at the bottom left of the window.

The transactions and reports that can be accessed through the Accountant Center are primarily limited to end of period activity.

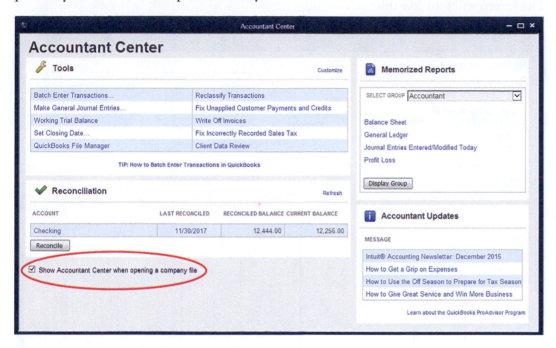

Centers (Customer, Vendor, Employee, Report)

QuickBooks has set up Centers where the user has access to information and certain forms related to a particular segment of the business (customers, vendors, etc.). Links are available in the Customer, Vendor, and Employee Centers that allow you to add or edit records, create new transactions, and prepare simple reports.

The Centers are accessed through either the main menu bar or the icon bar (**My Shortcuts** tab). We will cover Centers more thoroughly in the next few chapters.

Finding Transactions

You can find transactions in QuickBooks in **many** ways:

- You can use the **Find** feature to search using one or more filters.

- You can "drill down" (double-click) on a specific transaction in a report to see the transaction details.

- You can add a **Search** icon to **My Shortcuts** tab on the icon bar to search by keyword. (Click **Customize Shortcuts** to add the icon.)

- You can use the **Transaction History** button available on the **Reports** tab in various forms to see related transactions.

- You can find recent transactions with a specific customer or vendor on various sales and purchase forms.

The **Find** tool has the most flexibility.

The **Find** tool is accessed by either:

- Selecting the **Find** option on the **Edit** menu (main menu bar).

- Using CTRL F on your keyboard.

The screen will look like this:

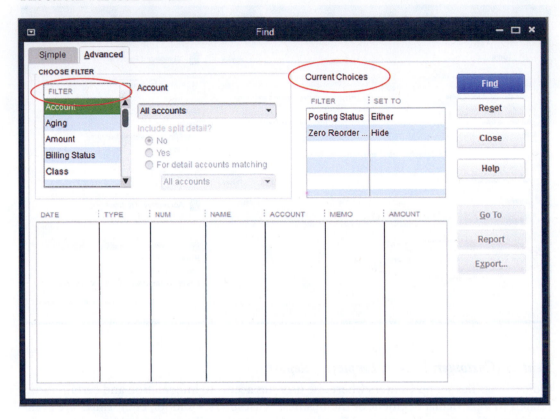

As you can see there are two tabs.

The **Advanced** tab (which you see in the accompanying screenshot) allows you to look for transactions meeting one or more criteria (filters). For instance, you might want to look at all transactions dated 6/5. Or you might want to look for all transactions over $100 entered during October.

The filters are selected first (in the box at the far left of the screen under **Choose Filter**).

For each filter selected (there can be more than one), you must enter the specific criteria for that filter using the options indicated to the right of the filter selection box. All filters selected will appear in the **Current Choices** box.

After the **Find** button is clicked, the transactions that meet the criteria will be displayed in the lower half of the screen.

Highlighting a displayed transaction and clicking the **Go To** button will take you to the transaction itself.

The **Simple** tab screen looks like this:

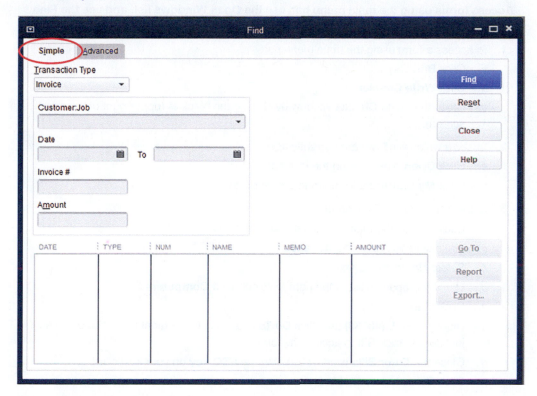

This tab provides a simplified version of the **Find** tool (fewer filtering options). It will appear automatically when you're working in a specific type of transaction (writing a check for example) and you access the **Find** tool.

You can always switch to the **Advanced** tab for more flexibility in filtering.

Open Windows

A "window," in QuickBooks, is an open form, list, tool, or report. Most of the time, a window will have a **Save & Close** or **Close** button that is used to save a transaction and automatically exit the window. There are times, though, when the window has to be closed manually (when you're viewing a report for example). You have two options:

✓ Use the ESC button on your keyboard.

✓ Click the ✖ in the top right corner of the open window.

> **! WARNING: Be careful to click the ✖ in the open window. The ✖ at the top right of the QuickBooks screen is for exiting QuickBooks.**

By the way, QuickBooks will allow you to have a number of windows (forms/lists/reports) open at the same time. Having multiple reports and lists open while you're working will not generally cause a problem, but having a form open might cause a problem if you want to begin a new transaction of the same type.

To show a list of open windows, click the **Open Windows** tab at the bottom of the icon bar.

To close all open windows, select the **Close All** option on the **Window** dropdown menu (main menu bar).

Access forms using the main menu bar, use the Open Windows list, and use the Find feature in Sac City Accounting to locate specific transactions.

1. To access a form using the main menu bar:
    a. Click **Banking**.
    b. Click **Write Checks**.
    c. Close the **Write Checks** window by clicking the black ✖ (upper right of the check screen).

2. To show which windows are currently open:
    a. Click **Open Windows** on the icon bar.
    b. Click **My Shortcuts** to return to the list of icons.

3. To search using the Find feature:
    a. Click **Edit** on the main menu bar and select **Find**.
    b. Make sure you're on the **Advanced** tab.
    c. Select **Name** as the filter.
    d. Use the dropdown list to the right to select "**Dell Computers**."
    e. Click **Find**.
    f. Highlight **BILL (#8788)** and click **Go To** to access the original form. You can also just double-click **Bill** to access the form.
    g. Close the **Enter Bills** window by using the **ESC key** on your keyboard.
    h. Click **Close** to exit the **Find** window.

QUICKBOOKS PRO ORGANIZATION

The Importance Of "Lists"

QuickBooks Pro uses "lists" as part of the organizational structure.

Chart Of Accounts

Account A record of the additions, deductions, and balances of individual assets, liabilities, stockholders' equity, dividends, revenues, and expenses.

The primary list is the **Chart of Accounts**. An **account type** must be selected for each **account** used by an organization. The account type chosen will determine:

*   The financial statement on which an account will appear.
*   Where on that statement the account will be displayed.
*   Which QuickBooks features are available for that account.

Classified balance sheet A balance sheet in which items are classified into subgroups to facilitate financial analysis and management decision making.

QuickBooks prepares **classified balance sheets** and **multistep income statements**. There are lots of groupings and subtotals in those statements (as you remember from your previous classes), so QuickBooks has an expanded list of account types. Here's a list of account types used by QuickBooks:

Multistep income statement An income statement in which items are classified into subgroups to facilitate financial analysis and management decision making.

Financial Accounting Classifications				
Assets	**Liabilities**	**Equity**	**Revenues**	**Expenses**
QuickBooks Account Types				
Bank	Accounts payable	Equity	Income	Cost of goods sold
Accounts receivable	Credit card		Other income	Expense
Other current asset	Other current liability			Other expense
Fixed asset	Long-term liability			
Other asset				

You can have many different accounts with the same **account type** in your chart of accounts.

Here are some examples of the way **account type** determines placement in a financial statement. Let's say you are going to set up an account called Petty Cash. You would want to set the account up as type **Bank** so that it shows up at the top of the balance sheet along with any checking or savings accounts the company has. (Checking and savings accounts would also be set up with the **account type Bank**.) A Salaries Payable account would be set up as type **Other Current liability**. That way it shows up on the balance sheet as a current liability along with accounts such as Interest Payable and Payroll Taxes Payable.

Here are some examples of the way **account type** is associated with various features in QuickBooks: If an account were set up as an **Accounts Receivable** type, you would be able to use that account when preparing customer invoices. You would also be able to pull an accounts receivable aging report for that account. You would not be able to do either of those things with an account set up as an **Other Current Asset** type. You will learn more about these features as you go through the textbook. For now, just be aware that selecting the appropriate account type is important for a variety of reasons.

Adding, Editing, or Deleting Accounts

To add, edit, or delete accounts, you will need to click **Lists** (on the menu bar) and then **Chart of Accounts**. The screen will look something like this:

NAME	⚡	TYPE	BALANCE TOTAL	ATTACH
◇ Checking		Bank	12,256.00	
◇ Accounts receivable		Accounts Receivable	2,280.00	
◇ Inventory		Other Current Asset	4,000.00	
◇ Supplies on hand		Other Current Asset	600.00	
◇ Prepaid expenses		Other Current Asset	0.00	
◇ Undeposited funds		Other Current Asset	0.00	
◇ Accumulated depreciation		Fixed Asset	-736.00	
◇ Computer and office equipment		Fixed Asset	10,600.00	
◇ Office furniture		Fixed Asset	4,400.00	
◇ Security deposit - office space		Other Asset	1,200.00	
◇ Accounts payable		Accounts Payable	4,300.00	
◇ Payroll taxes payable		Other Current Liability	0.00	
◇ Sales tax payable		Other Current Liability	0.00	
◇ Note payable-computers		Long Term Liability	5,553.00	
◇ Opening balance equity		Equity	0.00	
◇ Partners' capital		Equity	25,000.00	
◇ Student name		Equity	12,500.00	
◇ Student, capital balance		Equity	12,500.00	
◇ Student, draws		Equity	0.00	
◇ Student, earnings current year		Equity	0.00	
◇ Williams		Equity	12,500.00	
◇ Williams, capital balance		Equity	12,500.00	
◇ Williams, draws		Equity	0.00	
◇ Williams, earnings current year		Equity	0.00	
◇ Retained earnings		Equity		
◇ Accounting services fees		Income		
◇ Financial statement reviews		Income		
◇ Bookkeeping services		Income		

Account ▼   Activities ▼   Reports ▼   Attach   ☐ Include inactive

Adding an Account

To add an account, click **Account** (bottom left corner of the **Chart of Accounts** screen) and then click **New**. The screen will look like this:

Click the appropriate account type and click **Continue**. The screen will look like this:

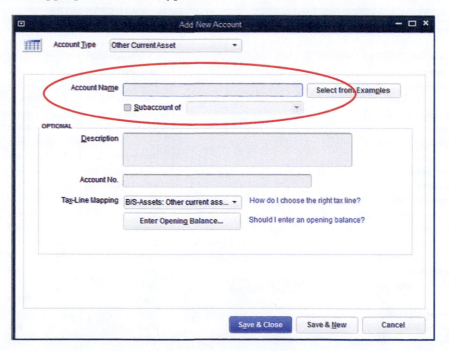

Account Name is what appears on the financial statements.

To group similar accounts together for presentation purposes, you can create a primary account and then identify other accounts as **subaccounts** of the primary account.

An optional description field is there if you want to include additional detail about the contents of the account.

You can use account numbers in QuickBooks. (The number must be indicated in the **Account No.** field on the **Add New Account** window.) However, we will not be using them in this course.

Editing an Account

To edit an account, highlight (on the **Chart of Accounts** list) the account you want to change.

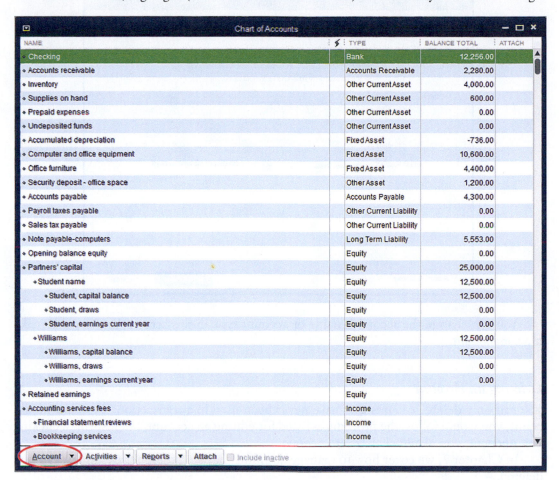

Click **Account** (bottom left corner of screen) to open the following screen:

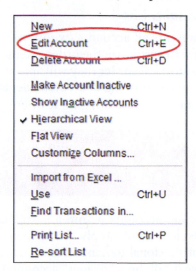

Click **Edit Account**.

The screen will look something like this:

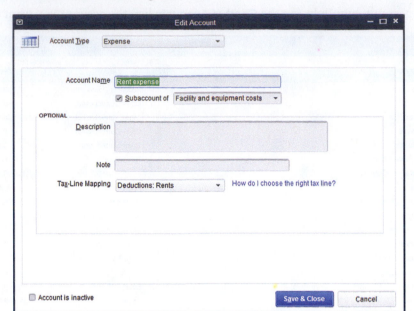

You can change the account's name or account type in this screen. You can also make it a **subaccount**.

Deleting an Account

You can only delete accounts that have never been used in a transaction. To delete an account, you would follow the procedures listed for editing an account, but instead of clicking **Edit Account**, you would click **Delete Account**.

In Chapter 7, we cover how to manage accounts that are no longer useful but can't be deleted.

Organizing the Chart of Accounts List

QuickBooks automatically presents all accounts (within each **account type**) in alphabetic order. Most users would prefer to customize the order. (Remember, the order the accounts are listed in the **Chart of Accounts** is the order they will appear on financial statements.) Rearranging the order is easily done within the **Chart of Accounts** list by clicking the diamond bullet to the left of the account name and dragging it where you want it to go.

 WARNING: You can only reorder accounts that are located within the same account type.

Many users also prefer to group accounts within a particular classification (particularly income and expense accounts) instead of simply listing them. This allows the user to prepare more informative and professional looking income statements. To group accounts, a primary account is created (we'll call them "header" accounts). You then identify secondary accounts as subaccounts to the appropriate header account.

> **!** **WARNING:** If header accounts are used, no transactions should be posted to those accounts. If transactions **are** posted to header accounts, Quick-Books will create (for reporting purposes only) a separate account for those transactions, which can be confusing.

True or False? QuickBooks will allow you to set up your Notes Payable account as an Expense account type. (Answer at end of chapter.)	**Quick**Check **1-1**

Work with Sac City Accounting's Chart of Accounts.

(Sac City needs a miscellaneous expense account and wants to rearrange some existing accounts.)

PRACTICE EXERCISE

1. Click **Lists**.

2. Click **Chart of Accounts**.

3. To add a new account.

    a. Click **Account** button.

    b. Click **New**.

    c. Choose account type **Expense**.

    d. Click **Continue**.

    e. Type in "Miscellaneous expense."

    f. Click **Subaccount of** and select **Other Costs**.

    g. Click **Save and Close**.

4. To edit an account:

    a. Highlight **Equipment rental**. (It's the first **Expense** account listed.)

    b. Click **Account**.

    c. Click **Edit Account**.

    d. Change the name to "Equipment rental expense."

    e. Click **Subaccount of** and select **Facility and equipment costs**.

    f. Click **Save and Close**.

5. To move an account:

    a. Grab the diamond bullet to the left of **Equipment rental expense** (left click and hold).

    b. Move account below **Repairs and maintenance expense**.

    c. Click the diamond bullet to the left of **Accumulated Depreciation** and drag the account below **Office Furniture**. (Accumulated Depreciation is a **Fixed Asset** account type.)

6. To delete an account:

    a. Highlight **Travel expense** (subaccount of **Labor related costs**).

    b. Click **Account**.

    c. Click **Delete Account**.

    d. Click **OK**.

7. Exit out of the Chart of Accounts window by clicking the Esc key on your keyboard.

Other Lists in Quickbooks

There are a number of other lists used in QuickBooks.

The **item list** contains information about every product sold or service provided by the organization. **Items** are used when billing customers and when purchasing **inventory** in QuickBooks. The **payroll item list** contains information about every type of compensation and every employer and employee payroll tax specific to the organization. **Payroll items** are used when entering timesheets and when creating paychecks in QuickBooks.

Inventory Goods purchased or produced for sale to customers.

Some lists represent options that might be used. For example, there is a list of customer messages that can be accessed and included on a customer invoice. There's also a list of shipping methods (UPS, FedEx, USPS, etc.) that might be used in a merchandising or manufacturing company.

Finally, some lists are additional "grouping" tools. There's a **customer type list** that can be used to group customers. For example, a company that sells products to consumers and to resellers might set up two customer types (retail and wholesale). A **vendor type list** serves a similar purpose. Another grouping tool (**classes**) can be used to track segments of a business (department, location, etc.). We'll be using **classes** in a later chapter.

You can organize **most** of these other lists in much the same way you can organize the Chart of Accounts list.

- The order of the lists can be changed.

- Header items can be used to group items in the list.

These (and other) lists will be covered in more detail in later chapters but, just for practice, we'll take a look at editing **items** here.

Editing An Item

The **item list** can be accessed through the **Lists** menu (main menu bar).

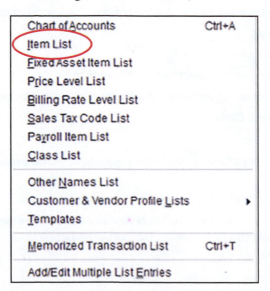

Select the menu option **Item List**.

The screen will look something like this:

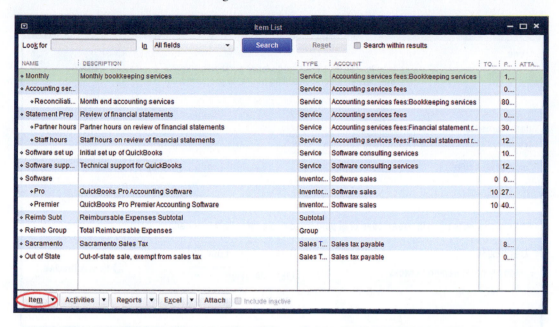

Highlight the **item** you want to edit and click **Item** (bottom left of screen) to open the dropdown menu.

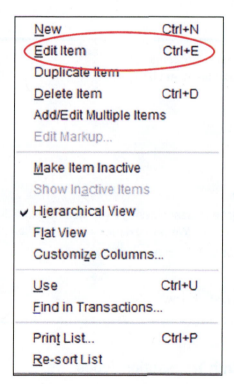

Click **Edit Item**.

The next screen will look something like this:

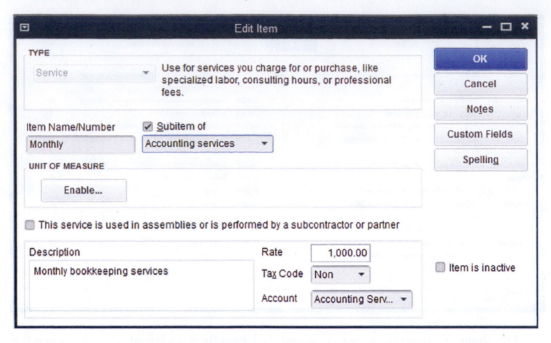

You can make changes in various fields in this screen. Clicking **OK** saves the changes.

Work with Sac City Accounting Items.
(Sac City wants to organize the **Item List**.)

1. Click **Lists**.

2. Click **Item List**.

3. Highlight **Monthly**.

   a. Click **Item**.

   b. Click **Edit Item**.

      i. You may get a message asking if you want to add/edit multiple items. Exit out of the window. We will cover adding multiple items in Chapter 12.

   c. Click **subitem of** and select **Accounting services**.

   d. Click **OK**.

4. Exit out of the **Item List** window.

Behind The Scenes With Transaction Types

Journal A tabular record in which business transactions are analyzed in debit and credit terms and recorded in chronological order.

In a manual accounting system, the mechanics of accounting work something like this:

✓ Documentation (for transactions) is received from outside sources or prepared internally.

✓ Details from the documents are recorded in **journals**.

✓ Journal entries are posted (transferred) to the **general ledger** and, as appropriate, to **subsidiary ledgers**.

✓ A **trial balance** is prepared.

✓ Financial statements are prepared from the trial balance, and subsidiary ledger reports are prepared from the subsidiary ledgers.

In QuickBooks, the mechanics work like this:

✓ Certain documents are prepared directly in QuickBooks (invoices and checks, for example) using specific "forms." Documents received from outside sources (vendor invoices, for example) are entered into QuickBooks using other "forms."

✓ That's all the user has to do (other than making those pesky adjusting journal entries!).

General ledger A grouping of all of a business's accounts that are used to prepare the basic financial statements.

Subsidiary ledger A ledger that provides detailed information about an account balance.

Trial balance A list of the account titles in the general ledger, their respective debit or credit balances, and the totals of the debit and credit balances.

> **BEHIND THE SCENES** The journal entries related to transactions are automatically created by QuickBooks and posted to the general ledger when the "form" is completed (saved). Subsidiary ledgers, trial balances, and financial statements are also automatically updated every time a transaction is entered.

Each form is identified as a specific **transaction type** in QuickBooks. Knowing the various **transaction types** allows you to easily find transactions or create or modify reports.

There are many **transaction types**. Here are a few of them (see Appendix C for a list of all transaction types):

- **Sales receipt** (cash sales).

- **Invoice** (sales on account).

- **Payment** (collections from customer for sales on account).

- **Check** (payments by check NOT including payments on account or payroll checks).

- **Bill** (purchases from vendors on account).

- **Bill payment** (payments to vendors for purchases on account).

- **Journal** (adjusting entries).

Transaction type names in QuickBooks are **very** specific.

In business, we might "bill" a customer OR we might receive a "bill" from a vendor. In QuickBooks, we **invoice** customers and we record **bills** from vendors that we will be paying at a later date. You cannot enter a sale to a customer, on account, using a **bill**.

In business, we write "checks" to pay for something on the spot. We write "checks" to pay the phone bill we recorded in the general ledger last month. We also write checks to pay our employees. In QuickBooks those are three different **transaction types**. **Check** is the **transaction type** used when we pay for something on the spot. Checks written to vendors to pay account balances are **bill payment transaction types**. **Paycheck** is the **transaction type** for employee payroll checks.

BEHIND THE SCENES There is a journal entry behind every completed form **except** (there are always exceptions, right?):

- Purchase and sales orders (not accounting transactions).
- Estimates (not accounting transactions).
- Timesheets. (Timesheets are not considered an accounting transaction by QuickBooks. Wages are only recorded in QuickBooks when payroll checks are created or when general journal entries are made. Interestingly enough, timesheets are not even considered a **transaction type** in QuickBooks so you can't use the **Find** feature to look up timesheets. More about payroll later.)

QuickCheck
1-2

> Why aren't purchase orders, sales orders, and estimates considered accounting transactions? (Answer at end of chapter.)

REPORTING

There are lots of reports already set up in QuickBooks. You'll be using many of those reports during the class term, so this chapter won't go into much detail. Most, if not all, reports in QuickBooks can be customized, and you'll need to be able to customize many of the reports required in the homework assignments.

There are many ways you can customize reports:

- You can add or delete the types of information that appear on the report and/or the order in which the information is presented.

- You can specify which transactions are included in the report.

- You can modify the appearance of the reports (fonts, titles, etc.).

Report Modification

Simple Report Modification

Certain report modifications can easily be made on the face of most reports using the menu bars. (For the **Sales by Item Summary**, the menu bars will look like this:)

These modifications would include:

- Changing the date range of the report (under **From** and **To**).

- Changing the amount of detail presented (under **Show Columns**).

- Changing how the information in the report is sorted (under **Sort by**).

- Changing the column widths (done by clicking the separator bar just to the right of the column name and dragging left to decrease the width and dragging right to increase the width).

To be sure all changes are reflected, click the **Refresh** button at the top right of the window.

If lists are set up with headers (discussed earlier in this chapter), reports can be created with differing levels of detail for different users. For example, a creditor might need less detail on an income statement than an owner. If the **Chart of Accounts** list is set up with header accounts, the income statement can easily be modified to:

- Show all subaccounts with subtotals by header.

- Show only header account subtotals.

QuickBooks calls changing this level of detail **expanding** or **collapsing** a report.

When a report is initially opened, the report will show all detail. A **Sales by Item Summary** report (slightly customized), for example, would appear something like this:

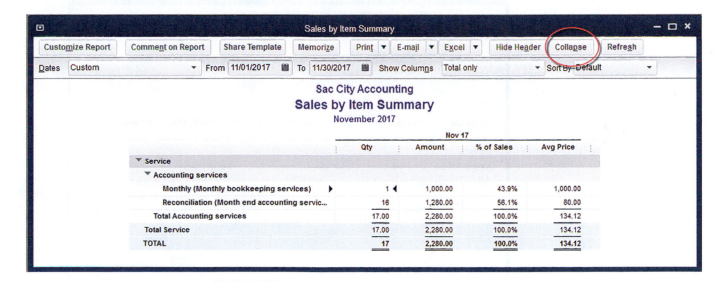

If you click the **Collapse** button on the tool bar (the tool bar is at the top of the report under the report title), only the primary (header) information will appear.

The preceding **Sales by Item Summary** report would look something like this when **collapsed**:

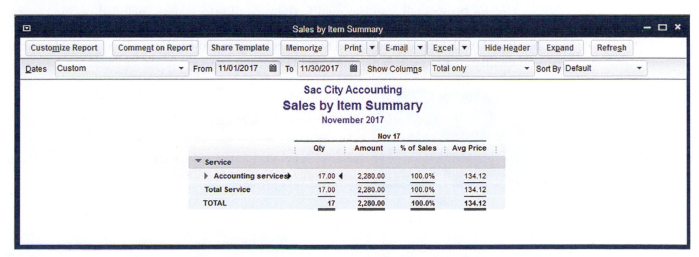

To return to the more detailed report, you would just need to click the **Expand** button on the tool bar.

Advanced Report Modification

Sometimes, a company might want to limit the type of information included in a report or do more extensive modifications to how the report looks. For example, a company might want to limit a sales report to include only sales greater than $1,000 to certain customers. Or, a company might want to change the report name or the font used.

Modifying the **type of information that is included in a report** is done through a filtering process. Modifying the appearance of a report is done through a selection process. Both are done through a modification window.

To more extensively modify a report, click the **Customize Report** button at the top left of any report screen. You'll see a screen that looks something like this (different reports have different modification options so the screens will differ):

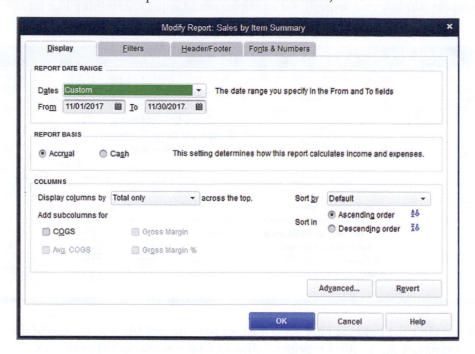

As you can see in the screenshot, there are four tabs: **Display**, **Filters**, **Header/Footer**, and **Fonts & Numbers**. The **Display** tab is open when **Customize Report** is first clicked.

On the **Display** tab, you can modify the type of information included on the report (the columns displayed) and the order of the presentation. The options that appear on the **Display** tab will differ depending on the report being modified. The options available when you modify a **Sales by Item Summary** report are:

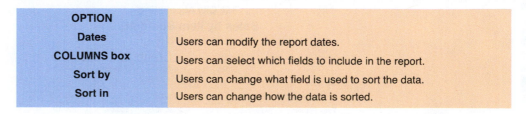

OPTION	
Dates	Users can modify the report dates.
COLUMNS box	Users can select which fields to include in the report.
Sort by	Users can change what field is used to sort the data.
Sort in	Users can change how the data is sorted.

If you click the **Filters** tab, the screen will look like this:

On the **Filters** tab, you choose the type of information you want filtered in the **CHOOSE FILTER** section. After you highlight the filter, the middle section of the screen will change to show you the filtering options available. In the screenshot, the **Account** filter is selected, so you're able to use the dropdown menu under **Account** to select the accounts you'd like included on the report. You can choose multiple filters. Each time you choose a new filter, the middle section will change.

You can remove filters by highlighting the filter in the **CURRENT FILTER CHOICES** section and clicking **Remove Selected Filter**.

The other two tabs in the **Modify Report** window (**Header/Footer** and **Fonts & Numbers**) contain additional options. On the Header/Footer tab, you can change information appearing in the header or footer of the report. For example, you could change the report title or remove page numbers on the Header/Footer tab. On the **Fonts & Numbers** tab, you can change the fonts used. You can also change how numbers are presented.

PRACTICE EXERCISE

Modify and print reports for Sac City Accounting.

(Sac City wants a hard copy of its chart of accounts and general journal.)

1. Modify and print a chart of accounts.

   a. Click **Reports** in the main menu bar.

   b. Click **List**.

   c. Click **Account Listing**.

   d. Click **Customize Report**.

(continued)

e. On the **Display Tab**, uncheck all options except the **(left margin)**, **Account**, and **Type** options. (Checkmarks are removed by clicking them.) You'll need to scroll down to see all the options available.

f. Click **OK**.

g. Grab the separator bar at the top right of the **Account** column. Drag the bar to the right until you can see the entire account name.

h. Click **Print** (at the top of the open window) and select **Report** (or simply click CTRL P to access the print menu).

  i. Choose **Landscape Orientation**.

  ii. Select **Fit report to 1 page(s) wide**.

i. Click **Preview**.

j. Click **Close**.

k. Click **Cancel**.

l. Close the window.

2. Modify a Journal report.

a. Click **Reports** in the main menu bar.

b. Click **Accountant & Taxes**.

c. Click **Journal**.

  i. You may get a message about collapsing and expanding transactions. Click **OK**.

d. Click **Customize Report**.

e. Click the **Filters** tab.

  i. Highlight Date.

  ii. Enter "08/1/17" to "11/30/17" as the filter choices.

  iii. Highlight **Transaction Type** and select **Bill** from the dropdown menu.

  iv. Click **OK**.

f. Select **date** in the **Sort By** dropdown menu at the top of the report screen.

g. Close the window.

CUSTOMIZING QUICKBOOKS PRO

One of the reasons QuickBooks is so popular is that it can be used in different types of organizations and in many different industries. That flexibility, however, presents some challenges. The tools needed by a retail store (the ability to track inventory held for sale, for example) are not the same as the tools needed by a construction contractor (the ability to create estimates, for example). If all the tools needed in all the different industries were visible all the time, users might justifiably complain that the menu options are a little **too** extensive.

QuickBooks solves this by allowing companies to easily customize the program. Users can select or deselect features (known as **preferences**). If you don't need to track inventory, you don't turn that feature on. If you don't create estimates, you don't turn that feature on. Not all features can be turned on or off, but many can—and that makes the program more streamlined and user friendly.

You can customize the features available in QuickBooks in a variety of ways:

- As part of the initial company setup (covered in Chapter 12).
- By changing the **preferences** in an existing company.

Editing Preferences

To change preferences, click **Edit** (main menu bar) then **Preferences**. The screen will look something like this (depending on which category and which tab you choose):

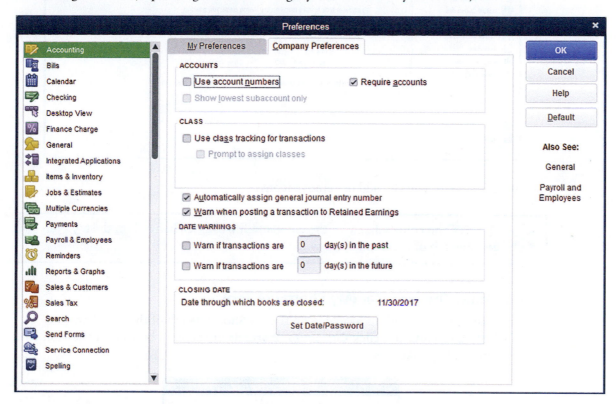

Preferences are grouped by category (left side of page). For most categories, there are **Company Preferences** and **My Preferences** (preferences specific to a single user). The screenshot shows the **Company Preferences** for the **Accounting** category.

> **WARNING: When you make changes in *Preferences*, options on the main menu bar and icons on the Home page may change.**

Customizing The Look Of Quickbooks

You can also customize the look of the Home page and the icon bar.

Customizing the Home Page

The icons available on the Home page are, for the most part, determined by the preferences selected in the initial company setup. However, you can also make changes through the **Desktop View** tab of the **Preferences** window. The **Company Preferences** tab of **Desktop View** looks like this:

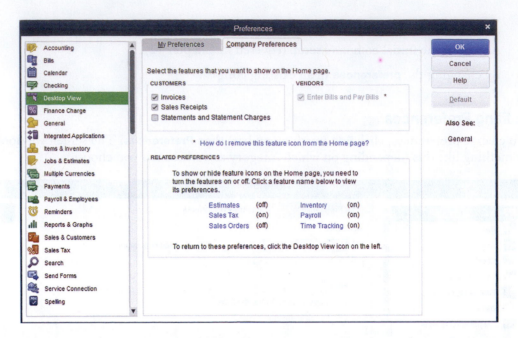

On this screen, you can add or remove icons.

 HINT: The color scheme of the company file can be changed on the **My Preferences** tab of the **Desktop View**.

Customizing The Icon Bar (My Shortcuts Tab)

You can customize the options available on the **My Shortcuts** tab of the icon bar.

Click **My Shortcuts** and click **Customize Shortcuts** at the very bottom of the icon bar. The screen will look like this:

You can delete options by highlighting the item and clicking **Delete**. You can also change the order by clicking the diamond bullet to the left of the icon name and dragging it up or down.

To add options to **My Shortcuts**, click **Add**.

The screen will look like this:

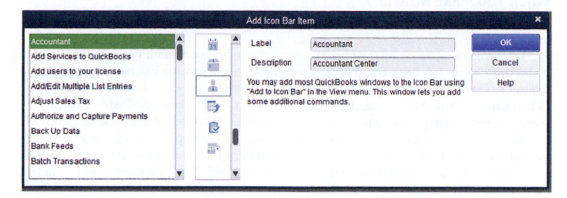

Highlight the option you want to add. Choose the icon you want to have associated with the function. Change the **Label** and **Description** if you prefer and then click **OK**.

Customize QuickBooks for Sac City Accounting.
(Sac City wants to reduce some of the pop-up warnings.)

1. Change a **Preference**.
   a. Click **Edit**.
   b. Click **Preferences**.
   c. Click **Accounting** (on left bar of screen).
   d. Click **Company Preferences** tab.
   e. For both date warnings, click **Warn if transactions are** and enter "180" for the number of days.
   f. Click **OK**.

PRACTICE
EXERCISE

A FEW GENERAL GUIDELINES

Messages

You will soon get used to seeing pop-up messages. There are three types of messages:

- Invitations to purchase QuickBooks products.
  - You will not need to purchase additional products for this course so if you want, you can turn those messages off.
    - Select the **Preferences** menu option on the **Edit** menu (main menu bar).
    - Select the **General** option (left side of window).
    - On the **My Preferences** tab, check the **Turn off pop-up messages for products and services**.

- Informational (reminder) messages.

- Warning messages.

Read the informational and warning messages carefully to begin with. You **will** be able to turn some of the messages off as you become more familiar with QuickBooks. The option to turn off a message, if available, is selected within the message itself.

When You Make Mistakes

QuickBooks is very forgiving. You can change, void, or delete most transactions pretty much at will.

Just remember, in a regular company, transactions are not generally changed or deleted if the transaction has been completed. (For example, the invoice has been sent out, or a deposit has been brought to the bank.) Why? Because the transaction has actually occurred. (The customer has the invoice. The bank has recorded the deposit.) Instead, errors are corrected by creating a new transaction. (A credit memo is issued. An additional deposit is recorded.) In some cases, transactions can be voided. For example, a check was written but not mailed. The check physically exists, but it can be voided and not sent out.

That being said, we're not in a real business, so you will probably want to edit or delete transactions that you enter incorrectly in your homework assignments.

> **BEHIND THE SCENES** In QuickBooks, deleted transactions don't appear on reports. Voided transactions do appear but with zero dollar amounts. Keeping track of voided transactions is a good internal control policy.

There is one more thing you need to know before you start changing or deleting transactions. Often times, transactions are related. You invoice a customer. The bookkeeper pays the bill. You deposit the payment. QuickBooks connects all three transactions. If you've made an error in the customer payment amount, you'll need to delete the deposit (or at least delete that specific payment from the deposit) before you can change the payment amount. So, when you find an error, consider first whether it's connected to other transactions. If so, work backward. Delete, or correct, the transactions in date order (most recent to least recent).

Suggestions For Finding Mistakes

You will be given "check figures" to help you as you complete your homework assignments. If all your numbers agree to the check figures, you have a reasonably good chance of having completed the assignment correctly. (Agreeing to check figures is not a **guarantee** that all the entries are recorded correctly, but it's certainly a comfort!)

What if you don't agree? Where do you start looking? Here are some suggestions.

- CHECK DATES. Entering an incorrect date is the single most common cause of student errors (and student headaches!). QuickBooks enters default dates when you first open a form. It defaults to the current date when you start entering transactions during a work session. If you change the date on the first invoice, it will default to that new date when you enter the second invoice. If you open a new form, however, it will default back to the current date. Accounting is date-driven, so your financial statements won't match the check figures if you enter a transaction in the wrong month. First thing to do? Pull a report of transactions dated BEFORE the first transaction date in the assignment and then one of transactions dated AFTER the last transaction date of the assignment. Make sure you're only checking transactions that you entered. (There are some transactions that were entered in the initial setup of the company files. Those should not be changed.)

- **There are always two sides to every story.** This is **double-entry accounting**, so if one account is wrong, then at least one other account is also wrong. It's hard to find errors in cash, accounts receivable (A/R), and accounts payable (A/P) due to the sheer volume of transactions that affect these accounts. So, if your numbers don't match the check figures, see if you can find the other account(s) that is(are) also off. If you can find and correct the other error(s), these accounts will, of course, fix themselves!

- **Debits** on the left, **credits** on the right. QuickBooks gets the debit and credit part down really well when it comes to standard transactions (invoices, checks, etc.). However, when it comes to journal entries, QuickBooks relies completely on you. It will debit (credit) whatever you tell it to debit (credit). We're all human. Sometimes we get our journal entries reversed. You can often spot those errors pretty easily by looking at the balance sheet. Does Accumulated Depreciation show a debit balance? That's a problem. Look at supplies accounts, prepaid accounts, and accrued expense accounts and see if the balances look reasonable. Adjusting journal entries are frequently made to those accounts.

- **Math hints.** Errors can also be found, sometimes, by checking the difference between the check figure and your total. Is the number divisible by nine? You may have a transposition error (for example, you entered 18 instead of 81). All differences due to transposition errors are divisible by nine. Is the difference equal to the amount of a transaction? Maybe you forgot to enter it (or entered it on the wrong date). Is the difference equal to twice one of your transactions? You may have entered in a journal entry backwards (watch those debits and credits!).

Double-entry accounting A method of accounting that results in the recording of equal amounts of debits and credits.

Debit (entry) An entry on the left side (or in the debit column) of an account.

Credit (entry) An entry on the right side (or in the credit column) of an account.

WHEN YOU'RE DONE FOR THE DAY

If proper closing procedures are followed and files become corrupted, you may be able to get help from Intuit (at a cost, of course) to recover your data. If proper closing procedures are NOT followed, it may be impossible for them to help you.

So, close all your open windows and close the company file before you exit QuickBooks. Make sure you also use the "Safely remove hardware" feature on your computer if you're using a USB drive.

Close down Sac City Accounting's QuickBooks file.

1. Close all open windows.
   a. Click **Window**.
   b. Click **Close All**.

2. Make a backup copy of your company file.
   a. Click **File**.
   b. Click **Back Up Company**.
   c. Click **Create Local Backup**.
   d. Select **Local Backup**.
   e. Select **Save it now**.
   f. Modify the file name, if appropriate, and click **Save**.

(continued)

PRACTICE
EXERCISE

3. Close the company file.

  a. Click **File**.

  b. Click **Close Company**.

4. Close QuickBooks.

  a. Click **File**.

  b. Click **Exit**.

5. Safely eject your USB drive, if applicable.

ANSWER TO
QuickCheck
1-1

Yes. The user creates the account name and chooses the account type. Be careful that the account type you select is correct.

ANSWER TO
QuickCheck
1-2

Sales orders, purchase orders, and estimates are not considered **accounting transactions** because the **accounting equation** does not change when orders are placed or estimates are given.

Accounting transaction An economic event that requires accounting recognition; an event that affects any of the elements of the accounting equation—assets, liabilities, or stockholders' equity.

Accounting equation An expression of the equivalency of the economic resources and the claims upon those resources of a business, often stated as Assets = Liabilities + Stockholders' Equity.

CHAPTER SHORTCUTS

To create a new working file from a backup file

1. Open QuickBooks Pro
2. File/Open or Restore Company
3. Restore a backup copy/Next
4. Browse for location on server where backup is located/Open
5. Next
6. Browse for location on USB where you want file created/Save
7. OK

To open a company working file

1. Open QuickBooks Pro
2. File/Open or Restore Company
3. Open a Company File/Next
4. Browse for file on USB drive and double click

To back up a company file

1. File/Create Backup
2. Local backup/Next
3. Browse for location on USB where you want file saved/Next

  a. Date and time stamp to clearly identify your backup files

  b. Complete verification

4. If you are saving to the USB containing your .QBW file, you will get a warning message; click Use this Location
5. Save it now/Next
6. Check location and change name if desired

To restore a backup file when you're in a working file

1. File/Open or Restore Company
2. Restore a backup copy/Next
3. Local Backup/Next
4. Browse for location of backup file/Open
5. Next
6. Continue
7. Enter YES

To change the company name

1. Click Company/Company Information

To change the Icon Bar

1. Click View/Customize Icon Bar

To see what windows are open

1. Click View/Open Window List

To change preferences

1. Click Edit/Preferences

To add an account

1. Click Lists/Chart of Accounts
2. Click Account/New

To edit an account

1. Click Lists/Chart of Accounts
2. Highlight account to change
3. Click Account/Edit Account

To delete an account

1. Click Lists/Chart of Accounts
2. Highlight account to delete
3. Click Account/Delete Account

CHAPTER REVIEW (Answers available on the publisher's website.)

Matching

Match the term or phrase (as used in QuickBooks) to its definition

1. .QBB file
2. .QBW file
3. Find
4. Transaction type
5. Item
6. Payroll item
7. Expanding or collapsing
8. Preference

_____ Name given to a specific form

_____ Specific type of compensation, payroll tax, or other labor-related charge

_____ File extension used with company backup files

_____ Command used to search for (query) data

_____ Specific type of customer or inventory charge

_____ Options for modifying the level of detail included on a report

_____ Customizable feature

_____ File extension used with company working files

Multiple Choice

1. The company file used to record transactions has the file extension _____ .
   a. .QBW
   b. .QBB
   c. .working
   d. .qbx

2. Which QuickBooks **account type** should be selected when setting up the general ledger account "Buildings"? (Assume the buildings are used as the corporate headquarters.)

   a. Other asset

   b. Property, plant, and equipment

   c. Asset

   d. Fixed asset

3. Your company files should be stored on _____ .

   a. the server at your school

   b. a local drive on the school lab computers

   c. either a USB drive or your personal computer

4. Which of the following statements is false?

   a. General ledger accounts can be added in QuickBooks at any time.

   b. You can have more than one account set up as an "Accounts receivable" **account type** in QuickBooks.

   c. A subaccount doesn't need to be the same account **type** as the primary account.

   d. The chart of accounts is considered a **list** in QuickBooks.

5. In QuickBooks, the **transaction type** for recording a sale on account is _____ .

   a. Sale

   b. Sales receipt

   c. Bill

   d. Invoice

ASSIGNMENTS

Assignment 1A

At Your Service

Assignments with the MBC are available in myBusinessCourse.

Your nephew, Gilbert Greenjeans, was given a $6,000 check from his grandparents for his 16th birthday. They encouraged him to deposit the check in a college savings account. Gilbert understood their point of view, but he was a very ambitious young man and thought he'd be better off using that money to start a small lawn-mowing business. He believed he could make more money mowing lawns than he could earn, in interest, on money in a savings account. The fact that he lived near a very exclusive neighborhood full of palatial homes and large yards was a real bonus. He came to you for advice.

After you cautioned him on all the risks of going into business for himself, you realized that he was very serious about this new venture, so you decided to give him some help. You first told him that he'd have to come up with a business name and business structure. Gilbert decided to set the company up as a sole proprietorship under the name "At Your Service."

On 10/20/17, Gilbert used $700 of his grandparents' gift to purchase, for cash, a good lawnmower, a lawn edger, and some rakes ($600) and a big supply of yard waste bags ($100).

He convinced his father to co-sign on a loan for a truck. The truck, which he purchased on 11/1, cost $20,000. He put $5,000 down and financed the balance with First Sacramento Bank over three years. His monthly payment (including interest at 5 percent) was set at $450. The first payment was due on 12/1.

He set up the following fee schedule to start:

- Weekly lawn mowing with edging
  - Large yard: $200 per week
  - Medium yard: $125 per week
  - Small yard: $75 per week

- Other gardening services
  - Leaf raking: $25 per hour

He signed up three clients in November and started working right away.

Gilbert has been tracking his business transactions in QuickBooks Pro 2015. He has no accounting knowledge though, and it's taking him so long to do his accounting that he's falling behind on his homework! His parents have asked you to help him out. He has entered all the basic transactions through November 30. You will be entering all the December transactions and helping him prepare all the financial reports as of 12/31/17, the company's year-end.

To begin you need to create a working file (.QBW file). Here is a refresher!

a. Open QuickBooks Pro.

b. Click the **File** dropdown menu and select **Open or Restore Company**.

c. At the **What type of file do you want to open or restore?** prompt, choose **Restore a backup copy**.

d. Click **Next**.

e. At the **Is the backup copy stored locally or online?** prompt, select **Local** and click **Next**.

f. Locate the .QBB file "At Your Service 2017 (Student Data)." Your instructor will give you instructions on where to find the file.

g. Highlight the file name and click **Open**.

h. At the **Where do you want to restore the file?** prompt, click **Next**.

i. Save the file to your USB drive (or your computer) using the **Save in** box (upper left corner). [**TIP:** There can sometimes be problems if you save the file using the same file name as the backup file. Consider replacing *Student Data* with your last name. Also consider setting up a separate folder on your USB drive for *At Your Service* so that you can easily find your files in the future.]

j. Click **Update Now** if asked about updating the company file and click **Yes** to confirm.

k. Set up your password if prompted.

l. Click **OK** at the **Your data has been restored successfully** message.

> **!** **WARNING:** QuickBooks has now created your new working file (.QBW file). This is the file you will be using to enter transactions. You will open this file each time you work on At Your Service. Do NOT continue to create new working files.

You'll also need to add your name to the company file.

a. Click **Company** (main menu bar).

b. Click **My Company**.

c. Click the edit icon (the pencil at the top right of the Company Information section of the window).

d. Change the company name by adding your first and last names before "At Your Service" under both the **Contact Information** and **Legal Information** tabs. (Use your actual name.) [**TIP:** Because the company name appears on all reports, this is how your homework assignments will be identified. Don't forget this step!]

e. Click **OK**.

f. Exit out of the window by clicking the small ✖ in the top right corner of the **My Company** window or by pressing the **ESC** button on your computer.

You are now ready to start your assignment!

CHART OF ACCOUNTS WORK

You take a look at the company's chart of accounts and notice that the revenue and expense accounts are listed in alphabetic order. You decide to organize the chart of accounts a little so that the presentation is more professional.

1. Currently, the largest source of revenue for your nephew is lawn mowing. He expects to add other gardening services next, so you move the Other Service Revenue account so that it will be the **last** income account to appear on the profit and loss statement.

2. You also notice that interest expense is appearing with all the operating expense accounts. You want interest expense to show under **Other Expenses** on the profit and loss statement, so you change the account **type**.

3. You think the operating expenses should be organized into groups (categories) of related expenses. [**TIP:** You will need to set up header accounts for each category. You won't be posting transactions to those accounts. They are used only for presentation purposes. The other accounts listed are already set up. You just need to edit them so they become subaccounts of the appropriate header accounts. Make sure your accounts are listed in the exact order given here. Ignore the Payroll Expenses account that's set up in your file. We won't be using that account.] The order of the categories (and their subaccounts) should be:

ACCOUNT NAME	
Equipment Expenses	Header Account
Gasoline Expense	Subaccount
Repairs and Maintenance Expense	Subaccount
Depreciation Expense	Subaccount
Supplies Expenses	Header Account
Gardening Supplies Expense	Subaccount
Office Supplies Expense	Subaccount
Business Promotion Expenses	Header Account
Advertising Expense	Subaccount
Taxes and Professional Services	Header Account
Insurance Expense	Subaccount
Business Licenses and Taxes	Subaccount
Other Operating Expenses	Header Account
Bank Service Charges	Subaccount
Miscellaneous Expense	Subaccount

4. You also look at the balance sheet accounts. You move Accumulated Depreciation so that it is listed AFTER the Computer Software account.

ITEM LIST WORK

You talk with your nephew about services he plans to provide. Lawn mowing is the main service, but he provides some other gardening services (like leaf raking) as well. He's open to providing other services in the future, but he's not yet sure what those might be.

1. You organize the item list. The primary (header) items (Mowing, Other Gardening Services, Other Services) have already been set up. You edit the other **items** (Large Weekly, Medium Weekly, Small Weekly, and Leaf Raking) so they are appropriately classified as **subitems**. You make sure the items are listed in the order shown here:

ITEM NAME	
Mowing	**Header item**
Large Weekly	Subitem
Medium Weekly	Subitem
Small Weekly	Subitem
Other Gardening Services	**Header item**
Leaf Raking	Subitem
Other Services	**Header item**

✳ **HINT:** It's a good idea to do a backup after each chapter assignment. Remember, though, the backup is just used in case your working file is damaged in some way.

REPORTS TO CREATE FOR ASSIGNMENT 1A

All reports should be in portrait orientation; fit to one page wide. Both reports can be found under the **Lists** option of the **Reports** menu (main menu bar).

- Account listing
  - Modify the report so just the **(left margin)**, **account**, and **type** columns appear. Make sure the account name column is wide enough to see the entire name. Remember: Clicking on and moving the separator bars between the column headings allows you to change the width of the column.

- Item listing
  - Modify the report so that only the following columns appear:
    - **Item**
    - **Description**
    - **Type**
    - **Account**
    - **Price**
  - Decrease the column widths so that the report fits well in portrait orientation.

Your sister Monica started a dog-walking business in November 2017 as a way to earn money for college tuition. She decided to operate as a sole proprietorship for now because her operations are fairly simple.

She already has a few regular customers and is excited about the possibility of attracting new ones. She currently offers the following services:

- Dog walks
  - Daily: $20
  - Weekly (5 walks a week): $75 (walks occur Monday through Friday)

- Dog care
  - Dog transport to veterinarian or grooming appointments: $25 per hour
  - In-home visits: $15 per hour

She didn't have a need for any special equipment, but she did purchase a used van that she uses to transport the dogs. The van cost her $7,600. She put $4,000 down and financed the rest with

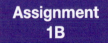

**Assignment
1B**

Dancing with
Dogs

**Assignments with the
📕 are available in
myBusinessCourse.**

Friendly Freeport Bank. The loan is for 60 months at 8 percent interest. The monthly payment is $73 with the first payment due on December 1, 2017.

She took your advice and has been tracking her business transactions in QuickBooks Pro 2015. She has no accounting knowledge though, and she's asked you so many questions that you've decided that it would be easier to just do the accounting for her—at a fee, of course! She has entered all the basic transactions through November 30. You will be entering all the December transactions and helping her prepare all the financial reports as of 12/31/17, the company's year-end.

To begin you need to create a working file (.QBW file). Here is a refresher!

a. Open QuickBooks Pro.

b. Click the **File** dropdown menu and select **Open or Restore Company**.

c. At the **What type of file do you want to open or restore?** prompt, choose **Restore a backup copy**.

d. Click **Next**.

e. At the **Is the backup copy stored locally or online?** prompt, select **Local** and click **Next**.

f. Locate the .QBB file "Dancing with Dogs 2017 (Student Data)." Your instructor will give you instructions on where to find the file.

g. Highlight the file name and click **Open**.

h. At the **Where do you want to restore the file?** prompt, click **Next**.

i. Save the file to your USB drive (or your computer) using the **Save in** box (upper left corner). [**TIP:** There can sometimes be problems if you save the file using the same file name as the backup file. Consider replacing *Student Data* with your last name. Also consider setting up a separate folder on your USB drive for *Dancing with Dogs* so that you can easily find your files in the future.]

j. Click **Update Now** if asked about updating the company file and click **Yes** to confirm.

k. Set up your password if prompted.

l. Click **OK** at the **Your data has been restored successfully** message.

> **! WARNING:** QuickBooks has now created your new working file (.QBW file). This is the file you will be using to enter transactions. You will open this new .QBW file each time you work on Dancing with Dogs assignments. Do NOT continue to create new working files.

You'll also need to add your name to the company file.

a. Click **Company** (main menu bar).

b. Click **My Company**.

c. Click the edit icon (the pencil at the top right of the window).

d. Change the company name by adding your first and last names before "Dancing with Dogs" under both the **Contact Information** and **Legal Information** tabs. (Use your actual name.) [**TIP:** Because the company name appears on all reports, this is how your homework assignments will be identified. Don't forget this step!]

e. Click **OK**.

f. Exit out of the window by clicking the small ✖ in the top right corner of the **My Company** window or by pressing the **ESC** button on your computer.

You are now ready to start your assignment!

CHART OF ACCOUNTS WORK

You take a look at the company's chart of accounts and notice that the revenue and expense accounts are listed in alphabetic order. You decide to organize the chart of accounts a little so that the presentation is more professional.

1. Currently, the largest source of revenue for your sister is dog walking, so you move the Dog Walking Income account so that it will appear **first** on the profit and loss statement.

2. You also notice that interest expense is appearing with all the operating expense accounts. You want interest expense to show under **Other Expenses** on the profit and loss statement, so you change the account **type**.

3. You think the operating expenses should be organized into groups (categories) of related expenses. [**TIP:** You will need to set up an account for each category (header accounts). You won't be posting transactions to those accounts. They are used only for presentation purposes. The other accounts listed are already set up. You just need to edit them so they become subaccounts of the appropriate header accounts. Make sure your accounts are in the exact order given here.] The order of the categories (and their accounts) is:

ACCOUNT NAME	
Supplies and Helper Expenses	Header Account
Dog Supplies Expense	Subaccount
Office Supplies Expense	Subaccount
Vehicle Expenses	Header Account
Gas Expense	Subaccount
Repairs and Maintenance Expense	Subaccount
Depreciation Expense—Vehicles	Subaccount
Business Promotion Expenses	Header Account
Advertising Expense	Subaccount
Client Relations Expense	Subaccount
Taxes and Professional Services	Header Account
Insurance Expense	Subaccount
Business Licenses and Permits	Subaccount
Legal Fees	Subaccount
Other Operating Expenses	Header Account
Bank Service Charges	Subaccount
Miscellaneous Expense	Subaccount

4. You also look at the balance sheet accounts. You move Accumulated Depreciation so that it is listed AFTER the vehicle account.

ITEM LIST WORK

You talk with your sister about services she plans to provide. Dog walking is the main service, but she does some dog care as well. She plans to have some special events in the future, but she's not yet sure what these events will be.

5. You organize the item list. The primary (header) items (Walks, Care, and Specials) have already been set up. You edit the other **items** (Daily Rate, Weekly Rate, Home Visits, and Transport) so they are appropriately classified as **subitems**. [**TIP:** Header items have already been set up for the three main categories (Walks, Care, and Specials). You will just need to edit the other **items** so that they are appropriately classified as **subitems**. Make

sure the items are listed in the exact order shown.] You make sure the items are listed in the order shown below.

ITEM NAME	
Walks	**Header item**
Daily Rate	Subitem
Weekly Rate	Subitem
Care	**Header item**
Home Visits	Subitem
Transport	Subitem
Specials	**Header item**

 HINT: It's a good idea to do a backup after each chapter assignment. Remember, though, the backup is just used in case your working file is damaged in some way.

REPORTS TO CREATE FOR ASSIGNMENT 1B

All reports should be in portrait orientation; fit to one page wide. Both reports can be found under the **Lists** option of the **Reports** menu (main menu bar).

- Account Listing
  - Modify the report so just the **(left margin)**, **account**, and **type** columns appear. Make sure the account name column is wide enough to see the entire name. Remember: clicking on the separator bars between the column headings allows you to change the width of the column.

- Item Listing
  - Modify the report so that only the following columns appear:
    - **(left margin)**
    - **Item**
    - **Description**
    - **Type**
    - **Account**
    - **Price**
  - Decrease the column widths so that the report fits well in portrait orientation.

APPENDIX 1A MULTI-USER MODE

Many companies using QuickBooks have more than one employee working in the accounting department at the same time, and they all need access to the company file. Simultaneous access to company files is possible if QuickBooks is configured for multi-user access (**multi-user mode**).

QuickBooks must be installed on each user's computer and all computers must be networked within the company. QuickBooks Premier allows installation of the program on up to 5 computers. QuickBooks Enterprise allows installation on up to 30 computers.

HINT: You can add additional users to a QuickBooks license by clicking **Manage My License** on the *Help* dropdown menu (main menu bar) and selecting **Buy Additional User License**.

If multi-user mode were needed, one computer would be designated as the **host** computer. In addition, all company files would need to be prepared for multi-user access.

In most companies, the **host** computer would contain the company data files. Let's say Joe's computer is the **host** computer. Beverly's computer has QuickBooks installed and her computer is networked to Joe's. **Multi-user mode** is turned on. When transactions are entered or operations are performed by Beverly, a message is sent to Joe's computer. The company file is appropriately updated in Joe's computer and the updated file is made accessible to Beverly.

INITIAL CONFIGURATION

A computer can be designated as the **host** computer as part of the original installation of the program on the computer. (The **multi-user host installation** option should be selected.)

If the program has already been installed on the computer, open QuickBooks but do not open a company file. Click **File** and then click **Utilities**.

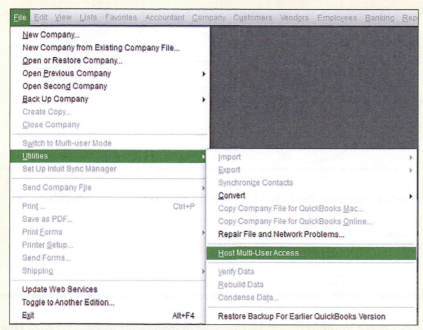

Click **Host Multi-User Access**. If you have set an administrator password, you will be asked to enter that. You will also be asked to confirm your request to set the computer as the **host**. If you answer **Yes**, the following screen will appear:

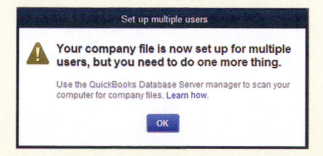

The company data files are prepared for multi-user use through the **QuickBooks Database Server Manager**. Go to the **Start button** on your computer and click **QuickBooks**. Then open the **QuickBooks Database Server Manager**.

Click the **Scan Folders** tab and select the folders that contain company data files. The company files are ready for multi-user access once the scan is complete.

WORKING IN MULTI-USER MODE

You can turn on **multi-user mode** before you open a company file or when you're working in a company file.

To open a company in **multi-user mode**, click **Open or restore an existing company** in the **No Company Open** window.

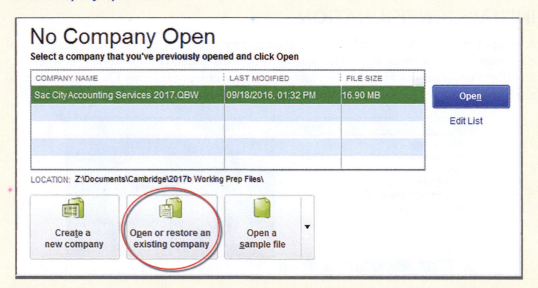

Search for the company file (.QBW file) you want to open, and highlight it.

Put a checkmark in the box next to **Open file in multi-user mode** and click **Open**.

If you're already in a company file but are working in **single-user mode**, click **File** on the main menu bar.

Select **Switch to Multi-user Mode**. The option will show **Switch to Single-user Mode** if you're already in **multi-user mode**.

QuickBooks

Service Companies

Businesses are frequently classified according to primary source of revenue as follows:

- Service companies earn revenue by charging a fee for services they perform.

- Merchandising companies earn revenue by buying products from one company and selling those products to consumers (or to distributors).

- Manufacturing companies earn revenue by making products and selling them to consumers (or to merchandisers).

QuickBooks Pro can handle the accounting for all three types of companies. It works best, though, for smaller companies—especially for small service and merchandising companies. Larger companies, especially larger manufacturing companies, would be better served by software that could handle the volume and complexity of their operations.

In this textbook, we'll be looking at how QuickBooks can function in service and merchandising companies. We will not be covering the QuickBooks features that would apply to manufacturing companies.

We'll look at service companies first because the accounting for service companies is fairly straightforward.

SECTION OVERVIEW

Chapter 2 covers the sales cycle in a service company.
Chapter 3 covers the purchase cycle in a service company.
Chapter 4 covers end of period accounting in a service company.

Selling Services
(Service Company)

After completing Chapter 2, you should be able to:

1. Add, edit, and delete customers.

2. Add, edit, and delete service items.

3. Record sales on account, cash sales, and customer credit memos.

4. Record customer payments on account.

5. Record deposits to bank.

6. Create and modify sales and receivables reports.

Objectives

WHAT IS THE SALES CYCLE IN A SERVICE COMPANY?

The sales cycle in a service company normally follows these steps:

✓ Get the job (client).

✓ Provide the service.

✓ Bill for the service.

✓ Collect the fee.

Getting the job (or the client) is outside the accounting function, but the accounting system **does** have to maintain records related to the transactions with every customer.

At the very least, the following information must be maintained for each customer:

● Contact information.

● Terms of payment.

● Shipping instructions.

● Record of past transactions.

● Record of any unpaid invoices.

Before any transactions can be recorded, of course, the customer (client) needs to be set up in QuickBooks.

MANAGING CUSTOMERS

Adding a Customer

Customers are entered through the **Customer Center**. The **Customer Center** can be accessed through the **Customer** dropdown menu on the main menu bar or from the icon bar (**My Shortcuts** tab). It can also be accessed by clicking the **Customers** tab on the Home page.

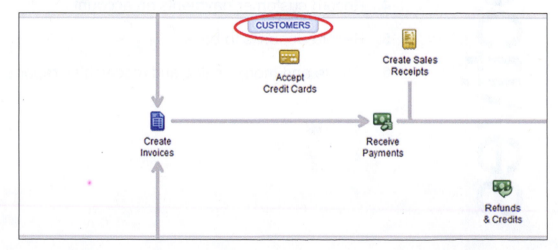

In the **Customer Center**, you can enter new customers, edit existing customers, or delete customers.

> **WARNING:** You cannot delete customers, vendors, accounts, or items that have transactions associated with them. You can, however, make them inactive. Inactive customers (accounts, vendors, items) are still in QuickBooks (and can be reactivated), but they are not available for new transactions. To make a customer inactive, right-click the customer name and click *Make Customer: Job Inactive.*

The initial screen in the **Customer Center** looks something like this:

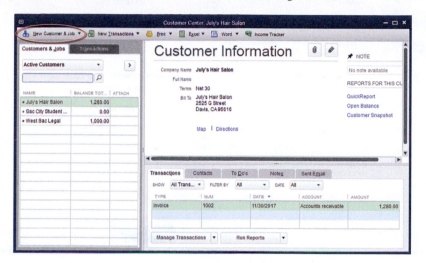

When you click the dropdown menu next to **New Customer & Job** and select **New Customer**, you get this screen:

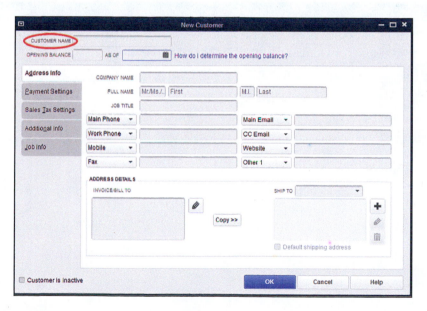

The **Customer Name** field at the top of the screen is used to enter a customer identifier. It could be a number or a shortened version of the name. This **customer name** is used for internal purposes only. It would not appear on any customer invoices. In this class, we'll use the company name as the identifier.

As you can see in the preceding screenshot, there are five tabs in the window. The basic contact information is included on the **Address Info** tab. The **Company Name** and address information entered on this tab will appear on customer invoices.

Credit terms, preferred shipping information, account numbers, and other information related to customer payments are all included on the **Payment Settings** tab.

Sales tax information specific to the customer is included on the **Sales Tax Settings** tab.

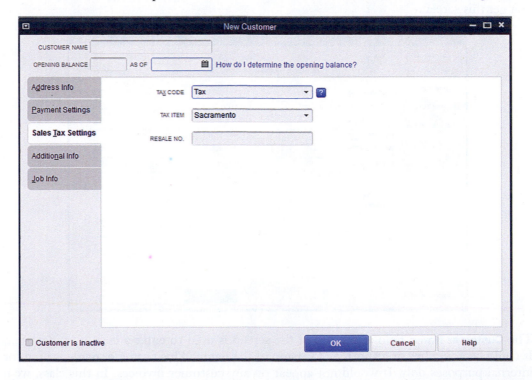

The **Additional Info** tab is used to identify sales reps and customer types. Users can also create custom fields on this tab. Custom fields are covered in Chapter 11, Appendix 11A.

If the company were tracking particular projects for a customer, that information would be included on the **Job Info** tab. (You'll learn more about **jobs** in Chapter 9.)

Changing a Customer Record

Customer information can be changed at any time. The **Customer Center** must be open, and the appropriate customer name must be highlighted.

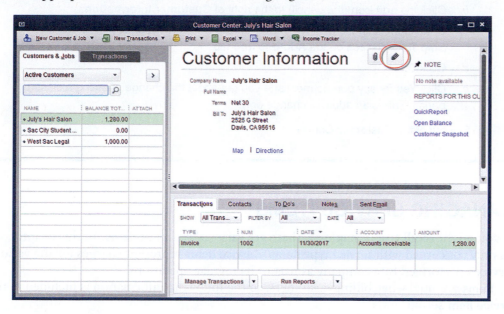

The pencil icon at the top right of screen takes you to the customer's master record. (The pencil icon represents the edit feature.) The tabs on the screen in the **Edit Customer** window are identical to the tabs shown on the previous page for adding customers. In the **Edit Customer** window, you can change customer addresses, payment terms, sales tax settings, and more.

Add and edit customers for Sac City Accounting.
(Sac City gets a new client and receives an address change for an existing client.)

1. Click **Customers** (icon bar or Home page).

2. Add a customer (New customer name: Accounting Student Tutoring Center).

   a. Click the **New Customer & Job** dropdown menu and select **New Customer**.

   b. Enter "Accounting Student Tutoring Center" in the **Company Name** field on the **Address Info** tab.

      i. NOTE: The **Customer Name** (top of screen) will automatically default to the **Company Name** whenever you enter the **Company Name** first.

   c. Enter "Steve Oster" in the **first** and **last name** fields.

   d. Enter "916-199-2222" in the **Main Phone** field.

   e. In the **Address Details** text box (**Invoice/Bill To**), and add the following address information just below the contact name:

      1515 Ravenna Blvd
      Sacramento, CA 95822

   f. Click **Payment Settings** tab and select **Payment Terms** of Net 30.

   g. Although we are not currently selling products at Sac City Accounting, go ahead and select **Tax** as the **Tax Code** and **Sacramento** as the **Tax Item** on the **Sales Tax Settings** tab.

   h. Click **OK**.

(continued)

> 3. Edit a customer. (Edit billing address for West Sac Legal.)
>
>   a. Highlight West Sac Legal (left side of Customer Center window).
>
>   b. Click the **edit** icon (the pencil) to the right of **Customer Information**.
>
>   c. Change the address to "1010 Capital Avenue" for the **Invoice/Bill To** and the **Ship To** addresses on the **Address Info** tab.
>
>   d. Click **OK**.
>
>   e. Click **Yes** for any pop-up message you get about the change affecting a closed period. This is an address change only.
>
> 4. Exit out of the **Customer Center**.

MANAGING SERVICE ITEMS

As you might recall from Chapter 1, there are various "types" of **items**. In this chapter, we are only concerned with **service** type **items**. **Service items** represent charges for the various **services** performed by a company as part of its regular operations.

Items are used when billing customers, so the following information is included in the **service item** set-up:

✓ The standard rate (price) to be charged to the client.

✓ The description that should appear on a client invoice.

✓ The income account that should be credited when the client is charged.

Each **item** can only be associated with one general ledger account, but one general ledger account can be associated with many **items**. This allows the company to keep considerable detail in subsidiary ledgers and still keep the general ledger (and the financial statements) reasonably concise.

Items are set up through the **Item List** option on the **Lists** dropdown menu.

You can add, edit, or delete **items** through this screen using the **Item** button at the bottom left of the screen. The **Item** dropdown menu looks like this:

Adding a Service Item

To add a new service **item**, select the **New** option on the **Item** dropdown menu. The screen will look like this:

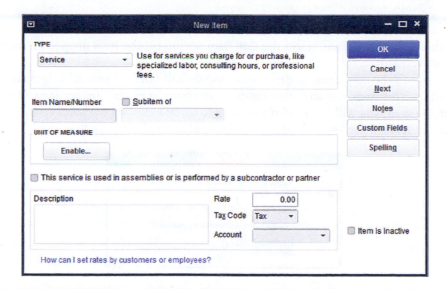

Every service **item type** **must** have an **Item Name/Number** and must be associated with a specific general ledger account.

You can set up a default invoice description and default billing rate when you're adding an **item**.

Because most services are not taxable in most states, you would select **Non** as the **Tax Code** if you were creating a service **item**.

As discussed in Chapter 1, **items** can be "grouped" to organize the **item** list. Click **Subitem** to include an **item** in a group.

> **BEHIND THE SCENES**   The rate (sales price) you set up is a default amount only. You can change the rate when you're creating an invoice. You can also change the description that will appear on the invoice.

If you're going to put an amount on an invoice or a sales receipt, you must first set it up as an **item**.

Editing and Deleting Items

Items can be edited at any time. Items can only be deleted if they have never been used in a transaction.

To edit or delete an item, you must first highlight the item in the Item List screen.

To edit the highlighted item, select the Edit Item option on the Item dropdown menu (bottom left of screen).

You can edit the item name or description, the default rate, the general ledger account associated with the item, and any other fields. If you edit the general ledger account associated with the item, you will be asked if you want to update existing transactions in addition to changing the account for future transactions. The dialog box looks like this:

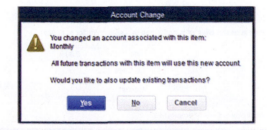

> **WARNING:** Most *item types*, including *service items* can't be changed in QuickBooks. The field will be greyed out if it can't be changed. If you made an error selecting the *type* in the setup, you would need to create a new *item*.

To delete a highlighted item, select the Delete Item option on the Item dropdown menu (bottom left of screen) to open the following dialog box:

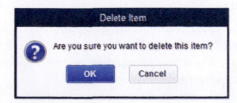

If you try to delete an item that's been used in a transaction, you will get an error message.

Add and edit items for Sac City Accounting.

(Sac City has decided to do more consulting work. They intend to assist clients with budget development and might expand into other areas of consulting in the future, so they want to set up a new item category (Consulting). All consulting income is to be tracked in a new general ledger account (Consulting Services). They also need to make an adjustment in the tax code assigned to one of their existing items.)

PRACTICE
EXERCISE

1. Add an item.
   a. Click **Lists**.
   b. Click **Item List**.
   c. Open **Item** dropdown menu (bottom left of window).
   d. Click **New**.
   e. Select **Service** as the type.
   f. Enter **Item Name/Number** as "Consulting" (new item category).
      i. Leave **Description** blank. (This is the "header" item for the new item category. It won't be used on an invoice and doesn't need a description.)
      ii. Leave **Rate** blank.
      iii. Select **Non** for **Tax Code**.
      iv. Select **Add New** for **Account** (top of **Account** dropdown menu).
      v. Select **Income** as the **Account Type**.
      vi. Enter "Consulting Services" as the **Account Name**.
      vii. Click **Save & Close**.
   g. Click **Next** on the **New Item** screen.
   h. Select **Service** type.
   i. Enter **Item Name/Number** as "Budget prep."
      i. Check **subitem of** and choose "Consulting."
      ii. Enter "Assistance with budget preparation" for **Description**.
      iii. Enter "125" for **Rate**.
      iv. Select **Non** for **Tax Code**.
      v. Select **Consulting Services** for **Account**.
   j. Click **OK**.

2. Edit an item. (Item had an incorrect tax code.)
   a. Highlight **Accounting Services**.
   b. Open **Item** dropdown menu (bottom left of window).
   c. Click **Edit Item**.
   d. Change **Tax Code** to **Non**.
   e. Click **OK**.
   f. Exit out of **Item List** window.

RECORDING SALES REVENUE

In a manual accounting system, an invoice is created. The invoice is then recorded in the sales journal. The sales journal is posted, in total, to the general ledger, and each transaction in the sales journal is posted to the appropriate customer's subsidiary ledger.

In QuickBooks, a form is completed for each sale. QuickBooks automatically does the rest. Because everything is done automatically, the form must include all the relevant information needed.

✓ Who is the customer? (Customer name is needed for posting to the subsidiary ledger.)

✓ What are we charging them for? (What general ledger account should QuickBooks credit?)

✓ Have they paid already, or will they pay later? (What general ledger account should QuickBooks debit?)

Accounts receivable
A current asset that is created by a sale of merchandise or the provision of a service on a credit basis. It represents the amount owed the seller by a customer.

We've already got the customers and the items set up so QuickBooks knows which subsidiary ledger should be updated and which income accounts should be credited when the sales form is completed. But how does QuickBooks know which account to debit in a sale? Should it be Cash or **Accounts receivable**? QuickBooks solves that problem by setting up two different forms (two separate transaction types).

> **BEHIND THE SCENES** For processing purposes, QuickBooks assigns certain default accounts for common transactions. For example, the default debit account for recording a sale on account is Accounts receivable. The default credit account for recording a bill from a vendor is Accounts payable. These accounts are automatically set up (categorized with the proper account **type**) by QuickBooks. The user can change the name of the account but not the **type**.

Recording Sales On Account

Sales on account A sale of merchandise or the provision of a service made on a credit basis.

The form (transaction type) used to record **sales on account** is **invoice**. The default debit account for **invoices** is, of course, Accounts receivable. If needed, multiple accounts can be set up as **accounts receivable account types**. This might be useful for companies that want to track receivables by region or by product line. If multiple accounts are used, the user must identify the appropriate account when the **invoice** is created. (QuickBooks automatically adds a field to the form for that purpose if more than one **accounts receivable** type account exists.)

The credit account(s) in the journal entry underlying an **invoice** transaction will depend, of course, on the **items** included on the **invoice**. As explained earlier, the credit account associated with a specific **item** is set up through the **item list**.

The **invoice** form is easily accessed through the main menu bar on the dropdown menu for **Customers**. It can also be accessed through the Home page (**Create Invoices** button).

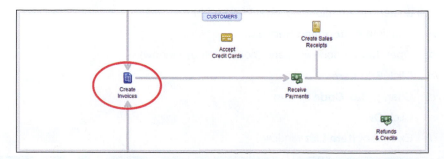

The form looks like this if the "Intuit Service Invoice" template is used (other templates can be accessed using the dropdown menu in the **Template** field in the top middle of the screen):

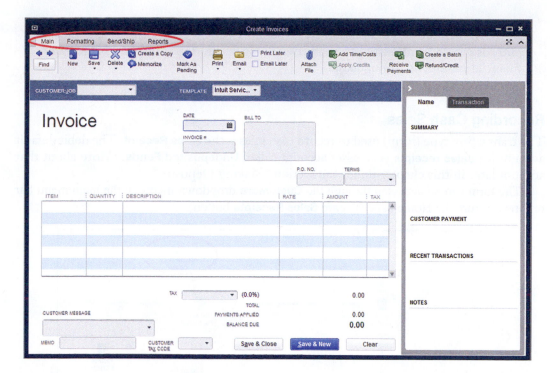

There are various tabs on this and most other forms in QuickBooks. (The tabs are at the top of the window in the menu bar.)

The **Main** tab is used to enter all transaction data. Other tabs include additional tools that might be needed for the specific type of transaction. For example, the **Formatting** tab has options for spell checking and inserting or deleting lines. The **Reports** tab provides easy access to particular information related to the transaction.

To complete an **invoice**, you must enter the customer name, the sale date, the credit terms, and the **items** to be charged to the customer on the **Main** tab.

Common credit terms are automatically set up in QuickBooks. They are accessible through the dropdown menu in the **Terms** field.

Setting up new credit terms will be covered in Chapter 3.

You can add a **customer message** at the bottom of the invoice if you'd like. QuickBooks automatically sets up common customer messages, but users can create additional messages as needed. New messages are set up by selecting **<Add New>** in the dropdown menu next to the **Customer Message** field.

For this class, the **Print Later** and **Email Later** options should not be checked (middle section at the top of the form). Those options allow you to create batches to be processed later. Because we won't be printing or emailing, you can avoid that step.

Click **Save & Close** (or **Save & New** if you are recording multiple **invoices**) to record sales on account.

> **BEHIND THE SCENES** Remember: As soon as you save a transaction, a journal entry is created and posted to the general ledger, and the subsidiary ledgers and financial statements are updated.

Recording Cash Sales

The transaction type (form) used to record cash sales is the **Sales Receipt**. The debit default account for **sales receipts** is an asset account called **Undeposited Funds**. (More about that account later in this chapter under the section "Making Deposits").

The form can be accessed through the **Customers** dropdown menu on the main menu bar or directly from the Home page (**Create Sales Receipts** button).

The form will look something like this if the **Custom Sales Receipt** template is used:

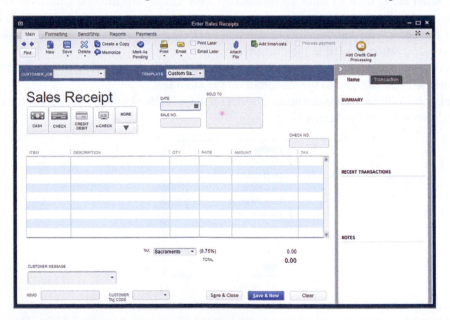

To complete a **sales receipt**, you must enter the customer name, the receipt date, and the **items** to be charged. You also select the payment method.

> ✱ **HINT:** In the QuickBooks Accountant Edition, the payment method is selected using icons. In other versions, the payment method may be selected using a dropdown menu under the **Payment Method** field.

If the customer is paying with a check, the customer's check number can be entered in the **Check No.** field.

HINT: If a company has a lot of walk-in customers and they don't want to track each cash customer's name, they can set up a "Cash Customer" or "Walk-in" customer.

You can also add a **customer message** at the bottom of sales receipts. Clicking **Save & Close** (or **Save & New**) records the transaction.

 HINT: You'll notice a number of options on the menu bar at the top of **invoice** and **sales receipt** forms. Appendix D provides a summary of the purpose of many of the options on these and other forms.

Record cash and credit sales for Sac City Accounting.

(Sac City does some account reconciliation work for July's Hair Salon. They invoice West Sac Legal for monthly bookkeeping services and for some budget preparation assistance. They also need to record cash collected at time of service for some review work they did for Sac City Student News.)

1. Create invoices.
   a. Click **Create Invoices** on Home page.
   b. Use **Intuit Professional Invoice** for invoice **template** (dropdown menu in the top center of the form).
   c. Invoice July's Hair Salon for 4 hours of account reconciliation work.
      i. Select **July's Hair Salon** as the **Customer:Job**.
      ii. Enter "12/5/17" for the **Date**, "1003" for the **Invoice #**. Select **Net 30** for the **Terms**.
      iii. Select **Reconciliation** as the **Item**.
      iv. Enter "4" as the **Quantity** (hours in this case).
      v. Total invoice balance should be $320. Click **Save & New**.
   d. Invoice West Sac Legal for monthly bookkeeping ($1,000) and for 4 hours of budget preparation assistance.
      i. Select **West Sac Legal** as the **Customer:Job**.
      ii. Enter "12/29/17" for the **Date**, "1004" for the **Invoice #**. Terms **Net 30**.
      iii. Select **Monthly** as the first **Item** (**Amount** should be $1,000).
      iv. Tab to second line and select **Budget Prep** as the second **Item**. Enter "4" as the **Quantity**.
      v. Total invoice balance should be $1,500. Click **Save & Close**.

2. Record a cash sale. [Sac City Student News paid $3,200 (by check #6789) for the financial statement review.]
   a. Click **Create Sales Receipt** on Home page.
   b. Select **Sac City Student News** as the **Customer:Job**.
   c. Click the **Check** icon.
   d. Enter "12/21/17" for the **Date** and "100" for the **Sale No**.
   e. Enter "6789" as the **Check No**.

(continued)

PRACTICE EXERCISE

> *f.* There are two items.
>   i. Select **Staff hours** for first **item** and enter quantity of 16.
>   ii. Select **Partner hours** for second **item** and enter quantity of 4.
> *g.* Click **Save & Close**.

QuickCheck **2-1**

What is the underlying journal entry for Invoice 1003 to July's Hair Salon? (Answer at end of chapter.)

Recording Customer Credits

Stuff happens! A client is mistakenly overbilled or maybe the work isn't done to the satisfaction of the client. In either case, a company will probably decide to credit the customer's account by issuing a **credit memo**.

Credit memo A document prepared by a seller to inform the purchaser the seller has reduced the amount owed by the purchaser due to a return or an allowance.

QuickBooks uses the transaction type (form) called **Credit Memo** for crediting customer accounts. It's easily accessible from the Home page (**Refunds & Credits** button).

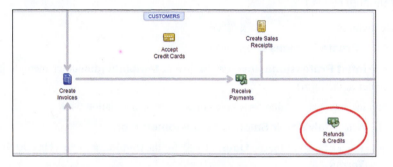

The form will look like this if the "Custom Credit Memo" template is used:

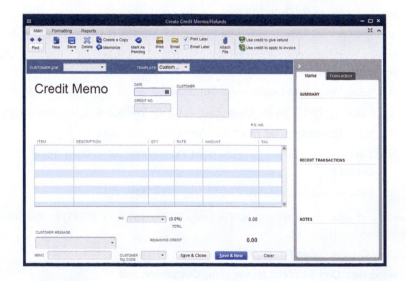

To complete a **credit memo**, you must enter the customer name, the date, and the **items** to be refunded.

You can also add a **customer message** at the bottom of **credit memos**. Clicking **Save & Close** (or **Save & New**) records the transaction.

> **BEHIND THE SCENES** When a credit memo is created, the account(s) associated with the **item**(s) selected are debited in the underlying journal entry. The accounts receivable account (**Accounts Receivable account type**) is credited.

As soon as you save the **credit memo**, QuickBooks will ask you what you want to do with the credit. The screen will look like this:

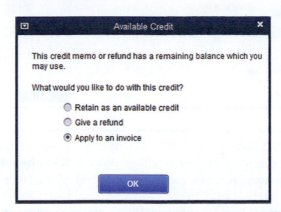

If you choose **Retain as an available credit**, QuickBooks will make the credit available for use with that customer at any point in the future.

If you choose **Give a refund**, the following window will appear:

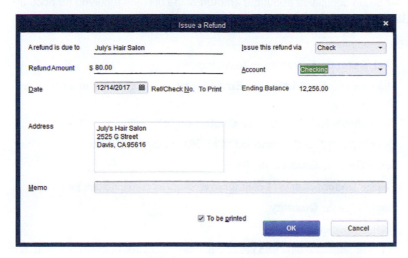

A refund check will automatically be created with this option. (Unchecking **to be printed** at the bottom of the window allows you to enter a manual check number.)

If you choose **Apply to an invoice**, a list of outstanding **invoices** for the customer will appear. You can then select the specific **invoice** to which the credit should be applied.

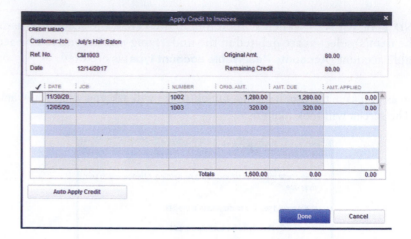

 HINT: You can also apply a credit (or issue a refund) by clicking one of the icons at the top right of the form (either **Use credit to give refund** or **Use credit to apply to invoice**). You can use that feature when you're creating the **credit memo** or at a later time.

PRACTICE EXERCISE

Record a credit memo for Sac City Accounting.
(July's Hair Salon complains about the amount of the bill they received for account reconciliation. Sac City decides to reduce the time billed by one hour.)

1. Create a credit memo.

   a. Click **Refunds & Credits** on Home page.

   b. Make sure the **Print Later** and **Email Later** options at the top of the page are not checked.

   c. Select **July's Hair Salon** as the **Customer:Job**.

   d. Enter "12/14/17" as the **Date** and "CM1003" as the **Credit No.**

   e. Select **Reconciliation** as the **Item**.

   f. Change **Description** to "Credit for overcharge on reconciliation project."

   g. Enter "1" as the **Quantity**.

   h. Total balance should be $80.

      i. The amount should be a positive number. QuickBooks knows to credit Accounts Receivable for the amount because it's entered using the **Credit Memo** form.

   i. In the **Customer Message** dropdown menu (in lower left section of the form), select **<Add New>**.

   j. Enter "Sorry for the miscommunication. You are a valued customer." in the **message** box.

   k. Click **OK**.

   l. Click **Save & Close**.

2. Apply the credit to a specific invoice.

   a. Click **Apply to an invoice**.

   b. Deselect Invoice 1002 by clicking the checkmark next to the date of Invoice 1002.

   c. Select invoice 1003 dated 12/5.

   d. Click **Done**.

RECORDING PAYMENTS FROM CUSTOMERS

Companies generally give customers or clients a number of payment options.

- Customers can pay with check, cash, or credit card at the time of service.
  - Recorded through **Sales Receipts** (already covered in this chapter).
- Customers can buy on account and pay later.

Most companies that sell to individuals would generally only accept cash or major credit cards. An exception would be retail outlets that have their own credit cards. (Macy's and Nordstrom are two examples.)

Most companies that sell to other companies would sell primarily on account. It would simply be impractical for most companies to pay cash or have checks or credit cards ready whenever goods or services are delivered.

In a manual accounting system, customer payments are recorded through the Cash Receipts Journal. The journal is posted, in total, to the general ledger, and each transaction is posted to the appropriate customer's subsidiary ledger (if paying on account). In QuickBooks, all of the steps are done when the form is saved.

Payments On Account

Customer payments on account balances are recorded using the **Receive Payments** form (**Payment** transaction type).

The form can be accessed through the **Customers** dropdown menu on the main menu bar or through the Home page (**Receive Payments** button).

The form looks like this:

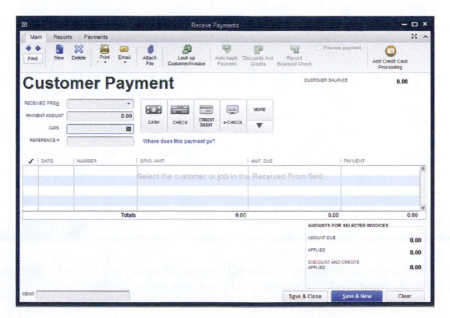

To enter a customer payment, you need to know the amount of the payment, the date, and how the payment should be applied. Unless you turn off the feature in **Preferences** (on the **Payments** tab), QuickBooks will automatically apply payments for you. (You can change the payment application if needed.)

If QuickBooks applies the payment, it will do so in this order:

✔ It will be applied first to an invoice of the **exact** same dollar amount as the payment.

✔ If there's no exact match, QuickBooks will apply the payment in due date order (oldest invoice first).

Full or partial payments can be entered. If a partial payment is received, you should make sure that the amount(s) entered in the **Payment** field(s) agree(s) to the payment amount that should be applied to the specific invoice.

If a partial payment is entered, QuickBooks will give you the option of either leaving the unpaid balance for the **invoice** in accounts receivable or writing it off using a screen that looks like this:

If there are unapplied credits available to the customer, you can apply those while you're recording the payment by clicking the **Discounts And Credits** button.

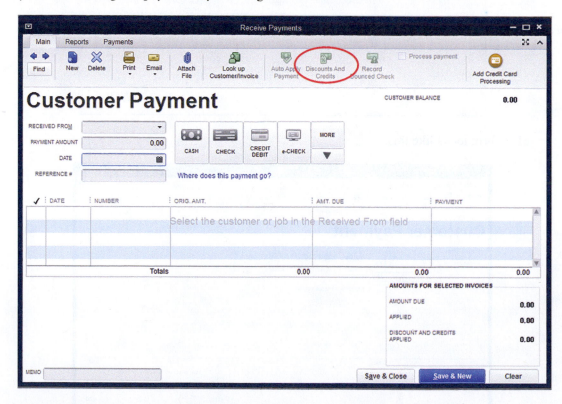

A screen showing all available credits will appear, allowing you to apply the credit to the **invoice** currently being paid. The screen would look something like this:

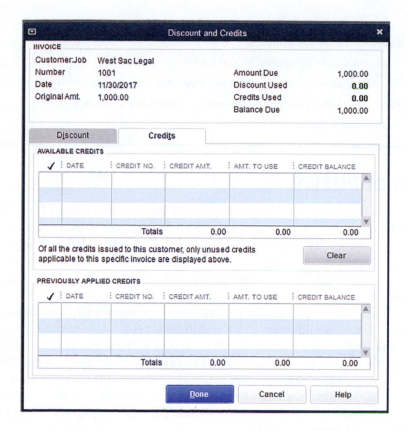

Any available credits would be listed. Previously applied credits would also be listed.

PRACTICE
EXERCISE

Record customer payments on account for Sac City Accounting.
(Sac City received payments from two of its customers.)

1. Record customer payment in full. (July's Hair Salon, check #5865 in the amount of $1,280 for Invoice #1002)

   a. Click **Receive Payments** on Home page.

   b. Select **July's Hair Salon** in the **Received From** field as the **Customer:Job**.

   c. Enter "1,280" as the **Amount**.

   d. Enter "12/7/17" for the payment **Date**.

   e. Click the **Check** icon.

   f. Enter "5865" as the **Check #**.

   g. Payment should be applied to Invoice 1002.

   h. Click **Save & New**.

   i. Click **Yes** if prompted about automatic application of payments.

2. Record customer partial payment. (West Sac Legal check #6899 dated 12/20 for $800 to be applied to Invoice 1001)

   a. Select **West Sac Legal** in the **Received From** field as the **Customer:Job**.

   b. Enter "800" as the **Amount**.

   c. Enter "12/21/17" as the payment **Date**.

   d. Click the **Check** icon.

(continued)

> e. Enter "6899" as the **Check #**.
>
> f. Payment should be applied to Invoice 1001.
>
> > i. Make sure 800 is entered in the **Payment** field for Invoice 1001.
>
> g. Click **Leave this as an underpayment** (bottom left of screen).
>
> h. Click **Save & Close**.

MAKING DEPOSITS

Before you learn how to record bank deposits, you need to understand how QuickBooks handles cash receipts. As you know, there's a journal entry behind every sales receipt (cash sale) and every customer payment on account. Based on your knowledge of accounting, you would probably expect that the debit account for each of the transactions would be Cash, right? (Debit Cash, Credit Revenue for the cash sales and Debit Cash, Credit Accounts Receivable for the customer payments on account).

Because QuickBooks updates the general ledger automatically and immediately for every transaction, that would mean there would be a debit entry to the cash account for every check and cash payment received. Why is that a problem? Well, it's not if you're depositing every payment separately. But most companies group checks when they're making deposits. On the bank statement, the actual deposit amount is shown (not each check that makes up the deposit). It would be difficult (not impossible, but difficult) to reconcile the bank account every month if QuickBooks didn't group the payments together to correspond to the actual deposit amount.

So, here's what QuickBooks does. Instead of debiting Cash for every customer payment, an account called "Undeposited Funds" is debited. Undeposited Funds is an **Other Current Asset** account **type** (not a **Bank** account **type**). You can think of it as a temporary holding account.

When a deposit is actually made, QuickBooks credits the Undeposited Funds account and debits the Cash account for the total of the funds deposited. Now the entries in the Cash account agree (hopefully!) to the entries on the bank statement.

> **HINT:** The preceding process is the QuickBooks default procedure. If you want to change that (decide for yourself where you want the debit to go), you just have to remove that feature on the **Payments** tab of **Preferences**.

Deposits are recorded using the **Make Deposits** form.

This form is accessed through the **Banking** dropdown menu on the main menu bar or through the **Record Deposits** button on the Home page.

If there are undeposited checks, cash, or credit card payments in the Undeposited Funds account, the following screen will appear first:

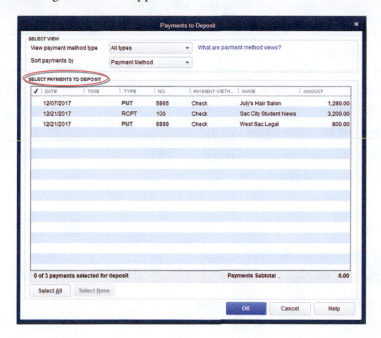

You would select all payments (receipts) that are being included in the day's bank deposit and click **OK**. You can select all the payments or just some of them.

The next screen is the actual **Make Deposits** form. The screen looks something like this:

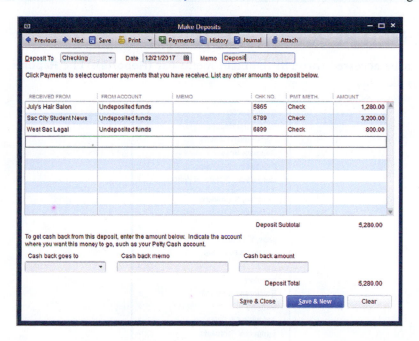

You want to first make sure the correct bank account is showing in the top left **Deposit To** field. (A company might have multiple deposit accounts.)

You can enter additional cash receipts (non-customer receipts) on this screen as well. We'll cover non-customer receipts in a later chapter.

If you want to create a deposit summary report, click **Print** (tool bar at top of screen) and select **Deposit Summary**.

Save & Close records the transaction.

HINT: If there are **no** Undeposited receipts in the Undeposited Funds account, only the second screen (the **Make Deposits** form) will appear when you click **Record Deposits**.

PRACTICE EXERCISE

Make a deposit for Sac City Accounting.
(Sac City deposits cash received during December.)

1. Click **Record Deposits** (Home page).

2. Click **Select All** (bottom left of screen).
   a. Total should be $5,280.

3. Click **OK**.

4. **Date** should be 12/21/17.

5. Click arrow to right of **Print** icon.

6. Click **Deposit Summary** to see checks selected for deposit.

7. In the **Print Lists** window, click **Preview**.
   a. Click **Close**.
   b. Click **Cancel**.

8. Click **Save & Close** in the **Make Deposits** form.

CUSTOMER REPORTS

Reports can be accessed through the main menu bar (**Reports**). The **Reports** dropdown menu looks like this.

Reports can also be accessed through the **Reports** icon on the **My Shortcuts** tab on the icon bar. (The icon bar is just left of the Home page.)

For this chapter, we're most interested in two report categories:

- **Customers and Receivables**

  - Reports on uncollected accounts and general customer information.

- **Sales**

  - Reports on types of revenues earned.

As discussed in Chapter 1, reports can be modified as needed. (Refer to the "Reports" section of Chapter 1 for a refresher on report modification.)

In most reports, additional detail can be obtained by double-clicking (drilling down) on report line items.

PRACTICE EXERCISE

Prepare sales and receivable reports.

(Sac City needs an A/R aging and a sales by type of service report.)

1. Prepare an accounts receivable aging report.

   a. Click **Reports**.

   b. Click **Customers & Receivables**.

   c. Click **A/R Aging Summary**.

   d. Change date to 12/31 and click **Refresh**.

   e. Drill down (double-click) on the Total column for West Sac Legal to see detailed information.

   f. Exit out of both report screens.

2. Prepare a sales report by service type including amounts, average rates, and percentage distribution of revenue sources.

   a. Click **Reports**.

   b. Click **Sales**.

   c. Click **Sales by Item Summary**.

   d. Change dates to 11/1-12/31.

   e. Click **Customize Report**.

   f. On **Display** tab, unclick **COGS**.

   g. Click **OK**.

   h. Exit out of report screen.

ANSWER TO QuickCheck 2-1

Accounts receivable	$320	
Bookkeeping services		$320

CHAPTER SHORTCUTS

Add a customer
1. Open Customer Center
2. Click New Customer & Job/New Customer

Edit a customer
1. Open Customer Center
2. Highlight customer name
3. Click Edit Customer

Delete a customer
1. Open Customer Center
2. Highlight customer name
3. Right-click/Delete Customer:Job

Add item
1. Click List/Item List
2. Click Item/New

Edit item
1. Click List/Item List
2. Highlight item to change
3. Click Item/Edit item

Delete item
1. Click List/Item List
2. Highlight item to delete
3. Click Item/Delete item

Record cash sale
1. Click Create Sales Receipts on Home page

Record sale on account
1. Click Create Invoices on Home page

Record customer credit memo
1. Click Refunds & Credits on Home page

Record customer payments on account balances
1. Click Receive Payments on Home page

Record deposits
1. Click Record Deposits on Home page

CHAPTER REVIEW

Matching

Match the term or phrase (as used in QuickBooks) to its definition.

1. Customer Name
2. Company Name
3. Sales receipt
4. Invoice
5. Deposit
6. Credit Memo
7. Undeposited Funds
8. Payment

_____   Transaction type used for recording cash sales

_____   The name used as a specific customer identifier

_____   Transaction type used to record bank deposit

_____   Default account used to initially record cash received

_____   Transaction type used for recording customer payments on account

_____   Transaction type used to record sales on acccount

_____   Transaction type used to record credit given to customer

_____   The name appearing on an invoice in the Bill To field

Multiple Choice

1. A **service item** in QuickBooks:
   a. can be linked to more than one account.
   b. must be linked to one, and only one, account.
   c. can only be linked to an accounts receivable **type** account.
   d. can be, but doesn't need to be, linked to an account.

2. The account "Undeposited Funds" in QuickBooks represents:
   a. all cash sales.
   b. the balance in accounts receivable.
   c. cash, checks or credit card payments received and recorded but not yet deposited.
   d. none of the above.

3. The account that is credited when a credit memo is completed in QuickBooks will have the account type _____.
   a. Bank
   b. Accounts receivable
   c. Accounts payable
   d. Other current asset
   e. Other current liability

4. The default account Undeposited Funds has the account **type** _____.
   a. Bank
   b. Other current asset
   c. Other asset
   d. Other current liability
   e. Accounts receivable

5. There is an underlying journal entry behind every completed form listed below **except**:
   a. Invoice
   b. Credit memo
   c. Make deposit
   d. Sales receipt
   e. None of the above are correct.

ASSIGNMENTS

Background information from Chapter 1: Your nephew, Gilbert Greenjeans, was given a $6,000 check from his grandparents for his 16th birthday. They encouraged him to deposit the check in a college savings account. Gilbert understood their point of view, but he was a very ambitious young man and thought he'd be better off using that money to start a small lawn-mowing business. He believed he could make more money mowing lawns than he could earn, in interest, on money in a savings account. The fact that he lived near a very exclusive neighborhood full of palatial homes and large yards was a real bonus. He came to you for advice. After you cautioned him on all the risks of going into business for himself, you realized that he was very serious about this new venture, so you decided to give him some help. You first told	**Assignment 2A** **At Your Service**

him that he'd have to come up with a business name and business structure. Gilbert decided to set the company up as a sole proprietorship under the name "At Your Service."

On 10/20/17, Gilbert used $700 of his grandparent's gift to purchase, for cash, a good lawnmower, a lawn edger, and some rakes ($600) and a big supply of yard waste bags ($100).

He convinced his father to co-sign on a loan for a truck. The truck, which he purchased on 11/1, cost $20,000. He put $5,000 down and financed the balance with First Sacramento Bank over three years. His monthly payment (including interest at 5 percent) was set at $450. The first payment was due on 12/1.

He set up the following fee schedule to start:

- Weekly lawn mowing with edging
  - Large yard: $200 per week
  - Medium yard: $125 per week
  - Small yard: $75 per week

- Other gardening services
  - Leaf raking: $25 per hour

He signed up three clients in November and started working right away.

Gilbert has been tracking his business transactions in QuickBooks Pro 2015. He has no accounting knowledge though, and it's taking him so long to do his accounting that he's falling behind on his homework! His parents have asked you to help him out. He has entered all the basic transactions through November 30. You will be entering all the December transactions and helping him prepare all the financial reports as of 12/31/17, the company's year-end.

12/1/17

✓ You receive payments from customers for services performed (and invoiced) in November:
- Check #18899, dated, 12/1, from Darren Buffet for $300 in payment of Invoice #100.
- Check #78923, dated 12/1, from Oprah Zinfrey for $800 in payment of Invoice #101.

✓ You prepare new invoices for Oprah Zinfrey and Darren Buffet. Both clients should be billed for two weeks of weekly lawn mowing (December 2–December 15). Terms are Net 15. Use the Intuit Professional Invoice as the template. (Add the dates of service to the invoice. You can use the line below the service description or simply add the dates at the end of the description.) Since all revenue will be earned during the month, you don't worry about recording the charges as unearned revenue.
- The invoice for Ms. Zinfrey (#102) totals $400 (large yard).
- The invoice for Mr. Buffet (#103) totals $150 (small yard).
- Go ahead and update the terms for both customers if prompted.

✓ Jenny Lopez is going out of town for a few days, so she brings you a check (#12378) as payment for two weeks of lawn mowing (medium yard). The check, dated, 12/1, covers lawn mowing for the first two weeks of December (12/2–12/15). (Sales Receipt #101: $250).

12/4/17

✓ You drive down to the bank to deposit the three checks received so far in December into the checking account. The deposit total is $1,350.

12/5/17

✓ Your nephew decides to expand his services. He decides to offer a one-time shrub trimming special. It will be called "Saturday Snip" and he will charge $35 per job. He decides to accept cash only for this service, and he puts flyers around the neighborhood hoping to gain some new clients.

- You **will** need to set up a new service **item**, however, so you can include it on invoices (or sales receipts). You name the new item "Shrubs" and set it up as a subitem of **Other Gardening Services**. You use "Saturday Snip" as the description. The rate is $35 per shrub. You already have an income account set up for other gardening services.

12/8/17

✓ When your nephew is at Jenny Lopez's house, he mentions to her that if she agrees to be a regular customer, she wouldn't have to pay in advance every time. She says that would be great. You prepare an invoice for her for four weeks of medium yard lawn mowing (December 18–January 12). Terms are Net 15. The invoice (#104) totals $500.

- You realize that some of the revenue just invoiced to Jenny will not be earned until January. (The four weeks will be up on January 12th.) You decide to wait until the end of the month to make any necessary adjustments to the income statement. [**TIP: You'll do this as part of the homework for Chapter 4, so don't worry about it now.**]

12/9/17

✓ Four customers take advantage of the shrub trim special (one shrub each). All of them pay cash ($140 in total). [You decide to create one sales receipt (#102) for all payments, using **Cash Customer** as the customer name instead of creating a receipt for each client.]

✓ One of the customers, Johnny Chan, decides to also sign up for two weeks of lawn mowing (medium lawn). He pays an extra $250 cash for those services. Your nephew schedules the service for 12/14 and 12/21.

- Because he may be an ongoing customer, you decide to set him up as a customer and prepare a separate receipt for the mowing (#103). His address is 2525 Martial Drive, Sacramento, CA 95822. His phone number is 916-444-8282. Credit terms are Net 15.

12/15/17

✓ You prepare two invoices: One for Darren Buffet (#105) and one for Oprah Zinfrey (#106). Terms are Net 15 for both.

- Mr. Buffet has sold his home, so he only needs his lawn mowed for the next two weeks (through 12/29). He has a small yard, so the invoice total is $150.
- You invoice Ms. Zinfrey for four weeks of lawn mowing (December 18–January12). Your nephew tells you that Ms. Zinfrey also asked him to do some leaf raking for her last week that took two hours. She has a large yard, so the invoice total (including the raking) is $850.

12/19/17

✓ Your nephew gets a call from Billy Gates, a neighbor of Darren Buffet. Mr. Gates heard that your nephew is very reliable and very ambitious and is hoping that Gilbert would be willing to run some errands for him. Your nephew is up for new challenges and agrees to do pickup services for the Gates family.

- **Item** name is "Pickups" and it should be a subitem of **Other Services**.
- Description should be "Pickup services."
- Enter a rate of $20. Gilbert will charge by the hour.
- Don't forget to attach the **item** to an income account. [**TIP:** Look at the chart of accounts to pick an appropriate account.]

✓ You also set up Billy Gates as a customer.

- 2 Windows Avenue, Sacramento, CA 95822. 916-343-4444.
- Terms are Net 30.

12/20/17

✓ A local law firm (Curly & Moe, LLC) called your nephew today. It has a small flower garden behind its office building and would like your nephew to do weekly weeding. He agrees to provide that service for $25 per hour.

- You'll need to set up a new service **item**. Name: Weeding. Description: Garden weeding. (Don't forget to associate the item with the appropriate income account. Consider whether it should be a subitem of an existing group.)

- The law firm address is:
  - 2943 Barrister Lane
    Sacramento, CA 95822
  - 916-444-8999
  - Terms: Net 15

12/21/17

✓ You receive two customer payments in the mail.

- Check #78945, dated 12/21, for $400 is received from Oprah Zinfrey in payment of Invoice #102.

- Cash of $150, dated 12/21, is received from Darren Buffet. Mr. Buffet didn't note the invoice number being paid so you apply it to the oldest outstanding invoice.

✓ You go down to the bank and deposit all the cash received from the event on 12/9 and the cash and check received today (12/21). The total deposit equals $940.

12/26/17

✓ Your nephew spent two hours on 12/21 and one hour on 12/22 weeding the Curly & Moe garden (three hours total). You invoice the law firm for his time. (Invoice #107 for $75. Terms are Net 15.)

✓ Mr. Gates's wife, Belinda, calls and asks your nephew to pickup some dry cleaning and some groceries. He spends three hours in total ($60 in total). Terms on the invoice (#108) are Net 30.

12/27/17

✓ Your nephew tells you that he forgot to mow Jenny Lopez's lawn yesterday because he was so busy running errands for the Gates family. He called her to apologize. She let him know that she was out of the country, so it was okay to miss one week. You prepare a credit memo for her (CM104: $125).

- Use **Medium Weekly** for the item because the original charges were recorded using that **item**.

- Change the description to "Credit for missed mow."

- Don't forget to click off the **Print Later** box.

- Apply the credit to Invoice #104.
  - QuickBooks will prompt you to select an option when you click **Save and Close**.
  - NOTE: You can also do it before you save and close the form by clicking **Use credit to apply to invoice** at the top right of the **invoice**.

12/29/17

✓ Johnny Chan called. He was angry that your nephew missed mowing his side yard. Your nephew decides to give him a $25 refund. You prepare a check for the refund. [**TIP:** You must create a **credit memo** (CM103) **first**.]

- Use **Medium Weekly** for the item.

- Change the description to "Credit for missing the side yard."

- Enter $25 as the amount.
    - Ignore any messages you get about setting up price levels or changing rates. This is just a partial refund.
- Choose the option **Give a refund** when you **Save & Close**.
- Don't forget to click off the **to be printed** box on the screen when you prepare the refund check so you can enter the check number. Use 1006 for the refund check number. (You can put the check number in the **Ref/Check No.** field as long as the **To be printed** box is not checked.)

✓ You receive two checks from customers and deposit both in the bank.
- Check #98743, dated 12/29, from Jenny Lopez for $375 in payment of the remaining balance due on Invoice #104.
- Check #45678, dated 12/29 from Oprah Zinfrey for $850 in payment of invoice dated #106.
- The deposit should total $1,225.

Don't forget to do a backup!

Check numbers 12/31

    Checking account balance $3,860

    December Sales Revenue . . . . . $2,675 (Gilbert was a very busy student!)

REPORTS TO CREATE FOR ASSIGNMENT 2A

All reports should be in portrait orientation; fit to one page wide.

- Journal—12/01 through 12/31 transactions only.
    - Put entries in date order.
    - Remove columns for **Tran #** and **Adj**.
- Sales by Item Summary (December sales only).
- A/R Aging Summary dated 12/31.

Background information from Chapter 1: Your sister, Monica, started a dog-walking business in November as a way to earn money for college tuition. She decided to operate as a sole proprietorship for now because her operations are fairly simple.

    She already has a few regular customers and is excited about the possibility of attracting new ones. She currently offers the following services:

- Dog walks
    - Daily: $20
    - Weekly (5 walks a week): $75 (walks occur Monday through Friday)
- Dog care
    - Dog transport to veterinarian or grooming appointments: $25 per hour
    - In-home visits: $15 per hour

She didn't have a need for any special equipment, but she did purchase a used van that she uses to transport the dogs. The van cost her $7,600. She put $4,000 down and financed the rest with Friendly Freeport Bank. The loan is for 60 months at 8 percent interest. The monthly payment is $73 with the first payment due on December 1, 2017.

    She took your advice and has been tracking her business transactions in QuickBooks Pro 2015. She has no accounting knowledge though, and she's asked you so many questions that you've decided that it would be easier to just do the accounting for her—at a fee, of course! She has entered all the basic transactions through November 30. You will be entering all the December transactions and helping her prepare all the financial reports as of 12/31, the company's year-end.

Assignment 2B

Dancing with Dogs

12/1/17

✓ You receive payments from customers for services performed (and invoiced) in November.

- Check #18899, dated 12/1, from Jeremy Wang for $150 in payment of Invoice #105.
- Check #78923, dated 12/1, from Janet Reyes for $150 in payment of Invoice #104.

✓ You prepare invoices for Janet Reyes and Jeremy Wang. Both clients should be billed for two weeks of weekly dog walking (December 2–December 15). Terms are Net 15. Use the Intuit Professional Invoice as the template. (Add the dates of service to the invoice. You can use the line below the service description or simply add the dates to the end of the description line.) Since all revenue will be earned during the month, you don't worry about recording the charges as unearned revenue.

- The invoice for Janet (#107) totals $150.
- The invoice for Jeremy (#108) also totals $150.

12/5/17

✓ You receive check #12378, dated 12/5, from Martha Stuart of $75 for November services (Invoice #106).

✓ You drive down to the bank to deposit the three checks received so far in December into the checking account. The deposit total is $375.

12/8/17

✓ You prepare an invoice for Martha Stuart for two weeks of weekly dog walking (December 8–December 21). Terms are Net 15. The invoice (#109) totals $150.

✓ Your sister decides to expand her services and offer her first "special event." It will be called "Dog Day at the Park," and she will charge $35 (each) to bring the dogs to a local park that has an "off-leash" area. She decides to accept cash only for this service, and she puts flyers around the neighborhood hoping to gain some new clients.

- You **will** need to set up a new service **item** so you can include it on invoices (or sales receipts). You name the new item "Park" and set it up as a subitem of **Specials**. You use "Dog Day at the Park" as the description. You set $35 as the rate. You already have an income account set up for special events.

12/9/17

✓ Eight dogs (and their owners!) show up for the Day at the Park event. All clients pay cash ($280 in total). You decide to create one sales receipt (#102) for all special event payments, using "Cash Customer" as the customer name instead of creating a receipt for each client.

✓ One of the owners at the event, Frank Beagle, decides to also sign up for two future dog-walking sessions (at the daily rate). He pays an extra $40 cash for those services (#103). Your sister schedules the walks for 12/12 and 12/15.

- Because he may be an ongoing customer, you decide to set him up as a customer and prepare a separate receipt for the dog walks (#103). His address is 2525 River Drive, Sacramento, CA 95822. His phone number is 916-444-8282. Credit terms are Net 15.

12/15/17

✓ You prepare two invoices: one for Jeremy Wang (#110) and one for Janet Reyes (#111). Both invoices are for two weeks (12/18–12/29) of dog walking (weekly rate). Terms are Net 15.

12/16/17

✓ Your sister gets a call from Freeport Vet Clinic. They are interested in hiring her to come in on weekends to care for dogs under their care. They agree to a rate of $20 per hour. You set up a new **item**.

- **Item** name is "Vet Care," and it should be a subitem of **Care**.
- Description should be "Weekend visits with dogs under care."

- Enter a rate of $20.
- Don't forget to attach the **item** to an income account. [**TIP:** If you're unsure of which account to choose, look at the income account used for other **items** included in the **Care** group.]

You also set up the clinic as a customer.

- 3044 Freeport Ave, Sacramento, CA 95822. 916-343-4444.
- Terms are Net 30. (Your sister gives business clients slightly longer terms.)

12/18/17

✓ Frank Beagle's dog (a beagle, of course) seems to benefit from the two dog walks, so Frank signs up for four weeks of twice-weekly dog walking (December 18–January 12). Your sister decides to charge him $35 per week.

- You'll need to set up a new service **item**. Name: Half week rate. Description: Twice a week dog walks. (Don't forget to associate the item with the appropriate income account. Consider whether it should be a subitem of an existing group.)
- You prepare an invoice (#112), totaling $140, with terms of Net 15.
- You realize that some of the revenue just invoiced to Frank will not be earned until January. (The four weeks will be up on January 12.) You decide to wait until the end of the month to make any necessary adjustments to the income statement. **(You'll do this as part of Chapter 4's homework, so don't worry about it now.)**

12/23/17

✓ You receive two customer payments in the mail that you apply to their account balances.

- Check #78945 for $150, dated 12/23, is received from Janet Reyes in payment of Invoice #107.
- Cash of $150, dated 12/23, is received from Jeremy Wang. Jeremy didn't note the invoice number being paid, so you apply it to the oldest outstanding invoice.

✓ You invoice Martha Stuart (#113) for two weeks of dog walking (12/25–1/5) at the weekly rate. Terms are Net 15.

✓ You go down to the bank and deposit all the cash received on 12/9 and the cash and check received today. The total deposit equals $620.

12/26/17

✓ Your sister spent two hours on 12/24 and one hour on 12/25 caring for the dogs at Freeport Vet Clinic. You invoice the clinic for her time. (Invoice #114 for $60.)

12/27/17

✓ Your sister tells you that Jeremy's and Janet's dogs weren't along for the 12/26 walk. You prepare a credit memo for each of them ($15 each). (Credit memo numbers should be 115 and 116, respectively.)

- Use **Weekly Rate** for the item because the original charges were recorded using that **item**.
- Change the description to "Credit for missed walk on 12/26."
- Change the rate to $15.
- Ignore any messages you get about setting up price levels.
- Don't forget to click off the **Print Later** box.
- The credits for each should be applied to the invoices dated 12/15 for both customers.

12/29/17

✓ Jeremy Wang's poodle had to be taken (transported) to the vet for a checkup. The total time spent by your sister was two hours ($50 in total). Terms on the invoice (#117): Net 15.

- Be careful to choose the correct item.

✓ You receive two checks from customers and deposit both in the bank.

- Check #98743, dated 12/29, from Martha Stuart for $150 in payment of the invoice #109.

- Check #45678, dated 12/29, from Frank Beagle for $140 in payment of the invoice #112.

- The deposit should total $290.

12/30/17

✓ Martha Stuart called. She was angry that your sister was late picking up her Irish Setter last week. Your sister decides to give her a $15 refund. You prepare a check for the refund. [**TIP:** You must create a **credit memo** (#118) first and then issue the refund check.]

- Use **Weekly Rate** for the item.

- Change the description to "Credit for late pickup."

- Don't forget to click off the "to be printed box" on the screen when you prepare the refund check. Use 1015 for the refund check number. (You can put the check number in the **Ref/Check No.** field as long as the **To be printed** box is not checked.)

Don't forget to do a backup!

Check numbers 12/31

    Checking account balance **$1,680**

    December Income (sales revenue) . . . **$1,425**

REPORTS TO CREATE FOR ASSIGNMENT 2B

All reports should be in portrait orientation; fit to one page wide.

- Journal—12/01 through 12/31 transactions only.
  - Put entries in **date** order.
  - Remove **Trans #** column.
  - Remove **Adj** column.

- Sales by Item Summary (December sales only).

- A/R Aging Summary dated 12/31.

Incurring Costs
(Service Company)

Objectives

After completing Chapter 3, you should be able to:

1. Add, edit, and delete vendors.

2. Enable 1099 vendor tracking.

3. Record purchases on account.

4. Set up new credit terms.

5. Record purchases by cash or credit card.

6. Void checks.

7. Record payments of vendor account balances.

8. Create and modify purchase and payables reports.

WHAT IS THE PURCHASE CYCLE IN A SERVICE COMPANY?

The purchase cycle in a service company, like the sales cycle, is pretty straightforward.

- Incur the cost.
- Receive a bill for the cost.
- Pay the vendor.

Service companies can

- Pay at the time of purchase of goods or services.
- Pay later (buy "on account" or "on credit").

Before any purchases can be recorded in QuickBooks, a vendor has to be set up.

  HINT: In QuickBooks, there are four types of "names": Customer/Job, Vendor, Employee, Other Name. In business, a vendor is a company (or person) from whom another company purchases goods or services. In QuickBooks, many users use the "vendor" name type for any company (or person) to whom a company would regularly issue payments. That might include owners, lenders, and tax authorities. This is because the "other name" category can be a little less accessible in QuickBooks.

MANAGING VENDORS

Vendors are entered through the **Vendor Center**. The **Vendor Center** can be accessed through the **Vendor** dropdown menu on the main menu bar or from the icon bar (**My Shortcuts** tab). It can also be accessed by clicking the **Vendors** tab on the Home page.

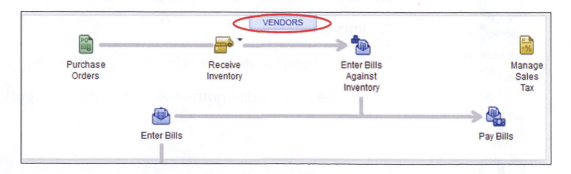

In the **Vendor Center**, you can enter new vendors, edit existing vendors, or delete vendors. The initial screen looks like this:

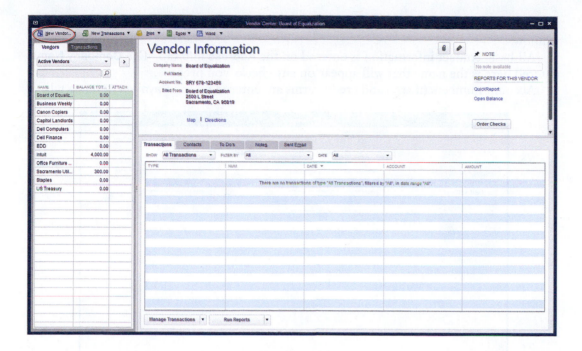

Adding a Vendor

Vendors are added by selecting **New Vendor** from the **New Vendor** dropdown menu at the top left of the window.

This screen appears:

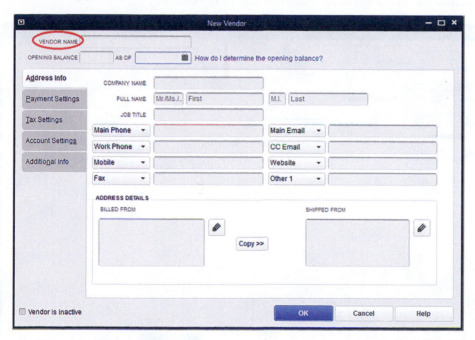

The first step is to create a **Vendor Name**. **Vendor names** are used as identifiers in Quick-Books. They can be a shortened version of the vendor's name or a number. In this class, we'll use the actual name of the vendor as the identifier.

Additional information about vendors is entered on the five tabs in the **New Vendor** window.

All basic contact information is entered on the **Address Info** tab. The **Company Name** entered here is the name that will appear on any checks you prepare.

Account numbers (if any) and credit terms are entered on the **Payment Settings** tab.

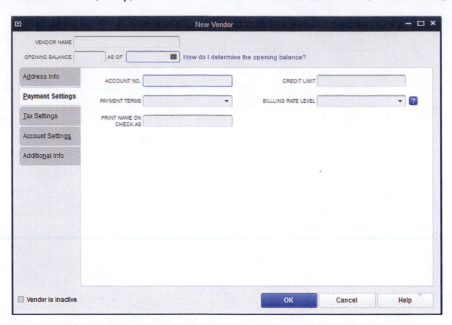

Required tax information for "1099 vendors" is entered on the on **Tax Settings** tab. (See next section for additional information about 1099 vendors.)

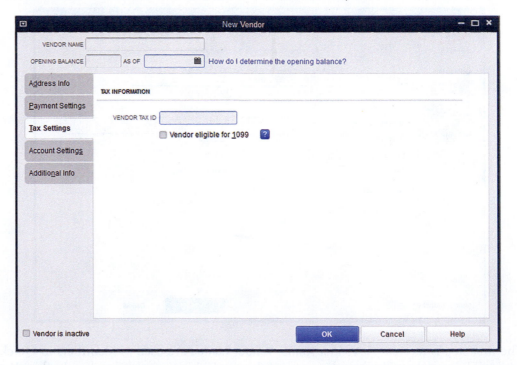

If you want QuickBooks to automatically display certain accounts when bills are entered for the vendor, you can enter those on the **Account Settings** tab. The screen looks like this:

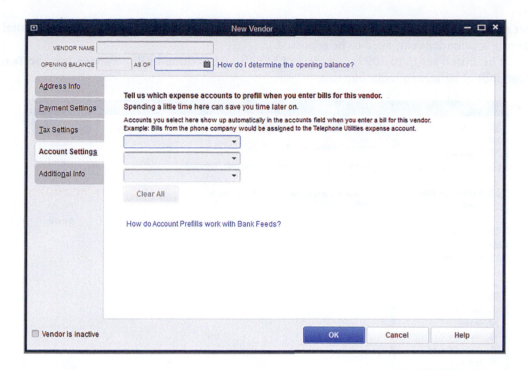

You can always change accounts when you enter transactions.

Vendor types and custom fields are entered on the **Additional Info** tab. **Custom fields** can be created for vendor or customer names. They can be useful for companies that want additional tracking by region, department, etc. Custom fields are covered in the appendix to Chapter 11.

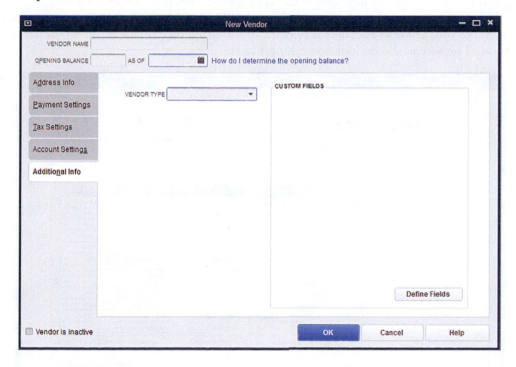

Setting Up 1099 Vendors

"1099 vendors" are vendors for whom you're required to report information to the IRS (using Form 1099) about certain payments made to those vendors. 1099 vendors include independent contractors, attorneys, landlords, etc. For each type of payment, the IRS has set annual threshold amounts. Only payments to vendors that exceed the threshold, in total during a calendar year, need to be reported.

The initial setup of 1099 tracking in QuickBooks is done in **Preferences** (on the **Tax: 1099** tab). The screen looks like this:

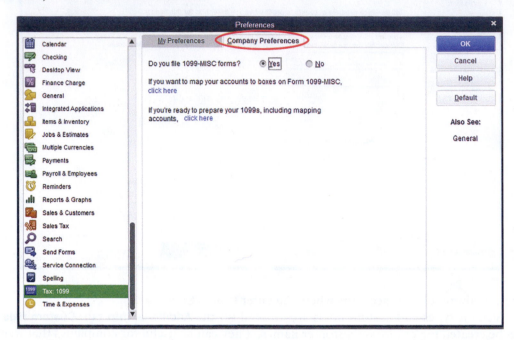

For each type of 1099 payment, you must map (connect) the general ledger account that might include that type of payment to the appropriate field (box) on Form 1099.

To map accounts, select the first **click here** option as shown on the preceding screenshot. Make sure **Show all accounts** is selected in the dropdown menu at the top of the new window. The screen should look something like this:

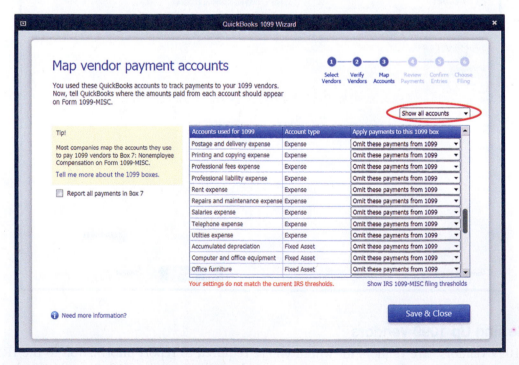

For every account that might include payments to 1099 vendors, select the appropriate 1099 box. In this class, all of the 1099 eligible payments will either be mapped to Box 1: Rent or to Box 7: Nonemployee Compensation. The screen would look something like this:

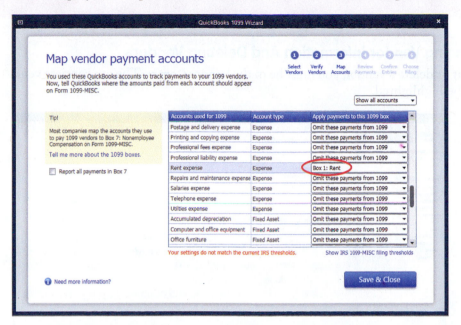

As noted earlier, the IRS establishes various thresholds for different types of 1099 payments. You can make sure the threshold amounts are up to date by clicking the **Show IRS 1099-MISC filing thresholds** at the bottom right of the **Map vendor payment accounts** window.

On the threshold window, click the **Reset to IRS thresholds** button. The screen will now look something like this:

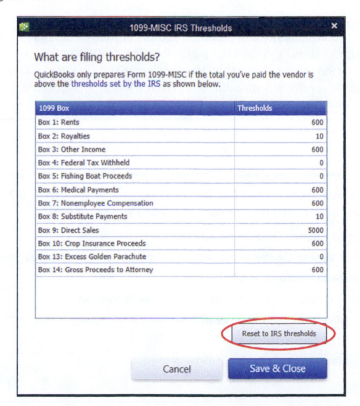

WARNING: QuickBooks will only track payments (to 1099 vendors) that are debited to the accounts mapped in the *Preference* setup.

Changing Vendor Information And Deleting Vendors

To edit or delete a vendor, you must be in the **Vendor Center**. The appropriate vendor name must be highlighted.

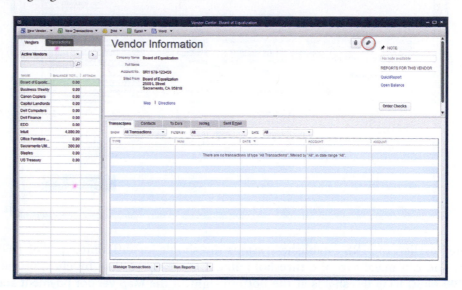

To edit vendor information, click the **edit icon** (the pencil at the top right of the screen).

To delete a vendor, choose the **Delete Vendor** option on the **Edit** dropdown menu (main menu bar).

HINT: You cannot delete vendors, accounts, or items that have transactions associated with them. You can only make them inactive. To make a vendor inactive, right-click the vendor name in the **Vendor Center** and click **Make Vendor Inactive**. An inactive vendor will appear in reports but will not be accessible when entering transactions. If necessary, you can reactivate a vendor.

PRACTICE
EXERCISE

Set up and edit vendors for Sac City Accounting.
(Sac City adds two new vendors and edits an existing vendor's record.)

1. Enter a new vendor: "Office Supplies Shop."

    a. Select **Vendor Center** on the **Vendor** dropdown menu in the main menu bar.

    b. Click **New Vendor** (top left of screen).

    c. Enter the following information on the **Address Info** tab:

        i. Office Supplies Shop (**Vendor Name** and **Company Name** fields)

           2121 Capital Avenue

           West Sacramento, CA 95691

(continued)

    d.   Click on the **Payment Settings** tab and select **Net 15** on the **Terms** dropdown menu.

    e.   Click **OK** and exit out of window.

2. Set up 1099 vendor tracking for independent contractors.

    a.   Click on **Edit**.

    b.   Click on **Preferences**.

    c.   Click on **Tax: 1099**. [HINT: You'll need to scroll down the Preferences icon bar.]

    d.   Click **Company Preferences** and click **Yes** for **Do you file 1099-MISC forms?**

    e.   Click the link "click here" after **"If you want to map your accounts to boxes on Form 1099-MISC."**

    f.   Select the option **Show all accounts** on the dropdown menu.

    g.   Link the account "Rent expense" to Box 1 and the accounts "Contract labor" and "Prepaid expenses" to Box 7.

    h.   Click **Show IRS 1099-MISC filing thresholds** at the bottom right.

    i.   Click **Reset to IRS thresholds**.

    j.   Click **Save & Close**. (You'll need to click Save & Close twice.)

3. Enter a new 1099 vendor: Beverly Okimoto (accountant who may be hired as contract labor to assist with consulting work).

    a.   Click **Vendor Center** on the **Vendor** dropdown menu on the main menu bar.

    b.   Click **New Vendor** (top left of screen).

    c.   Enter the following information on the **Address Info** tab:

        i.   Beverly Okimoto as the **Vendor Name**

        ii.   Beverly as the **First Name** and Okimoto as the **Last Name**

            2525 Paradise Road

            Suite 2502

            Sacramento, CA 95822

    d.   Click **Payment Settings** tab and enter **Terms** of Net 15.

    e.   Click **Tax Settings** tab.

        i.   Enter **Tax ID** number as 444-22-9898.

        ii.   Check the box next to **Vendor eligible for 1099**.

    f.   Click **OK**.

4. Edit a vendor.

    a.   Highlight "Capital Landlords" in the **Vendor Center**.

    b.   Click on the **edit icon** (the pencil).

    c.   Enter **Main Phone** number 916-375-5511.

    d.   Click on **Tax Settings** tab.

    e.   Enter **Tax ID** number as 91-1112222.

    f.   Check the box next to **Vendor eligible for 1099**.

    g.   Click **OK** and exit out of the **Vendor Center**.

RECORDING PURCHASES

In a service company, most purchases are made "on account." It's just an easier, more efficient way to do business. There are times, however, when payment is made at the time of purchase (by cash/check or by credit card). As you can probably guess by now, QuickBooks has a separate form for each alternative. The transaction types are:

- **Bill**—used for purchases on account.

- **Check**—used when payment is made at the time of purchase (or when the bill wasn't first entered into QuickBooks).

- **Credit Card**—used when payment is made by credit card.

Purchasing on Account

In a manual accounting system, a bill is received from the vendor. The bill is recorded in the purchases journal. The purchases journal is posted, in total, to the general ledger, and each transaction in the purchases journal is posted to the appropriate vendor's subsidiary ledger.

In QuickBooks, the form for entering a purchase on account is called a **bill**. (Remember, the vendor might call it an invoice but QuickBooks calls it a **bill**. Only charges to customers are called **invoices** in QuickBooks.) All accounts, ledgers, and statements are updated automatically when the **bill** is saved so the form must include all relevant information needed.

That information includes:

- Who's the vendor? (This is needed for posting to the subsidiary ledger.)

- What are we buying? (What account should QuickBooks debit?)

- When do we have to pay for it? (What are the vendor's credit terms?)

> **HINT:**   You can set up multiple accounts payable accounts in QuickBooks if you want. Each account, however, must have an **accounts payable** account **type.** If you set up an account called, say, "Accounts Payable for Inventory" with an **Other Current Liability account type**, it would not be accessible to you when you're entering a **bill** because it doesn't have the appropriate account **type.** If you do have multiple accounts payable, you will need to select the specific account you want to credit when you complete the form. QuickBooks will display all accounts of the appropriate **type.**

You can easily access the "form" **Bill** by selecting **Enter Bills** on the Home page.

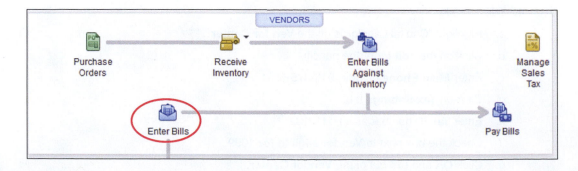

The screen looks like this:

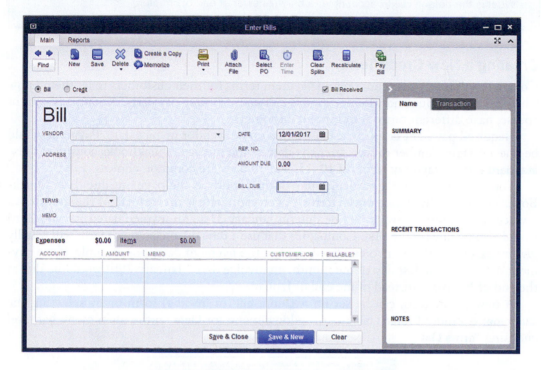

To complete a **Bill**, you must enter the vendor name, date of the bill, amount, and which accounts you want QuickBooks to charge (debit).

The vendor reference number (vendor invoice #) should be entered in the **Ref No.** field.

You also need to know when the bill is due (credit terms). If you've already set up the credit terms for the vendor, these will show up automatically in the **Terms** field. If you haven't, you will need to enter the terms on the form. QuickBooks uses the terms to keep track of any available early payment discounts, so it's important to make sure the date and the terms are entered correctly.

There are two memo fields on a **bill**. Anything entered into the memo field right under **Terms** will appear on the check created when the **bill** is paid. Information entered into the memo field just to the right of the **Amount** column appears only in journal reports.

As you can see in the preceding screenshot, there are two tabs on the bottom half of the form. Both are used to specify the account(s) to be **debited**.

- **Expenses** tab
  - Used to record charges not tracked as **items**. Most likely, you would be debiting an asset or expense account on this tab, but you could debit any type of account.

- **Items** tab
  - Used to record inventory purchases and charges tracked as items. Inventory will be covered in Chapter 6.

You can enter multiple accounts in the account distribution section of the form. You can even enter negative amounts, which would, of course, appear as credits in the underlying journal entry. A negative amount would be entered if, for example, the vendor gives you a discount and you decide to track discounts in a separate account. The sum of all the distributions must, of course, equal the total amount of the bill. (This is, after all, still accounting! The underlying journal entry must balance.)

What is the default **credit** account for a **bill**? (Answer at end of chapter.)

Creating a New Credit Term

Companies that sell on account set up payment terms for their customers to let them know when payment is due and whether there's a discount if they pay early. A company can, of course, have different terms for different customers.

Required payment dates are usually based on the vendor invoice date. Payment would be due a certain number of days after the date of the invoice. QuickBooks considers these **standard** terms. Payment terms of 10, 15, and 30 days are common choices.

Some companies set a particular day of the month as the payment due date. QuickBooks considers these **date driven** terms. A common date is the last day of the month. An invoice dated January 3rd would be due on January 31st. An invoice dated January 23rd would also be due on the 31st. Companies that use a **date driven** payment term will usually give an extra month for invoices dated close to the payment date. For example, if the payment date were the last day of the month, an invoice dated January 29th would be due at the end of February instead of the end of January.

A new credit term can be set up within a **bill** (or **invoice**) form or by selecting the **Customer & Vendor Profile Lists** (on dropdown menu for **Lists** on the main menu bar) and choosing **Terms List**.

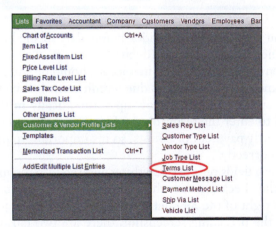

To set up a new term within a **bill**, use the dropdown menu in the **Terms** box and select **<Add New>**.

If the payment due date is determined by the invoice date, select **Standard** and enter the number of days and any discount percentage for early payment. The screen will look like this:

If the payment due date is set as a particular day of the month (regardless of the invoice date), select **Date Driven** and enter the due date and any discount percentage for early payment. The screen will look like this:

Enter bills for Sac City Accounting and set up a new credit term.
(Sac City enters several bills received in the mail.)

PRACTICE
EXERCISE

1. Click **Enter Bills** on the Home page.

2. Enter the utilities bill [$535 bill for December ($250 for telephone; $285 for utilities)].

    a. Select **Sacramento Utilities** as **Vendor**.

    b. Enter "12/1/17" as the **Date**.

    c. Enter "118-1119" as the **Ref. No.**

    d. Enter "535" as the **Amount Due**.

    e. Select **Net 30** for **Terms**.

    f. On the **Expenses** tab, select **Telephone expense** as the **Account** and enter "250" as the **Amount**.

    g. On the second line, select **Utilities expense** as the **Account** and enter "285"as the **Amount**.

    h. Click **Save & New**.

3. Enter a $450 bill for an ad placed in the "Business Weekly" (December 4th edition), and create a new credit term.

    a. Select **Business Weekly** as **Vendor**.

    b. Enter "12/1/17" as the **Date**.

    c. Enter "120117" as the **Ref No.**

    d. Enter "450" as the **Amount**.

    e. Enter a new credit term.

        i. Click **Add New** in the **Terms** dropdown menu.

        ii. Name the term "EOM."

        iii. Click **Date Driven**.

        iv. Use the 31st (QuickBooks will automatically adjust in months with less than 31 days) and the other defaults.

(continued)

v. Click **OK**.

f. On the **Expenses** tab, select "Advertising/Promotion expense" as the **Account** and enter 450 as the **Amount**.

g. Click **Save & New**.

h. If prompted, accept the change of information.

4. Enter a $750 bill from Office Supplies Shop for the purchase of a new printer ($216) and 10 cases of copy paper ($534).

a. Select **Office Supplies Shop** as the **Vendor**.

b. Enter "12/15/17" as the **Date**.

c. Enter "67-1313"as the **Ref. No.**

d. Enter "750" as the **Amount Due**.

e. Select **Net 15** for the **Terms**.

f. Distribute the printer purchase to the **Computer and office equipment** account ($216) and the copy paper purchase to the **Supplies on hand** account ($534). Include a description for each in the **Memo** field next to the amount.

   i. These purchases were both debited to asset accounts. The printer represents equipment that will be used for more than one year so it's debited to a **fixed asset** account type. The copy paper is expected to last for a few months so it's debited to an **other current asset** account type.

g. Click **Save & Close**.

Purchasing With Cash, Check, or Debit Card

In a manual system, cash payments are recorded in the cash disbursements journal. The journal is recorded, in total, to the general ledger.

In QuickBooks, cash payments made at the time of purchase (or to record a payment to a vendor when the bill wasn't first entered into QuickBooks) are entered through the form (transaction type) **Check**. We'll cover payments on vendor account balances later in the chapter.

 HINT: Payments using coin and currency, checks, or debit cards are all considered cash payments.

You can easily access the form **Check** from the Home page by clicking the **Write Checks** icon in the **Banking section**.

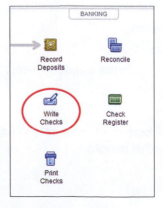

Your screen will look this:

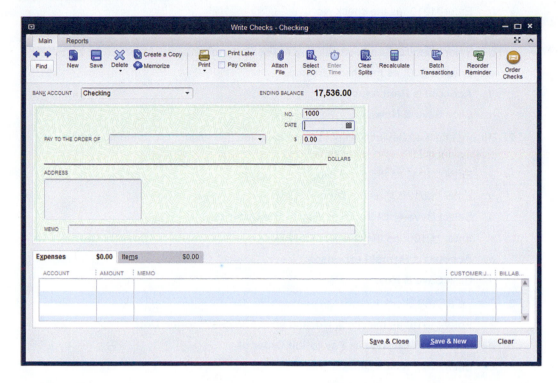

You need to enter the date, payee, and amount. You also need to enter the account you want debited. Your **Bank** account is the default credit account. If you have multiple **Bank type** accounts set up, you'd need to select the correct account in the **Bank Account** field at the top left of the screen.

You'll notice the form has the same tabs as the **Bill** form (**Expenses** and **Items**). Both tabs are used for entering the general ledger accounts to be debited (or credited if a negative is entered).

 HINT: For this class, leave the **Print Later** option unchecked whenever you enter checks. You'll want to enter the check numbers given in the homework assignments because you won't actually be printing checks.

 WARNING: QuickBooks will allow you to select an *Accounts Payable type* account for the account distribution on the *Check* form. If you do, QuickBooks will record the payment in the vendor subsidiary ledger, but the amount will need to be associated with a particular *bill* at a later date. Unless you're making an advance payment to a vendor (without a *bill*), it's best to use the method shown in the "Paying Vendor Balances" section covered later in the chapter.

PRACTICE EXERCISE

Enter checks for Sac City Accounting.
(Sac City pays its rent, makes a loan payment, and pays a retainer fee to a consultant.)

1. Record $1,200 December rent payment.

    a. Click **Write Checks** on the Home page.

(continued)

  b.   Enter "1010" as the check **No.**

  c.   Enter "12/1/17" as the **Date**.

  d.   Select **Capital Landlords** as **Pay to the Order of**.

  e.   Enter "1,200" as the check amount.

  f.   **Account** is **Rent expense**.

  g.   Click **Save & New**.

2. Record check to Beverly Okimoto for retainer fee. (Retainers are amounts paid to professionals for future services.)

  a.   Enter "1011" as the check **No.**

  b.   Enter "12/12/17" as the **Date**.

  c.   Select **Beverly Okimoto** as **Pay to the Order of**.

  d.   Enter "1,100" as the check amount.

  e.   **Account** is **Prepaid expenses**.

  f.   Click **Save & New**.

3. Record a $188 check for the loan payment.

  a.   Enter "1016" as the check **No.** and enter "12/29/17" as the **Date**.

  b.   Select **Dell Finance** as **Pay to the Order of**.

  c.   Enter "188" as the check amount.

  d.   There are two **account** distributions.

    i.   **Interest expense** for $37.

    ii.   **Note payable-computers** for $151 (principal).

  e.   Click **Save & Close**.

Voiding Checks

If a check is printed but contains an error and won't be distributed, it should be voided (not deleted) in QuickBooks. This ensures that all check numbers are properly accounted for.

  Voiding a check is done within the **Check** form, using the option **Void Check** on the **Edit** menu (main menu bar).

  Voided checks do appear on journal reports (0.00 dollar amounts) and are accessible using the **Find** feature.

Accounting period
The time period, usually one year or less, to which periodic accounting reports are related.

> **BEHIND THE SCENES** In most cases, QuickBooks uses the original check date to record a voided check. This can create problems if financial reports have already been distributed. For example, let's say a $100 check was written in December to pay for some travel expenses. In the December income statement, net income would, of course, be decreased by the $100 travel expense. Now let's say that the $100 check was lost; a new check was then issued and the original check was voided in QuickBooks in February. The replacement check would have a February date, but the original check would be voided by QuickBooks as of the original December check date. If you then prepared a new December Income Statement, net income would automatically be $100 higher than it was before due to the voided check. On the other hand, February's net income would be reduced by the $100 December travel expense. The expense is now reported in the wrong **accounting period**. If the amounts are significant, or if tax reports have already been filed, journal entries should be made to correct the balances.

The only exception to this treatment by QuickBooks is when a check written in a **closed period** is voided. (**Closed periods** are covered in Chapter 4.) If the account distributions are for **expense** accounts only, QuickBooks will ask the user whether the check should be voided in the current period (instead of the **closed period**). This option is not available if the account distributions include any balance sheet accounts.

Void a check for Sac City Accounting.

(Sac City voids a check prepared incorrectly. A replacement check is written.)

1. Void the check to Beverly Okimoto written for the wrong amount.

   a. Click **Edit**.

   b. Click **Find**.

   c. On the **Advanced** tab, select **Name** in the **Filter** box.

   d. Select **Beverly Okimoto** in the **Name** box.

   e. Click **Find**.

   f. Double-click check #1011. The original check form should appear.

   g. Click **Edit** on the main menu bar to access the dropdown menu.

   h. Select **Void Check**. The amounts on the check should now show as 0.00.

   i. Click **Save & New**. (Accept the change when prompted.)

2. Reissue a check to Beverly for the correct amount ($1,000).

   a. Enter "1012" as the check **No.**

   b. Enter "12/14/17" as the **Date**.

   c. Select **Beverly Okimoto** as the **Pay to the Order of**.

   d. Enter "1,000" as the **Amount**.

   e. The **account** selected should be **Prepaid expenses**.

   f. Click **Save & Close**.

   g. Exit out of the **Find** window.

PRACTICE EXERCISE

Purchasing with a Credit Card

Some companies obtain corporate credit cards. Owners or employees who need to be able to purchase items when they're traveling are the typical users of these cards.

Although the seller might see a payment by credit card as the same as cash, the purchaser is really buying on credit. The company that issued the card is the creditor.

In QuickBooks, credit cards are set up as a separate liability account type (**Credit Card** account **type**). When individual credit card charges are entered, the amounts are credited to the **credit card** account and debited to the appropriate expense or asset account. This allows the user to track the details of all purchases.

When the credit card statement is received, the user reconciles the amounts recorded in QuickBooks to the statement and processes the credit card bill for payment. (Credit card reconciliations are covered in Chapter 4.) At that point, the bill can either be paid immediately or transferred to an **accounts payable** account **type** to be paid at a later date.

Before you can enter credit card charges, the general ledger account must be set up. This is done through the **Chart of Accounts** list. Remember, the account must be set up as a **credit card** account type.

Once the credit card account is set up, the form for entering credit card charges (or credit card credits) is accessed through the main menu bar using the **Enter Credit Card**

Charges option on the **Banking** menu. The transaction type for credit card charges is **Credit Card**.

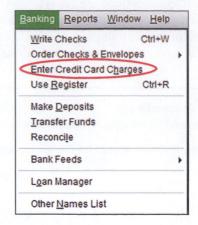

The screen looks like this:

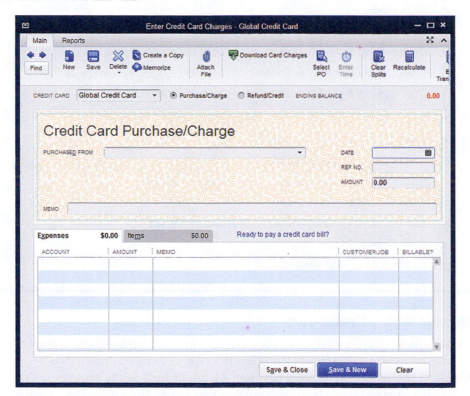

To enter a credit card charge, you need to enter the name of the business where the credit card was used, the date of the charge, and the account(s) you want QuickBooks to debit.

> **BEHIND THE SCENES** Remember, you will be paying the entity that issued the card, not the business where you used the card. The business name is entered here for informational purposes only.

The **Enter Credit Card Charges** form is very similar to the **Bill** and **Check** forms. The account credited will be the liability account set up as a **credit card** account type. If multiple **credit card** accounts are set up, the user will need to identify the appropriate account using the dropdown menu at the top left of the window. The accounts debited will be identified on the **Expenses** tab, the **Items** tab, or on both.

Set up and use a credit card in Sac City Accounting.
(Sac City uses its corporate credit card to make several purchases.)

1. Set up a credit card account.

   a. Click **Lists** on the main menu bar.

   b. Click **Chart of Accounts**.

   c. Click **Account**.

   d. Click **New**.

   e. Click **Credit Card** (for type of account).

   f. Click **Continue**.

   g. Enter "Global Credit Card" in the **Account Name** field.

   h. Click **Save & Close**.

   i. Click **NO** if prompted to consider online services.

   j. Exit out of the chart of accounts window.

2. To record a client lunch (paid with credit card).

   a. Click **Banking** on the main menu bar.

   b. Click **Enter Credit Card Charges**.

   c. Enter "Fancy Restaurant" (**Quick Add** and choose **Vendor** when prompted) in the **Purchased from** field.

   d. Enter "12/7/17" as **Date**.

   e. Leave **Ref. No.** blank.

   f. Enter "94.10" as **Amount**.

   g. On **Expenses** tab, select **Meals and entertainment expense** as **Account**.

   h. In the memo field (next to **Amount** field), enter "Lunch with July Summers".

   i. Click **Save & New**.

3. To record purchase of stamps with a credit card.

   a. Enter "USPS" in **Purchased From** field. **Quick Add** as **Vendor**.

   b. Enter "12/15/17" as the **Date**.

   c. No reference number.

   d. Enter "56" as **Amount**.

   e. **Account** is **Postage and delivery expense**.

   f. Click **Save & Close**.

PRACTICE EXERCISE

PAYING VENDOR BALANCES

Eventually vendors must be paid! Most companies pay vendors in batches. A check run might be processed once or twice a month. Check runs might be processed more frequently in larger companies.

In a manual system, checks are prepared and then entered in the cash disbursements journal. The totals of the journal are posted to the general ledger, and each transaction is posted to the appropriate vendor's subsidiary ledger.

In QuickBooks, the selection of bills to be paid is made through the **Pay Bills** window. You can pick and choose the bills that you want to pay. You can pay the bills in full or make partial payments.

You can pay bills using cash, checks, credit cards, or through online payments. In this textbook, we'll only cover paying vendor balances by check, which is the most common payment method in small to medium-sized companies.

Once you've selected the bills to be paid, QuickBooks creates a separate form (**Bill Payment** transaction type) for each check written. If you pay more than one bill for a particular vendor, only one **Bill Payment** form for that vendor would be created.

The **Pay Bills** screen is easily accessed from the Home page.

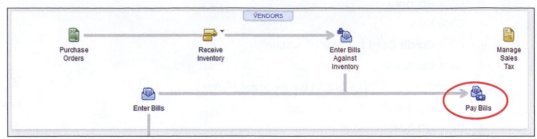

The screen will look something like this:

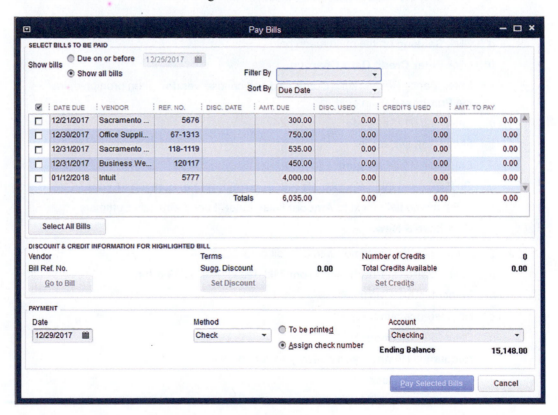

There is a lot to do on this screen, so take your time!

You can display all bills or just bills due on or before a particular date (see the choices listed at the top left of the screen).

Bills to be paid are selected by checking the box to the left of the specific bill. (There is a **Select All Bills** option in the middle of the window.) If you want to see the details of a particular bill, highlight the bill and then click **Go To Bill** in the lower left section of the screen. QuickBooks will display the original **bill**. If there are any available credits or discounts for a vendor, the amounts will be displayed in the middle of the screen **when the bill is highlighted**. Vendor credits are covered in Chapter 6.

Don't forget to enter the **payment date** and the **method** of payment. Because you're not printing checks in this course, you'll also need to check the **Assign check number** button at the bottom of the form.

When you choose the **Assign check number** option, another screen will appear after you click **Pay Selected Bills**. In that screen, you can input the check numbers or allow QuickBooks to automatically assign a number. (QuickBooks would assign check numbers starting with the next available number.)

The screen looks something like this:

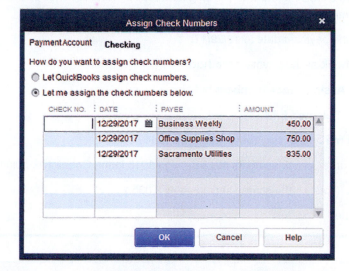

> **BEHIND THE SCENES** If multiple bills from the same vendor have been selected for payment, QuickBooks will automatically combine the amounts and create a single check for that particular vendor.

In the final screen, QuickBooks will show you a list of all checks recorded. The screen will look something like this:

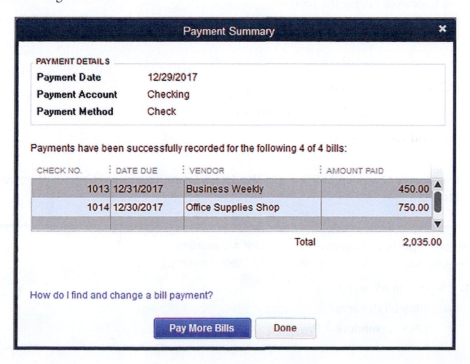

PRACTICE
EXERCISE

Record payment of bills for Sac City Accounting.
(Sac City pays several vendor balances.)

1. Click **Pay Bills** on the Home page.

2. Click the **Show bills due on or before** option and enter 1/5/18.

3. Click **Select All Bills**.

   a. There should be four bills showing for a total of $2,035 in the **Amt. To Pay** column.

4. Change the payment date to 12/29/17.

5. Select **Check** as the payment **Method**.

6. Click the **Assign check numbers** button.

7. Click **Pay Selected Bills**.

8. Click **Let me assign the check numbers below**.

9. Enter, in order, check numbers 1013 through 1015 in the **Check No.** column.

10. Click **OK**. (Total on the screen should show 2,035.)

11. Click **Done**.

QuickCheck 3-2

> Why did QuickBooks create only three checks when you selected four bills for payment? (Answer at end of chapter.)

VENDOR REPORTS

Reports can be accessed through the main menu bar (**Reports**) or through the **Reports** icon on the **My Shortcuts** tab on the icon bar.

For this chapter, we are most interested in the reports listed under **Vendors & Payables**. These include:

- Reports on payable balances.

- Reports of vendor activity.

- Reports listing general vendor information.

- Reports on 1099 activity.

Sales tax reports are also included in the **Vendors & Payables** group. These will be covered in Chapter 7.

**PRACTICE
EXERCISE**

Prepare reports on payables for Sac City Accounting.
(Sac City needs an A/P aging report and a 1099 summary.)

1. Prepare an A/P aging.

   a. Click on **Reports**.

   b. Click on **Vendors & Payables**.

(continued)

    c.   Click on **A/P Aging Summary**.

    d.   Change date to 12/31 and refresh the screen.

2. Prepare a 1099 payment summary report.

    a.   Click on **Reports**.

    b.   Click on **Vendors & Payables**.

    c.   Click on **1099 Summary**.

    d.   Change date to 1/1 to 12/31.

    e.   To filter out transactions that would **not** need to be reported to the IRS, the **1099 options** (top of report screen under menu bar) selected should include:

       i.   **Only 1099 vendors**.

       ii.   **Only 1099 accounts**.

       iii.   **Use thresholds**.

Accounts Payable.

ANSWER TO
QuickCheck
3-1

Two of the bills were for the same vendor ("Sacramento Utilities").

ANSWER TO
QuickCheck
3-2

CHAPTER SHORTCUTS

Add a vendor
1. Click Vendor Center
2. Click New Vendor

Edit a vendor
1. Click Vendor Center
2. Highlight Vendor
3. Click Edit Vendor

Delete a vendor
1. Click Vendor Center
2. Highlight Vendor
3. Right-click/Delete Vendor

Set up 1099 vendor tracking for independent contractors
1. Click Edit/Preferences
2. Select Tax:1099
3. Click Company Preferences
4. Check Yes
5. Click dropdown menu for Box 7 and select general ledger account(s) used

in recording payments to independent contractors

Record vendor bill
1. Click Home
2. Click Enter Bills

Record credit card purchase
1. Click Banking/Enter Credit Card Charges

Record checks (not including payroll checks or checks written to record payment of bills previously recorded in QuickBooks)
1. Click Home
2. Click Write Checks

Record payment of vendor account balance
1. Click Home
2. Click Pay Bills

CHAPTER REVIEW

Matching

Match the term or phrase (as used in QuickBooks) to the best definition below.

1. Bill   5. Vendor
2. 1099 vendor   6. Net 15
3. Bill Payment   7. Ref No. (on **bill**)
4. Credit card   8. Check

_____   Transaction type used for recorded invoices received from vendors

_____   Vendor invoice number

_____   Transaction type used to record payments to vendors on account

_____   Individual or company from whom goods or services are purchased

_____   An individual or company that receives payments that must be reported to the IRS

_____   A type of payment term

_____   Transaction type used to record payments to vendor at time of service

_____   Transaction type used to record purchases using a card issued by a bank or company

Multiple Choice

1. A purchase of a computer, on account, would be recorded on the _____ tab of a **bill** in QuickBooks.

   a. Items
   b. Fixed assets
   c. Expenses
   d. Computer equipment

2. Which of the following is not a "name" type in QuickBooks?

   a. Vendor
   b. Employee
   c. Owner
   d. Customer/Job
   e. All of the above are name types in QuickBooks.

3. When a purchase made with a credit card is recorded in QuickBooks,

   a. cash is credited.
   b. a liability account is credited (**account payable account type**).
   c. a liability account is credited (**credit card account type**).
   d. a liability account is credited (**other current liability account type**).

4. If a vendor bill is entered in the "Enter Bills" window in QuickBooks, the best option when recording the payment is to

   a. use "Write Check."
   b. use "Pay Bills."

    c. use either "Pay Bills" or "Write Check." There's no advantage in one over the other.

    d. use "Pay Bills," "Write Check," or "Transfer."

    e. prepare a journal entry.

5. Which of the following statements is true?

    a. You can only have one accounts payable account in QuickBooks.

    b. You can have multiple accounts payable accounts, but they must each have a different name and they must all have an **Accounts Payable account type**.

    c. You can have multiple accounts payable accounts, but they must each have a different name and only one can have **an Accounts Payable account type**.

ASSIGNMENTS

Background information from Chapter 1: Your nephew, Gilbert Greenjeans, was given a $6,000 check from his grandparents for his 16th birthday. They encouraged him to deposit the check in a college savings account. Gilbert understood their point of view, but he was a very ambitious young man and thought he'd be better off using that money to start a small lawn-mowing business. He believed he could make more money mowing lawns than he could earn, in interest, on money in a savings account. The fact that he lived near a very exclusive neighborhood full of palatial homes and large yards was a real bonus. He came to you for advice.

    After you cautioned him on all the risks of going into business for himself, you realized that he was very serious about this new venture, so you decided to give him some help. You first told him that he'd have to come up with a business name and business structure. Gilbert decided to set the company up as a sole proprietorship under the name "At Your Service."

    On 10/20/17, Gilbert used $700 of his grandparent's gift to purchase, for cash, a good lawnmower, a lawn edger, and some rakes ($600) and a big supply of yard waste bags ($100).

    He convinced his father to co-sign on a loan for a truck. The truck, which he purchased on 11/1, cost $20,000. He put $5,000 down and financed the balance with First Sacramento Bank over three years. His monthly payment (including interest at 5 percent) was set at $450. The first payment was due on 12/1.

    He set up the following fee schedule to start:

- Weekly lawn mowing with edging
  - Large yard: $200 per week
  - Medium yard: $125 per week
  - Small yard: $75 per week

- Other gardening services
  - Leaf raking: $25 per hour

He signed up three clients in November and started working right away.

    Gilbert has been tracking his business transactions in QuickBooks Pro 2015. He has no accounting knowledge though, and it's taking him so long to do his accounting that he's falling behind on his homework! His parents have asked you to help him out. He has entered all the basic transactions through November 30. You will be entering all the December transactions and helping him prepare all the financial reports as of 12/31, the company's year-end.

12/1/17

✓ Your nephew's insurance agent (at Goldman Insurance) advises him to purchase a liability insurance policy. You write the check (#1007) for the first six-month premium: $240. The policy is effective beginning 12/1. (An adjustment for insurance expense for the month of December will be made at the end of December as part of Chapter 4's assignment.)

Assignment 3A

At Your Service

✓   You convince your nephew to get a good desktop calculator and to purchase QuickBooks Pro. (He's been using a trial version of the software.) You know the calculator will last for some time, but you decide to expense it (office supplies) in December because the total cost ($55) is insignificant. You expect the software ($216) to last two years. He purchases everything from Sactown Office Supplies, on account. The vendor invoice number is 5266 ($271) and the terms are Net 30. Because you might get more bills from this vendor, you update the terms if prompted.

✓   You prepare the check (#1008) to First Sacramento Bank for the first vehicle loan payment of $450. Remember, the note was dated 11/1. You are paying November interest and some principal. [**TIP:** Interest for November was properly accrued in the **Interest payable** account, so check out the Balance Sheet for the interest portion of the December 1st payment.]

12/4/17

✓   Your nephew receives a credit card offer from a gas company in the mail. He decides to activate the card. You set up a new general ledger account. (You name it "Bolero Gas Card.") Remember: You must use the account type **credit card** so that you have the functionality you need. Ignore any messages about available online services.

•   You also set up the vendor for the credit card. The vendor in this case is:

Bolero Gas Company

1305 Main Street

New York, NY 10007

Credit Terms: Net 15

✓   Your nephew purchases some gardening supplies (yard waste bags and some oil for the lawnmower) from Harry's Hardware for $85, on account (Invoice #3659). He is tracking all gardening supplies as an **asset** (Gardening Supplies on Hand). At the end of the month, he'll determine how many supplies remain on hand, and you'll make any necessary adjustments. The terms are Net 15. (These will be the new terms for this vendor.)

12/8/17

✓   Your nephew hands you the receipt for the $80 of gas he purchased at Luxury Lanes Gas & Grub using his new credit card, and you enter the credit card charge in QuickBooks.

12/12/17

✓   Although the Saturday Snip special was a success overall, there was one small incident at one of the customer's homes. Your nephew tripped over a tree root and suffered a minor sprain to his ankle. He went to the 24 Hour Sprain Clinic and had his ankle X-rayed and bandaged. The cost was $300, and the clinic gave your nephew a bill (#121521).

•   The 24 Hour Sprain Clinic's address is 7500 Medical Boulevard, Sacramento, CA 95822. The phone number is 916-222-9999. The terms are Net 10. [**TIP:** You'll need to set up a new term.]

•   You decide to expense the cost to **Miscellaneous Expense**.

12/14/17

✓   You pay all bills due by 12/29/17.

•   There should be two bills totaling $385. Assign check numbers starting with check #1009.

12/18/17

✓   Your friend Nikolay Levin helped your nephew out on Saturday. Your nephew doesn't expect to use much help, so you won't be setting Nikolay up as an employee. If you pay him more than $600 per year, however, you'll need to file a 1099 for him at year-end. You decide to get everything set up just in case he's paid over the threshold next year.

- You set up a new general ledger account. You decide to name the account "Contract Labor Expense" and make it a subaccount of **Other Operating Expenses**.

- You set up QuickBooks to track 1099 vendors. [**TIP:** Use the preferences menu.] The account **Contract Labor Expense** is the only account you anticipate using for 1099 vendor payments. The account should be mapped to Box 7. Don't forget to update the IRS thresholds.

- You also set Nikolay up as a vendor. His address is 256 Paradise Road, Sacramento, CA 95822. His phone number is 916-345-3456 and his Social Security number (tax id number) is 555-44-3333. [**TIP:** 1099 vendor information is input on the **Tax Settings** tab. Don't forget to check the **Vendor eligible for 1099** box.] Select **Due on receipt** as the payment terms.

✓ Nikolay agreed to a $15 per hour pay rate and helped out for four hours. You write Nikolay a check (#1011) for $60.

✓ Your nephew decides to purchase some new business cards that list his expanded services, so he heads down to Sactown Office Supplies. He purchases, on account, the business cards ($50) and, while he's there, he purchases some holiday greeting cards ($15) to give to his clients. You expense the gifts but not the business cards, which he expects to last him for six months or so. You set up a new account ("Client Relations Expense" in the **Business Promotion Expenses** category) for the cost of the holiday cards. The Sactown Office invoice number is 3895. The terms are Net 30.

✓ You receive a bill in the mail from "Sactown News" for an ad your nephew placed in the paper advertising his services and listing his rates. The ad is set to appear in next Sunday's paper. The total cost is $80 (vendor invoice #12213). The bill is due on receipt.

12/19/17

✓ Your nephew hands you another gas receipt for $60. He purchased the gas at Luxury Lanes Gas and Grub using his gas credit card.

✓ On the way home, he stopped in at Bodies by Barney to ask about the cost of building some shelving and a lockbox for his supplies in the back of his truck. He also asked about the possibility of installing a cooler in the truck to keep any groceries he picks up for clients cool. Barney quoted him a price of $1,000. Gilbert agreed to bring the van back on 12/30 to have the work done. According to Barney, the additional storage should last at least as long as Gilbert plans to keep the truck.

12/29/17

✓ You pay all bills due on or before 1/5/18.
  - There should be two bills totaling $351. Start with check #1012.

12/30/17

✓ Your nephew brings his truck to Bodies by Barney and has the shelving, lockbox, and cooler installed. The actual price is the $1,000 quoted (invoice #9998). Terms are Net 30.

> **HINT:** Don't forget, the new equipment increases the functionality of the van.

✓ Your nephew has been working hard and decides to have some New Year's Eve fun. You write him a $100 check. (Use check #1014.) NOTE: Gilbert has already been set up in your company file. [**TIP:** He's the owner (sole proprietor) so this won't be classified as an expense. Distributions to sole proprietors are called draws.]

Check numbers as of 12/31

Checking account balance **$2,274.00**

Accounts Payable **$1,065.00**

Net income (December only) **$2,025.00**

REPORTS TO CREATE FOR ASSIGNMENT 3A

All reports should be in portrait orientation; fit to one page wide.

- Journal—12/01 through 12/31 (put in date order). Include only these transaction types: **Check**, **Credit Card**, **Bill**, and **Bill Payment**. Remove columns for **Tran #** and **Adj** (if selected).

- Vendor Balance Detail (12/1–12/31).

- Vendor Contact List
  - Include only **Vendor** and **Eligible for 1099** columns.

- Profit and loss statement (December only).

Assignment 3B

Dancing with Dogs

Background information from Chapter 1: Your sister, Monica, started a dog-walking business in November as a way to earn money for college tuition. She decided to operate as a sole proprietorship for now because her operations are fairly simple.

She already has a few regular customers and is excited about the possibility of attracting new ones. She currently offers the following services:

- Dog walks
  - Daily: $20
  - Weekly (5 walks a week): $75 (walks occur Monday through Friday)

- Dog care
  - Dog transport to veterinarian or grooming appointments: $25 per hour
  - In home visits: $15 per hour

She didn't have a need for any special equipment, but she did purchase a used van that she uses to transport the dogs. The van cost her $7,600. She put $4,000 down and financed the rest with Friendly Freeport Bank. The loan is for 60 months at 8 percent interest. The monthly payment is $73 with the first payment due on December 1, 2017.

She took your advice and has been tracking her business transactions in QuickBooks Pro 2015. She has no accounting knowledge though, and she's asked you so many questions that you've decided that it would be easier to just do the accounting for her—at a fee, of course! She has entered all the basic transactions through November 30. You will be entering all the December transactions and helping her prepare all the financial reports as of 12/31, the company's year-end.

12/1/17

- ✓ Your sister's insurance agent (at Premiere Insurance) advises her to purchase a liability insurance policy. You write the check (use #1007) for the first six-month premium: $120. The policy is effective beginning 12/1. (An adjustment for insurance expense for the month of December will be made at the end of December as part of Chapter 4's assignment.)

- ✓ You convince your sister to get a good calculator and a desk lamp. You know the equipment will last for some time, but you decide to expense them in December because the total cost ($75) is insignificant. She purchases them from Sactown Office Supplies, on account. The vendor invoice number is 5266 and the terms are Net 30.

- ✓ You prepare the check (#1008) to Friendly Freeport Bank for the first vehicle loan payment of $73. Remember, the note was dated 11/1. You are paying November interest and some principal. [**TIP:** Interest for November was accrued in the "Interest payable" account, so check out the Balance Sheet for the interest portion of the December 1st payment.]

12/4/17

✓   Your sister receives a credit card offer from a gas company in the mail. She decides to activate the card. You set up a general ledger account. (You name it "Union 67 Card.") Remember you must use the account type **credit card** so that you have the functionality you need. Ignore any messages about online services.

• You also set up the vendor for the credit card. The vendor in this case is:

Union 67 Gas Company

1305 Main Street

New York, NY 10007

Credit Terms: Net 15

12/7/17

✓   Your sister purchases $50 of supplies from Healthy Pets, on account (Invoice #3659). She is tracking all dog supplies as an asset (Dog Supplies on Hand). At the end of the month, she'll determine how many supplies remain on hand and you'll make any necessary adjustments. The terms are Net 15. (These will be the new terms for this vendor.)

✓   You pay the $50 amount due to Sactown Office on invoice #4577 (entered in November) with check #1009.

12/8/17

✓   Your sister hands you the receipt for the $25 of gas she purchased at "Neighborhood Gas" using her new credit card, and you enter the credit card charge in QuickBooks.

12/12/17

✓   Although Dog Day at the Park was a great success overall, there was one small incident. One of the dogs got a little aggressive and your sister sustained a dog bite. She went to the Dr. Fixup Clinic and had the wound cleaned and bandaged. The cost was $200, and the clinic gave your sister a bill (#121521).

• Dr. Fixup Clinic's address is 2020 R Street, Sacramento, CA 95822. The phone number is 916-222-9999. The terms are Net 10. [**TIP:** You'll need to set up a new term.]

• You decide to charge the cost to "Miscellaneous expense."

12/14/17

✓   Your friend Shanelle Carson helped your sister out at Dog Day at the Park. Your sister doesn't expect to use much help, so you won't be setting Shanelle up as an employee. If you pay her more than $600 per year, however, you'll need to file a 1099 for her at year-end. You decide to get everything set up just in case she's paid over the threshold next year.

• You set up a new general ledger account. You decide to name the account "Helper Expense" and make it a subaccount of **Supplies and Helpers**.

• You also set up QuickBooks to track 1099 vendors. [**TIP:** Use the preferences menu.] The account "Helper Expense" is the only account you anticipate using for 1099 vendor payments. The account should be mapped to Box 7. Don't forget to update the IRS thresholds.

• You set Shanelle up as a vendor. Her address is 9881 Ravenna Blvd, Sacramento, CA 95822. Her phone number is 916-345-3456 and the terms are **Due on receipt**. Her Social Security number (tax id number) is 555-44-3333. [**TIP:** 1099 vendor information is input on the **Tax settings** tab. Don't forget to check the **Vendor eligible for 1099 box**.]

✓   Shanelle agreed to a $10 per hour pay rate and helped out for four hours. You write Shanelle a check (#1010) for $40.

✓   Your sister decides to purchase some holiday gifts for her clients, so she heads down to Healthy Pets. She purchases, on account, some dog treats (as the gifts) for $40 and, while she's there, she purchases some additional supplies to have on hand for $10. You expense the gifts (to client relations) but not the supplies to have on hand. The Healthy Pets invoice number is 3895. Terms are Net 15.

✓ You prepare check #1011 for your sister to bring down to the "Sacramento Daily News" to pay for some additional advertising. The advertising will appear in next Sunday's paper. The total cost is $20.

12/19/17

✓ Your sister hands you another gas receipt for $20. She purchased the gas at Neighborhood Gas using her gas credit card.

✓ While she was heading home, she drove over some glass in the road and ruined one of her tires. She brought the van to Truxell Trucks and purchased a new tire for $100. (Truxell billed it to her account. Truxell's invoice number is 9978 with terms of Net 30. These are the normal credit terms for Truxell.) You expense the cost of the new tire.

✓ While she was at Truxell's, she talked to the owner about having some dog cages built into the van. She thinks the cages should last for four years and will help keep the dogs safe whenever she's transporting them. He quoted her a price of $600. She agreed to bring the van back on 12/30 to have the cages installed.

12/22/17

✓ You pay all bills due on or before 1/5/18. [**TIP:** You should be paying four bills with three checks. Assign check numbers starting with #1012. All three checks total $375.]

12/30/17

✓ Your sister brings her van to Truxell and has the dog cages installed. The actual price is the $600 quoted (invoice # 9998). Terms are Net 30.

 HINT: Don't forget that the cages are expected to last for four years.

✓ Your sister has been working hard and decides to have some New Year's Eve fun. You write her a $100 check. (Use check #1016.) NOTE: Monica has already been set up in your company file (on the **Other Name** list). [**TIP:** She's the owner (sole proprietor) so this **won't** be classified as an expense. Distributions to sole proprietors are called "draws."]

Check numbers as of 12/31

Checking account balance $902.00
Accounts Payable $700.00
Net income (December only) $905.00

REPORTS TO CREATE FOR ASSIGNMENT 3B

All reports should be in portrait orientation; fit to one page wide.

● Journal—12/01 through 12/31 (put in **date order**). Include only these transaction types: Check, Credit Card, Bill, and Bill Payment. Remove **Trans #** and **Adj** column.

● Vendor Balance Detail (12/1–12/31)

● Vendor Contact List
  ■ Include only Vendor and Eligible for 1099 columns. [**TIP:** You may need to resize the **Vendor** column to see **Eligible for 1099** column.]

● Profit and loss statement (December only).

End-of-Period Procedures

(Service Company)

BEFORE ISSUING FINANCIAL STATEMENTS

Sales, purchases, cash receipts, and cash payments make up the vast majority of transactions in a company. You've already learned how most of those standard transactions are entered in QuickBooks, and you've seen how QuickBooks does a lot of the work related to posting and tracking those transactions for you. As we discussed in Chapter 1, though, the accuracy and the usefulness of all that data are still dependent on the operator(s) of QuickBooks.

For most companies, the primary financial reports (like the profit and loss statement and the balance sheet) are prepared monthly. It's at the end of the month, then, that the accountant needs to make sure that:

- All accounting transactions have been recorded.

- All accounting transactions have been recorded in the proper accounts.

- All accounting transactions are recognized in the proper accounting period.

- No accounting transactions have been duplicated.

There is, unfortunately, no foolproof method for ensuring the accuracy of the financial statements. There are some tools though. They include:

- Reconciling account balances to external sources.
    - Cash accounts to bank statements.
    - Vendor payable balances to vendor statements.
    - Debt balances to lender reports.

- Reconciling account balances to internal sources.
    - Physical count of supplies on hand to supplies account balance.
    - Timesheets for the last period of the month to salaries payable account if all salaries have not been paid as of the end of a period.

- Reviewing accounts for reasonableness.
    - Most account balances should reflect their **normal balance** (assets should have debit balances, **contra** assets should have credit balances, expenses should have debit balances, etc.).
    - Relationships between accounts should make sense. For example, rent expense, hopefully, shouldn't be higher than income!
    - Account balances that are significantly higher or lower than the prior month should be investigated.

Normal balance The side (debit or credit) on which increases to the account are recorded.

Contra account An account with the opposite normal balance as other accounts of the same type.

As a result of all this reconciliation and review, it is virtually guaranteed that adjustments will need to be made! Without even thinking very hard, you can come up with a few examples. They might include:

- Bank charges that you weren't aware of until you saw the bank statement, which need to be recorded.

- Adjustments to the Supplies on Hand account that need to be made to record supplies used during the period.

- Adjustments to recognize depreciation expense for the period.

- **Accruals** that need to be recorded.

Accruals Adjustments that reflect revenues earned but not received or recorded and expenses incurred but not paid or recorded.

In this chapter, we'll cover:

- Using QuickBooks to reconcile bank accounts.

- Using QuickBooks to reconcile credit card statements.

- Recording adjusting journal entries in QuickBooks.

- Closing accounting periods.

BANK RECONCILIATIONS

QuickBooks has an account reconciliation tool that can actually be used for any balance sheet account (other than **Accounts Receivable** and **Accounts Payable account types**). In this textbook, we'll be using the tool for bank and credit card reconciliations only.

The reconciliation tool is accessible through the Home page (**Reconcile** icon) or within the **Banking** menu on the main menu bar.

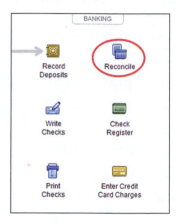

The initial screen looks like this:

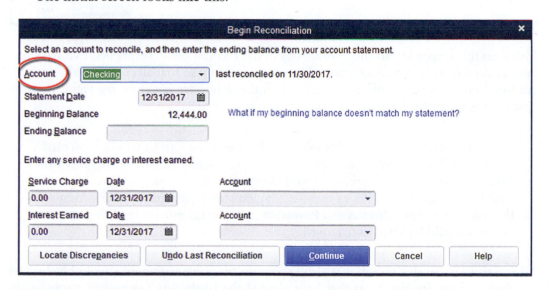

The account to be reconciled is selected first. The next three fields **must** agree to the bank statement you're reconciling.

- The **Statement Date** would be the ending date listed on the bank statement.

- The **Beginning Balance** is **automatically** filled in by QuickBooks. QuickBooks completes this field by using the ending bank statement balance from the prior period's reconciliation. QuickBooks will automatically enter $0.00 in the field if this is the **first** account reconciliation.

- The **Ending Balance** would be the ending **bank** balance listed on the bank statement you're reconciling.

Service charges and interest earned that appear on the bank statement but have **not** been previously recorded in QuickBooks would also be entered in this first screen. Watch the dates! You can use the dropdown menus under **Account** to select the general ledger account to which you want to debit the charges (or credit the interest).

Once you complete the initial screen, you can click **Continue** to start the reconciliation. The screen will look something like this:

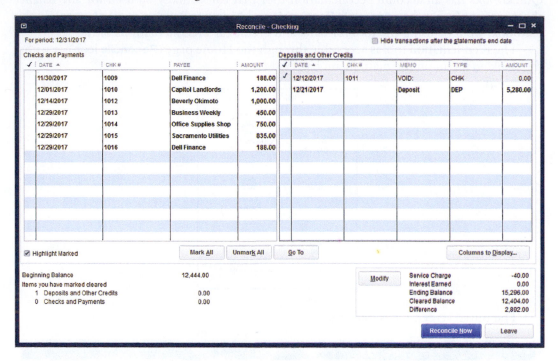

Listed on this screen are **all** the transactions in the account being reconciled that have **not** been cleared in a prior reconciliation. The screen is set up so that all credits to the account are listed on the left side of the screen and all the debits are listed on the right. (I know that sounds backward!)

> **BEHIND THE SCENES** QuickBooks actually uses terms similar to what you might see on a bank statement. You'll notice that the right side is titled **Deposits and Other Credits**. A debit to cash to record a bank deposit on the company's books is a credit (liability) on the bank's books because they now owe you that amount. Although the left side is titled **Checks and Payments**, any journal entries crediting the cash account would be listed here as well.

All transactions on this screen that also appear on the bank statement should be checked (marked). These are the items that have cleared the bank. Any unchecked items would represent outstanding checks or deposits in transit.

A few hints that might help with the reconciliation process:

- If you can't complete the reconciliation, you can click the **Leave** button at the bottom right corner of the screen. QuickBooks will save all your work until you return to complete the reconciliation.

- You can leave the reconciliation window open and create (or edit) a transaction if needed. QuickBooks will automatically refresh the screen for any changes.

- Clicking the **Modify** button will take you back to the first screen. You can change the date, ending balance amount, service charge, or interest income amounts.

- If you highlight a transaction and click on the **Go To** button (center of the screen), QuickBooks will take you to the original transaction where you can make changes, if needed.

- If you only want to display transactions that are dated prior to the bank statement closing date (the only transactions that **could** have cleared the bank), you can click the **Hide transactions after the statement's end date** at the top right of the screen. (This assumes, of course, that you've dated everything correctly.)

- You can change the information that appears on the screen using the **Columns to Display** button.

When you've reconciled the account, the **Difference** field in the bottom right corner of the screen will equal zero. Only then should you click the **Reconcile Now** button.

> **!** **WARNING:** Do not click the *Reconcile Now* button if you haven't finished the reconciliation. QuickBooks will give you a warning if you try, but, if you persist, it will allow you to "reconcile" without actually reconciling. That would leave what my former accounting professors would call a "dangling" credit or debit. Of course QuickBooks won't actually allow you to create an unbalanced transaction, so it will either debit (or credit) an account called "Reconciliation Discrepancy" for the *Difference* amount. You would then have to fix that at a later date.

Once you've reconciled the account, the following screen will appear:

The **Summary** report subtotals cleared and uncleared transactions by type. The **Detail** report lists all cleared and uncleared transactions separately. In most cases, you would want to print a **Detail** report.

> **HINT:** If you forget to print the report, you can access a pdf version of it through the **Banking** option on the **Report** dropdown menu on the main menu bar. **Previous Reconciliation** is the name of the report.

PRACTICE
EXERCISE

Reconcile the bank account for Sac City Accounting.
(Sac City receives its 12/31/17 bank statement. The ending balance is $15,296. Bank services fees are $40.)

1. Click **Reconcile** on the Home page.

2. Select **Checking** as the **Account**.

3. Enter "12/31/17" as the **Date** and "15,296" as the **Ending Balance**.

4. Enter "40" as a **Service Charge** with a 12/31 date.

5. Select **Bank service charges expense** as the **Account**.

6. Click **Continue**.

7. Mark all deposits and checks as cleared except for checks 1013 through 1016.

8. **Difference** should be 0.00.

9. Click **Reconcile Now**.

10. Click **Both**.

11. Click **Display**.

Fixing Bank Reconciliation Errors

The title of this section is actually a little misleading. You can't "fix" bank reconciliations in QuickBooks. A bank reconciliation is not a form that can be modified. QuickBooks will, however, allow you to "undo" the most recent reconciliation and start over.

> **!** **WARNING:** There can be some technical issues that arise when you undo a bank reconciliation. There's actually a lot more to the process than you might think. That's why QuickBooks will suggest that you make a backup of your company file before you undo a reconciliation.

To undo a bank reconciliation, you would go to the reconciliation screen (easily accessed by clicking the **Reconcile** icon on the Home page) and click the **Undo Last Reconciliation** button at the bottom of the screen.

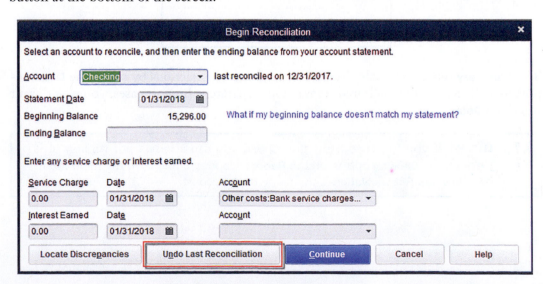

At that point, QuickBooks will suggest that you make a backup of your company file.

> **BEHIND THE SCENES** When you undo a reconciliation, QuickBooks "unclears" all the transactions that were cleared as part of the reconciliation. It does **not**, however, delete any service charge or interest income amounts you had entered. Those transactions will appear as entries on the second reconciliation screen when you make the next attempt to reconcile the account. You can change the amounts there if you need to. Do **not** re-enter them in the initial screen.

CREDIT CARD RECONCILIATIONS

You learned in Chapter 3 how company credit cards are handled in QuickBooks. A separate account is set up (**Credit Card** account **type**), and individual card transactions are posted to the account as they occur. There are a number of credit card forms (**transaction types**). These are listed in Appendix C. One thing they all have in common, though, is that because they are not **bills** or **bill credits**, they do not show up in the **Pay Bills** screen. That's a good thing as companies don't pay individual credit card charges; they pay the credit card statement balance.

At some point, though, the statement balance has to be paid. QuickBooks provides a couple of options. Both of these options are automatically offered after the credit card reconciliation process is complete.

> **BEHIND THE SCENES** It's important to reconcile credit card account activity to the statement. For one thing, there aren't a lot of controls on credit cards. Whoever holds the card can, generally, use the card. Companies need to make sure that all charges are legitimate. Additionally, most credit card transactions are fairly insignificant. Receipts get lost or don't get turned in. Again, companies need to make sure that all activities have been properly recorded.

The process for reconciling a credit card account is very similar to the bank reconciliation process.

The reconciliation tool is easily accessed through the Home page. The credit account to be reconciled should be select in the **Account** field. The screen looks something like this:

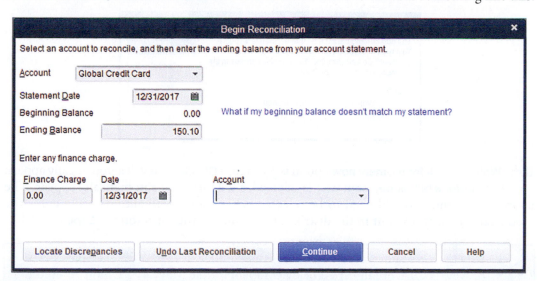

Like the bank reconciliation process, the dates and amounts entered on the initial screen are from the statement being reconciled. The next screen looks something like this:

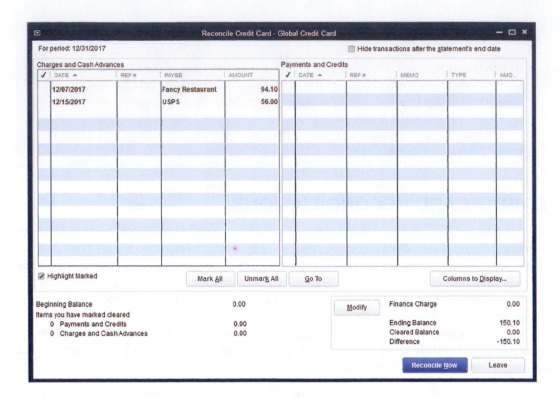

All displayed transactions that agree to items listed on the credit card statement should be checked (marked).

BEHIND THE SCENES If you discover that there's an error on one of the recorded transactions while you're in the reconciliation process, you can highlight the item, click **Go To**, and edit the form. You can also leave the reconciliation screen open while you create a new transaction. The new transaction will automatically appear in the reconciliation screen when it's saved.

Once the statement is reconciled, the following screen will appear:

If the **Write a check for payment now** option is selected, a **Check** form will automatically appear.

If the **Enter a bill for payment later** is selected, a **Bill** form will automatically appear. The appropriate vendor would need to be selected. QuickBooks will automatically enter the credit card liability account in the distribution section of the form (on the **Expenses** tab).

 HINT: Remember, credit cards are issued either by banks (for example, VISA or MasterCard credit cards) or by companies (like Macy's or Union 76 credit cards). You will need to set up the company that issued the credit card as a **vendor** in QuickBooks.

After the **Bill** is completed and saved, it would appear on the **Pay Bills** screen and would be included in the accounts payable account.

> What journal entry does QuickBooks make if you select the **Enter a bill for payment later** option after reconciling a credit card? (Answer at end of chapter.)

QuickCheck **4-1**

PRACTICE EXERCISE

Reconcile Sac City Accounting's credit card statement.
(Sac City received its December statement from Global Credit. The ending statement balance is $150.10. There were no service charges.)

1. Click **Reconcile** on the Home page.

2. Select **Global Credit** as the **Account**.

3. Enter "12/31/17" as the **Date** and "150.10" as the **Ending Balance**.

4. Click **Continue**.

5. Mark all charges as cleared.

6. **Difference** should be 0.00.

7. Click **Reconcile Now**.

8. Select **Enter a bill for payment later**.
   a. Close the reconciliation reports window that appears.
   b. Set up a vendor for the bank that issued the card.
      i. Click **Add New** in the **Vendor** dropdown menu.
      ii. Vendor name is America's Bank.
         1000 Wall Street
         New York, NY 10000
      iii. **Terms** are **Net 15**.
      iv. Click **OK**.

9. Make sure America's Bank shows as the vendor in the **Bill**.

10. Enter "Dec Stmt" as the **Ref. No.**

11. Click **Save & Close**.

MAKING ADJUSTING JOURNAL ENTRIES

All accounting transactions are recorded as journal entries, right? You only have to look at a **Journal** report in QuickBooks to see that all the **Invoices, Checks, Bills, Bill Payments,** etc., are listed (and they're in journal entry form, too).

> **BEHIND THE SCENES** Remember, only transactions that effect the accounting equation are considered accounting transactions. There are some activities (like ordering inventory for example) that can be recorded in QuickBooks but would not appear on the **Journal** report because they don't effect either assets, liabilities, equity, revenue, or expenses.

Adjusting journal entries are simply journal entries that are made to adjust account balances. Although they can be made at any time during an accounting period, the majority of them are made at the end of an accounting period.

In a manual system, adjusting journal entries are created in the general journal. The entries are then posted to the general ledger.

In QuickBooks, adjusting journal entries are created in an electronic version of the general journal. They are posted automatically to the general ledger.

The form used to create an adjusting entry (**Journal** transaction type) is accessed through the **Company** dropdown menu on the main menu bar. The menu option is **Make General Journal Entries**.

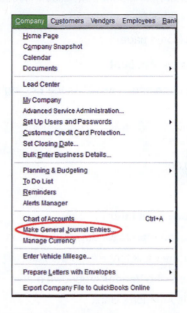

The journal entry screen looks like this:

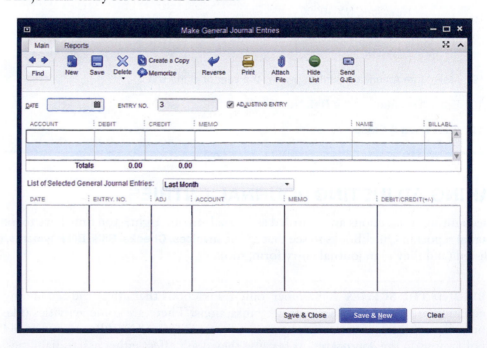

To complete the form, you need to enter the accounts and amounts involved. Although you **can** use the **Journal** form to create entries in accounts receivable, accounts payable, and cash accounts, it's generally better to use the standard forms for transactions that affect those accounts.

> **BEHIND THE SCENES** If you do make an adjusting journal entry to accounts receivable (payable), you would need to enter the name of the customer (vendor) in the **Name** field so that the subsidiary ledger is updated.

Here are some "good practice" points for working with adjusting entries:

- Include a brief description of the transaction in the **Memo** field of the form for future reference.

- Make one entry per type of adjustment. In other words, don't make one big entry with lots of different types of transactions on it. Companies should keep documentation to support adjusting journal entries, and it's easier to match the entry to the documentation if you keep the entries simple.

The mechanics of recording adjusting journal entries in QuickBooks is very simple. To help with the hardest part (knowing what adjustments need to be made), here's a list of common monthly entries for service companies:

- Depreciation.
- Accrual of:
  - Unpaid salaries and interest.
  - Other charges for which a vendor bill has not yet been received.
  - Unbilled revenue.
- Expiration (consumption) of
  - Prepaid expenses.
  - Supplies on hand.
- Recognition of deferred revenue as earned.

Record some adjusting journal entries for Sac City Accounting.
(Sac City records month-end adjustments for depreciation and supplies used.)

1. Click **Company** (main menu bar).

2. Click **Make General Journal Entries**.

3. Record depreciation expense of $379 for December.
   a. Enter "12/31/17" as the **Date**. You can leave the **Entry No.** as 3.
   b. Select **Depreciation expense** as the debit account and **Accumulated Depreciation** as the credit account.
   c. Enter "379" as the **Amount** for both lines.
   d. Enter "December depreciation" in the **Memo** field.
   e. Click **Save & New**.
      i. Ignore any messages you might get about Fixed Asset tracking in QuickBooks.

(continued)

**PRACTICE
EXERCISE**

4. Record supplies used during December. Count of supplies on hand totaled $450. Current account balance is $1,134.

   a. Enter "12/31/17" as the **Date**. Leave the **Entry No.** as 4.

   b. Select **Office supplies expense** (an expense) as the debit account and **Supplies on hand** (an asset) as the credit account.

   c. Enter "684"as the **Amount** for both lines.

      i. Remember, you want the balance sheet to show the cost of the supplies you have on hand at the end of the period. The cost of supplies on hand is $450, but the account shows $1,134 before the adjustment. You need to reduce the asset (using a credit) by $684 to bring the balance to $450.

   d. Enter "Supplies used in December" in the **Memo** field.

   e. Click **Save & Close**.

CLOSING A PERIOD

There are really two types of period closings:

- Closing a period after financial statements are prepared and distributed (generally every month).

- Year-end closing (closing the books at the end of the company's legal year (fiscal year).

Closing An Accounting Period

When we talk about closing a **period**, we are usually simply talking about not making any additional entries to that accounting period. An additional bill might come in that relates to the period or we might discover that we made an error in a reconciliation affecting the closed period, but, once financial statements have been prepared and distributed, we generally don't want to go back and make changes. Instead, we simply record those transactions in the current period.

Materiality An accounting guideline that states that insignificant data that would not affect a financial statement user's decisions may be recorded in the most expedient manner.

> **BEHIND THE SCENES** The constraint of **materiality** applies here. If the dollar amount of a potential adjustment is significant (would influence decisions of the users of the financial statements), the entry has to be made, whether the period is "closed" or not.

So what does all this have to do with QuickBooks? QuickBooks actually gives us a tool that's useful here. You probably have noticed by now, QuickBooks will let you enter any date you want for transactions. Many students (and clients) have spent hours trying to reconcile their financial statements, and it turns out they simply entered a wrong date on a transaction or two.

QuickBooks allows you to set a **Closing Date** in your company file. When a closing date is set, QuickBooks will warn you if you try to enter a transaction dated prior to that date. You can override the warning, but at least it's there.

Setting a closing date is done using the **Set Closing Date** option on the **Company** dropdown menu on the main menu bar.

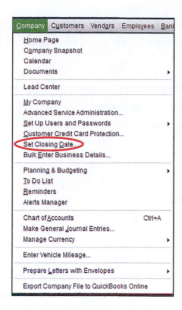

The screen looks like this:

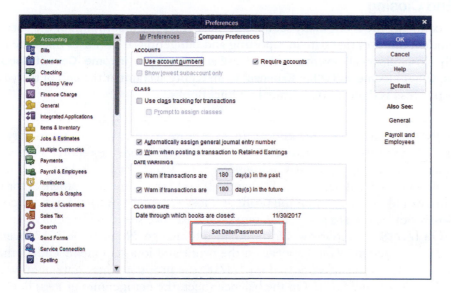

When you click **Set Date/Password** button, the screen looks like this:

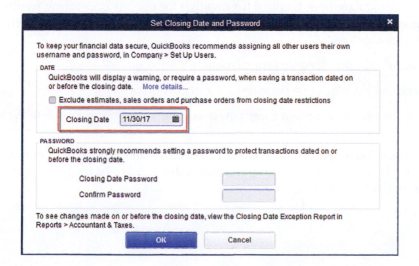

You enter the new **Closing Date** on the screen and click **OK** to close the window. You can also enter a password if there are multiple users of the file. That won't be necessary in this course.

PRACTICE EXERCISE

Set a closing date for Sac City Accounting.
(Sac City sets a 12/31 closing date in QuickBooks.)

1. Click **Company**.

2. Click **Set Closing Date**.

3. Click **Set Date/Password**.

4. Enter "12/31/17" as the **Closing Date**.

5. Click **OK**.

6. Click **No** if warned about passwords and prompted to add users.

Closing process A step in the accounting cycle in which the balances of all temporary accounts are transferred to the Retained Earnings account, leaving the temporary accounts with zero balances.

Year-End Closing

When a company file is originally set up, you must enter the first month of the fiscal (legal) year. QuickBooks uses that date in reporting and budgeting. It also uses that date to automatically close (clear) all revenue and expense account types (**Income**, **Cost of Goods Sold**, **Expense**, **Other Income and Other Expense**) to an equity account at the end of the year. The **closing process** is done automatically by QuickBooks.

> **BEHIND THE SCENES** QuickBooks doesn't create an entry to close temporary accounts that's visible in the **Journal**. It does, however, change the reports. For example, let's say a company started business on 3/1/17 and its year-end was 12/31/17. For all reports dated between 3/1/17 and 12/31/17, revenues and expenses for the period would be reported on the profit and loss statement. A total for net income or loss would show as a single line item on the balance sheet in the equity section.
>
> On 1/1/18, the reports would automatically change. None of the 2017 revenue and expense activity would appear on the profit and loss statement. Unless there were already some entries posted on 1/1/18, the profit and loss statement would show net income of $0.00. On the balance sheet, the net income (or loss) line (related to 2017 transactions) would also no longer appear. Instead, a default equity account would have been credited (or debited) for the 2017 operating results. The default equity account used by QuickBooks depends on the type of entity. The default accounts are:
>
> - Owner's Equity (for sole proprietorships).
>
> - Retained Earnings (for partnerships and corporations).
>
> You can change the names of these equity accounts but you can't delete them.

Although QuickBooks appropriately closes out revenue and expense accounts at year-end, there still may be some final housekeeping entries that need to be made. These entries vary depending on the type of entity.

- **For proprietorships:** Most companies set up separate capital investment and draw accounts (equity accounts) so that activity for the year is visible on the balance sheet. If so, those accounts should be closed out to **Owner's Equity** at the beginning of a new year.

- **For partnerships:** Most small partnerships set up separate capital investment, draw, and capital balance accounts (equity accounts) for each partner. If so, the capital investment, draw, and **Retained Earnings** accounts should be closed out to each partner's capital balance account at the beginning of a new year.

- **For corporations:** Most corporations set up a dividends account (equity account) so that current year distributions to shareholders are visible on the balance sheet. If so, the dividend account should be cleared out to **Retained Earnings** at the beginning of a new year.

Special Considerations For Partnerships

Partners may want to show their individual capital balances on the balance sheets at the end of every accounting period (generally monthly). If so, adjusting entries would need to be made monthly to distribute net income (or loss) to each partner's capital account. The offset account in the entry would be **Retained Earnings**.

PRACTICE EXERCISE

Record annual profit allocation to partner capital accounts.
(Sac City allocates profits of $1,211.90 to partners.)

1. Click on **Company**.
2. Click on **Make General Journal Entries**.
3. Enter "12/31/17" as the **Date** and use 5 for the **Entry No.**
4. Enter a
   a. debit to **Retained Earnings** for $1,211.90.
   b. credit to **Student, earnings current year** for $605.95.
   c. credit to **Williams, earnings current year** for $605.95.
5. Enter "Distribution of profit to partners" in **Memo** for each line.
6. Click **Save & Close**.
7. You will get two warning screens.
   a. The first screen will warn you that you're posting to a closed period. Ignore that warning by clicking **Yes**.
   b. The second screen will warn you that ordinarily you shouldn't be making entries to **Retained Earnings** (which is true!). You can ignore that warning by clicking **OK**.

PREPARING FINANCIAL STATEMENTS

As you know, there are four basic financial statements:

- **Balance sheet**.
- Profit and loss statement (**Income statement**).

Balance sheet A financial statement showing a business's assets, liabilities, and stockholders' equity as of a specific date.

Income statement A financial statement reporting a business's sales revenue and expenses for a given period of time.

Statement of stockholders' equity
A financial statement presenting information regarding the events that cause a change in stockholders' equity during a period. The statement presents the beginning balance, additions to, deductions from, and the ending balance of stockholders' equity for the period.

Statement of cash flows A financial statement showing a firm's cash inflows and cash outflows for a specific period, classified into operating, investing, and financing activity.

- Statement of retained earnings (or **Statement of stockholders' equity**).
- **Statement of cash flows**.

You can prepare a balance sheet, profit and loss statement, and statement of cash flows automatically in QuickBooks. In this course, we'll only be looking at the balance sheet and profit and loss statement.

Financial statements may be distributed to:

- Owners.
- Management.
- Lenders.
- Potential investors.
- Regulatory agencies.

They should be clear and professional in appearance. There are a few standard reporting conventions to consider:

- Assets are generally reported in descending order of liquidity (how quickly or easily they can be converted to cash).
- Liabilities are generally reported in descending order of their priority for payment.
- Revenue and expenses are generally reported in order of dollar amount (highest to lowest).
  - Categories are sorted first; then individual accounts within each category.

> **BEHIND THE SCENES** There are no absolute rules for presentation, particularly in the order of accounts on the profit and loss statement. For instance, there are some accounts that are generally reported last (like depreciation expense and miscellaneous expense) regardless of the dollar amount. As the accountant, your responsibility is to organize the information in the clearest and most meaningful manner possible.

Remember, you can change the order of account presentation in the **Chart of Accounts** list screen. Go back to Chapter 1 if you need a refresher!

PRACTICE EXERCISE

Prepare year-end financial statements for Sac City Accounting.
(Sac City needs a balance sheet and profit and loss statement.)

1. Review balance sheet.
   a. Click **Reports**.
   b. Click **Company & Financial**.
   c. Click **Balance Sheet Standard**.
   d. Change date to 12/31/17.
   e. Determine that all accounts appear to be in the proper order.
      i. NOTE: If you change the date to 1/1/18, you'll see that the **Net Income** and **Retained Earnings** lines disappear from the equity section.

(continued)

2. Review the income statement.

   a.   Click **Reports**.

   b.   Click **Company & Financial**.

   c.   Click **Profit & Loss Standard**.

   d.   Change dates to 1/1–12/31/17.

   e.   Change the order of the income accounts so that the category **Accounting Services Fees** appears first and that, within that category, **Bookkeeping Services** appears first.

      i.   Click **Lists**.

      ii.   Click **Chart of Accounts**.

      iii. Click and hold the diamond next to account **Accounting Services Fees** and move the category up so that it appears direct under **Retained Earnings**.

      iv.   Click and hold the diamond next to account **Bookkeeping Services** and move it so that it appears above **Financial Statement Reviews**.

   f.   Look at the order of the expense accounts.

      i.   Highest dollar amount categories would normally be listed first.

      ii.   Within each expense category, highest dollar amount accounts would be listed first.

      iii. There are exceptions. Many companies would list depreciation expense at bottom of the category (probably because depreciation is not a cash expenditure). Miscellaneous expense accounts are also frequently listed last.

   g.   Your statements might look like those that follow.

Sac City Accounting
Balance Sheet
As of December 31, 2017

	Dec 31, 17
ASSETS	
Current Assets	
Checking/Savings	
Checking	13,073.00
Total Checking/Savings	13,073.00
Accounts Receivable	
Accounts receivable	1,940.00
Total Accounts Receivable	1,940.00
Other Current Assets	
Inventory	4,000.00
Supplies on hand	450.00
Prepaid expenses	1,000.00
Total Other Current Assets	5,450.00
Total Current Assets	20,463.00
Fixed Assets	
Computer and office equipment	10,816.00
Office furniture	4,400.00
Accumulated depreciation	-1,115.00
Total Fixed Assets	14,101.00
Other Assets	
Security deposit - office space	1,200.00
Total Other Assets	1,200.00
TOTAL ASSETS	35,764.00
LIABILITIES & EQUITY	
Liabilities	
Current Liabilities	
Accounts Payable	
Accounts payable	4,150.10
Total Accounts Payable	4,150.10
Total Current Liabilities	4,150.10
Long Term Liabilities	
Note payable-computers	5,402.00
Total Long Term Liabilities	5,402.00
Total Liabilities	9,552.10
Equity	
Partners' capital	
Student name	
Student, capital balance	12,500.00
Student, earnings current year	605.95
Total Student name	13,105.95
Williams	
Williams, capital balance	12,500.00
Williams - Other	605.95
Total Williams	13,105.95
Total Partners' capital	26,211.90
Retained earnings	-1,211.90
Net Income	1,211.90
Total Equity	26,211.90
TOTAL LIABILITIES & EQUITY	35,764.00

Sac City Accounting
Profit & Loss
January through December 2017

	Jan - Dec 17
Ordinary Income/Expense	
Income	
Accounting services fees	
Bookkeeping services	3,520.00
Financial statement reviews	3,200.00
Total Accounting services fees	6,720.00
Consulting Services	500.00
Total Income	7,220.00
Gross Profit	7,220.00
Expense	
Facility and equipment costs	
Rent expense	2,400.00
Utilities expense	585.00
Telephone expense	350.00
Depreciation expense	1,115.00
Total Facility and equipment costs	4,450.00
General office costs	
Office supplies expense	684.00
Postage and delivery expense	56.00
Total General office costs	740.00
Marketing and client retention	
Advertising/Promotion expense	530.00
Meals and entertainment expense	94.10
Total Marketing and client retention	624.10
Other costs	
Bank service charges expense	40.00
Total Other costs	40.00
Total Expense	5,854.10
Net Ordinary Income	1,365.90
Other Income/Expense	
Other Expense	
Interest expense	154.00
Total Other Expense	154.00
Net Other Income	-154.00
Net Income	1,211.90

ANSWER TO
QuickCheck
4-1

Credit Card Payable	XXX	
Accounts Payable		XXX

CHAPTER SHORTCUTS

Void checks

1. Open check to be voided
    a. Click Edit/Find
    b. Enter check number, payee, date, or amount
    c. Highlight check
    d. Click Go To
2. Click Edit/Void Check

Reconcile an account

1. Click Home
2. Click Reconcile

Record adjusting journal entries

1. Click Company
2. Click Make General Journal Entries

CHAPTER REVIEW

Matching

Match the term or phrase (as used in QuickBooks) to its best definition.

1. Journal
2. Statement date
3. Accounting
4. Checks and Payments
5. Deposits and Other Credits
6. Filters
7. Undo Last Reconciliation
8. Closing Date

_____ Tab on **Modify report** screen used to identify categories of information to be included in a report

_____ Tab in **Preferences** where a closing date can be set.

_____ Date set by user used to limit entry of transactions dated prior to that date

_____ Date of statement received from bank

_____ Section of bank reconciliation screen listing all debits to the account being reconciled

_____ Command used to "unclear" transactions

_____ Transaction type used for recording an adjusting entry

_____ Section of bank reconciliation screen listing all credits to the account being reconciled

Multiple Choice

1. All transactions posted to an account being reconciled will appear on the bank reconciliation screen in QuickBooks **except**:
    a. transactions cleared in a prior period and uncleared transactions recorded through a general journal entry.
    b. transactions cleared in a prior period.
    c. uncleared transactions.
    d. uncleared **bill payment** transactions.

2. Which of the following accounts **could** be reconciled using the reconciliation tool in QuickBooks? (Select all the apply.)

   a. Cash (**Bank account type**)

   b. Prepaid expenses (**Other Current Asset account type**)

   c. Accounts payable (**Accounts Payable account type**)

   d. Unearned revenue (**Other Current Liability account type**)

3. The Journal report includes:

   a. all accounting transactions no matter where (how) they were recorded.

   b. only those accounting transactions recorded in the "Make General Journal Entries" form.

   c. only accounting transactions recorded through certain forms.

   d. only accounting transactions **not** recorded in the "Make General Journal Entries" form.

4. When **Undo Last Reconciliation** is selected,

   a. QuickBooks will "unclear" all transactions cleared in the prior reconciliation and delete any bank service charges or interest income credits entered in the prior period.

   b. QuickBooks will "unclear" all transactions cleared in the prior reconciliation but will not delete any bank service charges or interest income credits entered in the prior period.

   c. QuickBooks will "unclear" all transactions cleared during the fiscal year and delete any bank service charges or interest income credits entered during the year.

   d. QuickBooks will "unclear" all transactions cleared during the fiscal year but will not delete any bank service charges or interest income credits entered during the year.

5. On the first day of a new fiscal year, QuickBooks automatically closes

   a. all temporary accounts.

   b. all revenue and expense accounts.

   c. all revenue, expense, and equity accounts.

   d. all revenue, expense, and dividend accounts.

ASSIGNMENTS

Background information from Chapter 1: Your nephew, Gilbert Greenjeans, was given a $6,000 check from his grandparents for his 16th birthday. They encouraged him to deposit the check in a college savings account. Gilbert understood their point of view, but he was a very ambitious young man and thought he'd be better off using that money to start a small lawn-mowing business. He believed he could make more money mowing lawns than he could earn, in interest, on money in a savings account. The fact that he lived near a very exclusive neighborhood full of palatial homes and large yards was a real bonus. He came to you for advice.

After you cautioned him on all the risks of going into business for himself, you realized that he was very serious about this new venture, so you decided to give him some help. You first told him that he'd have to come up with a business name and business structure. Gilbert decided to set the company up as a sole proprietorship under the name "At Your Service."

On 10/20/17, Gilbert used $700 of his grandparent's gift to purchase, for cash, a good lawnmower, a lawn edger, and some rakes ($600) and a big supply of yard waste bags ($100).

He convinced his father to co-sign on a loan for a truck. The truck, which he purchased on 11/1, cost $20,000. He put $5,000 down and financed the balance with First Sacramento Bank over three years. His monthly payment (including interest at 5 percent) was set at $450. The first payment was due on 12/1.

Assignment 4A

At Your Service

He set up the following fee schedule to start:

- Weekly lawn mowing with edging
  - Large yard: $200 per week
  - Medium yard: $125 per week
  - Small yard: $75 per week
- Other gardening services
  - Leaf raking: $25 per hour

He signed up three clients in November and started working right away.

Gilbert has been tracking his business transactions in QuickBooks Pro 2015. He has no accounting knowledge though, and it's taking him so long to do his accounting that he's falling behind on his homework! His parents have asked you to help him out. He has entered all the basic transactions through November 30. You will be entering all the December transactions and helping him prepare all the financial reports as of 12/31/17, the company's year-end.

12/31/17

✓ Your nephew receives the December bank statement (included at end of assignment). You reconcile the statement to your records. [**TIP:** Look over the bank statement first. If there are any bank service charges, they should be entered on the first screen of the reconciliation.]

✓ He also receives his credit card statement from Bolero Gas Company (included at end of assignment). You reconcile the statement to his records and set up the balance due as a payable (**enter a bill for payment later** option). Remember: Bolero Gas Company is the vendor.

✓ You make adjusting journal entries for the month of December as needed. You carefully consider the following:

- Gilbert uses the straight-line method to determine depreciation expense each month.
  - Gilbert has determined that the truck's service life is four years. The truck was purchased on 11/1 for $20,000, and your nephew expects it to have a salvage value of $2,000. Depreciation for November was already recorded.
  - Gilbert says the gardening equipment (lawn mower and edger) will probably last two years. The equipment (purchased at the beginning of November) cost $600. He doesn't think there will be any salvage value.
  - The built-in storage units in the truck are expected to last as long as the truck. They were installed on 12/30, but he didn't start using them until 1/1/18.
  - The accounting software cost Gilbert $216 and was purchased and placed in service at the beginning of December. It should last two years with no salvage value.
- Your nephew tells you that he has $115 of supplies on hand at 12/31. The $115 includes gardening supplies ($90) and business cards ($25). Gilbert has already passed out half of his new cards. He's anxious to sign up new customers! NOTE: Your nephew tells you that all supplies on hand at 11/30 were gardening supplies.
- Your nephew purchased a $240 insurance policy in December. The policy term is six months (12/1/16–5/31/17).
- You check to make sure your nephew has, in fact, earned the revenue for all amounts billed in December. If not, you set up the necessary general ledger accounts for any unearned revenue. Remember: Your nephew earns the revenue when he performs the service (mows the lawns or weeds gardens for example). He bills his lawn-mowing

'clients in advance. [**TIP:** Jenny Lopez was billed for four weeks of lawn mowing starting 12/15 (one mow per week, four mows total) on invoice #104. Your nephew has mowed her lawn once since 12/15. He also gave her a credit for the mow he missed during the last week of December. He owes her two mows in January. Oprah Zinfrey was also billed for four weeks of lawn mowing starting 12/15 (one mow per week) on invoice #106. Your nephew mowed her lawn twice during that period.]

- You made one loan payment in December (on 12/1). Interest through November 30th was paid at that time. NOTE: Round any entry to the nearest whole dollar. Remember: The annual interest rate is 5%.

✓   You and your nephew agree that you should be paid something for the time you spent on his accounting. You agree to $100 per month (starting in December when you took over). You don't need the money right away, however, so you decide to set up an account called "Accrued Expenses" (an **other current liability account type**) instead of recording it in Accounts Payable. You decide to charge the $100 to an "Accounting Fees" expense account, which you set up as a subaccount of "Taxes and Professional Services."

✓   You are going to prepare a balance sheet and profit and loss statement for your nephew and want them to look professional. Take a look at the statements. Is the order of presentation reasonable? Make any account order changes to the chart of account you think are necessary to create a professional looking set of statements. NOTE: There is no one "right" answer here. There are some general presentation guidelines include in the chapter.

1/1/18

✓   At Your Service is a sole proprietorship and has a 12/31 year-end. Make any entries needed to ensure that all temporary accounts are closed appropriately to start the new year. [**TIP:** The **only equity** account that should appear on the 1/1/18 balance sheet is **Owner's Equity**. That is the capital account set up for the proprietorship. It should total $7,212.50.]

BOLERO GAS COMPANY
1305 Main Street
New York, NY 10007

Your Name At Your Service
3835 Freeport Blvd
Sacramento, CA 95822
Account # 157899400

December 31, 2017

	PAYMENTS	CHARGES	BALANCE
Beginning Balance, December 1,.			$ 0.00
12/8—Luxury Lanes Gas		$80.00	80.00
12/19—Luxury Lanes Gas		60.00	140.00
Ending Balance, 12/31			$140.00

Minimum Payment Due: $10.00   **Payment Due Date: January 15**

FIRST SACRAMENTO BANK
1551 Main Street
Sacramento, CA 95822
(916) 278-2788

Your Name At Your Service
3835 Freeport Blvd
Sacramento, CA 95822
Account # 134662   December 31, 2017

	CREDITS	CHARGES	BALANCE
Beginning Balance, December 1, ...			$ 420.00
12/2, Check 1005		$ 50.00	370.00
12/2, Check 1008		450.00	(80.00)
12/2, Overdraft charge		40.00	(120.00)
12/5, Deposit	$1,350.00		1,230.00
12/7, Check 1007		240.00	990.00
12/17, Check 1009		300.00	690.00
12/19, Check 1010		85.00	605.00
12/21, Deposit	940.00		1,545.00
12/26, Check 1011		60.00	1,485.00
12/30, Deposit	1,225.00		2,710.00
12/30, Check 1014		100.00	2,610.00
Ending Balance, 12/31			$2,610.00

Check numbers 12/31

> **Checking account balance** **$2,234.00**
> **Net income—December** **$625.00**
> **Net income for the year ending 12/31** **$1,312.50**
> **Total assets** **$23,841.00**
> **Total current liabilities** **$2,016.00**

REPORTS TO CREATE FOR ASSIGNMENT 4A

All reports should be in portrait orientation; fit to one page wide.

- Journal—include 12/31/17 and 1/1/18 transactions only.

- Balance Sheet (standard) as of 12/31/17.

- Profit & Loss (standard) for December 2017.
  - Add a subcolumn to the statement to include year-to-date information. (That option is available on the **Display** tab in the **Customize Report** window.)

- Balance Sheet (standard) as of 1/1/18.

Assignment 4B

Dancing with Dogs

Background information from Chapter 1: Your sister started a dog-walking business in November as a way to earn money for college tuition. She decided to operate as a sole proprietorship for now because her operations are fairly simple.

She already has a few regular customers and is excited about the possibility of attracting new ones. She currently offers the following services:

- Dog walks
  - Daily: $20
  - Weekly (5 walks a week): $75 (walks occur Monday through Friday)

- Dog care
  - Dog transport to veterinarian or grooming appointments: $25 per hour
  - In-home visits: $15 per hour

She didn't have a need for any special equipment, but she did purchase a used van that she uses to transport the dogs. The van cost her $7,600. She put $4,000 down and financed the rest with Friendly Freeport Bank. The loan is for 60 months at 8 percent interest. The monthly payment is $73 with the first payment due on December 1, 2017.

She took your advice and has been tracking her business transactions in QuickBooks Pro 2015. She has no accounting knowledge though, and she's asked you so many questions that you've decided that it would be easier to just do the accounting for her   at a fee, of course! She has entered all the basic transactions through November 30. You will be entering all the December transactions and helping her prepare all the financial reports as of 12/31/17, the company's year-end.

12/31/17

✓ Your sister receives the December bank statement (included at end of assignment). You reconcile that statement to your records. [**TIP:** Look over the bank statement first. If there are any bank service charges, they should be entered on the first screen of the reconciliation.]

✓ She also receives her credit card statement from Union 67 (included at end of assignment). You reconcile the statement to your records and set up the balance due as a payable. Remember, Union 67 Gas Company is the vendor.

✓ You make adjusting journal entries for the month of December as needed. You carefully consider the following:

- The van's service life is five years. The vehicle was purchased on 11/1 for $7,600, and your sister expects it to have a salvage value of $100 at the end of its life. She is using the straight-line method to determine depreciation expense each month. Depreciation for November was already recorded.

- The built-in dog carriers will be depreciated over the remaining life of the van. They were installed on 12/30, but they won't be placed in service until 1/1/18.

- Your sister tells you that she has $155 of dog supplies on hand at 12/31.

- Your sister has two insurance policies. Both have six-month terms.

  - The business insurance policy period began on 11/1. The total premium amount of $400 was charged to Prepaid Insurance. November insurance expense was recognized in November.

  - The term on the liability insurance policy she purchased in December began on 12/1. The total premium amount was $120.

- Your last loan payment was 12/1. Interest through November 30th was paid at that time. Remember: The annual interest rate is 8%.

- You make sure your sister has, in fact, earned the revenue for all amounts billed in December. If not, you set up the necessary general ledger accounts for any unearned revenue. Remember: Your sister earns her revenue when she performs the service (walks the dogs or works at the vet clinic), but she bills her dog walking clients in advance. [**TIP:** Martha Stuart was billed for two weeks of walks (five walks per week, ten walks in total) on invoice #113. Monica tells you that she had only walked Martha's dog five times by 12/31. Frank Beagle was billed for four weeks of walks (two walks per week, eight walks in total) on invoice #112. Monica tells you that Frank took his dog away for the holidays. He was walked twice during the last weeks of December. She has agreed to walk Frank's dog six more times after he gets back in January.]

✓ You and your sister agree that you should be paid something for the time you've been spending on her accounting. You agree to $100 per month (starting in December when you took over). You don't need the money right away, however, so you decide to set up an account called "Accrued Expenses" (a current liability account type) instead of recording it in Accounts Payable. You decide to charge the $100 to an "Accounting Fees" expense account, which you set up as a subaccount of "Taxes and Professional Services." You enter this as a **general journal entry**, not as a **bill**.

✓ You are going to prepare a balance sheet and profit and loss statement for your sister and want them to look professional. You take a look at the statements and consider the order of presentation. You make all changes to the order of the accounts (in the chart of accounts) you think are necessary to create a professional looking set of statements. NOTE: There is no one "right" answer here. There are some general presentation guidelines include in the chapter.

1/1/18

✓ Dancing with Dogs is a sole proprietorship and has a 12/31 year-end. Make any entries needed to ensure that all temporary accounts are closed appropriately to start the new year. [**TIP:** The **only equity** account that should appear on the 1/1/17 balance sheet is "Owner's Equity." That is the capital account set up for the proprietorship. It should total $5,293.99.]

UNION 67 GAS COMPANY
1305 Main Street
New York, NY 10007
(805) 544-3900

Your Name Dancing with Dogs
3835 Freeport Blvd
Sacramento, CA 95822
Account # 157899400   December 31, 2017

	Payments	CHARGES	BALANCE
Beginning Balance, December 1, ...			$ 0.00
12/8—Neighborhood Gas........................		$25.00	25.00
12/19—Neighborhood Gas.......................		20.00	45.00
Ending Balance, 12/31			$45.00

Minimum Payment Due: $10.00   **Payment Due Date: January 15**

FRIENDLY FREEPORT BANK
2199 Freeport Blvd
Sacramento, CA 95822
(916) 212-2801

Your Name Dancing with Dogs
3835 Freeport Blvd
Sacramento, CA 95822
Account # 134662   December 31, 2017

	CREDITS	CHARGES	BALANCE
Beginning Balance, December 1, ...			$ 445.00
12/1, Check 1005		$ 20.00	425.00
12/2, Check 1006		15.00	410.00
12/5, Check 1007		120.00	290.00
12/5, Deposit	$375.00		665.00
12/8, Check 1008		73.00	592.00
12/11, Check 1009		50.00	542.00
12/22, Deposit	620.00		1,162.00
12/22, Check 1011		20.00	1,142.00
12/26, Check 1013		100.00	1,042.00
12/27, Check 1012		200.00	842.00
12/28, Check 1014		75.00	767.00
12/29, Deposit	290.00		1,057.00
12/30, Check 1010		40.00	1,017.00
12/31, Service charge.		10.00	1,007.00
Ending Balance, 12/31			$1,007.00

Check numbers 12/31

> Checking account balance **$892.00**
> Net income—December. **$259.66**
> Net income for the year ending 12/31 . . . . . **$393.99**
> Total assets **$9,893.66**
> Total current liabilities **$1,048.67**

REPORTS TO CREATE FOR ASSIGNMENT 4B

All reports should be in portrait orientation; fit to one page wide.

- Journal—include only 12/31/17 and 1/1/18 transactions only. Remove **Trans #** and **Adj** column.

- Balance Sheet (standard) as of 12/31/17.

- Profit & Loss (standard) for December 2017.
  - Add a subcolumn to the statement for year-to-date information. (That option is available on the **Display** tab in the **Customize Report** window.)

- Balance Sheet (standard) as of 1/1/18.

APPENDIX 4A GETTING IT RIGHT

Most accountants work the hardest (use their brains the most!) at the end of an account-ing period. They know the income statement for the period should accurately reflect the earnings (or loss) for the period. They know the balance sheet as of the period end should accurately reflect the assets owned and the liabilities owed by the company. The difficulty doesn't lie in knowing the basic concepts. The difficulty lies in knowing what the "accu-rate" amounts are.

Often, students have the most difficulty with the assignments for Chapters 4 and 7 for the same reason. You have check numbers to refer to that will, hopefully, help, but if your numbers don't match those numbers, how do you figure out where you went wrong?

Some suggestions for finding mistakes were given at the end of Chapter 1. The following list includes those suggestions and adds a few more.

- Start by checking dates.

  - As noted in Chapter 1, entering an incorrect date is the **single most common** cause of student errors (and student headaches!). QuickBooks enters default dates when you first open a form. It defaults to the current date when you start entering transactions during a work session. If you change the date on the first invoice, it will default to that new date when you enter the second invoice. If you open a new form, however, it will default back to the current date. Accounting is date-driven, so your financial statements won't match the check figures if you enter a transaction in the wrong month. First thing to do? Pull a report of transactions dated **before** the first transaction date in the assignment and then one of transactions dated **after** the last transaction date of the assignment. Make sure you're only checking for transactions that **you** entered. (There were some transactions entered in the initial set up of the company files. Those should **not** be changed.)

- Really **look** at the balance sheet. [**TIP:** Start by changing the dates. Click **Customize Report** and enter the month you're working in (12/1 to 12/31/17 for Chapters 1 through 4) on the **Display** tab. That way, you can easily double-click on a balance in a specific account and see all the transactions you've entered for the period.]

  - The account balances will be positive if they reflect the normal balance for that type of account. Are any of the amounts on your balance sheet negative numbers? If so, should they be negative? If they are contra accounts, the answer would be yes. If there are no negative amounts on your balance sheet, should there be? Again, if you have any contra accounts, the answer would be yes. Accumulated depreciation is a contra account, so, if entries were made correctly, it would show as a negative number on the balance sheet. If accumulated depreciation isn't negative, you might have mixed up your debits and credits when making an entry. That's easy to do. Double-click on the amount, then double-click on the entry(ies) and make the necessary corrections.

  - Don't worry about errors in Cash, A/R or A/P until you are comfortable with the other balances. As noted in Chapter 1, this is double-entry bookkeeping, so, if one account is wrong, then at least one other account is also wrong. It's hard to find errors in cash, A/R, and A/P due to the sheer volume of transactions that affect these accounts. So, if you don't match the check figures, see if you can find the other account(s) that is(are) also off. If you can find and correct the other error(s), these accounts will, of course, fix themselves!

  - Pay particular attention to other current assets and to liabilities other than accounts payable. Are they adjusted properly? Does the supplies on hand account equal the amount given to you in the assignment? Does the balance in prepaid insurance represent the cost of future (unused) insurance coverage? Should there be any interest accrued on debt? Keep asking questions.

- Really **look** at the profit and loss statement.
  - Again, look for negative amounts that shouldn't be negative. There are some contra revenue and expenses accounts, of course. Sales discounts and purchase discount accounts are two examples of contra accounts that you'll be working with in future chapters.
  - Look at the detail for accounts that just look "odd." Is rent expense higher than income? That could happen, of course, but probably not in this class!

- If you're still off, you're going to have to do some detective work. Try to narrow down the possible errors first.
  - For example, let's say your A/R number is **higher** than the check figure given for A/R. You wouldn't start by looking for unrecorded invoices or cash sales. Why? Because missing invoices or cash sales wouldn't overstate A/R. You **would** start by looking for unrecorded customer payments or customer credits. Look through the assignment (day by day) and agree any customer payments or credits described to the **payment** and **credit memo transaction types** listed in your **journal**.
  - Here's another example. Let's say your cash number is **lower** than the check number given for cash. You might start by looking for undeposited checks by making sure there isn't a balance in the undeposited funds account. You might also look for duplicated customer payments. Then look through the assignment (day by day) and agree any payment transactions to **checks** and **bill payments** listed in your journal.
  - Don't give up. Keep checking transactions. You'll find the error.

- There is one other suggestion from Chapter 1. It's listed last here only because students tend to waste a lot of time looking for a specific amount when the difference is often the sum of several errors. That being said, sometime you just get lucky! So, determine the difference between the check figure and your total. Is the number divisible by 9? You may have a transposition error (for example, you entered 18 instead of 81). Is the difference equal to the amount of a transaction? Maybe you forgot to enter it (or entered it on the wrong date). Is the difference equal to twice one of your transactions? You may have entered a journal entry backwards (watch those debits and credits!).

QuickBooks

Merchandising Companies

In this section, we'll primarily be looking at how QuickBooks handles the unique needs of merchandising companies. However, some of the new processes and procedures you will learn can be, and are, also used by service companies.

Accounting in a merchandising company is a little more complex. For example, inventory purchases and sales need to be accounted for, and sales tax may need to be collected and remitted.

Merchandising companies are also, generally, larger than service companies. That means more employees, including more employees involved in accounting functions. Although internal controls are important in **any** company, the complexity and size of merchandising companies make the review and development of internal control systems even more important.

Two of the primary purposes of a good internal control system are:

- To safeguard assets.

- To ensure the accuracy of financial records.

QuickBooks has some features that can be part of a good internal control system.

Internal controls The measures undertaken by a company to ensure the reliability of its accounting data, protect its assets from theft or unauthorized use, insure that employees follow the company's policies and procedures, and evaluate the performance of employees, departments, divisions, and the company as a whole.

CONTROLS IN QUICKBOOKS

Limiting User Access

Many merchandising companies have multiple employees involved in the recordkeeping functions. Those employees must, of course, have access to the accounting software. Allowing every employee **full** access to the software, however, presents opportunities for fraud.

QuickBooks allows individual users to be limited in access to particular areas of the program and even to functions within those areas. QuickBooks

Fraud Any act by the management or employees of a business involving an intentional deception for personal gain.

149

requires that at least one user, the **administrator**, have access to all functions. The administrator sets up the other users.

> **BEHIND THE SCENES** The person who created the company file is automatically set up as the Administrator. Since you created the .qbw file for Sac City Accounting Services, you are the administrator.

Additional users are set up in the **Set up Users and Passwords** option of the **Company** menu (main menu bar).

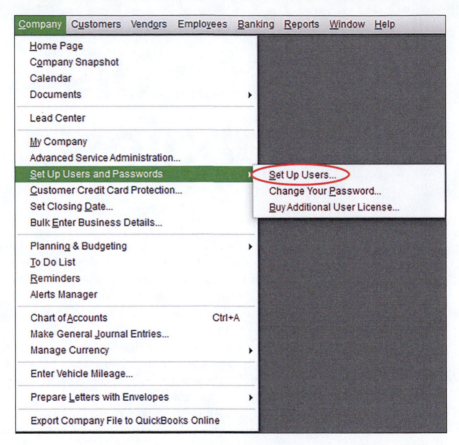

The initial screen displays a list of all current users:

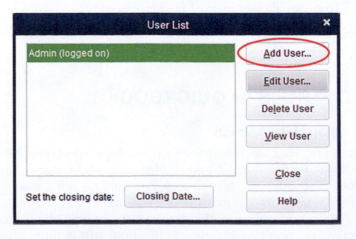

When you click **Add User**, the initial screen looks like this:

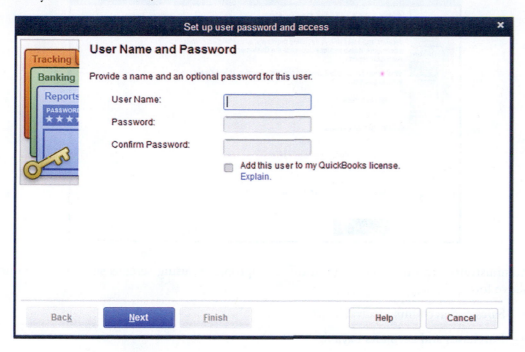

A different password should be set up for each user.

On the next screen, the administrator can limit the number of areas of access. The screen looks like this:

If **All areas of QuickBooks** is selected, the user would have unlimited access to QuickBooks, but the administrator would be able to pull reports on transactions initiated, changed, or deleted by that user. The **External Accountant** choice is generally selected for outside accountants hired to reconcile and prepare adjusting journal entries in a small company.

If **Selected areas of QuickBooks** is chosen, the next screen will look like this:

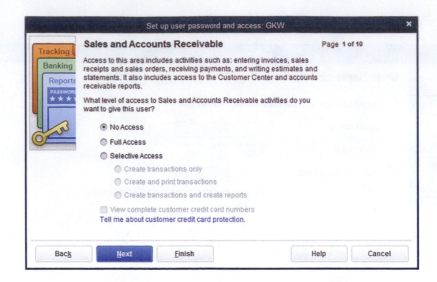

Administrators can turn access on or off, as appropriate, using screens similar to the one above for:

- Sales and accounts receivable.

- Purchases and accounts payable.

- Checking and credit cards.

- Inventory.

- Time tracking.

- Payroll and employees.

- Sensitive accounting activities (transferring funds, making general journal entries, etc.).

- Sensitive reporting (preparing and printing reports).

- Several other options relate to limiting a user's ability to change or delete transactions within their area(s) of access.

After the areas of access have been identified, the administrator must indicate whether the specific user should be allowed to edit transactions. The screen looks like this:

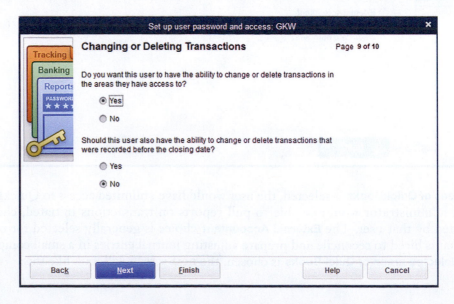

Once the final choices are made, QuickBooks displays a summary of the individual user's access. The screen would look similar to this:

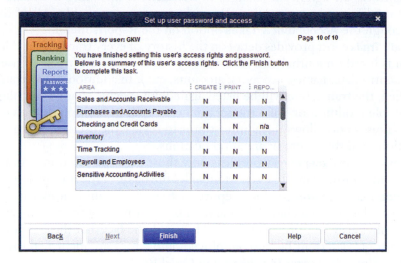

Editing Users

Users can be edited or deleted on the **User List** screen. (On the main menu bar, open the dropdown menu for **Company**, and select **Set Up Users and Passwords**, **Set Up Users**.)

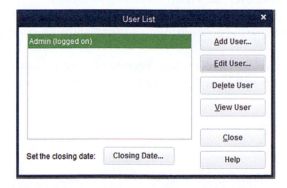

BEHIND THE SCENES If you'd like the set up a password for yourself, highlight **Admin** and click **Edit User**. The following screen will appear:

Creating a challenge question (with the answer of course) will allow you to reset your password in case you forget it.

Reporting On Transaction History

QuickBooks tracks all significant changes to transactions including the **name** of the user entering or modifying the transaction. Several reports are available. All of them can be accessed through the **Accountant & Taxes** option on the **Reports** menu.

The **Audit Trail** report provides detail on the history of every transaction. All significant information is listed (in journal entry form) for every transaction (name of user initiating transaction, entry date, names, accounts, amounts, etc.). In addition, if the transaction has been modified, the transaction will be listed again with specific changes highlighted (bold italics). Multiple modifications of a transaction will result in multiple entries on the **Audit Trail** report. This report allows the administrator to review the users entering and modifying transactions and the nature of any modifications.

The **Closing Date Exception Report** lists only those prior period transactions that were changed after the closing date. The report includes the name of the user making the change.

The **Voided/Deleted Transactions** reports list specific transactions that were either voided or deleted and also includes the name of the user making the modification.

Reports, obviously, can't prevent fraud. However, the fact that these reports are available acts as a fraud deterrent because employees know they are identified (by user name) with all transactions they enter (or change) in QuickBooks.

SECTION OVERVIEW

Chapter 5 covers the sales cycle in a merchandising company.
Chapter 6 covers the purchase cycle in a merchandising company.
Chapter 7 covers end of period accounting in a merchandising company.

We continue to use Sac City Accounting Services as the practice company. From now on, though, the company will be selling Intuit software to clients in addition to providing accounting services.

Selling Products
(Merchandising Company)

After completing Chapter 5, you should be able to:

1. Set up and edit sales tax codes and rates.

2. Set up and edit customer shipping addresses.

3. Set up and edit inventory items.

4. Record various types of customer discounts.

5. Write off uncollectible accounts.

6. Record customer credit card payments.

7. Process customer checks returned by the bank due to insufficient funds in the customer's bank account.

8. Record early payment discounts taken by customers.

9. Prepare sales reports by inventory item.

10. Create customer statements.

155

WHAT IS THE SALES CYCLE IN A MERCHANDISING COMPANY?

✓ Get orders.

✓ Fill orders.

✓ Bill for the products.

✓ Collect the sales price.

The sales cycle in a merchandising company, as you can see, is similar to that of a service company, and many of the accounting functions are the same. However, there are some differences. In this chapter, we cover those differences. We also cover some more advanced topics that apply to both service and merchandising companies.

MANAGING CUSTOMERS

Setting up and editing customers is covered in Chapter 2. This section covers:

- Entering sales tax information for customers.

- Entering shipping information for customers.

Customers And Sales Tax

Not all states have a sales tax, but the vast majority do (45 out of 50 states in 2015). Even if a business's primary location is in a state without a sales tax, it may still have to collect sales taxes on products sold and shipped to customers in states that do have a sales tax. Because sales taxes are more than likely an issue for every business, we cover how they are handled in QuickBooks here.

Sales of most tangible goods are subject to sales tax unless:

- The purchaser (customer) is out of state and the seller is not required to collect sales tax in that state.

- The purchaser (customer) is buying the product to sell to third parties. (The customer is a reseller of the product, not a consumer of the product.)

The seller is responsible for collecting sales tax, as appropriate, from its customers and for remitting those taxes to the appropriate taxing authority. Sales are reported and sales taxes are remitted to state agencies on a monthly, quarterly, or annual basis. NOTE: In most states, there are state and local sales taxes. Taxes are collected based on the specific rate set for the location of the buyer.

Tax codes and **tax items** are entered for each customer in their master record, in the **Customer Center**, on the **Sales Tax Settings** tab. The screen looks like this:

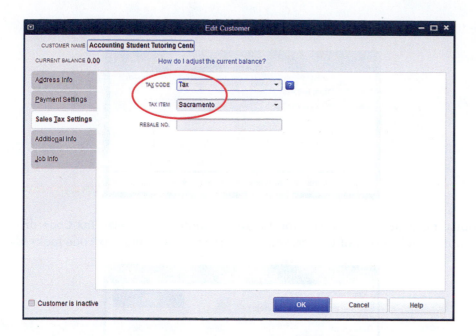

The **Tax Code** identifies the customer as taxable (subject to sales tax) or non-taxable (exempt from sales tax). (**Tax Codes** are also used when setting up items to indicate the taxability of the product or service.) The **Tax Item** identifies the taxing jurisdiction for the customer and the tax rate.

Sales Tax Codes

The **Tax Code** field identifies the overall taxability of the customer. There are two default tax codes set up automatically by QuickBooks:

- **Tax**—used for customers who are consumers (users) of products and subject to tax.

- **Non**—used for customers who are resellers of products or are otherwise not subject to tax.

Additional **tax codes** can be set up if needed. For example, you might want to set up a code for out-of-state customers and one for resellers so that you can track that information separately.

    Tax codes are set up through the **Sales Tax Code List** option on the **Lists** menu (main menu bar):

The initial screen looks like this:

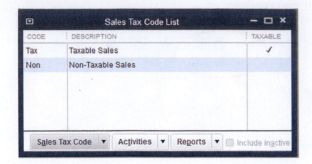

Additional tax codes are created using the **New** option on the **Sales Tax Code** dropdown menu (bottom left corner of the screen). The screen to add a new tax code looks like this:

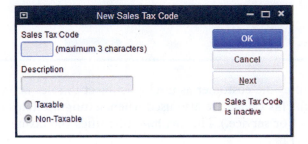

As you can see, the **sales tax code** is only used to differentiate taxable customers from non-taxable customers. **Sales tax codes** are **not** used to set up tax rates.

> **BEHIND THE SCENES** The company selling the product is responsible for collecting sales taxes. If the company purchasing the product identifies itself as a reseller and not subject to tax, the seller should obtain the reseller tax identification number from that customer. That number is input into QuickBooks on the **Sales Tax Settings** tab for the customer.

Sales Tax Items

The **Tax Item** field on the **Sales Tax Settings** tab of a customer data record in the **Customer Center** identifies the taxing jurisdiction (and the tax rate) for the customer.

A tax item must be set up for every state and local tax authority. Tax items are set up through the **Items** option on the **Lists** dropdown menu. Tax items have their own **item type** (**Sales Tax Item**).

The screen to set up a **sales tax item** looks like this:

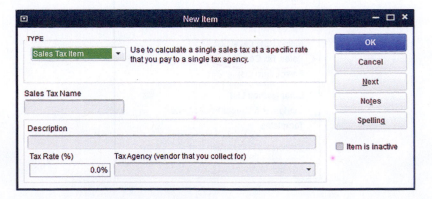

You must know the rate and the tax agency to create a **sales tax item**. For this textbook, we will be using 8.75% as the sales tax rate of every jurisdiction. In reality, this rate varies by jurisdiction.

PRACTICE EXERCISE

Setting up sales tax codes and rates for Sac City Accounting.
(Sac City wants to create a special tax code for resellers and needs to create a new sales tax item for sales made to West Sacramento customers. The company also wants to create a sales tax item for exempt sales for tracking purposes.)

1. Create a tax code for resellers.
   a. Click on **Lists**.
   b. Click on **Sales Tax Code List**.
   c. Open **Sales Tax Code** dropdown menu (bottom left of the screen).
   d. Click **New**.
   e. Enter "RSL" as the **Sales Tax Code**.
   f. Enter "Reseller" as the **Description**.
   g. Click **Non-taxable**.
   h. Click **OK** and exit out of window.

2. Create a new sales tax item for the city of West Sacramento.
   a. Click on **Lists**.
   b. Click on **Item List**.
   c. Open **Item** dropdown menu (bottom left of the screen).
   d. Click **New**.
   e. Select **Sales Tax Item** as the type.
   f. Enter "West Sac" as the **Sales Tax Name** and "West Sacramento Sales Tax" as the **Description**.
   g. Enter "8.75%" as the **Rate**.
      i. You **must** enter the % sign.
   h. Select **Board of Equalization** as the **Tax Agency**.
      i. Click **Next**.

3. Create a new sales tax item for exempt sales.
   a. Select **Sales Tax Item** as the type.
   b. Enter "Exempt" as the **Sales Tax Name** and "Exempt from sales tax" as the **Description**.
   c. Enter 0.0% as the **Rate**.
   d. Select **Board of Equalization** as the **Tax Agency**.
   e. Click **OK** and exit out of the window.

Shipping Addresses

Merchandising companies often ship products to customer warehouses or to various customer locations with addresses different than the customer's billing address. Billing **and** shipping addresses (including multiple shipping addresses for a single customer) can be maintained in QuickBooks.

Shipping addresses are entered on the **Address Info** tab of the customer data screen (**Customer Center**). The initial screen looks like this:

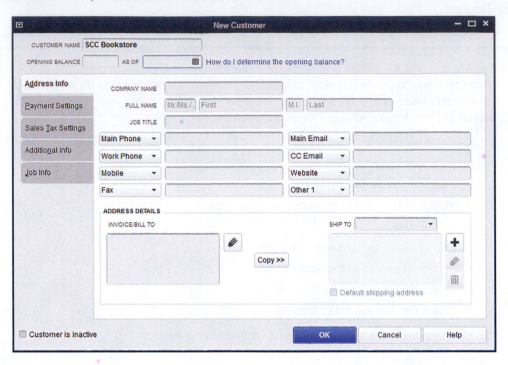

If the billing and shipping addresses are the same, you can use the **Copy** button on the **Address Info** tab (bottom center of screen).

To enter a shipping address that differs from the billing address, you would click the **+** (plus sign) in the bottom right section of the window. The following screen appears:

Each shipping address for a customer is identified by the **Name** given in the set up. If there are multiple addresses, one address can be selected as the default by checking the option at the bottom left of the screen.

Managing shipping addresses for customers of Sac City Accounting.
(Sac City has a new customer, SCC Bookstore, with multiple shipping addresses.)

1. Set up a new customer:

    a. Open the **Customer Center** from the **Home** screen or from **My Shortcuts** tab on the icon bar.

    b. Click on **New Customer** from the dropdown menu at the top left of the screen).

    c. New customer is:

    SCC Bookstore (Use for **Customer Name** and **Company Name**.)

    3835 Freeport Blvd

    Sacramento, CA 95822

    d. Click the **Copy** button.

    e. Enter "Main Campus" for the **Address Name**.

    f. Check that the address is correct.

    g. Make sure **Default shipping address** is clicked.

    h. Click **OK**.

2. Enter a second shipping address (you should be on the **Address Information** tab for SCC Bookstore).

    a. Click the **+** sign to the right of the shipping address text box.

    b. Enter "West Sac Campus" as the **Address Name**.

    c. Address should be:

    SCC Bookstore

    1115 West Capital Avenue

    West Sacramento, CA 95691

    d. **Default shipping address** should **not** be checked.

    e. Click **OK**.

3. Finish set up of new customer.

    a. Click on **Payment Settings** tab.

    b. Select **2% 10 Net 30** for **Terms**.

    c. Click on **Sales Tax Settings** tab

    d. Select **RSL** as the **Tax Code**.

    e. Select **Exempt** as the **Sales Tax Item**.

    i. Enter "5783992" as the **Resale No.**

    f. Click **OK**.

    g. Exit out of the Customer Center.

MANAGING ITEMS (MERCHANDISING COMPANY)

The biggest single difference between service and merchandising companies is, of course, inventory. There are several systems used by merchandising companies to track inventory

Periodic inventory A system that records inventory purchase transactions during the period in an expense account; the Inventory account and the cost of goods sold account are not updated until the end of the period when a physical count of the inventory is taken.

Perpetual inventory A system that records the cost of merchandise inventory in the Inventory account at the time of purchase and updates the Inventory account for subsequent purchases and sales of merchandise as they occur.

Specific identification method An inventory costing method involving the physical identification of goods sold and goods remaining and costing these amounts at their actual costs.

First-in, first-out (FIFO) An inventory costing method that assumes that the oldest (earliest purchased) goods are sold first.

Last-in, first-out (LIFO) An inventory costing method that assumes that the newest (most recently purchased) goods are sold first.

Weighted average method An inventory costing method that calculates an average unit purchase cost, weighted by the number of units purchased at each price, and uses that weighted average unit cost to determine the cost of goods sold for all sales.

(**periodic** and **perpetual**) and a number of acceptable methods used to value inventory (**specific identification**, **first-in, first-out** (**FIFO**), **last-in, last-out** (**LIFO**), **weighted average**, etc.).

Merchandising companies can use QuickBooks whether they choose to use periodic or perpetual inventory systems. However, the program is most effectively used as a perpetual tracking system. QuickBooks values inventory using the weighted average method. (FIFO is an option in the Enterprise Platinum version of QuickBooks.)

A company will need to set up an **item** for each and every product that they sell. There are two **item** types that can be used for inventory:

- **Inventory part**
  - Used for products that a company sells, maintains in inventory **and** tracks using a perpetual inventory system.

- **Non-inventory part**
  - Used for products that a company sells but does not track.
    - Generally insignificant items.
    - More frequently used by manufacturing companies.
  - Used for products that a company purchases to order (for a particular customer, for example) and doesn't maintain in inventory.
  - Can be used in a periodic tracking system.

Setting Up Inventory Items

The process for setting up **inventory items** is very similar to the process for setting up **service items**. Inventory items are set up through the **Item List** option of the **Lists menu**.

Setting Up Non-Inventory Part Items

When a new **item** is set up as a **non-inventory part**, the screen initially looks like this:

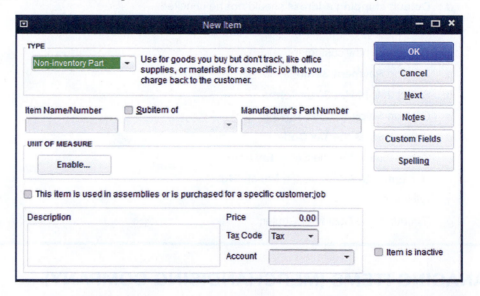

Products that a company sells but doesn't track are entered through this screen.

If a product might be purchased for a particular customer or project, additional information will be needed for tracking purposes. Checking the box next to "This item is used in assemblies or is purchased for a specific customer:job" will allow for that additional input when the product is purchased. The screen will now look something like this:

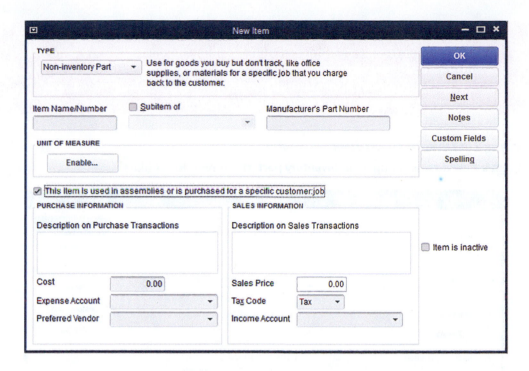

Items can be identified using names or numbers. If the **item** list is organized in groups (a very good idea), an **item** can be identified as a **subitem** of a group. (See Chapter 1 for help with setting up **item** groups.) The **Manufacturer's Part Number** (the vendor's part number) can be entered but is not required.

Because a merchandising company is purchasing the inventory item from another company, the **preferred vendor** and the description used on vendor bills (which often differs from the description on sales invoices) is normally entered in the **PURCHASE INFORMA-TION** section of the screen.

The **cost** field is a default amount used when preparing purchase orders or entering **bills**. The actual cost, if different, would be entered when the product is purchased.

> **BEHIND THE SCENES** Only the actual cost would be used when updating the inventory value.

The **Expense Account** field identifies the default debit account for entering purchases of the part.

> **BEHIND THE SCENES** There are a lot of possibilities here. The company might record all purchases of non-inventory parts in an inventory account or in a Purchases (expense) account if the company uses a periodic inventory system. If the non-inventory part costs are so insignificant that no tracking is done, the company might record the purchases directly to a parts expense account.

In the **SALES INFORMATION** section of the screen, the **Description on Sales Transactions** field should be completed with the preferred **item** description to appear on **invoices** or **sales receipts**.

A default selling price, **tax code**, and the income and cost of goods sold accounts associated with the particular **item** are also entered in this section of the screen.

> **WARNING:** The *tax code* selected should be *Tax* if the *item* is <u>ever</u> taxable. If a particular <u>customer</u> is non-taxable, the customer *tax code* will automatically override the *item tax code* when an *invoice* or *sales receipt* is created. You can also manually override the default *item tax code*, if needed, when preparing *invoices* or *sales receipts*.

Setting Up Inventory Part Items

When a new **item** is set up as an **inventory part**, the screen looks like this:

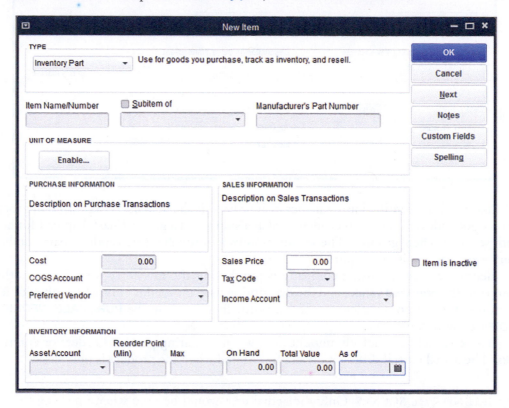

As you can see, this screen is very similar to the screen for entering **non-inventory part items** purchased to order. Defaults applicable to recording purchases of **inventory part items** are included in the **PURCHASE INFORMATION** section. Defaults applicable to recording sales of **inventory part items** are included in the **SALES INFORMATION** section.

    The **INVENTORY INFORMATION** section includes additional information. Because **inventory part items** are used in a perpetual tracking system, an inventory account must be entered here. The **Asset Account** field is used to identify the general ledger inventory asset account.

BEHIND THE SCENES QuickBooks automatically creates the following journal entry when an **inventory part** is purchased:

	Inventory (using the asset account specified in **item** setup)		
	Accounts payable (or cash)		

QuickBooks automatically creates the following journal entry when an **inventory part** is sold:

	Accounts Receivable (or Undeposited Funds if cash sale)		
	Cost of goods sold account (based on a weighted average cost at time of sale)		
	Income (using the income account specified in **item** setup)		
	Inventory (using the asset account specified in **item** setup)		

You can also set a **reorder point** for the **item**. A reorder point indicates the lowest level of inventory that should be maintained for a particular **item**. (Reorder points will be discussed further in Chapter 6.)

Adding a new inventory part item for Sac City Accounting.
(Sac City has decided to sell Quicken as well as QuickBooks and expects to purchase the software from Intuit for $25 and sell it for $40. Sac City will be selling the product to consumers.)

1. Click **Lists**.

2. Click **Item List**.

3. Click **New** (through **Item** menu at bottom left on screen).

4. Select **Inventory Part** as the type.

5. Enter **item name/number** as "Quicken."

6. Click **subitem** and select **Software**.

7. Enter "Quicken software" as **description** for purchase and sales transactions.

8. Enter "25" as **Cost**.

9. Select **Cost of software sold** for **COGS account**.

10. Select **Intuit** for **Preferred vendor**.

11. Enter "40" as **Sales Price**.

12. Select **Tax** for **Tax Code**.

13. Select **Software sales** for **Income Account**.

14. Select **Inventory** for **Asset Account**.

15. Enter "5" as the **Reorder Point (Min)** and click **OK**.

PRACTICE
EXERCISE

RECORDING SALES REVENUE

Merchandising companies, like service companies, make cash and credit sales. We learned how to record **Invoices** and **Sales receipts** in Chapter 2. In this chapter, we cover:

- Customer discounts.

- Handling uncollectible accounts.

Neither discounts nor uncollectible accounts are unique to merchandising companies. The processes outlined here would be used in service companies as well.

Customer Discount And Subtotal Items

Companies often give discounts to customers. They might include:

- Price breaks for large orders.

- Discounts for nonprofits, senior citizens, students.

- Early payment discounts.

QuickBooks actually has many different options for modifying prices charged to certain customers. We cover one method for giving these types of discounts in this textbook.

Early payment discounts are handled in a very specific way. We cover that later in this chapter.

As we learned in Chapter 2, if something is going to appear on an **invoice** (or a **sales receipt**), it must be set up as an **item**. If the company wants the discount to appear on the invoice or receipt given to the customer, then an **item** must be created.

Setting up discount items is done within the **Items** list. The list is accessed by selecting the **Item List** option on the **Lists** menu (main menu bar).

Once you've opened the **Item List** window, the **New** option on the **Item** dropdown menu must be selected.

The **item type** selected should be **Discount**. The screen looks something like this:

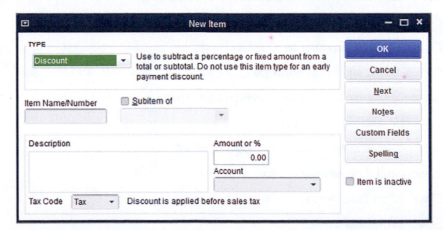

The **Item Name/Number** is used to identify the type of discount (student, nonprofit, etc.). The **Description** field is what will appear on the sales form (**invoice** or **sales receipt**).

The **Amount** entered for the discount can be a flat dollar amount or a percentage (%). If a percentage is entered, the actual discount will be calculated when the invoice is prepared. If you want to give a percentage discount, you **must** enter the % sign in the field.

If a percentage discount is used on an **invoice** (or **sales receipt**), QuickBooks will apply the percentage to the line item immediately preceding the discount **item**. If a company wants to apply a discount to multiple **items** on a sales form, a **Subtotal** has to be created first.

Subtotal items are set up within the **item list**. The screen to create a new **Subtotal item** looks like this:

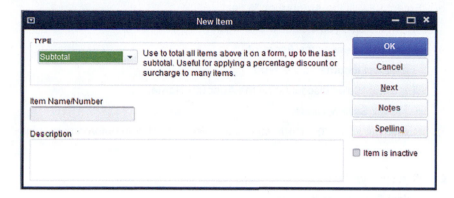

An **Item Name/Number** is set by the user, as is the **Description**.

> **BEHIND THE SCENES** A **Subtotal** item is used only as a calculator by Quick-Books, so no general ledger account association is necessary.

You can set up multiple subtotals. Multiple subtotals would only be needed if the company wants various descriptions.

> **! WARNING:** **When applying a discount to multiple items, the sales items must be listed on the sales form first, followed by the *Subtotal* item, and then the appropriate *Discount* item. QuickBooks will then calculate the discount on the subtotal amount.**

Any discounts given to customers will be debited to the **Account** identified on the **New Item** screen in the underlying journal entry.

> **BEHIND THE SCENES** Sales discounts are commonly set up as contra revenue accounts (**Income account type** in QuickBooks).

You must also indicate whether the discount is applied before or after sales tax using the **Tax Code** field. **Tax** (i.e., before tax) would be the most common choice.

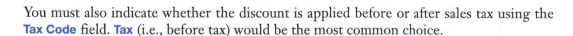

PRACTICE
EXERCISE

Setting up and giving discounts in Sac City Accounting.
(Sac City has decided to give a discount on all sales to educational institutions. SCC Bookstore will receive the discount on the shipment of 8 QuickBooks programs.)

1. Create a discount for educational institutions.
   a. Click on **Lists**.
   b. Click on **Item List**.
   c. Click **New** (from the **Item** menu at the bottom of the screen).
   d. Select **Discount** as the **Type**.
   e. Enter "Educational" as the **Item Name**.

(continued)

  f. Enter "10% educational institution discount" as the **description**.

  g. Enter "10%" in the **Amount or %** field.

   i. Make sure you include the % sign.

  h. Select **Add New** as the **Account**.

   i. Select **Income** as the **Type**.

   ii. Enter "Sales discounts" as the **Account Name**.

   iii. Click **Save & Close**.

  i. Select **Tax** as the **Tax Code** so that the discount is taken before tax is applied.

  j. Click **Next**.

2. Create a subtotal item.

  a. Select **Subtotal** as the **Type**.

  b. Enter "Subtotal" as the **Item Name/Number** and "Total before discount" as the **Description**.

  c. Click **OK**.

  d. Exit out of **item list**.

3. Give a discount to a customer.

  a. Click on **Create Invoice** (Home page).

  b. Select **SCC Bookstore** as the **Customer:Job**.

  c. Select **Intuit Professional Invoice** as the **Template**.

  d. Enter "1/4/18" as the **date** and "1006" as the **invoice #**.

  e. Select **2% 10 Net 30** for the **Terms** and **RSL** as the **Customer Tax Code** (bottom of screen).

  f. Select item **Pro** and enter "5" as the **quantity**.

   i. You can ignore any messages you get about changes to tax codes.

  g. Select item **Premier** and enter "3" as the **quantity**.

  h. Select item **Subtotal**.

   i. Note the automatic calculation of the total to be discounted.

  i. Select item **Educational**.

  j. Invoice total should be $2,317.50.

  k. Click **Save & Close**.

Recording Uncollectible Accounts

Bad debt expense
The expense stemming from the inability of a business to collect an amount previously recorded as receivable. It is normally classified as a selling or administrative expense.

Unfortunately, companies don't always collect the balances owed to them by their customers. Merchandisers will often try to get the product back when the customer defaults but, depending on the type and value of the products sold, that may not be feasible or even possible.

  If the company has exhausted all reasonable collection methods, the **invoice** must be written off. Deleting or voiding the **invoice** in QuickBooks would not be good accounting. The company did make the sale and should show the revenue. They should also report that uncollectible sales (recorded as **bad debt expenses**) are a real cost of selling on credit.

There are two methods for accounting for uncollectible accounts: the **allowance method** and the **direct write-off method**. Only the allowance method is acceptable under generally accepted accounting principles (GAAP).

Allowance Method Refresher

Under the allowance method, an estimate of the amount of uncollectible receivables is made at the end of an accounting period. The initial entry to establish an allowance for those amounts is:

	Bad debt expense		
	Allowance for doubtful accounts		

The allowance account is a contra asset account (contra to accounts receivable). Accounts receivable net of the allowance is referred to as the net realizable value of receivables (amount that the company actually expects to collect or "realize"). When a **specific** customer account is determined to be uncollectible, the account is written off. The entry is:

	Allowance for doubtful accounts		
	Accounts receivable		

If a previously written off amount is subsequently received, the entry is:

	Cash		
	Allowance for doubtful accounts		

> **BEHIND THE SCENES** Some companies make two entries to record the recovery of a bad debt. In the first entry, the customer balance is re-established (DR Accounts receivable, CR Allowance for doubtful accounts). The second entry records the customer payment (DR Cash, CR Accounts receivable). The two-entry method would likely be used if the recovery amount is significant and the company is aware of the recovery before the cash is actually received.

At the end of each accounting period, the allowance account is adjusted to reflect the amount that is currently considered uncollectible. For example, if the end of period balance in the allowance account is estimated to be too low, the entry is:

	Bad debt expense		
	Allowance for doubtful accounts		

Direct Write-Off Method Refresher

Companies that historically do not have many uncollectible accounts often use the direct write-off method. Under this method, bad debt expense is only recognized when a specific customer account is determined to be uncollectible. This method violates generally accepted accounting principles but is sometimes used when the amount of bad debts is insignificant.

The entry is:

	Bad debt expense		
	Accounts receivable		

Which accounting principle is violated under the direct write-off method? (Answer at end of chapter.)

QuickCheck
5-1

Allowance method
An accounting procedure whereby the amount of bad debts expense is estimated and recorded in the period in which the related credit sales occur.

Direct write-off method An accounting procedure whereby the amount of bad debts expense is not recorded until specific uncollectible customer accounts are identified.

Either the allowance or the direct write-off method can be used in QuickBooks.

If the allowance method is used, the entry to set up or adjust the allowance account should be made as a general journal entry (**Journal** transaction type). See Chapter 4 if you need help with making adjusting journal entries.

The actual write-off of an **invoice** (under either the allowance or direct write off method) can be done through the **Receive Payment** screen, which looks like this:

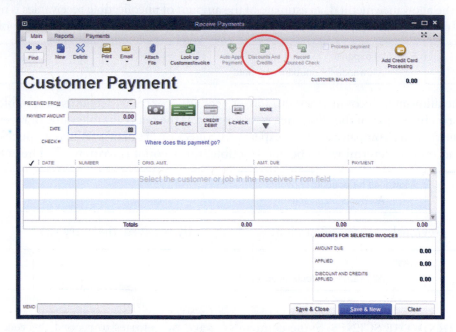

The customer with an uncollectible account would be entered in the **received from** field. The **payment amount** field should be left at zero. The **date** entered should be the date that the write-off should be recorded (recognized).

The invoice to be written off should be **highlighted**. (The check mark field should not be used to identify the invoice to be written off.)

The **Discounts and Credits** window should be opened using the **Discounts and Credits** icon at the top of the screen. The screen will look something like this:

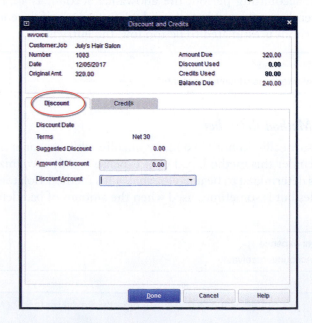

The amount to be written off is entered in the **Amount of Discount** field on the **Discounts** tab.

The **Discount Account** selected would be:

- **Allowance for doubtful accounts** (if the allowance method is used).
- Bad debt expense (if the direct write-off method is used).

> **HINT:** If the **invoice** being written off is for the sale of a product and sales tax has been collected, the sales tax liability will need to be adjusted. Sales tax adjustments are covered in Chapter 7.

Allowance for doubtful accounts A contra-asset account with a normal credit balance shown on the balance sheet as a deduction from accounts receivable to reflect the expected\ uncollectible amount of accounts receivable.

PRACTICE
EXERCISE

Recording an uncollectible account at Sac City Accounting.
(July's Hair Salon has gone bankrupt. Sac City Accounting has very few uncollectible accounts and has elected to use the direct write-off method to account for bad debts.)

1. Click **Receive Payments** on the Home page.

2. Select **July's Hair Salon** in the **Received From** field.

3. Leave the **payment amount** as 0.00.

4. Enter "1/5/18" as the **date**.

5. Highlight Invoice #1003.

    a. If you get a message about QuickBooks automatic application of payments, click **Yes** to keep the preference.

6. Click the **Discounts and Credits** icon at the top of the screen.

7. On the **Discounts** tab, enter "240" as the **amount of discount** and select **Bad debt expense** as the **account**.

    a. If bad debt expense doesn't exist in the chart of accounts, select **Add New**.

    b. Select **Expense** as the **Account Type**.

    c. Enter "Bad debt expense" as the **Name**.

    d. Make it a **subaccount** of the account **Other Costs**.

    e. Click **Save & Close**.

8. Click **Done**.

9. Click **Save & Close**.

RECORDING PAYMENTS FROM CUSTOMERS

Chapter 2 outlines the process for recording cash (or check) payments from customers. This chapter covers:

- Customer payments by credit card.
- Customer checks returned by the bank due to insufficient funds (NSF checks).
- Early payment discounts.

Customer Payments By Credit Card

Most retail stores accept credit cards as a form of payment. Credit card payments are considered almost the equivalent of cash. "Almost" because:

- The company pays a fee to the financial institution processing credit card receipts for the company (commonly called the merchant bank) on all credit card receipts.

- The merchant bank generally makes the deposits directly to the merchandiser's account (net of any fees) within a few days in batches that correspond to the credit card type (VISA, MasterCard, etc.).

Credit card payments can be received at the time of sale or as payment on an account balance.

> **HINT:** Users can purchase a credit card processing service through Quick-Books. Credit card receipts are processed automatically when entered. The processes described herein assume that the company does **not** have that service.

Recording Receipt Of Customer Credit Card Payment

Most companies receive credit card receipts from the merchant bank within a few days, so sales paid by credit card, at point of sale, are normally recorded as **Sales Receipts** (cash sales). The type of credit card used (VISA, MasterCard, etc.) is selected as the **payment method**. QuickBooks allows users to enter the credit number and expiration date. We will not be entering that information in this class.

When customers use credit cards to pay account balances, the payment is recorded through the **Receive Payment** window (similar to payments of account balances by cash or check). The type of credit card used (VISA, MasterCard, etc.) is selected as the **payment method**.

PRACTICE
EXERCISE

Recording customer credit card transactions for Sac City Accounting.
(The merchant bank is America's Bank. The transaction fee is 3% of credit card receipts.)

1. Record cash sale using a credit card. (Sac City News purchases QuickBooks Pro for internal use.)
   a. Click **Create Sales Receipts** (Home page).
   b. Select **Sac City Student News** as **Customer:Job**.
   c. Click the **Credit/Debit** icon and select **VISA**.
   d. Click **Done**.
   e. Enter "1/5/18" in the **Date** field.
   f. Enter "101" in the **Sale No.** field.
   g. Select **Pro** as the item and enter "1" as the **quantity**.
   h. Total (after tax) should be $299.06.
   i. Click **Save & Close**.

2. Record customer payment of an account balance with a credit card (West Sac Legal pays $200 invoice balance with a credit card.)
   a. Click **Receive Payments** (Home page).
   b. Select **West Sac Legal** as the **Customer:Job**.
   c. Enter "200" as the **Amount**.
   d. Enter "1/5/18" as the **Date**.
   e. Click the **Credit/Debit** icon and select **VISA**.
   f. Click **Done**.
   g. Make sure "Invoice 1001" is selected (checkmark in the left column).
   h. Click **Save & Close**.

"Depositing" Credit Card Receipts

As you learned in Chapter 2, unless the default preference is changed, QuickBooks debits **Undeposited Funds** for all payments received from customers through **Sales Receipt or Payment** forms. The receipts are transferred, in batches that correspond to the actual deposit amounts, from the **Undeposited Funds** account to the cash account through the **Make Deposits** form.

The same considerations have to be made for credit card receipts. The merchant bank makes deposits to the merchandiser's bank account in batches (grouped by credit card type), net of any transaction fees charged. The deposit in QuickBooks for credit card receipts should be made in corresponding batches, net of the fees. Checks and cash receipts should not be included on the same **deposit** form in QuickBooks as credit card receipts because they would show as separate transactions on bank statements.

Recording a deposit of credit card receipts is done using the **Make Deposits** form accessed from the Home page (**Record Deposits** icon). The first screen that will appear includes all undeposited receipts and looks something like this:

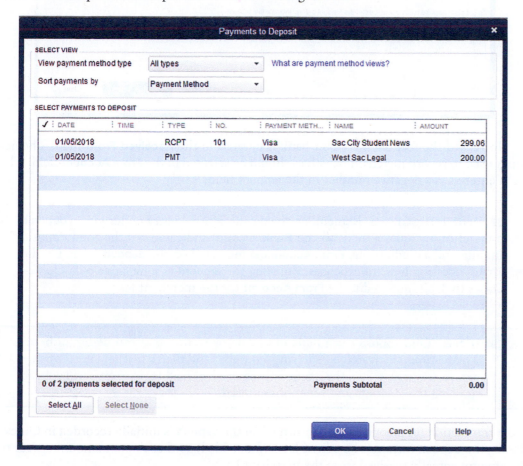

The user should mark (check) all receipts of the **same credit card type** for deposit.

 HINT: There are options for filtering and sorting transactions at the top of the screen.

Clicking **OK** takes the user to the final screen.

The transaction fee should be recorded on the final screen. The final screen looks like this:

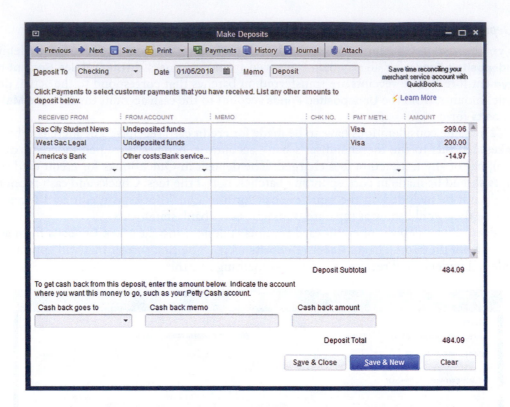

To record the fee, the merchant bank is entered in the **Received From** field. The account used to record merchant bank fees should be selected in the **From Account** field. The fee is entered as a negative number in the **amount** field.

BEHIND THE SCENES Remember, the default journal entry underlying a **deposit** transaction includes a debit to the **Bank** account indicated for the total deposit amount and a credit to the **From Account(s)** indicated on the **deposit** form. Credit card processing fees are expenses. Entering the **amount** as a negative tells QuickBooks to debit, not credit, the **From Account** for the merchant fees.

 HINT: QuickBooks has a built-in calculator feature that can be useful here. The feature is activated by entering a number and then a mathematical operator (+, −, *, or /). When the operator is entered, a small register tape will appear showing the amounts and functions entered.

If the transaction fee amount is not known when the **deposit** is initially recorded in QuickBooks, the **deposit** form can be edited later (fees added) so that the net amount agrees to the amount actually received from the merchant bank.

PRACTICE EXERCISE

Making a deposit of credit card receipts for Sac City Accounting.
(Sac City processes its VISA credit card receipts.)

1. Click **Record Deposits** (Home page).
2. Mark all VISA transactions.
    a. Total should be $499.06.

(continued)

3. Click **OK**.

4. Change **date** to 1/5/18.

5. Enter new line.

    a.   Select **America's Bank** as **Received From**.

    b.   Select **Bank service charges expense** as **From Account**.

    c.   Enter "Credit card fees" in the **Memo** field.

    d.   Enter the 3% transaction fee ($14.97) as a negative in **Amount** field.

6. **Deposit Subtotal** should be $484.09.

7. Click **Save & Close**.

Customer Checks Returned By Bank Due To Insufficient Funds (NSF Checks)

Every company that accepts checks from customers accepts a risk that the customer does not have sufficient funds in the bank to cover the check.

When customer checks are returned NSF (non-sufficient funds), the companies will normally choose from the following:

- Attempt to redeposit the check.

- Write off the **invoice** as a bad debt.

- Re-invoice the customer (for the amount of the check plus processing fees).

Regardless of the choice made, an NSF check must be recorded in the accounting records.

Remember, when the customer check was originally recorded in QuickBooks, the entry was:

Undeposited Funds			
Accounts receivable (or income)			

When the check was deposited, the amount was transferred from **Undeposited Funds** to the Cash account. Cash is now overstated by the amount of the NSF check. The entry underlying the **invoice** created will need to affect (credit) the cash account, not an income account.

The QuickBooks process for recording NSF checks allows the user to reinstate the invoice and credit cash, create an additional invoice to processing fees to be charged to the customer, and record any NSF fees charged to the company by the bank in one screen.

> **BEHIND THE SCENES** The QuickBooks feature for handling NSF checks assumes that the company will attempt to collect the full amount. The original invoice is reinstated, and a new invoice is created for any processing fees the company might decide to charge the customer. If the company decides that the amount is uncollectible, the following procedures should still be followed so that there is a record of the NSF check associated with the customer. The reinstated invoice should then be written off as described earlier in the "Recording Uncollectible Accounts" section of this chapter.

QuickBooks uses the term "bounced check" instead of NSF check so that term will be used in describing the process and in the practice exercise.

Recording A Customer Bounced Check And Associated Fees

The first step is to open the original payment screen for the check that has been returned by the bank.

 HINT: You can find the payment by using the **Find** feature. Filter using the customer name and the transaction type **Payment**.

The screen (on the **Main** tab) looks like this:

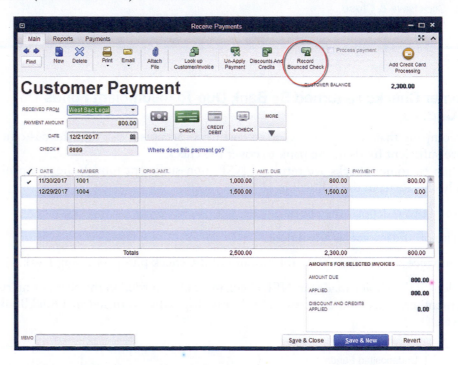

When you click the **Record Bounced Check** icon (at the top right of the window), a new window will open that looks like this:

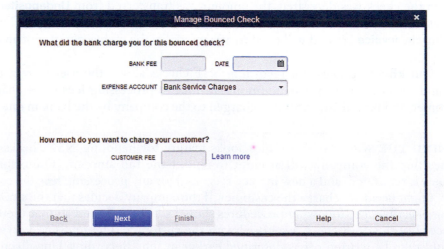

The amount and date of any fee charged by the bank should be entered in the top section. (This is the fee charged to the company, not the fee the company intends to charge to its customer.) The date entered should be the date the bounced check was returned (the date the bank recorded the return and the fee), not the date of the original payment.

The account that should be debited for the fee would be selected next. An **expense account type** would normally be selected.

In the bottom section, the amount of the processing fee, if any, the company wants to charge back to the customer would be entered. Clicking **Next** would open a window that looks like this:

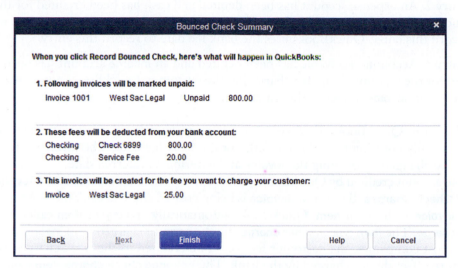

The entries that have just been created by QuickBooks are summarized in this window. Clicking **Finish** closes the window.

The customer payment screen now looks something like this:

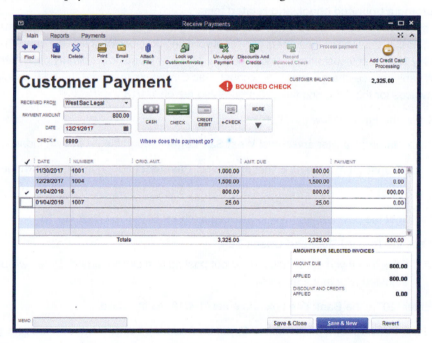

It's important to understand the entries QuickBooks creates when a bounced check is recorded. As an accountant, you need to determine that the dates and the accounts used in the transactions are the dates and accounts that you would have used if you were creating the entries manually.

Remember: In QuickBooks, up to three entries have been made when an NSF check is recorded.

✓ Entry 1: Accounts receivable has been debited and cash has been credited for the amount of the NSF check. QuickBooks uses a **journal transaction type** to record this entry.

QuickBooks records this entry using the bank fee date entered on the **Manage Bounced Check** screen. (The screen that appears after you click the **Record Bounced Check** icon on the **payment** screen.)

✓ Entry 2: An expense account has been debited and cash has been credited for the amount of the fee charged by the bank. QuickBooks uses a **journal transaction type** to record this entry. QuickBooks uses the bank fee date to record this entry.

✓ Entry 3: Accounts receivable has been debited and an **income** account has been credited for the amount of any fee charged to the customer. QuickBooks automatically creates an **invoice** to record this entry.

The default in QuickBooks is to record the **invoice** using the **current date** (the date the user is actually entering the information), not the bank fee date. The **invoice** date can, of course, be changed by opening the **invoice** and entering a preferred date.

The account credited by QuickBooks in this entry is a default **income** account called **Returned Check Charges**. Because an **invoice** is being created and you can't include something on an **invoice** without an **item**, QuickBooks automatically creates an **item** called **bounced check charge**. The **item** type is **other charge** and the account charged is an **income** account.

In most companies, the customer fee would be credited to the bank charges expense account to offset the fee charged by the bank. The **bounced check charge item** would need to be edited to change the account and add a description.

PRACTICE EXERCISE

Recording a bounced check and related fees.

(The check received from West Sac Legal #6899 for $800 was returned on 1/4/18 marked NSF. Sac City charges its customers $25 for processing bounced checks. The bank charges Sac City $20 for any customer bounced checks. Sac City wants to credit any customer fees to the bank service charge expense account. Sac City wants to record the NSF check and the invoices for the $800 and the $25 processing fee on 1/4/18.)

1. Open the **Find** window (CTRL F).

2. Click **Name** as a filter and select **West Sac Legal** through the dropdown menu.

3. Click **Transaction Type** as a filter and select **Payment** through the dropdown menu.

4. Click **Find**.

5. Highlight the payment from West Sac Legal (check 6899) and click **Go To**.

6. Click the **Record Bounced Check** icon.

   a. Click **Yes** if you get a message about posting to a closed period. Dates will be adjusted later in the exercise.

7. Enter "20" in the **Bank Fee** box and enter "1/4/18" as the **Date**.

8. Using the dropdown menu next to **Expense Account**, select **Bank service charges expense** as the account (under **Other costs**).

   a. WARNING: **Be careful here.** Make sure you select the correct account. QuickBooks creates a new account (called Bank Service Charges) by default. The new account should **not** be used.

9. Enter "25" in the **Customer Fee** box.

(continued)

10. Click **Next**.

11. Review the screen to make sure the information is correct.

    a. Invoice 1001 should show in 1#.

    b. The $800 check amount and the $20 service fee amount should show in #2.

    c. The fee being charged to West Sac Legal ($25) should show in #3.

12. Click **Finish**.

13. Click **Save & Close** to exit the **Receive Payments** form.

14. Adjust the account distribution, invoice numbers and transaction dates.

    a. Click **Item list** on **Lists** menu.

    b. Highlight **Bounced Check Charge**.

    c. Click the arrow next to **Item** at the bottom left of the screen and select **Edit Item**.

    d. Enter "Processing fee related to returned check" in the **Description** box.

    e. Because you may charge different fees to different customers, leave the **Amount or %** box as 0.00.

    f. Make sure the **Tax Code** field shows **Non**.

    g. Change **Account** field to **Bank service charges expense** (subaccount of **Other Costs**).

    h. Click **OK**.

    i. Click **Yes** to update existing transactions.

    j. Exit out of the **Item List** window.

    k. Re-open the **Find** window if closed (CTRL F).

    l. Click **Name** as a filter and select **West Sac Legal** using the dropdown menu.

    m. Click **Transaction Type** as a filter and select **Invoice** through the dropdown menu.

    n. Click **Find**.

    o. Double-click the invoice for the $25 fee (or highlight the invoice and click **Go To**).

    p. Change the date to 1/4/18.

    q. Make sure the description shows as edited. If not, enter "Processing fee related to returned check" as the **description**.

    r. Click **Save & Close**.

    s. Exit out of the **Find** window.

Early Payment Discounts

Companies often give customers discounts if credit sales are paid before the due date. Any available early payment discounts are included as part of the credit terms listed on the invoice.

Examples of credit terms with early payment discounts include:

- 2/10, Net 30
    - Discount of 2% of the invoice total if paid within 10 days of the due date. Balance is due in full 30 days from the invoice date.

- 1/15, Net 45
    - Discount of 1% of the invoice total if paid with 15 days of the due date. Balance is due in full 45 days from the invoice date.

All credit terms used by the company (for customers or vendors) are set up in the **Terms** menu option on the **Customer & Vendor Profile Lists** menu accessed through **Lists**.

The credit terms granted to a **specific** customer are entered on the **Payment Settings** tab of the customer record. These credit terms are automatically included on **invoices** prepared for the customer. They can be changed on a specific invoice if necessary. Early payment discounts are not recognized in QuickBooks until the customer actually takes the discount (i.e. at the time payment is made).

When a customer remits a payment, the screen for entering a payment on account looks something like this:

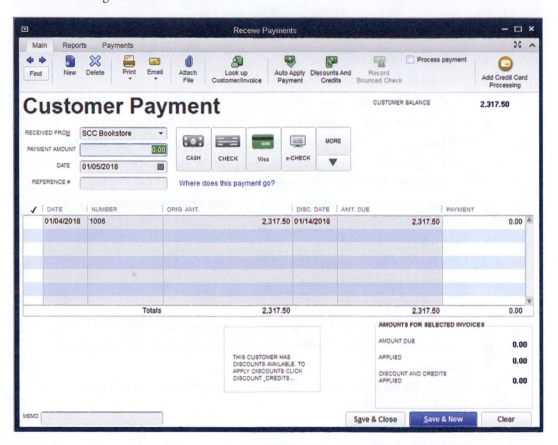

When the actual payment amount entered is less than the **invoice** amount, QuickBooks automatically displays two options for handling the underpayment at the bottom left of the screen. The unpaid balance can be written off or the unpaid balance can be left as a receivable.

If the underpayment represents an early payment discount, however, the company would want to record the underpayment as a discount.

 HINT: QuickBooks actually reminds the user of any available discounts in the message box just to the right of the underpayment message.

Clicking the **Discounts and Credits** icon at the top of the window opens a window that looks like this:

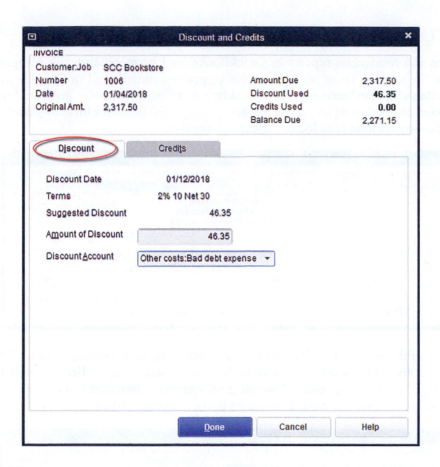

QuickBooks automatically calculates the expected amount of the early payment discount (based on the credit terms attached to the **invoice**). You can accept the amount or enter a different amount. A **discount account** must be selected for the debit entry. Early payment discounts, like other customer discounts, are typically reported in contra revenue accounts (**income** type accounts in QuickBooks).

PRACTICE

EXERCISE

Recording an early payment discount taken by a customer of Sac City Accounting.
(SCC Bookstore takes a 2% discount on Invoice #1006.)

1. Click **Receive Payment** (Home page).

2. Select **SCC Bookstore** as the **Customer:Job**.

3. Enter "2,271.15" in the **Payment Amount** field.

4. Enter "1/12/18" in the **Date** field.

5. Click the **Check** icon and enter "369990" in the **Check #** field.

6. Highlight outstanding invoice #1006.

7. Click **Discounts & Credits** icon at the top of the screen.
   a. Accept the discount amount of $46.35.
   b. Select **Sales discounts** as the **Discount Account**.
   c. Click **Done**.

8. Click **Save & Close**.

CUSTOMER REPORTS

The sales and receivables reports in QuickBooks used by merchandising companies are generally the same as those used by service companies (introduced in Chapter 2). However, the **Sales by Item Summary** report used by a merchandising company would normally include **cost of goods sold** and **gross margin** (gross profit) fields for **inventory part items**. A report of **inventory item** sales looks something like this:

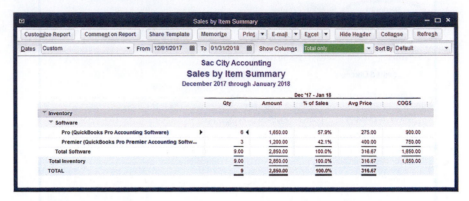

One useful report that we haven't looked at yet is the **Open Invoice** report. The report lists the invoice and due dates and can be helpful when making collection calls to tardy customers! The report is accessed through the **Customers & Receivable** menu option on the **Reports** menu (main menu bar). The report looks something like this:

<table>
<tr><td rowspan="2">PRACTICE
EXERCISE</td><td>**Preparing various sales and receivable reports.**</td></tr>
<tr><td>

1. Click on **Reports**.
   a. Click on **Sales**.
   b. Click on **Sales by Item Summary**.
   c. Change dates to 12/1/17-1/31/18.
   d. Click **Customize Report**.
   e. On **Display** tab, make sure all **COGS** and **Gross Margin** subcolumns are checked.
   f. On **Filters** tab:
      i. Click **Item**.
      ii. In the dropdown menu, select **All inventory items**. (This removes all **service items**.)
      iii. Click **OK**.

(continued)

</td></tr>
</table>

2. Click on **Reports**.
   a. Click on **Customers & Receivables**.
   b. Click on **Open Invoices**.
   c. Enter "1/31/18" as the **date**.

3. Exit out of report window.

CUSTOMER STATEMENTS

Companies will often send statements to customers on a monthly basis. Statements, for the most part, are simply summaries of activity over some period of time. They generally include a beginning balance, a list of all invoices and payments during the period, and an ending balance. Statements can be an effective way of communicating with customers.

For internal control purposes, most companies will not pay from a statement. (Companies choose to only pay from original invoices to avoid the risk of making duplicate payments.) For that reason, statements rarely include new charges (amounts not previously billed using an invoice). The most common exception would be finance charges assessed on past due balances. We do not cover finance charges in this course.

Statements can be prepared in QuickBooks and are easily accessed through the **Create Statements** option on the **Customer** menu (main menu bar).

The screen looks something like this:

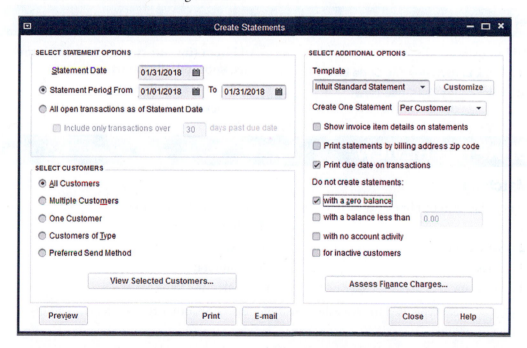

A **statement date** is entered. A company can choose the data that will appear on the statements. If the **Statement Period** option is selected (upper left corner of screen), the statement will show the beginning balance, a list of transactions for the period, and the ending balance. If the **All open transactions as of Statement Date** option is selected (upper left corner of screen), the statement will show a list of unpaid (or partially paid) invoices.

The company can also choose which customers will receive statements. Specific customers can be selected using the options at the bottom left of the screen in the **SELECT CUSTOMERS** section. In the **SELECT ADDITIONAL OPTIONS** section (right side of the screen), additional filtering choices can be made.

PRACTICE EXERCISE

Preparing statements for Sac City Accounting.
(Sac City decides to send statements to all customers with unpaid balances.)

1. Click **Customers** (main menu bar).

2. Click **Create Statements**.

3. Enter "1/31/18" as the **statement date**.

4. Click **Statement Period** and enter "1/1/18" to "1/31/18".

5. Click **All Customers** (bottom left section of screen).

6. Check **Print due date on transactions** (right section of screen).

7. Under **Do not create statements**, check **with a zero balance** (right section of screen).

8. Click **Preview** to see an example of a statement.

9. Click **Close**.

10. Click **Close** again to exit out of **Create Statements** window.

ANSWER TO QuickCheck 5-1

> The matching (expense recognition) principle

CHAPTER SHORTCUTS

Add sales tax code
1. Click **Lists/Sales Tax Code List**
2. Click **Sales Tax Code/New**

Add item (inventory part, non-inventory part, subtotal, discount)
1. Click **Lists/Item List**
2. Click **Item/New**

CHAPTER REVIEW

Matching

Match the term or phrase (as used in QuickBooks) to its best definition.

1. Inventory part
2. Statement
3. Sales tax code
4. Discount
5. Bounced check
6. Non-inventory part
7. Subtotal
8. Sales Tax Item

_____ Item type used for recording customer discounts other than early payment discounts.

_____ **Item** used to sum amounts charged for services or products.

_____ Product available for sale that is being tracked in a perpetual tracking system.

_____ **Item** used to identify sales tax rates and tax agencies.

_____ Field used to identify items (or customers) as taxable or nontaxable.

_____ Report sent to customer to summarize activity for a period or unpaid invoices.

_____ Product available for sale that is not being tracked in a perpetual tracking system.

_____ Customer check returned by bank due to insufficient funds in account.

Multiple Choice

1. When a customer makes a purchase using his or her credit card, it would normally be recorded as a(n):
   a. invoice.
   b. bill.
   c. sales receipt.
   d. credit card charge.

2. When a bounced customer check is recorded, which account does QuickBooks credit for the amount of the customer check?
   a. Cash (or Checking)
   b. Bad debt expense
   c. Accounts payable
   d. Unearned revenue
   e. Undeposited funds

3. The inventory valuation method used by QuickBooks Pro or Premier is:
   a. FIFO.
   b. LIFO.
   c. specific identification.
   d. weighted average.
   e. Any of the above can be selected by the user.

4. **Tax codes** are used in QuickBooks when setting up _____. (Select all that apply.)
   a. State and local tax rates
   b. Customers
   c. Items
   d. Accounts

5. What **account type** would be credited to record the amount of sales tax charged to the customer on an invoice?
   a. Accounts receivable
   b. Expense
   c. Other current liability
   d. Income

ASSIGNMENTS

You are one of three owners of Software 2 Go, a small retail store specializing in computer software. You have been in business for almost two years and have been fairly profitable both years. The business is a corporation with a 12/31 year-end.

The owners share business responsibilities.

- Rey Martinez runs retail operations at the shop and handles all merchandise purchasing.

- Elena Turgenev manages commercial sales.

- You handle all the accounting and administrative functions.

Assignment 5A

Software 2 Go

MBC

The company's primary commercial customers are professional service firms in Sacramento, although they also sell to a private tutoring center for children (Computer Fun Park). Credit terms for these customers are currently Net 30.

You also sell to walk-in customers. (You take cash/checks or credit cards.) Cash and checks are held in the safe and deposited once a week, on Fridays. Credit cards receipts are batched and transmitted to the merchant bank (Bank of Sutterville) every Friday. It generally takes one business day for the bank to process the receipts and deposit the funds in Software 2 Go's account. Bank of Sutterville charges a processing fee of 2% of the credit card total.

In November, the buyer for Komputer Kidz called Rey and asked about purchasing software from Software 2 Go. Komputer Kidz is a tutoring center specializing in children ages 6–12. Unlike Computer Fun Park, it will be reselling the software titles to its customers. (Actually, Komputer Kidz will be selling to its customer's parents!) It means you'll have to increase your inventory levels for certain titles, but you're all very happy for the increase in sales volume!

Your current inventory includes financial, educational, graphic, and simulation software. All items are taxable (except, of course, any sales to resellers like Komputer Kidz).

You took out a loan from Bank of Sutterville when you first started the business. The balance at 11/30/17 is $6,673.00. The monthly payment (due on the 30th of each month) is $200 (including interest). The interest rate on the note is 5%.

You rent the shop for $1,500 per month under a five-year lease.

Before you start your assignment:

✓ Change the company name to Your Name Software 2 Go. (Use your first and last names.)

✓ Change "Student" to your name on the **Other Names List**. (You decided to enter stockholder names on the **Other Names** list.)

- ○ Click on **Lists/Other Names List**.
- ○ Highlight "Student."
- ○ Click **Other Names** button.
- ○ Click **Edit Other Name**.
- ○ Change name to your name and click **OK**.

12/1/17

✓ The first order for your new customer, Komputer Kidz, is being delivered today and you realize you haven't yet set the customer up in QuickBooks, so you do that first.

- • Because Komputer Kidz will be selling the software to its students, you won't need to collect sales tax from them. You set up:
  - ○ A new sales tax code with the description "Resellers."
    - ❑ Remember, sales tax codes are created in the **Sales Tax Code List**. Use "RSL" for the code name.
  - ○ A new sales tax item that you name "Exempt." (Use Board of Equalization as the tax agency.)
    - ❑ Remember, sales tax items are created in the **item list**.
- • Billing information for Komputer Kidz is:

  Komputer Kidz

  3200 Riverside Blvd

  Sacramento, CA 95822

  (916) 346-3456

  Terms: 2%/10, Net 30

  Don't forget to enter the sales tax information.

  The store's resale number is SRY-333-444916.

- You will be shipping to two locations. The shipping address for the main location is the same as the billing address. The shipping address for the Curtis Park location is 445 Sunrise Blvd, Sacramento, CA 95822.

✓ Elena lets you know that the software got delivered to Komputer Kidz. You prepare the invoices using the S2G invoice template. (The dropdown menu for choosing a template is in the top middle of the **invoice** form.) Komputer Kidz has asked you to prepare **separate** invoices for each shipping address. Start with invoice #2011.

- Main location shipment
    - 30 "Grammar"; 30 "Math."
    - Invoice totals $4,200.00.
- Curtis Park location shipment
    - 20 "Grammar" 20 "Math."
    - Invoice totals $2,800.00.

12/4/17

✓ You realize that in order to grow, you're going to need to have sufficient cash on hand. The three of you have decided to try to avoid borrowing from the bank. Unfortunately, none of you have additional cash to invest personally right now. You decide to offer early payment discounts to your customers to help get the cash in faster. You edit all existing customers (except Store Customer, of course) to include terms of 2%/10, Net 30. (Komputer Kidz is already set up with the correct terms.)

- Ignore any messages you might get about the change affecting transactions in closed periods. QuickBooks will not change the terms on any open invoices.

✓ Computer Fun Park calls Elena to place an order. The company is thrilled with the new credit terms and orders five each of the "Grammar," "Math," and "Creations" titles. It also orders one copy of "People" for its own internal use. Elena ships the products out, and you create the invoice (#2013) that totals $2,121.18.

✓ RKO Seedman also calls Elena. The company to purchase 10 copies of "Golf" to give out to its very best clients. Elena packs up the order and ships it out. You prepare the invoice (#2014), which totals $4,340.00.

✓ Rey gives you the detail for Friday's in-store sales for recording. Sales figures were higher than normal for the store. Twenty medical students came in to purchase the "Anatomy" title on Friday alone. They were all getting a head start on spring semester! (All sales were made at the standard prices.) Use **Store Customer** as the customer name and 570 as the first **Sale No.**

- You will need to complete two forms. One for the cash sales; one for the credit card sales. (Software 2 Go treats customer payment by credit card the same as payment by cash. Remember to use the right form and to uncheck the **Print Later** box if necessary.)
- Cash sales of $3,330.95 (all paid with checks—ignore the **CHECK NO.** field):
    - 5 "Anatomy."
    - 2 "Drive."
    - 1 "Golf."
- Credit card sales of $8,459.75 (all VISA—ignore the **CARD NUMBER and EXP DATE** fields):
    - 15 "Anatomy."
    - 3 "Calculate."

✓ You deposit the checks and credit card receipts. (You'll be making two deposits. One for the checks. One for credit card receipts.)

 ○ The bank charges a 2% fee on all credit card sales. You record the fee with the deposit and charge the fee to Bank Charges. You do not need to enter a name in the **Received From** column for these charges.

 ○ The cash deposit should total $3,330.95.

 ○ The credit card deposit should total $8,290.55 (after the bank's fee).

12/5/17

✓ Legal Beagle's office manager, Brian, called Elena and placed an order for five copies each of "Calculate" and "Plan," and 10 copies of "Client."

12/6/17

✓ Elena ships the Legal Beagle order, and you create the invoice (#2015) totaling $3,846.33.

12/7/17

✓ You record the following checks received in the mail (all were dated 12/7):

 • Check #57890 from Erector Engineering for $3,083.57 (paying invoice 2006).

 • Check #58333 from Computer Fun Park for $325.50 (paying invoice 2009).

 • Check #883789 from Komputer Kidz for $6,860.00.

  ○ Komputer Kidz took all available sales discounts.

 HINT: When a customer is taking discounts on multiple invoices, it's sometimes easier to apply the early payment discount on each invoice first (before entering the check amount). Think about what account you should use to record the discounts.

12/8/17

✓ Rey gives you the detail for the in store sales for the week. (All sales were at the standard price.) Poor Rey didn't have much company this week.

 • Credit card sales (all MasterCard) totaling $1,908.52. If **Visa** appears, click that button and select MasterCard in the **PAYMENT** dropdown menu.)

  ○ 1 "Calculate."

  ○ 4 "CPA."

  ○ 1 "Grammar."

✓ You deposit all customer payments received during the week.

 • The check deposit totals $10,269.07.

 • The credit card deposit totals $1,870.35. (Don't forget the fees.)

12/12/17

✓ You receive two checks in the mail.

 • Check #59900 for $2,078.76 from Computer Fun Park dated 12/12 (paying invoice 2013).

 • Check #124675 for $4,900.95 from RKO Seedman dated 12/12 (paying invoices 2007 and 2014). [**TIP:** There's an early payment discount available on just one of the invoices RKO Seedman paid.]

✓ Elena ships out orders for two customers, and you invoice them as follows:

 • Erector Engineering ($1,367.10 invoice 2016)

  ○ 5 "Calculate."

  ○ 3 "Client."

- RKO Seedman ($2,777.60 invoice 2017)
    - 10 "Calculate."
    - 5 "Plan."
    - 2 each of "Client" and "People."

✓ You receive notice from the bank that the $325.50 check (#58333) from Computer Fun Park that was recorded on 12/7 (deposited on 12/8) was returned for insufficient funds. You call your contact there (Walter White). He apologizes profusely. He says cash flow has been a little tight lately, but they just got a much-needed loan from the bank so he assures you that this won't happen again. He agrees to pay your $30 processing fee. The bank charges Software 2 Go $20 for customer NSF checks (dated 12/12).

   - Remember: You need to start by opening the **receive payment** window for the bounced check.
       - **Do not** accept the default **Bank Service Charges** account created by Quick-Books. Use the dropdown menu to select the **Bank Charges** account under **Other Costs**.
   - After you've recorded the transaction, you edit the **Bounced check charge** item. You add the description "Processing fee for returned check," and you change the **account** related to the **item** to **Bank Charges** under **Other Costs**. (Software 2 Go chooses to offset the fees charged to the customer against the charges assessed by the bank.) You accept the option to change existing transactions.

12/14/17

✓ The accountant at Erector Engineering calls and says that when she opened one of the boxes of "Calculate" purchased on 12/12, the disk was missing. You issue a credit memo (#CM 2016) for $107.42 and apply it to invoice #2016 dated 12/12. Uncheck the **Print Later** box if necessary.

✓ Rey drives over to the Erector Engineering and picks up the empty box. He'll need to return it to the vendor.

12/15/17

✓ Rey gives you the detail for the in-store sales for the week. (All sales were at the standard price.)

   - Cash sales of $214.83 (paid with cash):
       - 2 "Calculate."
   - Credit card sales of $2,359.88 (all VISA):
       - 5 "Creations."
       - 3 "CPA."

✓ You deposit all customer payments received during the week.

   - Cash and checks deposit totals $7,194.54. VISA deposit totals $2,312.68. [**TIP:** Make sure the credit card fees are being charged to the **Bank Charges** under **Other Costs**.]

12/19/17

✓ One of the partners at RKO Seedman (Sal Seedman) calls Elena about one of his clients, a non-profit organization that provides assistance to start-up businesses in West Sacramento. He thinks that these start-ups would really benefit from the business planning and human resource management software that Software 2 Go stocks, but the current costs are a little high for a non-profit. Elena agrees to offer the company a 20% discount on all purchases.

✓ You set up three new **items** to handle the new customer.

   - A **sales tax item** is set up for West Sacramento. You name it "WSac". All taxes are remitted to the Board of Equalization. The tax rate is 8%.

- You set up a **discount item**. Use nonprofit as the name. The discount will be applied before the total before tax. Software 2 Go decides to group the non-profit discount with other sales discounts in the general ledger. Remember, the discount rate is 20%.

- Since the discount will apply to all items on any invoice, you set up a **subtotal item**.

✓ Sal calls back. His client accepts the offer and orders 20 copies of "Plan" and 10 copies of "People." Elena ships the order, and you prepare the invoice.

- The nonprofit company name is Own Your Future.

- Other information:
  ○ 2529 Freeport Blvd (billing and shipping) West Sacramento, CA 95691
  ○ Main Phone: (916) 444-9898
  ○ Terms: 2%/10, Net 30. Don't forget to enter the tax rate.

- The invoice (#2019) totals $4,147.20.

12/21/17

✓ A customer comes in to the shop carrying an opened box of "Golf Like a Pro." He is obviously very unhappy. "I'll say one thing," he says. "Playing outdoors on a green is NOT the same thing as playing indoors on a screen! I didn't get anything out of this software that helped me in the office tournament. As a matter of fact, I think I played worse. Now I'll never get that promotion." Rey says he understands and agrees to a **partial** refund of $100 (plus tax). He gives the customer a $108.50 refund (check #2476). You create a credit memo (101). (The **Customer:job** is **Store Customer**. The customer lives in Sacramento.)

- Ignore any messages you may get about custom prices.

- When you enter the **refund**, enter the check number in the **Issue this refund via** field on the **Issue a Refund** screen.

✓ You receive the following checks in the mail:

- Check #46866 for $4,637.40 from Legal Beagle dated 12/21 (paying invoices 2008 and 2015).
  ○ Legal Beagle took the discount on invoice 2015 but didn't pay during the discount period, so you leave the $76.93 balance on its account and give its accountant a call. The accountant agrees to pay the balance in the next few weeks.

- Check #13895 for $7,062.05 from RKO Seedman dated 12/21 (paying invoices 2010 and 2017). [**TIP:** Remember to highlight the invoice with the available discount before you click the **Discounts and Credits** icon.]

✓ Sweet Locations calls and places an order for two copies of "Space." Elena ships the order, and you prepare the invoice (#2020 for $4,557.00).

12/22/17

✓ You get a notice in the mail that one of your customers (One Stop Legal) has filed bankruptcy. It doesn't look like you'll be getting paid by them, and even if you could get the software back, you'd have no way to sell the used software. You decide to write off the amount they owe you ($215.92) to bad debt expense. (Software 2 Go uses the direct write-off method because it has historically had very few uncollectible accounts.) You'll need to set up a new expense account. You consider bad debt expense to be a subaccount of "Sales and marketing costs."

> **HINT:** It's easiest to write off invoices through the **Receive Payments** form. The write-off is recorded on the **Discount** tab of **Discounts and Credits**.

✓ Rey gives you the detail for the week's sales. (All sales were at the standard price.)

- Credit card sales of $1,178.31 (Receipt # 575, all VISA):
  ○ 1 "Golf."

- ○ 4 "Calculate."
- ○ 2 "Math."
- ○ 2 "Fly."
- ✓ You deposit all customer payments received during the week.
  - • Checks: $11,699.45.
  - • VISA: $1,154.74.

12/28/17

- ✓ The three of you decide to close the store to in-store sales between 12/25 and 12/29 so that you can do end-of-year inventory and store cleanup.

Check numbers 12/31

Checking account balance.	$94,393.59
Accounts receivable.	$10,396.31
Total income (December)	$43,921.23
Total cost of goods sold (December)	$25,374.00

REPORTS TO CREATE FOR ASSIGNMENT 5A

All reports should be in portrait orientation; fit to one page wide.

- • Journal—12/01 through 12/31 transactions only:
  - ▪ Put report in date order.
  - ▪ Columns should be Type, Date, Num, Name, Memo, Account, Debit, Credit.
- • Sales by item Summary (December only):
  - ▪ On the **Display** tab, uncheck the **COGS** subcolumn box. NOTE: This will automatically remove other subcolumns.
  - ▪ You might want to resize columns.
- • Open Invoices dated 12/31 (remove **P.O. #** and **Aging** columns).

You are one of three owners of The Abacus Shop, a small retail store specializing in books and supplies for accountants. You have been in business for a few years and, although the operation has been profitable, you and the other owners would like to grow the business a bit this year. You have hired an outside accountant, Martin Schmidt, to help you develop a business plan. The business is a corporation with a 12/31 year-end.

The owners share business responsibilities.

- • Marvena Smith runs retail operations at the shop and handles all merchandise purchasing.
- • Brandon Nguyen manages sales to the accounting firms.
- • You handle all the accounting and administrative functions.

The company's primary regular customers are accounting firms in Sacramento. Credit terms for these customers are 2%/10, Net 30.

You also sell to walk-in customers (cash/checks or credit cards only). Cash and checks are held in the safe and deposited once a week, on Fridays. Credit cards receipts are batched and transmitted to the merchant bank (Bank of Sutterville) every Friday. It generally takes one business day for the bank to process the receipts and deposit the funds in The Abacus Shop's account. Pocket Bank charges a fee of 2% of the credit card total.

In September, the buyer for Sactown College Bookstore called Marvena and asked about purchasing specialty textbooks from The Abacus Shop. The bookstore is understaffed and overcrowded and would like Abacus to handle some of the accounting course textbook orders. The margin will be smaller than normal for Abacus but the volume is good, so the three of you agree to accept the bookstore's order. The textbooks for spring semester arrived on 9/30.

Assignment 5B

The Abacus Shop

Your current inventory includes financial analysis software, calculators, accounting books, desk lamps, high-quality stationary paper, and, of course, the textbooks. All items are taxable.

You took out a loan from Pocket Bank when you first started the business. The balance at 9/30/17 is $3,556.44. The monthly payment (due on the 30th of each month) is $129 (including interest). The interest rate on the note is 9%.

You rent the shop for $800 per month.

Before you start your assignment:

✓ Change the company name to Your Name The Abacus Shop. (Use your first and last name.)

✓ Change "Student" to your name on the **Other Names List**.

- ○ Click on **Lists/Other Names List**.
- ○ Highlight "Student."
- ○ Click **Other Names** button.
- ○ Click **Edit Other Name**.
- ○ Change name.

10/2/17

✓ You come in extra early because you know a big order for a new customer, Sactown College, needs to be delivered today and you want to get the customer set up in QuickBooks.

- • Sactown College will be selling the textbooks to its students, so you set up:
  - ○ A new tax code for resellers (use RSL for the code and Reseller for the description).
  - ○ A new sales tax item that you name "Exempt" (use Board of Equalization as the tax agency and Exempt from sales tax as the description).
    - ❏ Remember, sales tax items are created in the **item list**.
- • Customer information for Sactown College is:

  Sactown College Bookstore

  3635 Freeport Blvd

  Sacramento, CA 95822

  (916) 855-5558

  Terms are 2%/10, Net 30

  Don't forget to enter the sales tax information. The bookstore's resale number is SRY-333-444444.

- • You will be shipping to two locations. The shipping address for the main campus is the same as the school address. The shipping address for the Roseville Campus is 445 Roseville Drive, Roseville, CA 95661.

✓ The textbooks got delivered to the two Sactown College locations as promised. You prepare the invoices using the Abacus invoice template. (The dropdown menu for choosing a template is in the top right hand corner of the Invoice form.) Sactown has asked you to prepare **separate** invoices for each shipping address. Start with Invoice #1100.

- • Main Campus shipment
  - ○ 160 "Financial," 130 "Managerial," and 20 "Cost."
  - ○ Invoice totals $44,100.
- • Roseville campus shipment
  - ○ 40 "Financial" and 30 "Managerial."
  - ○ Invoice totals $10,100.

✓ You notice that some of your larger customers are slow paying. To finance growth, you want to have sufficient cash available, so you decide to offer early payment discounts to your customers. You edit all existing customers (except Store Customer and Sactown College Bookstore) to include terms of 2%/10, Net 30.

- Ignore any messages you might get about the change affecting transactions in closed periods. QuickBooks will not change the terms on any open invoices.

✓ Abbey & Abbey calls Brandon and orders 2 financial analysis software packages and 5 cartons of stationary paper. The company is thrilled with the new credit terms. Brandon ships the products out, and you create the invoice (#1102) totaling $5,383.13.

✓ A new customer has called Brandon and placed an order for 2 cartons of stationary paper. The customer is located in Stockton. NOTE: The sales tax rate for Stockton is 9% so you'll need to create a new **sales tax item**. Taxes are remitted to the Board of Equalization.

- The new customer is Stockton Accounting Services

  2525 Riviera Blvd, Stockton, CA 95201 (billing and shipping)

  Office number: (209) 444-4343

  Credit terms: 2%/10, Net 30

  [**TIP:** Don't forget to set up the correct tax item for the customer.]

10/03/17

✓ Brandon ships the order to Stockton Accounting Services, and you create the invoice (1103) totaling $414.20.

10/5/17

✓ You record the following checks received in the mail:

- Check #57890 dated 10/5 from Abbey & Abbey for $1,386.56.
- Check #883789 dated 10/5 from Sactown College Bookstore for $53,116.00.
  - Sactown College took all available discounts.

 HINT: When a customer is taking discounts on multiple invoices, it's sometimes easier to apply the early payment discount on each invoice first (before entering check amount). Highlight each invoice and then click **Discounts and Credits**. The Abacus Shop records early payments in the Sales Discount account.

- Check #4789 from Juanita's Bookkeeping for $2,175.00 dated 10/5.

10/6/17

✓ Marvena gives you the detail for the in-store sales for recording. (All sales were made at the standard prices.) Use "Store Customer" as the customer name.

- You will need to complete two **sales receipts**. One for the cash sales; one for the credit card sales. (Abacus treats customer payment by credit card the same as payment by cash.) Remember to use the right form and to uncheck the **Print Later** box.
- Cash sales of $271.66 (all paid with check) Receipt #556:
  - 2 copies of "How They Cooked the Books."
  - 2 copies of "Using Numbers Effectively."
  - 1 calculator—standard model.
- Credit card sales of $299.06 (all VISA)—#557. If **MasterCard** appears, click that icon and select VISA in the **PAYMENT** dropdown menu.)
  - 1 desk lamp.
  - 2 calculators—standard model.
  - 1 calculator—deluxe model.

✓ You deposit all the cash, checks, and credit card receipts received. [**TIP:** You'll be making two deposits. One for cash and checks. One for credit card receipts.]

- The cash and check deposit should total $56,949.22
- The bank charges a 2% fee on all credit card sales. You record the fee with the deposit. Charge the fee to "Bank Charges." Do not enter a name in the **Received From** column.
- The credit card deposit should total $293.08 (after the fee).

10/10/17

✓ You receive check #59900 dated 10/10 for $5,275.47 from Abbey & Abbey. Abbey & Abbey took the early payment discount on invoice #1102.

10/11/17

✓ Brandon delivers orders for two customers, and you invoice them as follows:

- Grant, Thorpe and Romanov ($2,794.88, invoice 1104)
    - 3 cartons of stationary paper.
    - 1 financial analysis program.
- Price, Marwick and Coopers ($5,758.20, invoice 1105)
    - 5 cartons of stationary paper.
    - 3 calculators—deluxe model.
    - 2 copies of "How They Cooked the Books."
    - 2 financial analysis programs.

✓ You receive notice from the bank that the $1,386.56 check from Abbey & Abbey that was recorded on 10/5 (deposited on 10/6) was returned for insufficient funds. You call your contact there (Brittney Abbey), who apologizes and explains that the firm changed banks and the old account must have been closed out before the check cleared. She agrees to pay a $30 processing fee. The bank charges Abacus Shop $25 for customer NSF checks.

- Remember: You need to start by opening the **receive payment** window for the bounced check.
    - When you're entering the bank's $25 fee, **do not** accept the default **Bank Service Charges** account created by QuickBooks. Use the dropdown menu to select the **Bank Charges** account under **Other Costs**.
- After you've recorded the transaction, you edit the **Bounced check charge item**. You add the description "Processing fee for returned check," and you change the **account** related to the **item** to Bank Charges (a subaccount of **Other Costs**). Abacus chooses to offset the fees charged to the customer against the charges assessed by the bank. You accept the option to change existing transactions.
- Don't forget to change the date of the **invoice** to Abbey & Abbey for the processing fee to 10/11 if needed.

10/12/17

✓ One of the staff accountants at Price, Marwick and Coopers brings back one of the deluxe calculators purchased on 10/11. The calculator keypad had all the numbers in reverse order! Marvena takes the calculator back. (She'll need to return it to the vendor.) You issue a credit memo (CM 789) for $81.56 and apply it to invoice #1105 dated 10/11.

10/13/17

✓ Marvena gives you the detail for the week's sales. (All sales were at the standard price.)

- Credit card sales (all MasterCard) totaling $733.68:
    - 1 desk lamp.
    - 1 carton of stationary paper.

- ○ 1 calculator—standard model.
- ○ 1 calculator—deluxe model.
- ○ 5 copies of "How to Pass Accounting Classes Without Studying."
- ○ 2 copies of "Managing your Dollars."

✓ You deposit all customer payments received during the week.
- The check deposit totals $5,275.47.
- The credit card deposit totals $719.01. (Don't forget the fees.)

10/17/17

✓ One of the partners at Price, Marwick and Cooper (Steve Cooper) calls Brandon and asks for a favor. The company has a new client, a non-profit organization that is struggling to keep the doors open. Cooper would like to recommend the financial analysis software program, but the cost is more than the organization can afford. Brandon agrees to offer the client a 20% nonprofit discount on all purchases.

✓ You set up two new **items** to handle the new customer.
- You set up a **discount item**. Use nonprofit as the name. The discount will be applied before the total before tax. The Abacus Shop decides to group the non-profit discount with other sales discounts in the general ledger.
- Since the discount will apply to all items on any invoice, you set up a **subtotal item**.

✓ Steve Cooper calls back. His client accepts the offer and orders the software and three cartons of paper. Brandon ships the software and the paper to the client.
- The client is: Homes For All

  2529 Freeport Blvd (billing and shipping)

  Sacramento, CA 95822

  Main phone: (916) 444-9898

  Terms: 2%/10, Net 30
- The invoice (#1107) totals $2,235.90.

10/18/17

✓ A customer comes in to the shop carrying a "How to Pass Accounting Classes Without Studying." He wants a refund because he says he did **everything** the book said and still failed the course! Marvena agrees to a **partial** refund of $30 (plus tax) and gives the customer a $32.63 cash refund. You create a credit memo (CM791).
- When you enter the refund, select "cash" in the **Issue this refund via** field.

10/19/17

✓ You receive the following checks in the mail:
- Check #678997 dated 10/19 for $6,246.17 from Grant, Thorpe & Romanov. The customer took the early payment discount.
- Check #8994421 dated 10/19 for $13,693.98 from Price, Marwick and Coopers.
  - ○ You notice that the company took the early payment discount on the 10/13 invoice based on the original invoice amount (before the credit memo). The discount should have been taken on the balance after the credit memo (**Amt Due** column), but you decide to accept the check as payment in full because the difference is very small.
- Check #1245 dated 10/19 from Stockton Accounting Services for $405.92.
  - ○ Stockton took the discount but didn't pay during the discount period, so you leave the $8.28 balance on the account and give the accountant a call. The accountant agrees to pay the balance in the next few weeks.

10/20/17

✓ Marvena gives you the detail for the week's sales. (All sales were at the standard price.)

- Cash sales of $239.09 (all paid with cash, 559):
  - ○ 1 copy of "How to Pass Accounting Classes Without Studying."
  - ○ 2 copies of "Using Numbers Effectively."
  - ○ 1 desk lamp.
- Credit card sales of $945.85 (all VISA, 560):
  - ○ 3 cartons of stationary paper.
  - ○ 2 calculator—deluxe model.
  - ○ 5 copies of "Managing your Dollars."

✓ You deposit all customer payments received during the week:

- Cash and checks deposit totals $20,585.16.
- VISA deposit totals $926.93. (Don't forget the fees!)

10/25/17

✓ Accountants Plus calls and places an order for 10 standard calculators and 10 copies of "Brilliant Bookkeeping Techniques" to give out at a client appreciation party. The company also orders 3 cartons of paper. Brandon delivers all the items to them, and you create a $1,489.33 invoice (#1108).

✓ You review your **Open Invoices** report as of 10/25. Invoice #1081 to Somerset & Somerset has been outstanding since early September. You have been in contact with the firm but have yet to collect the amount owing. You try to call Gene Somerset (one of the owners) again but discover that the firm's phone has been disconnected. After further research, you discover that the firm has had to close and is in the process of filing for bankruptcy. You decide to write off the balance of $206.63 to bad debt expense. The Abacus Shop uses the direct write-off method because it has historically had very few uncollectible accounts. You'll need to set up a new expense account. You consider bad debts expense to be a subaccount of "Sales and marketing costs."

HINT: It's easiest to write off invoices through the **Receive Payments** form. Write-offs are recorded on the **Discounts** tab of **Discounts and Credits**.

10/27/17

✓ Marvena gives you the detail for the week's sales. (All sales were at the standard price.)

- Credit card sales of $3,572.44 (all VISA, 561):
  - ○ 1 financial analysis software program.
  - ○ 4 copies of "Fundamentals of Financial Accounting."
  - ○ 4 copies of "Introduction to Managerial Accounting."
  - ○ 1 calculator—standard model.
  - ○ 1 calculator—deluxe model.

✓ You deposit all customer payments received during the week:

- VISA—$3,500.99 (Don't forget the fees.)

10/30/17

✓ You decide to close the store both Monday and Tuesday to do some much needed cleaning.

Check numbers 10/31
Checking account balance $123,435.69
Accounts receivable $5,150.07
Total income (October) $74,926.73
Total cost of goods sold (October) . . . $28,703.34

REPORTS TO CREATE FOR ASSIGNMENT 5B

All reports should be in portrait orientation; fit to one page wide.

- Journal—10/01 through 10/31 transactions only:
  - Put report in date order. Remove **Trans #** and **Adj** from report.

- Sales by item Summary (October only):
  - Remove all the **subcolumns** (related to COGS and gross profit).

- Open Invoices dated 10/31 (remove **P.O. #**, and **Aging** columns).

6

Incurring Costs
(Merchandising Company)

Objectives

After completing Chapter 6, you should be able to:

1. Record purchase of inventory by check.

2. Set up reorder points for inventory items.

3. Create and edit purchase orders.

4. Record receipt of inventory with or without a vendor bill.

5. Enter bills for inventory previously received.

6. Enter and apply vendor credit memos.

7. Take early payment discounts on payments to vendors.

8. Prepare inventory and purchase order reports.

WHAT IS THE PURCHASE CYCLE IN A MERCHANDISING COMPANY?

✓ Place an order for products.

✓ Receive the products.

✓ Receive a bill for the products.

✓ Pay the vendor.

The single biggest cost in service companies is usually labor. The single biggest cost in merchandising companies is usually inventory.

Proper inventory management is critical to the success of a merchandising company because:

- It costs money to store inventory.
  - Costs include warehouse rent, insurance, utilities, security, interest, etc.

- Inventory held too long can become obsolete.
  - It's hard to charge full price (or sometimes any price!) for last year's model.

- You can't sell what you don't have.
  - Customers who can't find what they want to buy are not happy customers!

To determine the optimal level of product inventory, management needs information—information about sales volume, accessibility of products, product returns, gross margins, etc. That information frequently comes from the accounting system.

In this chapter, we cover transactions related to the purchase and management of inventory. We also add some topics that apply to both service and merchandising companies.

MANAGING VENDORS

There are no significant differences between managing service company vendors and managing merchandising company vendors in QuickBooks. We learned how to add and edit vendors in Chapter 3, so we won't cover the basics again here.

Entering accurate credit terms is important in all companies, but it's particularly important in merchandising (and manufacturing) companies. Most, if not all, purchases of inventory are done on credit, and many manufacturing and distribution companies offer early payment discounts.

Because inventory is such a large cost in a merchandising company, entering vendor credit terms accurately, so that no available discounts are missed, is very important. Although a 2% early payment discount on a single $500 purchase doesn't sound like much, 2% early payment discounts on five thousand $500 purchases starts to add up!

PRACTICE
EXERCISE

Editing vendor credit terms for Sac City Accounting.
(The accountant at Sac City Accounting called Office Supplies Shop and Intuit and negotiated better credit terms.)

1. Click the **Vendor Center** icon on the **My Shortcuts** tab on the icon bar.

2. Highlight **Office Supplies Shop**.

3. Click the **edit** icon (the pencil) at the top right of the screen.

(continued)

a.   Click **Payment Settings** tab.

b.   Change **Payment Terms** to **2% 10 Net 30**.

c.   Click **OK**.

4.   Highlight **Intuit**.

5.   Click the **edit** icon (the pencil).

a.   Click **Payment Settings** tab.

b.   Change **Payment Terms** to **2% 10 Net 30**.

c.   Click **OK**.

i.   Click **Yes** to any message you might get about how the change might affect prior periods. QuickBooks will not change the credit terms on previously entered **bills**.

6.   Exit out of the **Vendor Center**.

PURCHASING INVENTORY

In Chapter 2 and again in Chapter 5, we covered how the various **items** (**service**, **inventory parts**, **other charge**, **discount**, etc.) are used in the sales cycle. In a merchandising company, **inventory part items** are also used in the purchase and end of period cycles.

In summary, **inventory part items** represent products purchased and sold by the company. General information about each product is stored in the **inventory part** record. That information includes:

- The standard sales price.

- The expected unit cost.

- The name of the preferred vendor.

- The asset account (normally the inventory account) that should be debited if the item is purchased for future sales.

- The income account that should be credited if the item is sold.

- The expense account (cost of goods sold account) that should be debited if the item is sold.

In addition, information about inventory quantities and values is also maintained by QuickBooks for each **inventory part item**, including the quantity and value of units ordered, received, sold, and on hand.

Using **items** allows a company to maintain considerable detail without creating a gigantic chart of accounts. For example, a retail store might have only one income account called "Sales Revenue," but it can still generate a report that that lists sales quantities and dollars for each and every product sold in the store. A retail store might also have only one inventory (asset) account, but it can still track how many units are on hand at any point in time for each individual product.

In order to maintain that detail, of course, all transactions related to products must be recorded using **items**. That includes purchase and adjustment transactions as well as sales transactions.

WARNING: *Bill, Check,* and *Credit Card Charge* forms all have two distribution tabs. One tab is labeled *Expenses* and one is labeled *Items*. In order to properly adjust the subsidiary ledgers, the *Items* tab must <u>always</u> be used when entering inventory transactions. Charging a purchase to the "Inventory" account on the *Expenses* tab <u>will</u> result in a debit to the asset but will not adjust the inventory quantity in the subsidiary ledgers.

Paying At Time Of Inventory Purchase

In most cases, merchandise inventory is **not** purchased by going directly to the supplier's location and paying at time of purchase, but it could be. This might happen if the company needs to ship a particular order right away but doesn't have sufficient products on hand to fill the order. A company might pay for inventory at time of purchase using a check or credit card.

The only difference between entering checks or credit card charges for inventory purchases and entering checks and credit charges for other purchases is the tab used in the distribution section of the form. We use a purchase by check to demonstrate using the appropriate tab. (Refer to Chapter 3 for a refresher on entering credit card charges.)

If a company writes a check for the purchase, the **Write Check** window is accessed through the Home page.

Remember:

- The vendor name, date, and amount of purchase are all used by QuickBooks to credit the bank account and to prepare the check (if checks are printed directly from QuickBooks).

- The distribution section of the form is used to identify the debit account(s) in the underlying journal entry.

Purchases of inventory must be entered on the **Items** tab. The **Expenses** tab is used to enter the account distribution for all purchases other than purchases of inventory.

When the **Items** tab is selected, the **write checks** screen looks like this:

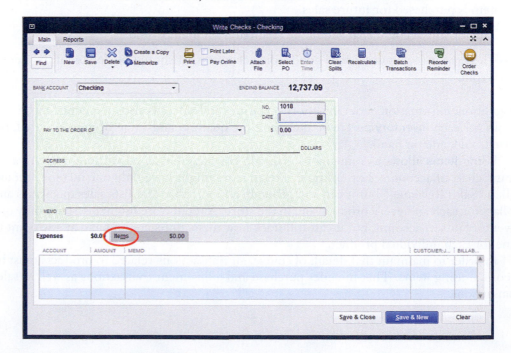

When distributions are entered on the **items** tab (and the form is saved), QuickBooks automatically:

- Debits the **asset account** specified in the **item** set up for the amount of the purchase.

- Updates the quantity records for the **item** purchased.

Purchasing inventory for Sac City Accounting with a check.
(Purchased one copy of Quicken for $30 to have on hand).

1. Click the **Write Checks** button on the Home page.

2. Enter "1018" for the check number and "1/5/18" for the date.

3. Select **Office Supplies Shop** as the **Pay to the Order of** and enter "30" as the check amount.

4. Click the **Items** tab (lower half of the screen).

5. Select Quicken as the **item** and enter "1" as the **Qty**.

6. Change the **Amount** to "30."

    a. This is a special purchase, so click **No** if asked if you want to update the item record.

7. Click **Save & Close**.

Ordering Inventory

Setting Reorder Points And Identifying Preferred Vendors

At the beginning of this chapter, we reviewed some important considerations in inventory management.

- Inventory levels should be high enough that customer orders can be promptly filled.

- Inventory levels should be low enough that costs and the risks of obsolescence are minimized.

Management generally puts considerable effort into determining what inventory level is appropriate for each product. As part of that process, the **minimum** amount of product that should be on hand at any point in time to safely meet customer demand is determined. When the quantity on hand reaches that minimum level, an order for more inventory is placed with the vendor. The minimum level is called the **reorder point**.

A reorder point can be set for every **inventory part item** in QuickBooks. Reports can then be generated that list products that should be ordered based on current inventory levels.

The reorder point is set on the **inventory part item** window. (As a reminder, the **item** window is accessed through the **Item List** option of the **Lists** menu on the main menu bar.) The screen looks something like this:

Reorder point The minimum level of inventory on hand that can safely meet demand until a new inventory order is received.

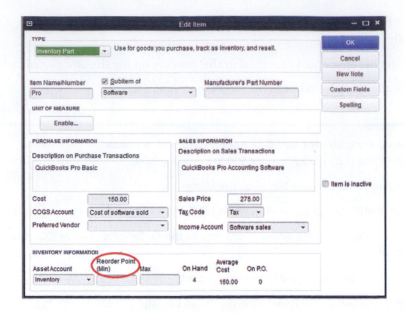

The reorder point is entered in the **Reorder Point (Min)** field at the bottom of the screen. The reorder point field should either be blank or contain a number greater than 0. Putting a 0 in the field can cause some confusion on reports.

Reports of current inventory levels (**Inventory Stock Status** reports) can be created through the **Inventory** option of the **Reports** menu.

BEHIND THE SCENES The words "**stock**" and "inventory" are often used interchangeably. In manufacturing companies, the word "stock" is sometimes used to refer specifically to finished goods held for sale. The word "inventory" is used to refer to finished goods held for sale and any of the materials used to manufacture those goods. QuickBooks uses the terms stock and inventory interchangeably.

Stock Inventory on hand

The **Inventory Stock Status by Vendor** report is particularly useful, in the ordering process because it groups items by vendor. The report can be accessed through **Reports** on the main menu bar:

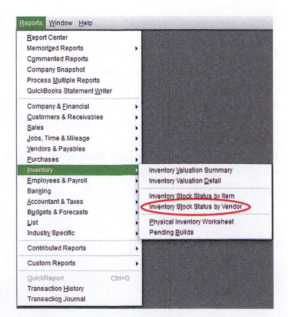

The report looks like this after you complete the practice exercise:

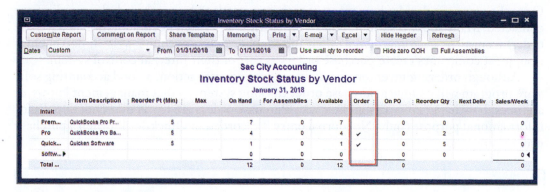

As you can see, products that should be ordered (products where quantity on hand is at or below the reorder point) are flagged (check marked).

 HINT: If you check the **Use avail qty to reorder** box (in the area right below the menu bar), QuickBooks will use available quantity, not on-hand quantity, to determine what needs to be ordered. Available quantity equals quantity on hand less any quantity **ordered** by a customer (on a **sales order**) but not yet shipped.

Editing inventory part items to include reorder points and preferred vendors and determining inventory needs for Sac City.

(Sac City wants to set reorder points for all items stocked.)

PRACTICE EXERCISE

1. Edit **inventory part items**.

   a. Select **Item List** option on **Lists** menu.

   b. Double click **Pro**.

      i.   Select **Intuit** as the **preferred vendor**.

      ii. Enter "5" as the **reorder point (min)**.

      iii. Click **OK**.

   c. Double click **Premier**.

      i.   Select **Intuit** as the **preferred vendor**.

      ii. Enter "5" as the **reorder point (min)**.

      iii. Click **OK**.

   d. Exit out of the **Items List**.

2. Prepare an **Inventory Stock Status by Vendor** report.

   a. Click **Reports**.

   b. Click **Inventory**.

   c. Click **Inventory Stock Status by Vendor**.

   d. Change dates to start (from) and end (to) on 1/31/18.

   e. Note that both **Pro** and **Quicken** are flagged for reorder.

3. Exit out of the report window.

Creating Purchase Orders

Once the company decides how many of each item needs to be purchased, the suppliers are contacted. Many suppliers will not fill an order without written documentation (a purchase order) from their customer. Even when the supplier doesn't require written documentation, most companies create purchase orders as part of their internal control system.

Although ordering inventory is not an accounting transaction, a good accounting software program will include a purchase order tracking system so that management knows, at all times, how many units are on their way. Purchase orders are tracked in QuickBooks for informational purposes only. No journal entry is recorded in QuickBooks when a purchase order is created.

QuickCheck
6-1

Why isn't ordering inventory an accounting transaction? (Answer at end of chapter.)

To create a purchase order, click the **Purchase Orders** icon in the **Vendors** section of the Home page:

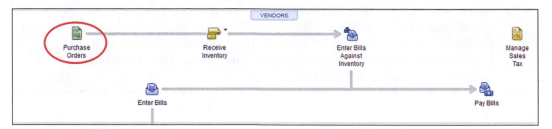

The form looks like this:

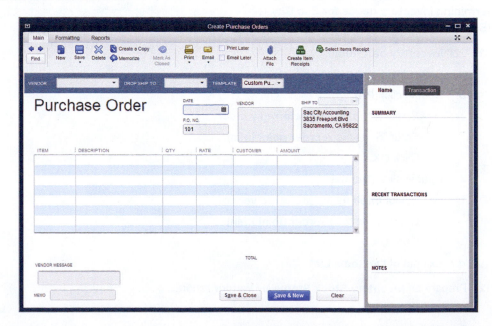

You need to enter the vendor name and the items being ordered to complete the form.

BEHIND THE SCENES QuickBooks will automatically enter the default cost when an **inventory part item** is selected. The unit cost can be changed at this point, if appropriate. The cost can also, of course, be changed later when the vendor **bill** is received.

Creating purchase orders for Sac City Accounting.
(Management decides to order 6 Pro, 9 Quicken, and 1 Premier. Two separate orders are placed.)

1. Click **Purchase Order** on the Home page.

2. Select **Intuit** as the **Vendor**.

   a. Enter "1/16/18" for the **date**.

   b. Enter "101" for the **P.O. No.**

   c. Enter two **items**.

      i.   Select **Pro** on the first line and enter "6" as the **qty.**

      ii. Select **Premier** on the second line and enter "1" as the **qty.**

   d. Use the default costs. The total should be $1,150.

   e. Make sure the **Print Later** box is not checked.

   f. Click **Save & New**.

3. Select **Intuit** as the **vendor**.

   a. Enter "1/19/18" for the **date**.

   b. Enter "102" for the **P.O. No.**

   c. Select **Quicken** as the **item** and enter "9" as the **qty.**

   d. Use the default cost. (Total cost should be $225.)

   e. Click **Save & Close**.

PRACTICE
EXERCISE

Receiving Ordered Inventory

Merchandising companies need to update their inventory records as soon as purchased goods arrive so that their inventory-on-hand quantities are accurate. However, many suppliers include a packing slip (detailing the products and quantities included in the carton) with their shipments but no bill (no vendor invoice). The bill (detailing total costs) frequently arrives after the shipment. This might be done:

- As part of a supplier's internal control system.

- Because a supplier's warehouse or store is physically separate from the supplier's accounting office.

QuickBooks provides a feature that allows the company to record the increase in inventory and the related liability in the accounting records at the anticipated cost (from the **purchase order**) through an **Item Receipt** form (**transaction type**) even if the **bill** has not yet been received. All inventory records are updated and the liability is recorded in the normal accounts payable account and in the vendor's subsidiary ledger. However, an **Item Receipt** is **not** available for payment through the **Pay Bills** screen. When the final **Bill** is received, any adjustments to costs are recorded and the **Item Receipt** becomes a **Bill**. It can then be paid through **Pay Bills**.

Sometimes, of course, the supplier sends the **Bill** with the shipment. We'll look at each situation separately.

Receiving Ordered Inventory Without A Bill

To create an **Item Receipt**, use the drop-down box next to the **Receive Inventory** button on the Home page to select **Receive Inventory without Bill**:

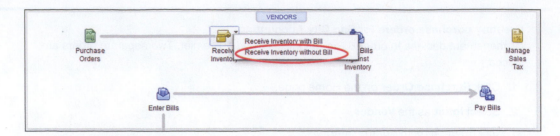

The screen looks like this:

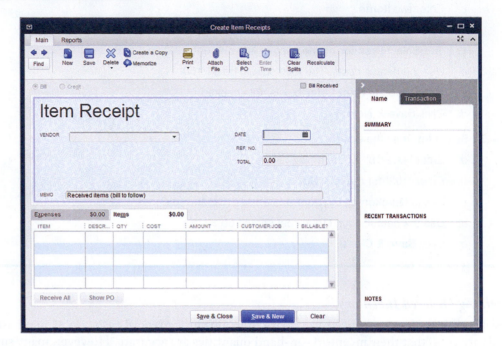

You first need to select the vendor name. If you have open **purchase orders** for the vendor selected, QuickBooks then prompts you with the following message:

If you answer yes, the next window lists all the open purchase orders for the vendor. The screen looks something like this:

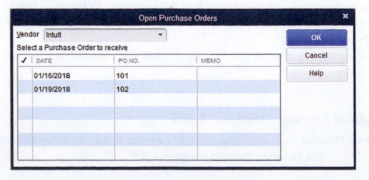

You need to put a check to the left of the appropriate purchase order(s). (You can't just highlight the PO.) The next screen looks something like this:

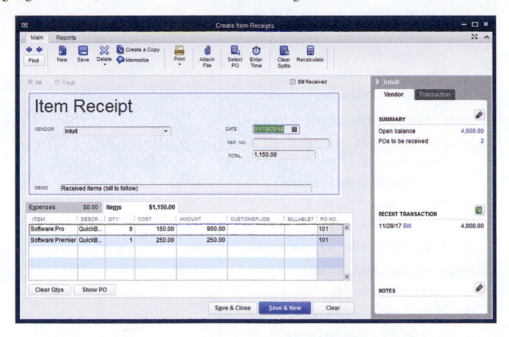

The date entered should be the date the items were received. QuickBooks will assume the quantity received was the quantity ordered. If only a partial shipment was received, the **Qty** can (and should be) changed.

> **BEHIND THE SCENES** If you receive a partial order, QuickBooks will keep the **purchase order** open. The **purchase order** will then be again available for processing when the remaining items are received.

Remember, the **item receipt** will be recorded in Inventory and in Accounts Payable but will not be available in the **Pay Bills** window.

As part of the following Practice Exercise, you'll get a chance to see how QuickBooks handles partial orders and orders received without a **bill**.

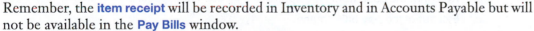

PRACTICE
EXERCISE

Receiving an inventory order without a bill for Sac City Accounting.
(Partial shipment of items on PO#101 is received from Intuit without a bill.)

1. Receive a partial shipment.

    a. Select **Receive Inventory without Bill** option on the drop-down menu next to **Receive Inventory** on the Home page.

    b. Select **Intuit** as the **vendor**.

    c. Click **Yes** at the prompt about open purchase orders.

    d. Check PO #101.

    e. Click **OK**.

    f. Enter "1/19/18" as the **date**.

(continued)

    g.   Leave the **Ref. No.** blank

    h.   Change quantities received (**QTY** column) to:

        i.   4 **Pro**.

        ii.   1 **Premier**.

    i.   Total should be $850.

    j.   Click **Save & Close**.

2. Check the status of the order in QuickBooks.

    a.   Click on **Reports** (main menu bar).

    b.   Select **Purchases**.

    c.   Select **Open Purchase Orders**.

    d.   Double click on PO #101.

        i.   Note that the **Pro** row shows 2 units backordered.

    e.   Exit out of the purchase order and report windows.

3. Check the status of the payable.

    a.   Click on **Reports** (main menu bar).

    b.   Click on **Vendors & Payables**.

    c.   Click on **A/P Aging Summary**.

    d.   Change **date** to 1/31/18.

    e.   Double click on total for Intuit.

        i.   Note that balance includes the **Item Receipt** created in step 1.

    f.   Exit out of report window.

4. Check whether the **item receipt** is available for payment in **Pay Bills** window.

    a.   Click on **Pay Bills** (Home page).

    b.   Note that the $850 **Item Receipt** from Intuit does not appear on the screen.

    c.   Exit out of the **pay bills** screen.

Receiving The Bill For Items Previously Received

Vendors will, of course, send a bill for any items shipped with a packing slip only.

    To enter a **bill** for items previously received, use the **Enter Bills Against Inventory** button on the Home page:

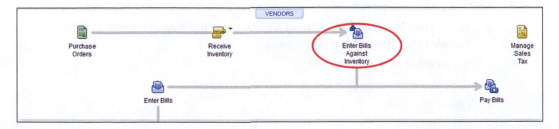

The screen looks like this:

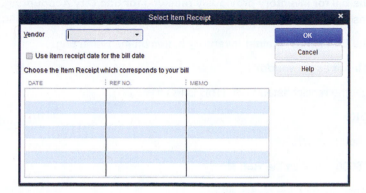

When you select a vendor name, all the open **Item Receipts** for that vendor appear on the screen. You need to highlight the appropriate **Item Receipt** and click **OK**.

The next screen represents the change of the inventory purchase from an **Item Receipt** to a **Bill**. The screen looks like this:

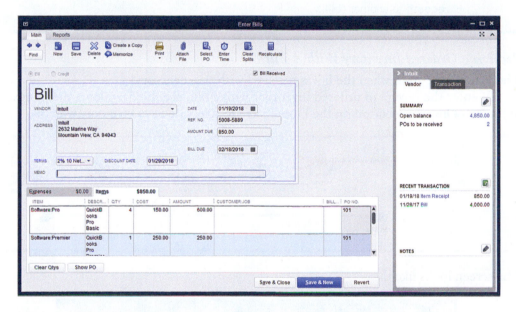

You need to enter a **Ref. No.** and review the **date** and the **terms**. You can change costs or add charges (late fees or freight charges, for example) on the screen if necessary to agree to the bill amount.

> **BEHIND THE SCENES** Late fees would not normally be considered a cost of inventory and should be distributed on the **Expenses** tab. Freight-in charges are product costs and should be added to the **item**'s cost on the **items** tab. (If an order includes multiple items, freight charges should be allocated to all items. Allocation could be based on weight, number of items, etc. Any reasonable method would be acceptable.)

> **WARNING: Once the *item receipt* is converted to a *bill*, the *item receipt* no longer exists. If the bill is later deleted or voided, the *item receipt* will <u>not</u> be reinstated.**

PRACTICE EXERCISE

Entering the bill for inventory previously received for Sac City Accounting.
(Bill for items received on PO #101 from Intuit was received. Total bill was $850.)

1. Click the **Enter Bills Against Inventory** button on the Home page.

2. Select **Intuit** as the **vendor**.

3. Highlight the receipt dated 1/19. (This is PO #101.)

4. Click **OK**.

5. **Date** should be 1/19/18.

6. Enter "5008-5889" as the **Ref. No.**

7. Make sure amount due shows as $850.

8. Click **Save & Close**.

9. Click **Yes** when prompted to record changes.

   a. The "change" you're agreeing to is the change from one **transaction type** (**item receipt**) to another (**bill**).

Receiving Ordered Inventory With A Bill

There are fewer steps when the bill is received with the inventory!

To enter the receipt of ordered inventory with a bill, use the dropdown menu next to the **Receive Inventory** button on the Home page to select **Receive Inventory with Bill**:

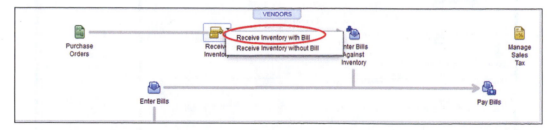

The screen looks like this:

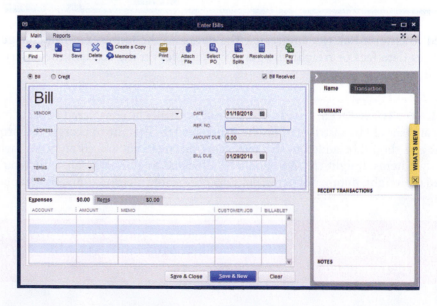

You first need to enter the vendor name. If you have open purchase orders, you receive a prompt like this:

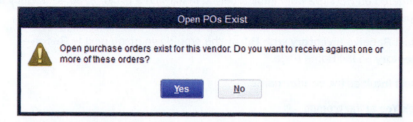

If you answer **Yes**, a window appears listing all open purchase orders for that vendor. You need to select (check) the appropriate one. The window looks something like this:

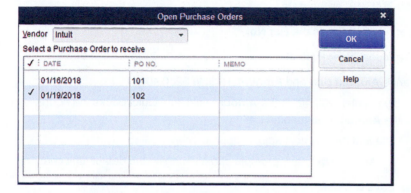

Once you select the appropriate **purchase order**, the next screen looks something like this:

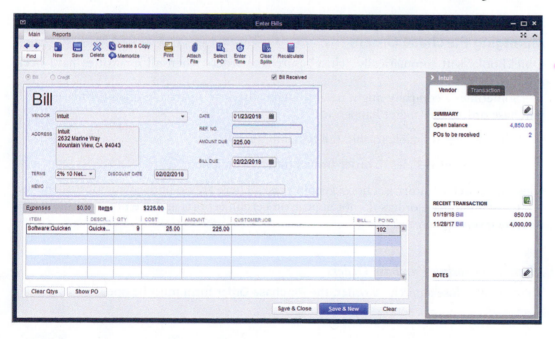

You need to enter the vendor reference number, review the credit terms and the date, and enter quantity and cost (if different than expected).

BEHIND THE SCENES Remember, if you receive a partial shipment, QuickBooks will leave the **Purchase Order** open for future shipments.

PRACTICE
EXERCISE

Receiving ordered inventory with a bill for Sac City Accounting.

(Items ordered on PO #102 from Intuit received in full with a bill for $230.40; slightly higher than expected.)

1. Select **Receive Inventory with Bill** on the drop-down menu next to **Receive Inventory** on the Home page.

2. Select **Intuit** as the **vendor name**.

3. Click **Yes** at the prompt.

4. Check **PO No.** 102.

5. Click **OK**.

6. Enter "1/23/18" as the **date**.

7. Enter "4998-4002" as the **Ref No.**

8. Leave quantity received at 9.

9. Change **Amount Due** and **Amount** fields to $230.40.

   a.   If you enter "230.40" in the **Amount** field first, QuickBooks will normally update the **Amount Due** automatically.

   b.   Note that the unit cost adjusts appropriately.

      i.   Answer **No** to any prompts about changing the default unit cost.

10. Click **Save & Close**.

Managing Purchase Orders

QuickBooks will automatically "close" purchase orders when all quantities have been received.

Sometimes a company might need to manually close a partially filled (or never filled) purchase order. This might happen when:

- The supplier is unable to ship the remaining items.
- The company decides to order from a different supplier.

Closing a purchase order is a housekeeping task. There are no underlying journal entries!

Closed purchase orders do not appear on certain reports and are not available in the **Receive Inventory** screens.

Manually Closing Purchase Orders

To manually close a purchase order, the **Purchase Order** form must be open:

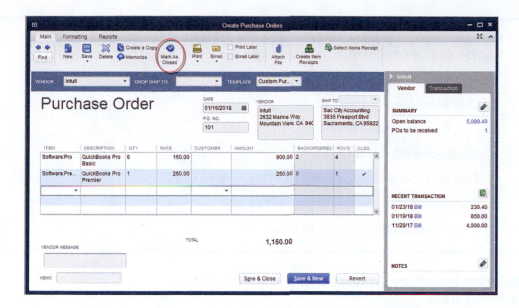

Clicking the **Mark As Closed** button (top of the screen) closes the entire **purchase order**.

Once you select that option, and save the form, the purchase order will be stamped **Closed**. The screen looks something like this:

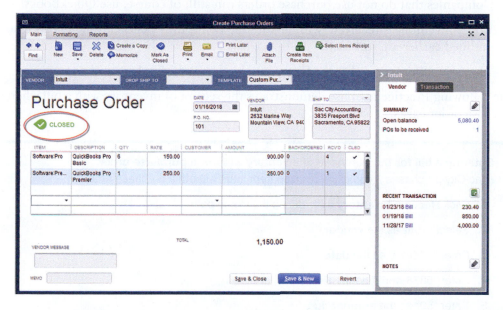

If you only want to close a particular **item** on a **purchase order**, you can click the **CLSD** field (far right column in the row) for that **item**.

 HINT: If all items on a purchase order were received, the green stamp would read **Received In Full**.

PRACTICE
EXERCISE

Manually closing a purchase order for Sac City Accounting.
(Sac City decides it doesn't need the remaining Pro copies and cancels the balance of PO #1.)

1. Click **Reports**.

2. Click **Purchases**.

3. Click **Open Purchase Orders**.

4. Double-click **PO No. 101**.

5. Click the **Mark As Closed** icon on the form menu bar.

6. Click **Save & Close** (accept change to transaction).

7. Close the **Open Purchase Orders** report.

Ordering Inventory Without Using The Purchase Order System

Given the importance of maintaining proper inventory levels, most companies want to track the status of orders they've placed with suppliers (purchase orders) and use the purchase order system outlined earlier.

Companies that do not use purchase orders can still, of course, use QuickBooks!

- When inventory is received (with or without a bill), the **Receive Inventory** processes outlined earlier are still used.

- The only difference is that the "open purchase orders" windows will not appear.

The following Practice Exercise demonstrates the receipt of inventory with a bill when no purchase order exists.

PRACTICE
EXERCISE

Entering a bill for the purchase of inventory without a purchase order.
(Sac City purchases 2 copies of Quicken from Intuit without a purchase order.)

1. Click **Receive Inventory with Bill** on the Home page.

2. Select **Intuit** as the **vendor**.

3. Enter "1/20/18" as the **date**.

4. Enter "5878-4662" as the **Ref No.**

5. Enter "50" as the **amount due**.

6. Select **Quicken** as the **item** (on **Items** tab) and enter "2" as the quantity.

7. Click **Save & Close**.

VENDOR CREDITS

Vendors issue credit memos for a variety of reasons. Those reasons might include the following:

- Goods were returned.

- There was an error on a previously issued bill.

- To give a "good faith" allowance when a customer isn't satisfied with goods or service.

Vendor credits aren't unique to merchandising companies. Service and manufacturing companies would also use the procedures outlined here.

Credit memos from vendors are recorded in QuickBooks as transaction type **Bill Credit**. (Remember: A credit issued to a customer is transaction type **Credit**.)

Vendor credit memos are a separate form (**transaction type**), but they are initially accessed through the **Bill** form window. At the top of the **Bill** form, there is a toggle button named **Credit**. Clicking this turns the **Bill** into a **Bill Credit**.

The form looks like this:

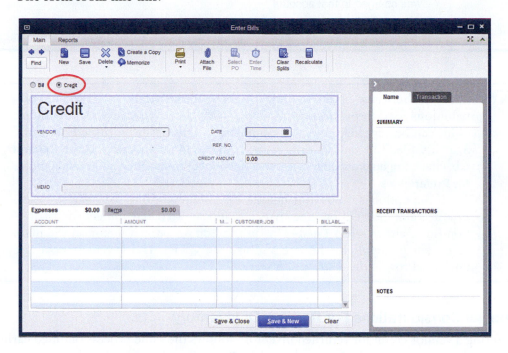

You need to enter the vendor name, date of the credit memo, reference number (that number often incorporates the original bill number), and the account that should be credited. The form includes some familiar tabs (**Expenses** and **Items**).

Unlike the customer credit memo form, QuickBooks does not ask you to apply the credit when the form is completed. Instead, QuickBooks tracks the credit separately in the vendor subsidiary ledger. All available credits are displayed whenever future vendor payments are being processed to allow the user to determine when and how a credit will be used.

> **HINT:** A preference can be changed so that QuickBooks automatically applies the credit to a specific bill when the credit memo is recorded. The preference change is made in the **Bill** tab on the **Preference** screen. Changing the preference removes the flexibility to apply the credit as considered appropriate, though, so most companies prefer applying credits as part of the bill paying process.

PRACTICE
EXERCISE

Entering a vendor credit for Sac City Accounting.
(Sac City receives a credit memo from Office Supplies Shop. It had been charged for two cases of paper never received.)

1. Click **Enter Bills** on the Home page.

2. Change the form to a **Bill Credit** by clicking the **Credit** button at the top left side of the form.

(continued)

3. Select **Office Supplies Shop** as the vendor.

4. Enter "1/5/18" as the **date**, "CM 67-1313" as the **Ref. No.**

5. Enter "106.80" as the **credit amount**.

   a. Select **Supplies on Hand** as the **account** (on **Expenses** tab).

      i. The Supplies on Hand account is selected here because the original invoice was charged to that account.

6. Click **Save & Close**.

HINT: There is an option in QuickBooks to automatically recall account distributions used in previous transactions with the same customer or vendor. (This can be very helpful or very annoying!) This has been turned off in the Sac City file. To turn that option on, go to **Edit/Preferences**. On the **General** tab, check the **automatically remember account or transaction information** under **My Preferences**.

If the option is on in your homework assignment files, you may see multiple account distributions automatically appear. To delete unneeded distribution lines, either select **Delete Line** in the **Edit** dropdown menu on the main menu bar or highlight the line and use the CTRL Del key to remove the unwanted row in the distribution section.

Special Considerations For Returns Of Inventory

Entering a vendor credit for returned inventory follows the same process outlined earlier. (You must, of course, use the **Items** tab, not the **Expenses** tab, in the distribution section.) However, understanding the underlying journal entry for **inventory part item** returns is important.

As you know, QuickBooks uses the weighted average method for valuing inventory. The average cost for items in inventory is adjusted in QuickBooks only when units are **purchased**. When an item is returned (through a vendor credit), QuickBooks credits the inventory account for the **average cost as of the return date**. That may or may not agree to the amount on the vendor credit. If it doesn't agree, QuickBooks will debit (or credit) the difference to the **costs of goods sold** account for that **item**.

For example, let's say the weighted average cost in QuickBooks for Product X is $40. A company returns one unit to the supplier. The current cost is $45, and that's the credit amount given by the supplier. The journal entry underlying the **Bill Credit** in QuickBooks would be:

Accounts payable	45	
Inventory		40
Cost of goods sold		5

Enter a vendor credit for return of inventory for Sac City Accounting.
(One Pro package was returned to Intuit due to damage.)

1. Click **Enter Bills** on the Home page.

2. Click **Credit** button at top of form.

3. Select **Intuit** as the **vendor** and enter "1/25/18" as the **date**.

4. Enter "CM 5777" as the **Ref. No.**

5. Enter "145" as the **credit amount**.

6. On the **items** tab, select **Pro** as the **item**.

7. Enter "145" as the **amount**.

    a.   QuickBooks will assume a quantity of "1."

8. Click **No** if prompted to update the **item** record.

9. If QuickBooks autofilled an account on the **Expenses** tab, you may need to delete that line before you can save the transaction.

10. Click **Save & Close**.

11. To view the underlying entry:

    a.   Click on **Reports**.

    b.   Click on **Accountant & Taxes**.

    c.   Click on **Journal**.

    d.   Enter report dates of 1/25/18 to 1/25/18.

    e.   Note that the entry for the credit from Intuit includes a debit to "Cost of Software Sales" for $5 (the difference between the weighted average cost and the credit memo amount).

    f.   Exit out of the report window.

PAYING VENDOR BALANCES

We covered the basics of paying vendor account balances in Chapter 3. In this chapter, we cover:

• Manually applying vendor credit when paying bills.

• Taking early payment discounts on payments to vendors.

Service, merchandising, and manufacturing companies use these procedures.

Applying credits and taking discounts is all done through the **Pay Bills** window. The **Pay Bills** screen is accessed from the Home page.

As a reminder, the screen looks something like this:

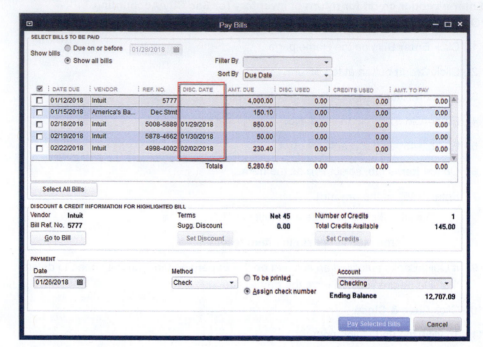

For any vendors with early payment discounts, the last day of the discount period will be displayed in the **Disc. Date** column. The screen can also be sorted by discount date.

If there are any available credits and/or early payment discounts for a vendor, the amounts will be displayed in the lower section of the screen **when a bill for that vendor is checked or highlighted**. Make sure you check that section of the screen. It's easy to miss a discount or a credit when you're busy selecting amounts to pay.

If there is a credit available and you want to take it to a specific invoice, you need to check that invoice and use the **Set Credits** button in the lower middle right of the window:

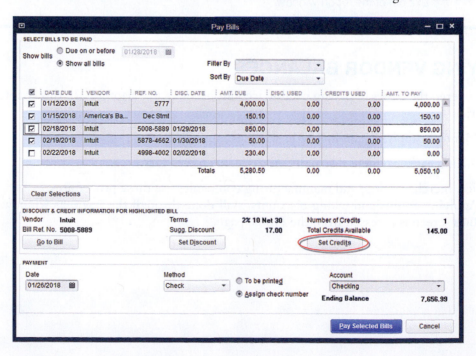

QuickBooks will then display the amounts of any available credits. You can apply some or all of the credits. The screen to apply credits looks something like this:

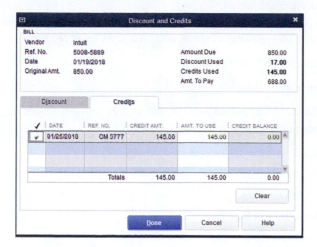

If there is an early payment discount available for the **bill**, you need to check the **bill** on the **Pay Bills** screen and use the **Set Discount** button in the lower middle of the screen. QuickBooks calculates the discount for you, but you can override the calculation. There is also an option for selecting the account the discount should be credited to. The account chosen depends on the invoice that's being paid. If the bill is for inventory, many companies credit a **cost of goods sold account type** (often named "purchase discounts"). If the discount relates to a bill for an expense, many companies either credit a "miscellaneous income" account (**Other Income account type**) or credit the original expense account. If the bill is for an asset, most companies credit the appropriate asset account. The screen for applying discounts looks something like this:

If there are both credits and discounts available on a single bill, you can enter them at the same time by switching tabs in the **Discounts and Credits** window.

> **BEHIND THE SCENES** Under GAAP, purchase discounts are properly accounted for as a reduction of the unit cost. If discounts taken relate to units on hand, the discounts should be credited to inventory. However, QuickBooks does not have the capacity to handle that level of complexity. As long as the error in inventory values (due to these discounts) is not material (not significant), crediting cost of goods sold for early payment discounts on inventory items is acceptable.

PRACTICE
EXERCISE

Recording payments of bills for Sac City Accounting taking vendor credits and early payment discounts.

(On 1/26/18, Sac City pays all bills due on or before 1/31—or with early payment discounts ending on or before 1/31—taking all credit and discounts as appropriate.)

1. Click **Pay Bills** on the Home page.

2. Click the **Show all bills** button.

3. Check all bills due on or before 1/31/18 and all bills with a discount date on or before 1/31/18. (There should be four bills checked.)

4. For the Intuit bill with the 1/29 discount date (#5777):

    a. Highlight the bill. (It should already be checked.)

    b. Click the **Set Credits** tab.

        i.   Check the row for **CM 5777**.

    c. Click **Discount** tab (middle of screen).

        i.   Accept QuickBooks calculation of $17 for the **amount of discount**.

            1. The discount is taken on the full amount of the vendor invoice ($850). The credit memo applied relates to a previous shipment.

        ii. Select **Add New** as the **Discount Account**.

            1. Select **Cost of goods sold** as the account **type**.

            2. Name the account "Purchase discounts."

            3. Do not enter as a **subaccount**.

            4. Click **Save & Close**.

    d. Click **Done**.

    e. **Amt To Pay** column should now show as $688 for Intuit **bill** 5008-5889."

5. For the Intuit bill with an 1/30 discount date (#5878-4662):

    a. Highlight the bill.

    b. Click **Set Discount** (lower middle right of the screen).

    c. Accept the $1 calculation.

    d. Select **Purchase discounts** as the **account**.

    e. Click **Done**.

6. Total amount to be paid for all four **bills** selected should be $4,887.10. (The total to be paid is displayed at the bottom of the **Amt To Pay** column.)

7. Enter "1/26/18" as the payment **date**. Select **Check** as the payment **method**.

8. Click the **Assign Check Number** button.

9. Select **Checking** as the **account**.

10. Click **Pay Selected Bills**.

11. Click **Let me assign check numbers below**.

12. Use check numbers 1020 and 1021.

    a. There will be two checks (A check to America's Bank for $150.10 and a check to Intuit for $4,737.00).

13. Click **OK**.

(continued)

14. The **Payment Summary** screen will display the four bills that have been paid.

15. Click **Done**.

VENDOR REPORTS

We reviewed some of the standard vendor and payables reports in Chapter 3. For this chapter, we're most interested in inventory and purchase reports.

Inventory reports are accessed through the **Inventory** option on the **Reports** menu (main menu bar). Commonly used inventory reports include:

- Inventory Valuation Summary
  - Gives a report of quantity, average cost, and total cost of units on hand by **item**.
- Inventory Stock Status (by Item or by Vendor)
  - Gives a report of quantities on hand and on order.
  - Also flags items with quantities at or below the reorder point.

Inventory purchase reports are accessed through the **Purchases** option on the **Reports** menu (main menu bar). A commonly used inventory purchase report:

- Open Purchase Orders
  - List of all unfilled purchase orders.

PRACTICE EXERCISE

Preparing reports on inventory and purchases for Sac City Accounting.
(Sac City wants an inventory valuation report and a report showing quantities on hand.)

1. Creating Inventory Reports.
   a. Click on **Reports**.
   b. Click on **Inventory**.
   c. Click on **Inventory Valuation Summary**.
       i.   Change date to 1/31/18 and refresh the screen.
       ii. Delete all columns relating to sales data.
            1. Click and hold the separator bar to the right of the column you want to delete. Drag the bar to the left.
       iii. Exit out of the report window.
   d. Click on **Reports**.
   e. Click on **Inventory**.
   f. Click on **Inventory Stock Status by Item**.
       i.   Change dates to 11/01/17 to 1/31/18 and click **refresh**.
       ii. Double click on **Pro** to see activity (units only) during the period.
       iii. Exit out of the report windows.

ANSWER TO QuickCheck 6-1

Because there is no change in the accounting equation when an order is placed.

CHAPTER SHORTCUTS

Record vendor credit
1. Click Home
2. Click Enter Bills
3. Click "Credit" (top of page)

Record purchase order
1. Click Home
2. Click Purchase Orders

Receive inventory without a bill
1. Click Home
2. Click dropdown menu next to Receive Inventory
3. Click Receive Inventory Without Bill

Receive inventory with the bill
1. Click Home
2. Click dropdown menu next to Receive Inventory
3. Click Receive Inventory With Bill

Record bill received after inventory receipt has been recorded
1. Click Home
2. Click Enter Bills Against Inventory

CHAPTER REVIEW

Matching

Match the term or phrase (as used in QuickBooks) to its best definition

1. Bill credit
2. Item receipt
3. Set Credits
4. Open Purchase Orders
5. Set Discount
6. Purchase order
7. Stock
8. Stock status by vendor

_____ Inventory

_____ Transaction type used to record inventory received without a vendor bill

_____ A report of **items** (grouped by preferred vendor) listing quantities on hand and on order

_____ Transaction type used to record credits received from vendors

_____ Command on the **bill payment** screen to attach a vendor credit to a specific bill

_____ Title of report listing all unfilled purchase orders

_____ Order for goods sent to vendor

_____ Command on the **bill payment** screen to take early payment discounts

Multiple Choice

1. A liability is recorded in QuickBooks Pro when: (Select all that apply.)
   a. inventory is ordered from the supplier.
   b. inventory is received without a bill from the supplier.
   c. inventory is received with a bill from the supplier.

2. Recording the receipt of **items** **not** accompanied by a **bill**:
    a. adjusts the quantity on hand for that **item**.
    b. adjusts the cost of inventory on hand.
    c. both a and b.
    d. neither a nor b.

3. If all items on a purchase order have been received,
    a. the purchase order is automatically marked as "closed" by QuickBooks Pro.
    b. the purchase order must be manually closed by clicking on the **CLSD** column for each **item** listed on the purchase order.
    c. the purchase order remains open until the **bill** has been paid.
    d. the purchase order is automatically deleted by QuickBooks Pro.

4. QuickBooks Pro adjusts the **unit** cost (cost per unit) on **inventory part items** when:
    a. **items** are received from a vendor.
    b. **items** are sold to a customer.
    c. **items** are returned to a vendor.

5. If multiple **bills** from the same vendor are paid at the same time, QuickBooks Pro will:
    a. Issue a separate check for each vendor **bill**.
    b. issue one check for the sum of the vendor **bill** amounts being paid.
    c. issue either one check for each **bill** or one check for all **bills** depending on the option selected by the user in the **pay bills** window.

ASSIGNMENTS

Background information from Chapter 5: You are one of three owners of Software 2 Go, a small retail store specializing in computer software. You have been in business for almost two years and have been fairly profitable both years. The business is a corporation with a 12/31 year-end.

The owners share business responsibilities.

- Rey Martinez runs retail operations at the shop and handles all merchandise purchasing.
- Elena Turgenev manages commercial sales.
- You handle all the accounting and administrative functions.

The company's primary commercial customers are professional service firms in Sacramento, although they also sell to a private tutoring center for children (Computer Fun Park). Credit terms for these customers are currently Net 30.

You also sell to walk-in customers. (You take cash/checks or credit cards.) Cash and checks are held in the safe and deposited once a week, on Fridays. Credit cards receipts are batched and transmitted to the merchant bank (Bank of Sutterville) every Friday. It generally takes one business day for the bank to process the receipts and deposit the funds in Software 2 Go's account. Bank of Sutterville charges a processing fee of 2% of the credit card total.

In November, the buyer for Komputer Kidz called Rey and asked about purchasing software from Software 2 Go. Komputer Kidz is a tutoring center specializing in children ages 6–12. Unlike Computer Fun Park, Komputer Kidz will be reselling the software titles to its customers. (Actually, Komputer Kidz will be selling to its customer's parents!) It means you'll have to increase your inventory levels for certain titles but you're all very happy for the increase in sales volume!

Assignment 6A

Software 2 Go

Your current inventory includes financial, educational, graphic, and simulation software. All items are taxable (except, of course, any sales to resellers like Komputer Kidz).

You took out a loan from Bank of Sutterville when you first started the business. The balance at 11/30/17 is $6,673.00. The monthly payment (due on the 30th of each month) is $200 (including interest). The interest rate on the note is 5%.

You rent the shop for $1,500 per month under a five-year lease.

12/1/17

✓ You pay the December rent ($1,500) to your landlord, Retail Space, Inc. (use check #2461).

✓ Rey hands you a bill for merchandise (inventory) received from Business Applications today. The shipment included 2 copies of "Client" **originally ordered on PO# 210**.

- The vendor reference number is 68993-33. The total due is $220.00. (Bill is dated 12/1. Terms are 1% 10, Net 30.)

✓ You review your unpaid bills report and notice that the early payment discounts for outstanding bills due to Computer Supply House and Business Applications expire today. You write the checks (net of the discount) and get them in the mail before you leave for the day. [**TIP:** There should be three bills but only two checks.]

- You set up an account called "Purchase Discounts" (**cost of goods sold** account type) for tracking vendor discounts.

  ○ Don't forget to change the check date first so you can "set" all available discounts.

- You pay $17,931.30 in total. You let QuickBooks assign the check numbers. The last check should be #2463.

12/5/17

✓ You receive the following bills in the mail:

> **HINT:** Always enter **bills** using the vendor invoice date so discounts can be properly tracked.

- A $900.00 bill, dated 12/5, from "Sactown News" for advertising in the Sunday papers (12/10, 12/17, and 12/24). The bill number is 128540. The terms are Net 15.

- A bill from Office Station (#81471) for $2,689.00, dated 12/5. The bill is for a new computer to use in the retail shop ($2,150.00), a new printer for your office ($389.00), and a supply of copy and printer paper to have on hand ($150.00). Terms are 2%/10, Net 30. (Accept the change in terms if prompted.)

  ○ You expect computer equipment to have a two-year life.

✓ Rey has reviewed the inventory stock status report (by vendor) and is ready to place some orders. He talks to Elena about sales of "Draw." Because that title has not been selling well, he thinks it should be discontinued. Elena agrees so Rey asks you to only prepare purchase orders for "Drive" and "Anatomy," as follows:

- Computer Supply House—14 copies of "Drive" (PO # 215, $546.00 total)

- Software Solutions—26 copies of "Anatomy" (Elena wants to be prepared for the next group of medical students!) (PO #216, $7,280.00 total)

✓ You notice that Software Design is still giving you Net 30 terms. You've been doing business with them for a while, so you give Cristina Rey (your rep) a call. She agrees to give you terms of 2%/10, Net 30 on all future bills. You edit the vendor record appropriately. (Ignore any messages about closed periods.)

12/7/17

✓ You pay all bills due on or before 12/22 **plus** any bills with early payment discounts expiring before 12/22.

- Early payment discounts on inventory purchases are credited to "Purchase Discounts" and early payment discounts on non-inventory purchases are credited to "Miscellaneous" Expense at Software 2 Go. [**TIP:** There should be six bills (two with a discount). Payment total should equal $8,476.02 (five checks). Let QuickBooks assign the check numbers. (The last check number should be 2468. You may need to scroll down to see the last check number.)]

12/8/17

✓ Rey hands you the packing slip for the Software Solutions order that was received today (PO #216). He has checked the shipment and all 26 copies were received. No bill was received with the shipment. You enter the **Item Receipt**.

✓ Elena and Rey have decided to expand the product line. Rey has had a number of customers ask for mouse pads and headsets when they're in the shop, so they decide to add some computer accessory items to their product line. They have found the following supplier:

- Better Buy

  2588 Bigbox Canyon Drive

  San Diego, CA 92104

  Main Phone: (619) 378-5432

  Terms: 2%/10, Net 30

- You decide to set up an **item** called "Accessories" as a "header item." Remember, a header **item** is just a tool for organizing the **item** list. It is not an actual product.

- Each **inventory part item** will have a reorder point of 10 (except **Accessories**, which has no reorder point) and will use "COGS-Accessories" and "Accessory Sales" as the COGS and Income accounts, respectively. (These are new accounts you'll need to set up.) Inventory will be recorded in the "Inventory" account. (Don't use the "Inventory Asset" account.) All **items** are taxable. The preferred vendor is Better Buy.

- New **items** in this category (i.e., **subitems** of Accessories) are:

  ○ Pad (description—mouse pad)—expected cost $2.50; selling price $8.00.

  ○ Headset (description—headset)—expected cost $22.00; selling price $50.00.

  ○ Speaker (description—set of speakers)—expected cost $15.00; selling price $35.00.

- You prepare the first purchase order (#217) for 15 of each new product. The PO totals $592.50.

12/15/17

✓ You receive the following bills in the mail:

- Sacramento Power—December utilities bill #W459-T45 for $212, dated 12/15 due 1/14/18.

- American Telephone—December phone bill #232-884 for $174, dated 12/15 due 12/30.

✓ Rey lets you know that he has received the following shipments:

- Computer Supply—Received all items ordered on 12/5 (PO #215).

  ○ Bill #918273 for $546 was included. Credit terms 2%/10, Net 30. Bill date 12/15.

- Better Buy—Received all items ordered on 12/8 (PO #217) **except for** five mouse pads.

  ○ Bill #444-8909 for $580 was included. Credit terms 2%/10, Net 30. Bill date 12/15.

12/18/17

✓ You receive two bills in the mail from Software Solutions for **shipments previously received**. Both have terms of 2%/10, Net 30.

- You are surprised to see that one of the bills covers a shipment you received in November (PO #213). (You figure someone at Software Solutions must have lost some paperwork!) The vendor invoice (#1010101), dated 12/12, is for $2,800.00.

- The other bill (#1010102) for $7,280.00 (also dated 12/12) is for the shipment you received on the 8th of December.

- Remember: The change QuickBooks is referring to in the prompt when you save the transaction is the change from **item receipt** to **bill**.

✓ You pay all bills due on or before 12/22 **plus** any bills with early payment discounts expiring on or before 12/22. [**TIP:** Make sure you're selecting the correct account for any discounts.]

- There should be two bills paid. One check for $9,878.40 (check # 2469).

12/19/17

✓ Rey lets you know that he has decided to return all 10 of the unsold copies of "Draw" to Software Design. The product just hasn't been selling well. (He will be returning them this week but he hasn't done it yet.)

- You delete the **reorder point** (remove, don't change to 0) for the **item** so it doesn't show up for reorder on the **Inventory Stock Status** report.

✓ Rey asks you to close out PO #212 to Software Design. He has contacted the supplier to say he wants to cancel the one copy of "Golf" that's on backorder. He'll create a new purchase order when he wants to restock the item. (Ignore any messages you might get about closed periods.) You close the PO as requested.

✓ The remaining five mouse pads from PO #217 are received from Better Buy. Bill #444-9992 for $12.50 dated 12/15 was included with the shipment. Credit terms are 2%/10, net 30.

12/22/17

✓ You pay all bills due on or before 12/31 **plus** any bills with early payment discounts expiring on or before 12/31. Let QuickBooks assign the check numbers.

- There should be four bills paid. Three checks totaling $1,289.73. Last check #2472.

✓ A credit memo for the 10 copies of "Draw" returned by Rey is faxed over from Software Design. The credit memo (#RP2699) is for $972.00. The credit memo included a 10% restocking fee charged by Software Design for the return of products.

- You charge the restocking fee ($108.00) to "Miscellaneous Expense." [**TIP:** The restocking fee must be entered as a negative on the **Expenses** tab because the fee reduces the credit allowed by the vendor. (A "negative credit" is really a debit, right?)]

✓ Rey reviews the Inventory Stock Status by Vendor report as of 12/22. He asks you to prepare purchase orders for the following:

- From Business Applications (PO 218 for $4,180.00):
  - 17 "People."
  - 25 "Plan."
- From Computer Supply House (PO 219 for $1,479.00):
  - 29 "Calculate."

12/23/17

✓ Rey hands you a credit memo (CM 51500 for $51.00, dated 12/23) he received from Computer Supply House today when he returned the damaged copy of "Calculate" the customer returned earlier this month. (Chapter 5 transaction.)

✓ You have your monthly staff meeting today at Plum Café. You decide to bring the monthly dividend checks to distribute ($2,500 for each owner). It's been a good month so far, but the owners want to leave plenty of cash in the business for future expansion. There should be three checks. (Don't forget to pay yourself!)

- Remember: Software 2 Go is a corporation. In a corporation, distributions to owners (other than salaries or expense reimbursements) are dividends.

✓ Lunch at the Plum Cafe costs $32.00, and you pay with check #2477.

- You charge the lunch to "Staff Meetings." (The "Labor costs" category includes any costs related to workers, not just wages.)

12/27/17

✓ You receive a bill (#76762) for $985 in the mail from the attorney at Parry & Broad, LLC. The bill, dated 12/27, is for professional work Andrea Parry did for Software 2 Go in December related to its lease agreement with Retail Space, Inc. (Software 2 Go is hoping to expand into some space its landlord owns next door.) The bill is due in 30 days.

12/28/17

✓ Rey hands you the bills for the shipments received today from Business Applications (PO 218) and Computer Supply House (PO 219).

- The bill from Business Applications (85991-11), dated 12/28, is for $4,180.00 (1%/10, Net 30).
- The bill from Computer Supply House (11W4788B), dated 12/28, is for $1,224.00. The shipment only contained 24 copies of "Calculate" (2%/10, Net 30).

✓ Rey gets a call from your new customer (Komputer Kidz). Apparently, software sales have been doing really well at both locations. The buyer just wanted Rey to know the company would soon be placing another large order.

- Rey decides to order 50 each of the titles purchased by Komputer Kidz earlier in the month ("Math" and "Grammar") from Computer Supply House at a total cost of $4,100.00.

✓ He also sees on the **Inventory Stock Status Report** that the quantity on hand of "Space" is below the reorder point. He orders six of them from Software Design at a total cost of $9,480.00.

✓ You prepare the purchase orders for Rey's orders from Computer Supply House and Software Design (PO 220 and 221).

12/28/17

✓ You prepare and mail January's $1,500 rent check (#2478) to your landlord (Retail Space). [**TIP:** Software 2 Go prepares monthly financial statements that it submits to the bank. The matching (expense recognition) principle applies here. You may need to create a new account.]

✓ You also pay all bills due by 1/12/18 and all bills with discounts expiring on or before 1/12/18.

- Don't forget to take all discounts **and any available credits**.
- There should be two bills (two checks) for a total payment of $5,286.72.
- Let QuickBooks assign check numbers. Last check number 2480.

Check numbers 12/31
    Checking account balance $40,999.42
    Inventory $46,093.50
    Accounts payable $225.00
    Net income (December) $14,742.50

REPORTS TO CREATE FOR ASSIGNMENT 6A

All reports should be in portrait orientation; fit to one page wide.

- Journal (12/1–12/31):
  - Transaction types: Check, Bill, Bill Credit, Bill Payment.
  - Put in date order.
  - Include Type, Date, Num, Name, Memo, Account, Debit, and Credit columns only.
- Inventory Stock Status by Item Summary Report as of 12/31:
  - Include columns for Item Description, Pref Vendor, Reorder Pt (Min), On Hand, Order, On PO only.
    - Use the separator bars to remove unnecessary columns.
- Unpaid Bills Detail as of 12/31.
- Open Purchase Orders as of 12/31. (To get open purchase orders as of 12/31, leave the **From** date field blank and enter "12/31/17" in the **To** date field.)

Assignment 6B

The Abacus Shop

Background information from Chapter 5: You are one of three owners of The Abacus Shop, a small retail store specializing in books and supplies for accountants. You have been in business for a few years and, although the operation has been profitable, you and the other owners would like to grow the business a bit this year. You have hired an outside accountant, Martin Schmidt, to help you develop a business plan. The business is a corporation with a 12/31 year-end.

The owners share business responsibilities.

- Marvena Smith runs retail operations at the shop and handles all merchandise purchasing.
- Brandon Nguyen manages sales to the accounting firms.
- You handle all the accounting and administrative functions.

The company's primary regular customers are accounting firms in Sacramento. Credit terms for these customers are 2%/10, Net 30.

You also sell to walk-in customers (cash/checks or credit cards only). Cash and checks are held in the safe and deposited once a week, on Fridays. Credit cards receipts are batched and transmitted to the merchant bank (Bank of Sutterville) every Friday. It generally takes one business day for the bank to process the receipts and deposit the funds in The Abacus Shop's account. Pocket Bank charges a fee of 2% of the credit card total.

In September, the buyer for Sactown College Bookstore called Marvena and asked about purchasing specialty textbooks from The Abacus Shop. The bookstore is understaffed and overcrowded and would like Abacus to handle some of the accounting course textbook orders. The margin will be smaller than normal for Abacus but the volume is good, so the three of you agree to accept the bookstore's order. The textbooks for spring semester arrived on 9/30.

Your current inventory includes financial analysis software, calculators, accounting books, desk lamps, high-quality stationary paper, and, of course, the textbooks. All items are taxable.

You took out a loan from Pocket Bank when you first started the business. The balance at 9/30/17 is $3,556.44. The monthly payment (due on the 30th of each month) is $129 (including interest). The interest rate on the note is 9%.

You rent the shop for $800 per month.

10/2/17

✓ You pay the October rent ($800) to your landlord, Retail Properties (use check #1916).

✓ Marvena hands you a bill for merchandise (inventory) received from Commercial Supplies today. The shipment included 3 standard calculators (partial shipment) and 2 desk lamps **originally ordered on PO# 157**.

  • The vendor reference number is 73734. The total due is $140. (Bill is dated 10/2. Terms are Net 15.)

✓ You review your unpaid bills report and notice that the early payment discounts for the outstanding bills due to Presley Publishing and Accounting Solutions are expiring. You write the checks (net of the discount) and get them in the mail before you leave for the day.

  • You set up an account called "Purchase discounts" (**cost of goods sold** account type) for tracking vendor discounts.

  • Total for both checks is $6,200.80. You let QuickBooks assign the check numbers. Last check number should be 1918.

10/4/17

✓ Marvena has reviewed the inventory stock status report and is ready to place some orders. She asks you to prepare purchase orders as follows:

  • The Paper Company—20 cartons of stationary paper: PO #181, $1,520 total.

  • Commercial Supplies—12 standard calculators, 15 deluxe calculators, and 5 desk lamps: PO #182, $890 total

  • Presley Publishing—8 each of all **regular** books **except** the "How to Pass Accounting Without Studying": PO #183, $512 total. (There are no textbooks in this order.)

✓ You decide to call both The Paper Company and Commercial Supplies about their credit terms. Both agree to give you terms of 2%/10, net 30 on all future bills. You edit the vendor records appropriately.

  • Ignore any messages about closed periods. QuickBooks won't change terms on existing **bills**.

✓ You receive a $450 bill in the mail, dated 10/4, from the "Accounting Journal" for advertising in the October issue. The bill reference number is A9888. The bill is due on 10/18.

✓ You drive down to Supplies to Go and purchase a new printer ($210) and a supply of copy and printer paper to have on hand ($185), on account. The bill (#5222) for $395 is dated 10/4. Terms are 2%/10, Net 30. (Accept the change in terms if prompted.)

  • You expect the printer to have a two-year life.

10/5/17

✓ Marvena hands you the packing slip for The Paper Company order that was received today (PO 181). She has checked the shipment and all 20 cartons were received. No bill was received with the shipment.

✓ You pay all bills due on or before 10/17 **plus** any bills with early payment discounts expiring before 10/17. [**TIP:** There should be 6 bills (two with discounts) totaling $23,164.60. There should be five checks. Let QuickBooks assign the check numbers. The last check number should be 1923.]

  • Discounts on inventory purchases should be credited to "Purchase Discounts." Discounts on non-inventory purchases should be credited to "Miscellaneous Expense."

10/6/17

✓ Brandon and Marvena have decided to expand the product line. Brandon has been getting requests from the local CPA firms for audit bags. Marvena has had a number of store customers ask about briefcases and computer bags. They have found the following supplier:

- Business Bags to Go

  1390 Freestone Road

  San Diego, CA 92104

  Main Phone: (619) 378-5432

  Terms: 2%/10, Net 30

- You decide to set up a "header category" called "Leather Goods" on the **Item** list to manage the new line of items. Remember, a header **item** is just a tool for organizing the **item** list. It is not an actual product.

- Each **inventory part item** will have a reorder point of 3 (except "Leather Goods") and will use "COGS-Accounting Supplies" and "Accounting Supplies Sales" as the COGS and Income accounts, respectively. Inventory will be recorded in the "Inventory" account. All **items** are taxable. The preferred vendor is Business Bags to Go.

- New **items** (**subitems** of Leather Goods) are:

  ○ Audit (description—audit bag)—expected cost $225; selling price $350.

  ○ Briefcase (description—leather briefcase)—expected cost $195; selling price $299.

  ○ Computer (description—computer bag)—expected cost $124; selling price $199.

- You prepare the first purchase order (#184) for 5 of each new product. The PO totals $2,720.00.

10/9/17

✓ You receive the bill for the paper received on 10/5 from The Paper Company. The bill (#0124567) totals $1,520. The terms are 2%/10, Net 30. The bill is dated 10/9.

- Remember: The change QuickBooks is referring to in the prompt when you save the transaction is the change from **item receipt** to **bill**.

10/12/17

✓ You receive the following bills in the mail:

- Sacramento Utilities October bill (for heat and light) #9976—$285.60, dated 10/12 due 11/11

- Horizon Phone October bill #121-775 for $194.28, dated 10/12 due 11/11.

✓ Marvena lets you know that she has received the following shipments on purchase orders dated 10/4:

- Commercial Supplies—Received all items ordered on 10/4 (PO 182).

  ○ Bill #87755 for $890 was included. Credit terms 2%/10, Net 30. Bill dated 10/12.

- Presley Publishing—Received all items ordered on 10/4 (PO 183) except for 2 copies of "How They Cooked the Books."

  ○ Bill #1238734 for $464 was included. Credit terms 1%/10, Net 30. Bill dated 10/12.

10/16/17

✓ Marvena lets you know that she has decided to return all of the unsold "How to Pass Accounting Without Studying" books (customers have been very disappointed!) and all the unsold textbooks (Sactown College is changing textbooks next semester). She will be returning them on 10/17:

- 5 "How to Pass Accounting Without Studying" books.
- 21 "Fundamentals of Financial Accounting" textbooks.
- 11 "Introduction to Managerial Accounting" textbooks.

✓ You delete the reorder points (remove, don't change to 0) for these products (and the "Cost Accounting" textbook) so they don't show up for reorder on the **Inventory Stock Status** report.

✓ Marvena also asks you to close out PO 157 to Commercial Supplies. She has contacted the supplier to say she doesn't need the two backordered standard calculators.

10/17/17

✓ Vendor credit memos are received for the books returned by Marvena. (See previous 10/16 entry for breakdown of textbooks returned.)

- Presley Publishing—CM#12399 for $80, dated 10/17, for the 5 "How to Pass Accounting Without Studying" books.
- Academic Texts Co—CM#4002-3 for $1,489.50, dated 10/17, for the 32 textbooks:
  - Academic Texts Co charged a 10% restocking fee. You decide to charge the $165.50 to "Miscellaneous Expense." [**TIP:** The restocking fee will show up as a negative on the expense tab since the fee reduces the credit allowed by the vendor. (A "negative credit" is really a debit, right?!)]

10/18/17

✓ The remaining two books on PO #183 are received from Presley Publishing. Bill #1238735 for $48 dated 10/18 was included. Credit terms were 1%/10, Net 30.

✓ Marvena also received the order from Business Bags to Go (the packing slip is dated 10/18). All but one audit bag is received. (The total amount received is $2,495.) The bill is expected to arrive in a few days.

✓ You pay all bills due on or before 10/25 **plus** any bills with early payment discounts expiring on or before 10/25.

- You apply the outstanding credit memo from Presley Publishing to invoice #1238734. (Take the early payment discount on the **original** invoice amount ($464), not on the amount currently due. The credit memo applied is not related to the products purchased on invoice #1238734.)
- There should be four checks totaling $3,191.16.
- The last check number should be #1927.

10/24/17

✓ Marvena lets you know that she returned the broken calculator (deluxe model) that the accountant from Price, Warwick and Coopers returned in mid-October (Chapter 5 transaction). You call Commercial Supplies and the accountant faxes you CM#12455 for $30, dated 10/24.

✓ You receive the bill from Business Bags to Go for the items received on 10/18 from PO #184. The bill (#1867) totaled $2,475 and was dated 10/24. The cost for the audit bags was lower than expected ($220 per bag instead of $225).

- Select "No" if prompted to change the **item** record.

10/25/17

✓ You have your monthly staff meeting today. You decide to bring the monthly dividend checks to distribute ($6,000 for each owner). It's been a great month, so the distribution is a little larger than usual. There should be three checks (1928–1930). (Don't forget yourself!)

- Remember: The Abacus Shop is a corporation. In a corporation, distributions to owners (other than salaries or expense reimbursements) are dividends.

✓ The three of you meet at Dick's Diner. Lunch costs $71, and you pay with check #1931.

- You charge the lunch to "Staff Meetings." (The "Labor costs" category includes any costs related to employees, not just wages.)

✓ Marvena reviews the Inventory Stock Status report when she gets back from the meeting.

- Marvena places an order with Accounting Solutions for 4 Financial Analysis Software products. You create PO # 185 for $3,200.

✓ You receive a bill (#3330) for $3,000 in the mail from your external accounting firm, Les & Schmidt. The bill, dated 10/25, is for work Martin Schmidt did for The Abacus Shop in October related to the development of a new business plan. The bill is due in 30 days. [**TIP:** This is a professional service.]

✓ You pay all bills due on or before 11/3 **plus** any bills with early payment discounts expiring before 11/4. (There should be 3 checks totalling $6,273.02. The last check #1934.)

10/30/17

✓ You write a check (#1935) to Pocket Bank for the $129 monthly installment on the loan. You pay interest through 10/31. (Remember: Interest is at 9%. Round interest expense to the nearest penny.)

✓ You plan to take a few days off, so you prepare and mail the November rent check (#1936) to your landlord (Retail Properties). [**TIP:** The Abacus Shop prepares monthly financial statements that it submits to the bank. The matching (expense recognition) principle applies here.] You may need to create a new account.

Check numbers 10/31
Checking account balance **$64,806.11**
Inventory **$8,182.27**
Accounts payable **$1,960.38**
Net income (October) **$41,587.05**

REPORTS TO CREATE FOR ASSIGNMENT 6B

All reports should be in portrait orientation; fit to one page wide.

- Journal (10/1–10/31):
  - Transaction types: Check, Bill, Bill Credit, Bill Payment.
  - Put in date order.
  - Remove **Trans #** and **Adj** columns.

- Inventory Stock Status by Item Report as of 10/31:
  - Remove the **Max**, **For Assemblies**, **Next Deliv**, **Available**, **Reorder Qty**, and **Sales/Week** columns using the separator bars between the column headings.

- Unpaid Bills Detail as of 10/31.

- Open Purchase Orders as of 10/31.
  - [**TIP:** Leave the **From** field blank and enter 10/31 in the **To** field.]

End-of-Period Procedures

(Merchandising Company)

After completing Chapter 7, you should be able to:

1. Adjust inventory quantities.

2. Manage and pay sales taxes.

3. Record cash receipts not related to normal sales transactions.

4. Record transfers between bank accounts.

5. Inactivate and merge accounts.

6. Add comments to reports.

7. Verify QuickBooks data.

Objectives

All of the "end-of-period" procedures we covered in Chapter 4 apply to merchandising companies as well as service companies. Bank accounts have to be reconciled. Adjusting journal entries have to be made. Remember: End-of-period procedures are focused on making sure the financial records are as accurate as possible. The financial statements should give internal and external users a fair picture of:

- The operations of the company for the period (profit and loss statement).

- The financial position of the company at the end of the period (balance sheet).

There are a few additional procedures unique to merchandising companies that we cover in this chapter.

- Inventory adjustments.

- Managing sales taxes.

We also look at a few additional procedures and QuickBooks features not covered in previous chapters:

- Recording non-customer cash receipts.

- Recording bank transfers.

- Inactivating and merging accounts.

- Adding comments to reports.

- Verifying data.

ADJUSTING INVENTORY

As you know, QuickBooks features a perpetual inventory tracking system for **inventory part items** so quantities are automatically updated when goods are received, sold, or returned.

If life were perfect, the inventory quantities in QuickBooks would **always** equal inventory quantities on hand (physically in the store or warehouse). Unfortunately, we know that that isn't always the case. Differences can occur because of:

- Theft.

- Unrecorded transactions (sales, item receipts, returns by customer or to vendor).

- Damaged goods.

In addition to needing to know the quantity on hand for valuing inventory, companies must have an accurate record of how many of each of their products they have available to sell. That's part of a good inventory management system. I'm guessing a few of you have asked a clerk about a book you can't find on the shelf at your favorite bookstore. The clerk looks the book up in the store's computer system and it says that they should have two in stock. You go back to the shelves with the clerk and neither of you can find the book. It may just be misplaced or it may have been stolen, but both you and the clerk have wasted time looking for it and you're a disappointed customer. The more accurate the inventory records, the smoother the operation and the more accurate the financial statements. So, periodically, the inventory on hand is physically counted, and the inventory records are adjusted as necessary.

Counts can be taken at any point during a year but are usually taken, at a minimum, at the end of the year. (Companies that need audited financial statements **must** take a count, with auditors present, at the end of the year.) Counts are frequently taken more often (quarterly, for example). It's usually a big job to take a physical inventory count, so many companies don't count inventory monthly. If there hasn't been a history of significant inventory adjustments, taking an annual physical inventory is probably sufficient. (If you're in the bookstore business and you have lots of books on shelves, you might want to consider more frequent counts!)

To get a good inventory count, it's usually best to take the count when products aren't moving (not being sold or received). Many companies take inventory counts after closing or on weekends. Counters are given a list of products and the unit of measure that should be used to count the products (units, cartons, pounds, etc.). As a control, the count sheets should not list the expected quantity. Why? For one thing, it's just too easy to see what you think you **should** see (i.e., what the count sheet says)!

Once the physical is taken, the count sheets are compared to the accounting records. Significant variations should be investigated. Documentation (particularly packing slips) related to transactions occurring close to the count date can often provide useful information. Goods might have been received or shipped out earlier or later than the customer invoice or vendor bill dates used in the accounting system. In practice, physical inventory counts usually involve a lot of recounts.

Once the company is confident that it has a good count and all known transactions have been recorded, the accounting records are adjusted to the count.

In QuickBooks, count sheets are accessed through the **Inventory Activities** under **Vendors** option on the main menu bar:

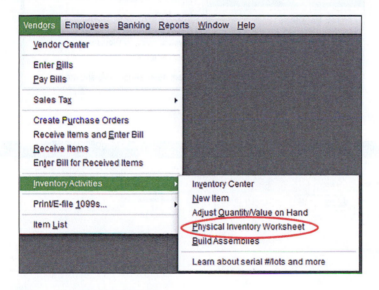

The worksheet looks something like this:

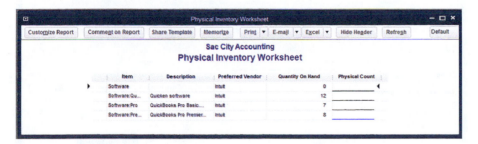

The worksheet can easily be modified using the **Customize Report** button. Remember, for an accurate count, the **Quantity On Hand** column should be removed.

HINT: You might have noticed that the date for the worksheet can't be changed. The count sheets **must** be printed on the day the count is taken.

After the count sheets are completed, the listed counts are compared to the inventory quantities in QuickBooks. As noted earlier, recounts are normally requested if the counts vary significantly from the perpetual records.

Once the company determines that the count is accurate, any necessary inventory adjustments are recorded through the **Adjust Quantity/Value on Hand** form:

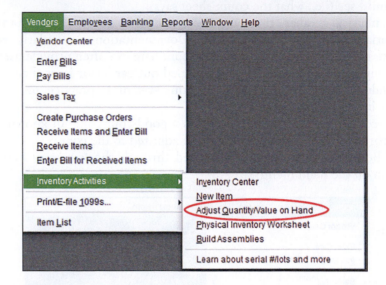

The new window looks like this:

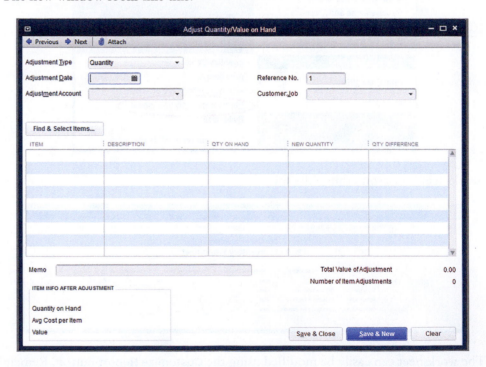

The **Adjustment Type** would normally be "Quantity."

> **BEHIND THE SCENES** Inventory values can also be adjusted. The only time a user would normally be adjusting the **value** of inventory would be to comply with the "**lower of cost or market**" rules under GAAP.

The **Adjustment Date** must be the date the count was taken.

The **Adjustment Account** is the choice of management. Most companies debit or credit inventory adjustments to a **cost of goods sold** account **type**. The offset account is, of course, the inventory (asset) account.

The **inventory part items** to be adjusted are selected using the **Find & Select Items** button in the upper left section of the window. The selection screen looks something like this:

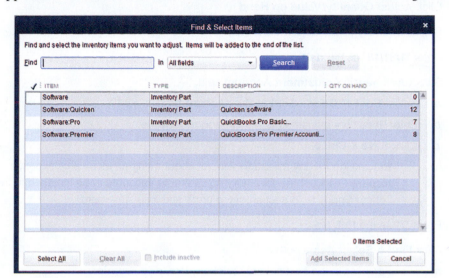

Once you've **added** the selected items, the **Adjust Quantity/Items on Hand** screen changes to look something like this:

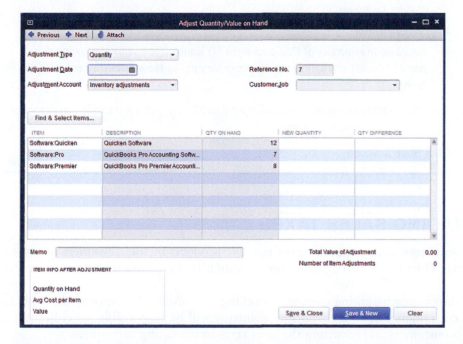

To adjust inventory, the correct quantity must be entered in the **New Quantity** column. QuickBooks will display the new inventory value for the highlighted item in the bottom

Lower of cost or market A measurement method that, when applied to inventory, provides for ending inventory to be valued on the balance sheet at the lower of its acquisition cost or current replacement cost.

left corner of the screen. QuickBooks will display the total adjustment to inventory (for all items) in the bottom right corner of the screen.

Adjusting inventory for Sac City Accounting.
(Inventory was counted on 1/31. There were 11 Quicken, 7 Pro, and 7 Premier packages on hand.)

1. Click **Vendors**.

2. Click **Inventory Activities**.

3. Click **Adjust Quantity/Value on Hand**.

4. Select **Quantity** as the **adjustment type**.

5. Enter "1/31/18" as the **date**.

6. Select **Add new** in **Adjustment Account** field.

   a.   Select **Cost of Goods Sold** as the **account type**.

   b.   Enter "Inventory adjustments" as the **account name**.

   c.   Click **Save & Close**.

      i.   You can ignore any message you get about using an income or expense account. We want the Inventory Adjustments accounts to be included in the Cost of Goods Sold section of the profit and loss statement.

7. Enter "7" as the **Ref. No.**

8. Click **Find & Select Items** button.

   a.   Place a check in the field next to **Quicken, Pro, and Premier**.

   b.   Click **Add Selected Items**.

9. Enter in the **New Quantity** column:

   a.   "11" for **Quicken**.

   b.   "7" for **Premier**.

   c.   Because the number of **Pro** packages (7) equals the number showing as on hand in QuickBooks, no entry is necessary in the **New Quantity** column for that item.

10. **Total Value of Adjustment** field should equal $275.87. (It's a decrease in the value, so the amount shows as a negative.)

11. Click **Save & Close**.

MANAGING SALES TAXES

Many states levy a tax on purchases of tangible products by the consumers (users) of those products. The tax is called a "sales" tax because it is charged to the customer at the point of sale.

Unless a merchandising company is selling to a reseller (a company that will, in turn, sell to consumers), the merchandising company will be responsible for collecting the tax from its customers and remitting the sales taxes to the taxing authorities.

You might remember that when you set up an **item**, QuickBooks requires you to indicate whether the **item** is taxable or not. In Chapter 4, we went over setting up various

tax codes and **sales tax items**. To sum up what we know already about sales taxes and QuickBooks:

- Whether or not QuickBooks calculates tax on a **particular** charge on an **invoice** or **sales receipt** is determined by two things:
  - First, is the customer a consumer or a reseller?
    - QuickBooks relies on the **tax code** associated with the **customer** to determine this.
  - Second, if the customer is the consumer, does the charge represent a sale of a taxable item?
    - QuickBooks relies on the **tax code** associated with the **item** to determine this.
- The **amount** of tax QuickBooks charges on a taxable item is determined by the **sales tax item** associated with the **customer**.
  - Remember: A **sales tax item** must be set up for every taxing jurisdiction.

The sales tax liability (for taxable sales) is increased automatically when an **invoice** or **sales receipt** is completed.

Sales taxes are remitted to taxing authorities on a periodic basis—generally annually, quarterly, or monthly, depending on the size of the company. Remember, the tax is on the consumer, but the responsibility to collect and remit the tax is the responsibility of the seller. In most states, sellers are responsible for remitting to the tax authorities the amount they **should** have charged (which, hopefully, agrees with the amount they actually **did** charge!).

> **BEHIND THE SCENES** In most cases, a company is required to report and remit sales taxes when the tax is **charged** to the customer. Some states allow a company to remit the tax when it's **collected** from the customer. The default in QuickBooks is the "charged" date (the date of the **invoice** or **sales receipt**). The default can be changed to the "collected" date in the **Sales Tax** option on the **Preferences** menu. (The **Preferences** menu is accessed through **Edit** on the main menu bar.) In the following example, and in the homework assignments, the default (charged) date will be used.

At the end of the tax-reporting period, a report should be prepared and reviewed, detailing sales and sales taxes charged, by taxing jurisdiction.

The **Sales Tax Liability** and **Sales Tax Revenue Summary** reports are accessed through the **Vendors & Payables** option on the **Reports** dropdown menu (main menu bar):

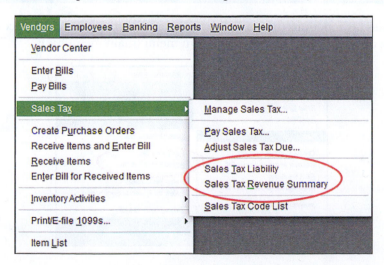

The **Sales Tax Liability** report looks something like this:

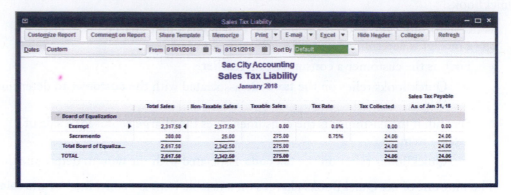

> ✳ **HINT:** QuickBooks will warn you if there are tax **items** on the report with no sales tax rate. If the **item** represents exempt sales, that warning can be ignored.

This report lists taxable and non-taxable sales by jurisdiction. As you can see, the tax rate and tax liability amounts are also included. This report would be used to prepare the various tax reports that are filed with the state and local tax agencies.

> **BEHIND THE SCENES** For control purposes, the company should carefully review its tax reports. Remember, QuickBooks is reporting what happened, not what **should** have happened.

The **Sales Tax Revenue Summary** report looks something like this:

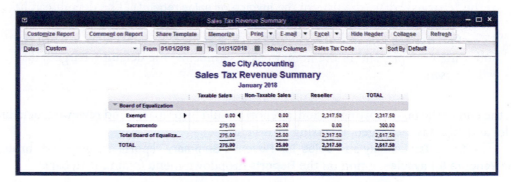

Other sales tax functions (like tax adjustments and payments) are also accessed through the **Sales Tax** option on the **Vendors** dropdown menu (main menu bar):

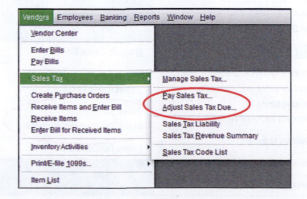

The tax liability can be adjusted through **Adjust Sales Tax Due**. The screen looks like this:

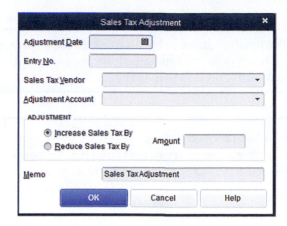

The liability might need to be adjusted because:

- An incorrect rate was input into QuickBooks.

- A specific customer was inadvertently over- or undercharged for sales tax.

- A customer took an early payment discount on a taxable sale.

- The company is located in a state that levies an additional tax (called an excise tax) on the **seller**.

> **BEHIND THE SCENES** Excise taxes are generally based on gross sales revenue. Excise taxes cannot be entered as a **sales tax item** because they are not charged to the customer. They are an expense of the seller.

The date of the adjustment is normally the ending date of the sales tax period. Adjustments due to corrections of errors would normally be charged to a miscellaneous expense or income account (hopefully, this doesn't happen very often!). Adjustments for excise taxes would normally be charged to a business tax expense account.

> **BEHIND THE SCENES** If a customer was overcharged, the company would generally want to reimburse him or her, if possible, by issuing a check or credit memo. If a customer was undercharged, the company might choose to **invoice** him or her for the tax. In that case, the company would need to set up an **Other Charge item** for uncollected tax. That **item** would, of course, be non-taxable.

Sales taxes are paid through the **Pay Sales Tax** option on the **Sales Tax** dropdown menu in the **Vendors** menu on the main menu bar. The screen looks something like this:

The check date and the tax period ending date (**show sales tax due through** date) must be entered.

> **HINT:** The tax liability can also be adjusted directly through this screen by clicking on the **Adjust** button. The screen that would appear is identical to the **Sales Tax Adjustment** screen shown earlier.

PRACTICE
EXERCISE

Paying sales taxes in Sac City Accounting.
(Sac City prepares the state sales tax return from QuickBooks sales data. According to the completed return, the actual tax was $24.07, not $24.06 as calculated by QuickBooks.)

1. Adjust the tax liability.
    a. Click **Vendors** on the main menu bar.
    b. Click **Sales Tax**.
    c. Click **Adjust Sales Tax Due**.
        i.   Enter "1/31/18" as the **Adjustment Date**.
        ii. Enter "8" as the **Entry No.**
        iii. Select **Board of Equalization** as the **sales tax vendor**.
        iv. Select **Miscellaneous Expense** as the **Adjustment Account**.
        v.   Select **Increase Sales Taxes By**.
        vi. Enter the **amount** as ".01".
    d. Click **OK**.

2. Pay the tax:
    a. Click **Vendors** on the main menu bar.
    b. Click **Sales Tax**.
    c. Click **Pay Sales Tax**.
        i.   Enter **Check Date** as 1/31/18.
        ii. Enter "1/31" in **Show sales tax due through** field.
        iii. Use "1022" for the **starting check no.**
        iv. Select (check) the **Sacramento** line and the $0.01 adjustment line.
            1. There is no amount due to West Sacramento because there were no product sales to that jurisdiction during the month.
        v.   Total to pay should equal $24.07.
            1. You may need to use the tab key to see the amounts due.
    d. Click **OK**.

QuickCheck
7-1

> What's the underlying journal entry for the sale, on account, of a taxable item? (Answer at end of chapter.)

ENTERING CASH RECEIPTS NOT RELATED TO NORMAL SALES TRANSACTIONS

In companies, most cash receipts come from customers (at least we hope they do!). As you know, cash receipts from customers are entered as **Sales Receipt** or **Payment** transaction types.

There are other sources of cash though:

- Borrowings.
- Sales of company stock.
- Sales of property or equipment.

When cash unrelated to sales transactions is received, the amounts can be entered in the following ways:

- Directly into a **Deposit** form.
- Through a general journal entry.

The most efficient way is to record these receipts is to enter them directly as a **Deposit**. The **Deposit** form can be accessed through **Record Deposits** on the Home page:

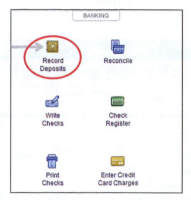

If there are no pending undeposited funds, the initial screen will look like this:

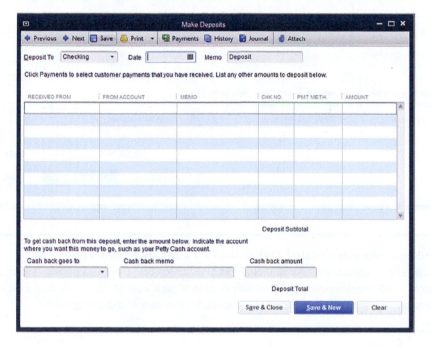

> **BEHIND THE SCENES** Remember, deposits should be grouped to correspond to the actual bank deposits. If a non-customer receipt is being deposited with customer receipts, it should be recorded in the same **make deposits** form. The customer receipts should be selected and added first. Non-customer cash receipts would be added to the final screen **after** the customer receipts were selected for deposit.

The appropriate **Bank** account and deposit date must be selected. For non-customer receipts, the payer's name should be selected in the **Received From** field, and the account to be credited should be selected in the **From Account** field.

Multiple entries can be recorded for one non-customer receipt. The **Deposit Subtotal** must, of course, equal the amount that's being deposited. An example is provided as part of the following Practice Exercise. The final screen from that exercise looks something like this:

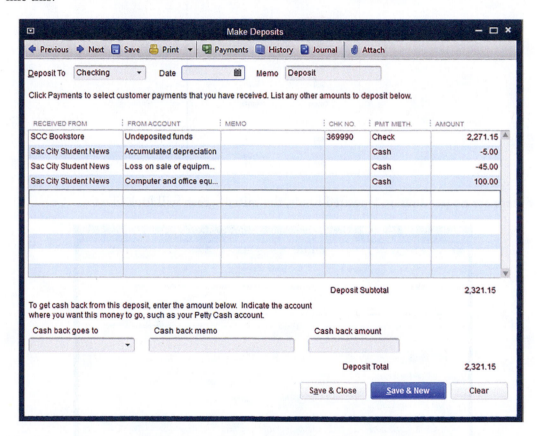

(continued)

PRACTICE EXERCISE

Recording a non-sales related cash receipt for Sac City Accounting.

(Sac City sold a used printer for $50 cash on 1/16/18 to "Sac City News." The printer originally cost $100. Accumulated depreciation at date of sale was $5. Sac City had a $45 loss on the sale. Remember: The journal entry to record the sale of the printer is:

	Cash	50.00	
	Accumulated depreciation	5.00	
	Loss on sale of equipment	45.00	
	Computer and office equipment		100.00

The debit to cash is automatically entered as the deposit total, but all the rest of the accounts must be individually entered on the form.

1. Click **Record Deposits** on the Home page.

2. On the **Payment to Deposit** screen, mark the SCC Bookstore receipt.

3. Click **OK**.

4. On the **Make Deposit** screen:

   a. Enter "1/16" as the **date**.

   b. On the line below the SCC Bookstore payment, select **Sac City Student News** in the **Received From** column.

      i. Select **Accumulated Depreciation** in the **From Account** column.

      ii. Select **Cash** as the **PMT. METH.**

      iii. Enter "5" as a negative in the **amount** column. You're debiting the accumulated depreciation account to remove the depreciation related to the printer. Positive numbers on deposits represent credits; negative numbers represent debits.

   c. On a new line, select **Sac City Student News** in the **Received From** column.

      i. Select **Add New** in **From Account** column.

         1. Create a new account—**Other expense** as the **account type**.

         2. Enter "Loss on sale of equipment" as the **account name**.

         3. Click **Save & Close**.

      ii. Select **Cash** as the **PMT. METH.**

      iii. Enter "45" as a negative in the **amount** column.

         1. Remember: You want to debit the Loss on sale of equipment account.

   d. On a new line, select **Sac City Student News** in the **Received From** column.

      i. Select **Computer and office equipment** in the **From Account** column.

      ii. Select **Cash** as the **PMT. METH.**

      iii. Enter "100" in the **Amount column**.

         1. You're crediting the asset account to remove the cost of the printer.

5. Make sure the deposit total equals $2,321.15. (Sac City received $2,271.15 from the bookstore and $50 from the sale of the printer.)

6. Click **Save & Close**.

Why was the "Loss on sale of equipment" account set up as an **other expense** account type? (Answer at end of chapter.)	**Quick**Check **7-2**

RECORDING BANK TRANSFERS

Many companies maintain more than one bank account. Other than the general checking account, a company will frequently have a separate checking account for payroll. It might also open a savings or a money market account as a way to earn some interest on funds not needed for immediate operations.

If the accounts are with the same bank, transfers between accounts can generally be made either electronically (through the bank's website) or by phone.

In QuickBooks, electronic or phone transfers are recorded through using the **Transfer** form. The **Transfer** form is accessed through the **Transfer Funds** option on the **Banking** menu (main menu bar). The screen looks like this:

The **Date** and **Transfer Amount** must be entered. The account selected in the **Transfer Funds From** field represents the account to be credited. The account selected in the **Transfer Funds To** field represents the account to be debited.

PRACTICE EXERCISE

Transferring funds between accounts for Sac City Accounting.
(Sac City decides to open a money market account at America's Bank with a $500 transfer from checking.)

1. Open a new account.
   a. Click **Lists**.
   b. Click **Chart of Accounts**.
   c. Click **Account** (bottom left of window).
   d. Select **New**.
   e. Select **Bank** as the **account type**.
   f. Click **Continue**.
   g. Enter "Money market" as the **account name**.
   h. Click **Save & Close**. (Ignore any messages about additional services.)
   i. Exit out of the **Chart of Accounts** window.

2. Transfer funds from the checking account to the money market account.
   a. Click **Banking**.
   b. Click **Transfer Funds**.
   c. Enter "1/31/18" as the **Date**.
   d. Select **Checking** as the **Transfer Funds From** account.
   e. Select **Money market** as the **Transfer Funds To** account.
   f. Enter "500" in the **Transfer Amount** field.

3. Click **Save & Close**.

INACTIVATING AND MERGING GENERAL LEDGER ACCOUNTS

Companies generally set up their initial chart of accounts based on expected activities and informational needs. As companies grow and change, the chart of accounts usually expands. Often, it expands substantially! An effective chart of accounts contains only those accounts that provide useful detail for owners and managers.

Periodically, a company should take a look at the structure of its chart of accounts to make sure it still meets the needs of the company. We already know how to group accounts. Accounts can be moved from one group to another (within the same **account type**), and "header" accounts can be added or deleted. But what do we do with accounts that are no longer needed or useful?

You cannot, of course, delete accounts that have activity. It doesn't matter that an account hasn't had activity in the last five years. If it ever had activity, it's there to stay. (Of course, you could go back and change all transactions that contained a distribution to that account, but that might be quite a job!)

QuickBooks provides two tools for managing unused accounts with previous activity:

- Inactivating the account:
    - Retains the account detail but restricts the use of the account.
        - An inactive account isn't available for use in future transactions.
        - It's also unavailable for filtering or searching.
    - An inactive account can be reactivated if necessary.
    - Inactive accounts **will** appear on reports when appropriate.

- Merging the account:
    - Deletes an account by transferring all the activity in the account to another existing account.
    - Merging an account is permanent. It can't be undone!

Inactivating An Account

Inactivating the account would be the best option when a company needs to maintain detail about past transactions. Let's use an example. Let's say that five years ago, a barbershop sold shampoo in addition to cutting hair. It has since discontinued selling products because of the high cost of maintaining inventory. It no longer needs the inventory account or the cost of goods sold account. The shop might, however, need that information in the future. That might be the case if it is ever audited or if it decides to reconsider merchandise sales.

To inactivate an account in QuickBooks, the **chart of accounts list** must be open. The selected account is highlighted. On the **Account** dropdown menu (bottom left of the screen), the option **Make Account Inactive** is selected:

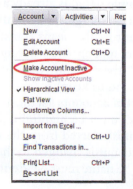

Once an account has been inactivated, it is no longer visible on the default **Chart of Accounts** screen.

To make inactive accounts visible, check the **Include inactive** box at the bottom of the **chart of accounts screen**. An ✖ to the left of the account name indicates all inactive accounts. The screen looks something like-this:

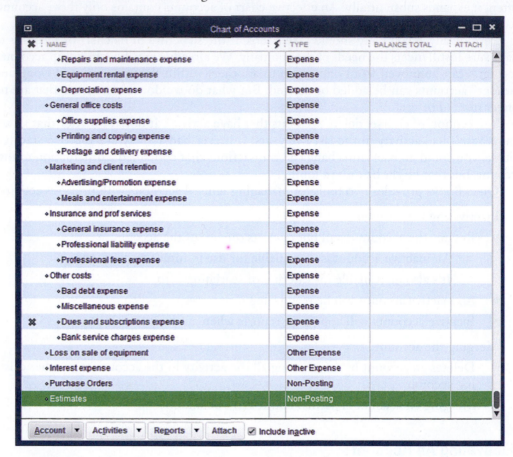

To reactivate an account, highlight the account in the **Chart of Accounts** screen and select the **Make Account Active** option on the **Account** drop down menu (bottom left of screen).

Merging Accounts

Merging an account would be the best option when an account does not (and maybe never did) provide useful detail. Let's use another example. Let's say the accountant for a barbershop set up separate general ledger accounts for every **service item**. There was an account for shampoos, another for haircuts, another for beard trims, etc. Those accounts were unnecessary because the revenue detail is already available by using the **Sales by Item** reports. It would make sense, then, to merge some or all of those accounts.

Remember, merging an account really means transferring activity out of the account you no longer wish to use **into** an appropriate existing account. There needs to be two accounts: the "transferor account" (the account you want to eliminate) and the "transferee account" (the account that you intend to keep).

To merge an account, the **chart of accounts list** must be open. The "transferor account" (the account you want to eliminate) must be highlighted.

The menu option **Edit Account** is selected from the **Account** dropdown menu (bottom left of screen). The **Name** of the account is changed to the name of the "transferee account" (the account you intend to keep). The name must be **identical** or you'll create a new account.

When you click **OK**, QuickBooks gives you the following message:

Yes should be selected. The screen looks like this if there are closed period transactions in the account to be merged:

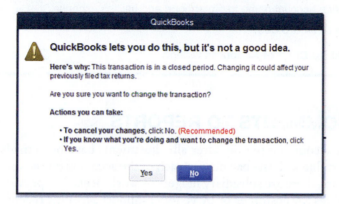

Because this action can't be reversed, QuickBooks gives you a final chance to cancel the merge. **Yes** should be selected if you're sure you want to merge the accounts.

Managing the chart of accounts in Sac City.

(The Dues and Subscriptions account is inactivated, and the Utilities expense and Telephone expense accounts are merged.)

1. Click on **Lists** (main menu bar).

2. Click on **Chart of Accounts**.

3. Inactivate an account.

    a. Highlight **Dues and subscriptions expense** (under **Other Costs**).

    b. Click **Account**.

    c. Click **Make Account Inactive**.

4. Merge an account.

    a. Highlight **Utilities expense**.

    b. Click **Account**.

    c. Click **Edit Account**.

    d. Enter "Telephone expense" in the **Name** field.

        i. Make sure you enter the name exactly as noted. If you have any differences, QuickBooks will simply change the name.

    e. Click **Save & Close**.

PRACTICE EXERCISE

(continued)

f.   Select **Yes** at the prompt to merge.

   i.   If this prompt doesn't appear, you probably made a spelling error when you entered the account name. Highlight the account and go back to step *4b*.

g.   Select **Yes** at the final prompt.

h.   As a final step, change the name of the remaining account to "Telephone and utilities expense."

   i.   Highlight "Telephone expense".

   ii.   Right click and select **Edit Account**.

  iii.   Change account name to "Telephone and utilities expense."

  iv.   Click **Save & Close**.

5.   Exit out of the **Chart of Accounts** window.

ADDING COMMENTS TO REPORTS

At the end of an accounting period, after all adjustments have been made, the accountant should be comfortable with the balances in each of the accounts on the financial statements. For many accounts, there are subsidiary ledgers or worksheets that provide documentation. For example, agings (by customer or by vendor) support accounts receivable and accounts payable account balances. Bank reconciliations support cash balances. Sales by item reports provide support for revenue and cost of goods sold amounts.

For other accounts (like prepaid or unearned revenue accounts), there may not be any standard, formal documentation. For control purposes (and in case of memory lapses!), the accountant would want to document the balances in those accounts as well.

QuickBooks has included a feature in all reports that allows the user to add comments to specific items in that report. This feature can be very useful to accountants as part of the end-of-period process. For example, instead of preparing an offline worksheet detailing the components of Prepaid Expenses, the accountant can simply include that detail in the balance sheet for the period by adding a comment next to the Prepaid Expenses account balance.

Other uses of this feature might include:

- Putting a note next to an inventory item on a stock status report, reminding the reader that the item was nearing obsolescence.

- Putting a note next to a purchase order on an open purchase order report, reminding the reader to contact the vendor and determine the status of a backorder.

A report must be open before comments can be added. Clicking **Comment on Report** on the report menu bar opens a new window:

If the comment were being made on a balance sheet, the new window would look something like this:

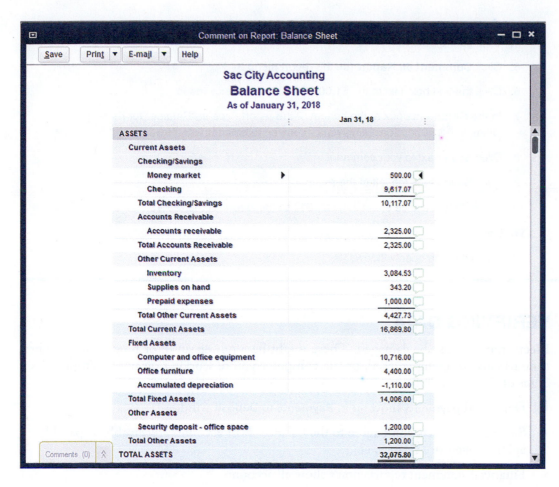

Just to the right of each amount is a small text box. Clicking the text box opens a **comments** box that looks like this:

Multiple comments can be made on the same report. Each comment will automatically be given a number. That number appears in the text box next to the appropriate amount.

Reports that contain comments can be saved with a unique name. Those reports can be accessed later through the **Commented Reports** option on the **Reports** dropdown menu (main menu bar). No changes, other than the name of the report, can be made to commented reports.

Adding a comment to a report.

(Sac City adds a comment to the balance sheet detailing the $1,000 retainer paid to Beverly Okimoto that is included in the Prepaid expenses account.)

1. Click on **Reports** (main menu bar).

2. Click on **Company & Financial**.

3. Select **Balance Sheet Standard**.

(continued)

PRACTICE EXERCISE

4. Change the date to 1/31/18.

5. Click **Comment on Report** (on the report menu bar)

6. Click the text box next to the $1,000.00 in **Prepaid expenses**.

7. In the **Comments** box at the bottom of the report, type in "Retainer for Beverly Okimoto—$1,000. Consulting work expected to be completed by July 31."

8. Click **Save** next to your comment.

9. Click **Save** at the top left of the report.

10. Enter "Final balance sheet January 31" as the **Name** of the report.

11. Click **OK**.

12. Exit out of the open windows.

VERIFYING DATA

Electronic data can be damaged. There might be a power surge or power outage when transactions are being entered, or the computer you're working on might simply crash. Signs of damage include:

- Deposited payments show up in **Payments to Deposit** window.

- Subsidiary reports don't agree to the balance sheet accounts (receivable or payable agings, inventory reports, etc.).

- Financial statement reports don't show all accounts.

This is, of course, one of the main reasons companies do backups. If the company file is damaged, a backup can be restored. Of course, you want to make sure your backups don't contain damaged transactions. Sometimes damage isn't noticed right away. In Chapter 1, doing a **Complete Verification** was recommended when making a backup. This is done to make sure there are no errors in the working file being backed up.

You can also verify data at other times (particularly if and when you first notice problems). The data verification tool is accessed through the **Utilities** option on the **File** menu (main menu bar):

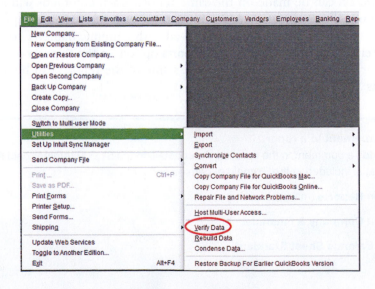

When **Verify Data** is selected, QuickBooks begins searching the working file for damaged transactions. Records of the damaged transactions (called "unexpected conditions" by QuickBooks) are maintained in a log.

If damaged transactions are found, a message will appear asking if you want to **Rebuild Data**. It is highly recommended that you talk to your instructor before choosing that option. Rebuilding data is a complex process and, if done incorrectly, can result in permanent damage to the company file. You would be better off to delete the damaged transaction, restore a backup copy, or contact QuickBooks Technical Support for assistance.

 HINT: To access the log listing any damaged transactions, press the F2 and then the F3 function keys. This opens the Tech help window:

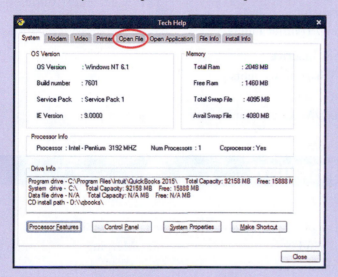

Click the **Open File** tab. Select **QBWIN.LOG** in the **Select a file to open** pane. Click the **Open File** button to view the contents of the log. Any damaged transactions will be reported at the end of the log. Before going any further, contact your instructor. If you can delete the damaged transaction, you should run the **Verify Data** utility again to make sure the file is working properly.

Accounts receivable	XXX	
Cost of goods sold	XXX	
Revenue		XXX
Inventory		XXX
Sales tax payable		XXX

ANSWER TO
QuickCheck
7-1

"Loss on sale of equipment" was set up as an **other expense** account type because losses on sales of property, plant, and equipment are not considered part of operations and aren't reported in the operating expense section of the income statement.

ANSWER TO
QuickCheck
7-2

CHAPTER SHORTCUTS

Adjust inventory quantities

1. Click Vendors/Inventory activities
2. Click Adjust Quantity/Value on Hand

Record payment of sales tax

1. Click Vendors
2. Click Sales Tax
3. Click Pay Sales Tax

Record bank transfer

1. Click Banking/Transfer Funds

Make an account inactive

1. Click Lists/Chart of Accounts
2. Highlight account
3. Click Account/Make account inactive

Merge two accounts

1. Click Lists/Chart of Accounts
2. Highlight one of the accounts
3. Click Account/Edit Account
4. Change name so that it is identical to the name of the other account

Verify data

1. Click File/Utilities
2. Click Verify Data

CHAPTER REVIEW

Matching

Match the term or phrase (as used in QuickBooks) to its best definition.

1. Quantity on hand
2. Inventory adjustment
3. Commented report
4. Transfer

5. Merging
6. Verify data
7. Inactive account
8. Sales Tax Liability report

_____ Number of **inventory part items** available at a point in time

_____ Transaction type used to record cash transfers between bank account

_____ Tool used to detect damage to a company's data file

_____ Tool used to transfer all activity from one account into another account

_____ Transaction type used to record corrections to **inventory part item** quantities or values

_____ Account that is unavailable for posting or searching

_____ Saved report that includes manually entered user comments

_____ Report of taxable and exempt sales revenue by jurisdiction

Multiple Choice

1. Adjustments to inventory can be made in QuickBooks:
   a. only to the quantity of inventory on hand.
   b. only to the value of inventory on hand only.
   c. to both the value and quantity of inventory on hand.

2. When sales tax is charged to a customer, the amount is credited to:

    a. an **accounts payable** account type.

    b. an **Income** account type.

    c. an **other current liability** account type.

    d. a **sales tax payable** account type.

3. When an **inventory part item** is sold in QuickBooks, at **least** _____ accounts are affected.

    a. two

    b. three

    c. four

    d. five

4. An **inactive** account in QuickBooks:

    a. can be used in transactions.

    b. can be used to filter reports.

    c. can be used in the search function.

    d. None of the above statements are true.

5. Recording proceeds from a bank loan could be done:

    a. through a general journal entry.

    b. by entering a deposit.

    c. either by creating a general journal entry or by entering the transaction as a deposit.

ASSIGNMENTS

Assignment 7A

Software 2 Go

Background information from Chapter 5: You are one of three owners of Software 2 Go, a small retail store specializing in computer software. You have been in business for almost two years and have been fairly profitable both years. The business is a corporation with a 12/31 year-end.

The owners share business responsibilities.

- Rey Martinez runs retail operations at the shop and handles all merchandise purchasing.

- Elena Turgenev manages commercial sales.

- You handle all the accounting and administrative functions.

The company's primary commercial customers are professional service firms in Sacramento, although they also sell to a private tutoring center for children (Computer Fun Park). Credit terms for these customers are currently Net 30.

You also sell to walk-in customers. (You take cash/checks or credit cards.) Cash and checks are held in the safe and deposited once a week, on Fridays. Credit cards receipts are batched and transmitted to the merchant bank (Bank of Sutterville) every Friday. It generally takes one business day for the bank to process the receipts and deposit the funds in Software 2 Go's account. Bank of Sutterville charges a processing fee of 2% of the credit card total.

In November, the buyer for Komputer Kidz called Rey and asked about purchasing software from Software 2 Go. Komputer Kidz is a tutoring center specializing in children ages 6–12. Unlike Computer Fun Park, it will be reselling the software titles to its customers. (Actually, Komputer Kidz will be selling to its customer's parents!). It means you'll have to increase your inventory levels for certain titles, but you're all very happy for the increase in sales volume!

Your current inventory includes financial, educational, graphic, and simulation software. All items are taxable (except, of course, any sales to resellers like Komputer Kidz).

You took out a loan from Bank of Sutterville when you first started the business. The balance at 11/30/17 is $6,673.00. The monthly payment (due on the 30th of each month) is $200 (including interest). The interest rate on the note is 5%.

You rent the shop for $1,500 per month under a five-year lease.

12/31/17

✓ You realize you need to make a loan payment to the bank. You're working from home this morning, so you call Rey and ask him to write a check for $200 and bring it down to the bank.

- When you get back to the office, you record the check Rey wrote to the Bank of Sutterville (#2481). The payment of $200 included interest (at 5%). [**TIP:** The last loan payment (in November) covered interest through 11/30.]

✓ You notice that you have a large balance in your checking account, so you call the bank and transfer $25,000 from your checking to your savings account.

✓ Elena was talking to the manager, Bridget, over at Own Your Future this morning. Bridget mentioned that her company was really short on computers. Elena knew that Software 2 Go had just purchased a new computer to replace an older model. She mentioned that to Bridget, who said Own Your Future would be very interested in purchasing the old one. Elena quoted her a price of $100 and Bridget drives over with a check to pick it up. Bridget is delighted!

- You deposit the check (#128999) in the bank. You decide to record the whole transaction on the **make deposit** screen. (Ignore the message about outstanding invoices for Own Your Future when you enter their name in the **Received From** column. This payment is not related any of the open invoices.)

  ○ The computer sold originally cost $1,000. Accumulated depreciation on the computer was $800 at 11/30, which is when Software 2 Go stopped using it. There was a small loss on the transaction, but you were happy to help out Bridget and all the aspiring entrepreneurs in West Sacramento! [**TIP:** You'll need to set up a new account. Remember, a loss on the sale of equipment is not a normal operating expense, so think about where you want it to show up on the profit and loss statement.]

 HINT: QuickBooks will credit accounts that have positive number listed on the deposit screen. If you want a debit, you'll need to enter the amount as a negative. (The offset, for the **deposit subtotal**, will be a debit to Cash–Checking.)

✓ You ask your neighbor, Kristine Jensen, if she'd like to help you count inventory. You let her know you'll pay her $12 an hour. She agrees. (She will only work for a few hours, so you won't need to pay her as an employee.) You don't think this will be a regular occurrence but you're not sure, so you go ahead and set her up as a 1099 vendor.

- You decide to set up an expense account named "Contract Labor Expense" for non-employee compensation. You make it a subaccount of "Labor Costs."

- You change the preferences in QuickBooks to track 1099 vendors and map "Contract Labor Expense" to Box 7 on the 1099-MISC form. Don't forget to update the IRS thresholds.

- You set up Kristine as a 1099 vendor. Her Social Security number is 312-89-5678. Her address is 1456 Hawthorne Avenue, Sacramento, CA 95822. You select **due on receipt** for the payment setting.

✓ Kristine counts the inventory after the shop closes and gives you this list:

Taken by Kristine Jensen	Inventory Count Sheet—12/31/17	Quantity on Hand
Accessories	Headset	15
	Mouse pad	15
	Set of speakers	15
Business	"Calculate!"	24
	"Client Connections"	28
	"Manage Your People"	30
	"Business Plan Creator"	30
Educational	"Anatomy Revealed"	29
	"CPA Exam Study at Home"	23
	"Gradeschool Grammar"	22
	"Math Refresher Course"	20
Graphic	"Cloud Creations"	14
Simulation	"Drive a Bus"	15
	"Fly to Mars"	13
	"Golf Like a Pro"	11
	"Design Space"	9

✓ You do a few rechecks to make sure the count is correct, which it is. You're surprised at the number of errors and decide to talk to Rey and Elena. You're going to look into the need for internal controls at the store.

✓ You adjust the inventory quantities in QuickBooks to agree to the count.

  • You decide to charge all inventory adjustment to cost of goods sold.

    ○ You notice that there's an account named "Cost of Goods Sold" in your chart of accounts that you're not using. You change the name of that account to "Inventory Adjustments." (You can delete the description that's listed when you edit the account.) [**TIP:** Ignore any messages about the **type** of account (Cost of Goods Sold) used.]

  • Use 1217INV for the **Reference No.**

  • The net adjustment should equal $630.00 (negative).

✓ Because Kristine is willing to stay a bit longer, you ask her to count the supplies on hand. She tells you that the total cost of supplies on hand equals $249.00. You adjust the supplies accounts appropriately.

✓ It took Kristine 5 hours to count the inventory and supplies. You write her a check (#2482) and charge the amount to the "Contract labor" account.

✓ You get ready to pay your sales tax liability.

  • You review your **Sales Tax Liability** report (in the **Vendors & Payables** section of the **Reports** menu). (Ignore any messages about 0% tax rates.) The total tax liability for December sales is $3,146.73.

  • You remember that, during December, you wrote off a November invoice to One Stop Legal. The November invoice included sales tax of $16.92. Because you remit sales taxes based on sales date (not on collection date), that $16.92 was remitted to the state when the November sales tax payment was made. Because One Stop Legal never paid you, you do not owe that tax.

  • You adjust the December sales tax liability by the $16.92 November overpayment. The deduction offsets bad debt expense. (Remember, the vendor is Board of Equalization.) [**TIP:** Use the **Vendors** dropdown menu to locate the appropriate form for the adjustment. Use 1207 as the entry number.]

  • You pay the balance of $3,129.81 due to the Board of Equalization with check #2483.

After month-end:

✓   You receive the December bank statements (checking and savings) and reconcile them to your records. (The statements are included at the end of the assignment.) [**TIP:** The only bank charge that you haven't recorded in the checking account is the $40 service fee charged at the end of the month.]

•   You notice that a November check to Plum Café is still outstanding (#2458). You make a note to call them next week to see if the check is lost.

✓   You review the account balances and make additional adjusting journal entries (dated 12/31) for December as needed. Carefully consider the following:

•   Total monthly depreciation expense on plant assets purchased prior to 11/30 (not including the computer sold to Own Your Future) is $383.00. None of the plant assets is fully depreciated yet. (All assets are being depreciated using the straight-line method.)

•   You expect the computer equipment purchased in December to have a two-year life with no salvage value. The equipment (computer and printer) was purchased on 12/5 and placed in service right away. Software 2 Go uses the straight-line method of depreciation. (Take a full month's depreciation and round any entries to the nearest dollar.)

•   Software 2 Go's insurance policy covers six months (9/1/17 to 2/28/18). [**TIP:** There were three months remaining on the policy at 11/30.]

•   Your last loan payment was made on 12/31 and covered interest through 12/31.

✓   You review your chart of accounts.

•   You aren't using the **Vehicle** expense account but you think you might need it in the future, so you make the account inactive.

•   You decide you don't need separate accounts for utilities and phone charges, so you merge **Utilities Expense** into **Telephone Expense**. You then change the account name to **Telephone and Utilities Expense**.

✓   You are going to present the balance sheet and profit and loss statement to the other owners, and you want both of them to be clear and concise. Take a look at the statements. Is the order of presentation reasonable? Make any changes you think necessary to create a professional looking set of statements.

Check numbers 12/31

Checking account balance . . . . $ 12,669.61
Net income—December . . . . $ 13,012.97
Net income for the year ended 12/31 . . . . $107,323.30
Total assets $116,240.10
Total liabilities . . . . $ 6,725.80

REPORTS TO CREATE FOR ASSIGNMENT 7A

All reports should be in portrait orientation; fit to one page wide.

•   Journal—include only 12/31 transactions:
   ■   Remove **Trans #** and **Adj** columns.

•   Bank reconciliation detail—Checking account only.

•   Balance Sheet (standard) as of 12/31.

•   Profit and Loss (standard) for December:
   ■   Add **Year to Date** as a subcolumn (On **Display** tab of **Customize Report**).

•   1099 Summary as of 12/31 (2017 calendar year, Only 1099 vendors, Only 1099 accounts, Ignore thresholds). [**TIP:** 1099 Summary Reports were covered in Chapter.]

BANK OF SUTTERVILLE
1500 Riverside
Sacramento, CA 95822
(916) 336-7882

Software 2 Go
3835 Freeport Blvd
Sacramento, CA 95822

Account # 4242878—Savings Account
12/31/17

	Deposits	Withdrawals	BALANCE
Beginning Balance, December 1			$ 8,013.33
12/31—Transfer from checking	$25,000.00		33,013.33
12/31—Interest at 2%.	$ 13.35		33,026.68
Ending Balance, December 31.			$33,026.68

BANK OF SUTTERVILLE
1500 Riverside
Sacramento, CA 95822
(916) 336-7882

Software 2 Go
3835 Freeport Blvd
Sacramento, CA 95822

Account # 4242879—Checking Account
12/31/17

	CREDITS	CHARGES	BALANCE
Beginning Balance, December 1, ...			$51,680.46
12/2, Check 2461		$ 1,500.00	50,180.46
12/2, Check 2456		130.00	50,050.46
12/2, Deposit	$ 3,330.95		53,381.41
12/4, Check 2460		2,402.20	50,979.21
12/5, Check 2462		11,860.20	39,119.01
12/5, Check 2463		6,071.10	33,047.91
12/5, VISA	8,290.55		41,338.46
12/9, Deposit	10,269.07		51,607.53
12/11, Check 2457		395.00	51,212.53
12/12, Check 2467		900.00	50,312.53
12/12, Check 2466		185.00	50,127.53
12/12, Check 2468		4,166.00	45,961.53
12/15, MasterCard	1,870.35		47,831.88
12/15, Check return		325.50	47,506.38
12/15, Check return fee		20.00	47,486.38
12/16, Deposit	7,194.54		54,680.92
12/18, Check 2465		3,007.22	51,673.70
12/18, Check 2464		217.80	51,455.90
12/19, Check 2469		9,878.40	41,577.50
12/22, VISA	2,312.68		43,890.18
12/23, Check 2476		108.50	43,781.68
12/23, Deposit	11,699.45		55,481.13
12/24, Check 2470		174.00	55,307.13
12/24, Check 2471		580.65	54,726.48
12/24, Check 2477		32.00	54,694.48
12/26, VISA	1,154.74		55,849.22
12/31, Check 2478		1,500.00	54,349.22
12/31, Transfer to savings		25,000.00	29,349.22
12/31, Check 2481		200.00	29,149.22
12/31, Deposit	100.00		29,249.22
12/31, Monthly bank fee		40.00	29,209.22
Ending balance, 12/31			$29,209.22

Background information from Chapter 5: You are one of three owners of The Abacus Shop, a small retail store specializing in books and supplies for accountants. You have been in business for a few years and, although the operation has been profitable, you and the other owners would like to grow the business a bit this year. You have hired an outside accountant, Martin Schmidt, to help you develop a business plan. The business is a corporation with a 12/31 year-end.

The owners share business responsibilities.

- Marvena Smith runs retail operations at the shop and handles all merchandise purchasing.

- Brandon Nguyen manages sales to the accounting firms.

- You handle all the accounting and administrative functions.

The company's primary regular customers are accounting firms in Sacramento. Credit terms for these customers are 2%/10, Net 30.

You also sell to walk-in customers (cash/checks or credit cards only). Cash and checks are held in the safe and deposited once a week, on Fridays. Credit cards receipts are batched and transmitted to the merchant bank (Bank of Sutterville) every Friday. It generally takes one business day for the bank to process the receipts and deposit the funds in The Abacus Shop's account. Pocket Bank charges a fee of 2% of the credit card total.

In September, the buyer for Sactown College Bookstore called Marvena and asked about purchasing specialty textbooks from The Abacus Shop. The bookstore is understaffed and overcrowded and would like Abacus to handle some of the accounting course textbook orders. The margin will be smaller than normal for Abacus but the volume is good, so the three of you agree to accept the bookstore's order. The textbooks for spring semester arrived on 9/30.

Your current inventory includes financial analysis software, calculators, accounting books, desk lamps, high-quality stationary paper, and, of course, the textbooks. All items are taxable.

You took out a loan from Pocket Bank when you first started the business. The balance at 9/30/17 is $3,556.44. The monthly payment (due on the 30th of each month) is $129 (including interest). The interest rate on the note is 9%.

You rent the shop for $800 per month.

10/31/17

✓ You notice that you have a large balance in your checking account. You call the bank and transfer $40,000 from your checking to your savings account.

✓ You receive a check (#21213) from Academic Texts Co. for $217.75 and deposit it into the bank account. The check is part of a rebate program Academic Texts has for its customers. At the end of each month, the company rebates 1% of the prior month's purchases. You consider this a "purchase discount."

✓ You ask your neighbor, Jerry DeAngelo, if he'd like to help you count inventory. You let him know you'll pay him $10 an hour. He agrees. (He will only work for a few hours, so you won't need to pay him as an employee.) You don't think this will be a regular occurrence but you're not sure, so you go ahead and set him up as a 1099 vendor.

- You decide to set up an expense account named "Contract Labor Expense" for non-employee compensation. You make it a subaccount of "Labor Costs."

- You change the preferences in QuickBooks to track 1099 vendors and map "Contract Labor Expense" to Box 7 on the 1099-Misc form.

- You set up Jerry as a 1099 vendor. His Social Security number is 222-98-9898. His address is 2589 Blake Street, Sacramento, CA 95822. You select **Due on Receipt** as the payment terms.

✓ Jerry counts the inventory after the shop closes and gives you this list:

Taken by Jerry DeAngelo	Inventory Count Sheet—10/31/17	Unit of Measure	Quantity on Hand
Leather	Computer	Items	5
	Briefcase.	Items	5
	Audit	Items	4
Other	Paper	Cartons	45
	Standard (calculators)	Items	22
	Deluxe (calculators)	Items	17
	Desk Lamps	Items	12
Books	"Brilliant"	Items	6
	"Cooking"	Items	15
	"Dollars"	Items	10
	"Numbers".	Items	12

✓ You do a few rechecks to make sure the count is correct, which it is. You're surprised at the number of errors and decide to talk to Marvena and Brandon about installing a security system and making sure all shipments received are carefully compared to the packing slips.

✓ You adjust the inventory quantities in QuickBooks to agree to the count.

- You decide to charge all inventory adjustment to cost of goods sold.

- You notice that there's an account named "Cost of Goods Sold" in your chart of accounts that you're not using. You change the name of that account to "Inventory Adjustments." You delete the default description when you edit the account.

- The net adjustment should equal $105.54.

✓ Because Jerry is willing to stay a bit longer, you ask him to count the supplies on hand. He tells you that there is $241 worth of supplies on hand. You adjust the supplies accounts appropriately.

✓ It took Jerry 5 hours to count the inventory and supplies. You write him a check (#1937) and charge the amount to the "Contract Labor Expense" account.

✓ You get ready to pay your sales tax liability.

- You review your **Sales Tax Liability** report. (Ignore any messages about 0% tax rates.) The total tax liability for October sales is $1,933.78.

- You remember that, during October, you wrote off a September invoice to Somerset and Somerset that included sales taxes of $16.63. Because you remit sales taxes based on sales date (not on collection date), that $16.63 had previously been remitted to the state when the September sales tax payment was made. Because Somerset and Somerset never paid you, you do not owe that tax.

- You adjust the October sales tax liability by the $16.63 overpayment. The deduction offsets bad debt expense.

- You pay the balance of $1,917.15 due to the Board of Equalization with check #1938.

After month-end:

✓ You receive the October bank statements (checking and savings) and reconcile them to your records. (The statements are included at the end of the assignment.) [**TIP:** The only bank charge that you haven't recorded in the checking account is the $40 service fee charged at the end of the month.]

✓ You review the account balances and make additional adjusting journal entries for October (dated 10/31) as needed, carefully considering the following:

- Total monthly depreciation expense on plant assets purchased through 9/30 is $250. None of the plant assets is fully depreciated yet. (All assets are being depreciated using the straight-line method.)

- You expect the printer purchased in October to have a two-year life with no salvage value. The printer was purchased on 10/4 and placed in service on 10/16. (The Abacus Shop uses the straight-line method of depreciation. Take a half month's depreciation.)
- The insurance policy was for six months (7/1–12/31). [**TIP:** There were three months remaining on the policy at 9/30.]
- Your last loan payment was made on 10/30 and covered interest through 10/31.

✓ You review your chart of accounts.

- You aren't using the "Vehicle Expenses" account but you think you might need it in the future, so you make the account inactive.
- You decide you don't need separate accounts for various types of equipment, so you merge Computer Equipment into Store Equipment. You leave "Store Equipment" as the name.

✓ You are going to present the financial statements to the other owners so you want them to be clear and concise. Take a look at the statements. Is the order of presentation reasonable? Make any changes you think necessary to create a professional looking set of statements.

Check numbers 10/31

Checking account balance	$23,016.71
Net income—October	$40,665.55
Net income for the 10 months ending 10/31	$148,830.68
Total assets	$95,232.17
Total liabilities	$5,414.49

REPORTS TO CREATE FOR ASSIGNMENT 7B

All reports should be in portrait orientation; fit to one page wide.

- Journal—include only 10/31 transactions.
    - Remove **Trans #** and **Adj** columns.
- Bank reconciliation detail—Checking account only.
- Balance sheet (standard) as of 10/31.
- Profit-and-loss (standard) for October:
    - Add **Year to Date** as a subcolumn (On **Display** tab of **Modify Report**).
- 1099 Summary (2017 calendar year, Only 1099 vendors, Only 1099 accounts, Ignore thresholds). [**TIP:** 1099 Summary Reports were covered in Chapter 3.]

POCKET BANK
1518 Florin Road
Sacramento, CA 95822
(916) 331-8765

The Abacus Shop
3835 Freeport Blvd
Sacramento, CA 95822
Account # 4242878—Savings Account   10/31/17

	Deposits	Withdrawals	BALANCE
Beginning Balance, October 1			$10,017.00
10/31—Transfer from checking	$40,000.00		50,017.00
10/31—Interest at 3%.	$ 25.04		50,042.04
Ending Balance, October 31.			$50,042.04

Pocket Bank
1518 Florin Road
Sacramento, CA 95822
(916) 331-8765

The Abacus Shop
3835 Freeport Blvd
Sacramento, CA 95822
Account # 4242879—Checking Account   10/31/17

	CREDITS	CHARGES	BALANCE
Beginning Balance, October 1, ...			$38,726.55
10/1, Check 1911		$ 85.00	38,641.55
10/1, Check 1912		129.00	38,512.55
10/2, Check 1913		328.00	38,184.55
10/2, Check 1915		1,402.53	36,782.02
10/3, Check 1914		152.00	36,630.02
10/3, Check 1916		800.00	35,830.02
10/7, Deposit	$56,949.22		92,779.24
10/8, Check 1917		5,488.00	87,291.24
10/8, Check 1918		712.80	86,578.44
10/10, VISA	293.08		86,871.52
10/10, Check 1919		21,339.50	65,532.02
10/14, Check return		1,386.56	64,145.46
10/14, Check return fee		25.00	64,120.46
10/14, Deposit	5,275.47		69,395.93
10/17, Deposit, MasterCard	719.01		70,114.94
10/16, Check 1920		1,060.00	69,054.94
10/16, Check 1921		128.00	68,926.94
10/17, Check 1922		250.00	68,676.94
10/17, Check 1923		387.10	68,289.84
10/19, Cash Withdrawal		32.63	68,257.21
10/21, Deposit	20,585.16		88,842.37
10/21, VISA	926.93		89,769.30
10/23, Check 1925		872.20	88,897.10
10/24, Check 1927		1,489.60	87,407.50
10/24, Check 1926		379.36	87,028.14
10/30, VISA	3,500.99		90,529.13
10/31, Deposit	217.75		90,746.88
10/31, Transfer to savings		40,000.00	50,746.88
10/31, Service fee		40.00	50,706.88
Ending balance, 10/31			$50,706.88

APPENDIX 7A OPTIONAL YEAR END CLOSING PROCESS

In Chapter 4, we covered closing accounting periods in QuickBooks. In summary:

- QuickBooks automatically closes all revenue and expense accounts on the first day of a new fiscal year.

- The user is required to make journal entries to close any temporary equity accounts like dividends or draws.

- The user can set a **closing date** in QuickBooks so that users are reminded that the period has been closed if they try to save a transaction to that period.

The company may also want to reduce the amount of data maintained in QuickBooks at the end of a fiscal year. Although QuickBooks can handle up to a maximum of 2 billion transactions, large numbers of transactions can slow processing time. And although QuickBooks maximum sizes for lists are generous, companies that have been operating for a long time may start to reach the size limits.

> **BEHIND THE SCENES** As a point of interest, these are the maximum sizes for certain lists in QuickBooks Pro and QuickBooks Premier.
>
> | List name | Maximum number of items |
> | --- | --- |
> | Chart of accounts . . . . | 10,000 |
> | Items . . . . | 14,500 |
> | Payroll items . . . . | 10,000 |
> | Total names: employees, customers, vendors, and other names combined . . . | 14,500 |

To see the file sizes in a particular company file, click the F2 function key. The list sizes are displayed in the far right column.

QuickBooks includes a utility called **condense data** that allows some or all transactions to be removed from a company file. It's a good idea, of course, to make a final backup copy o before beginning the process.

To condense files, click **File** and then click **Utilities**.

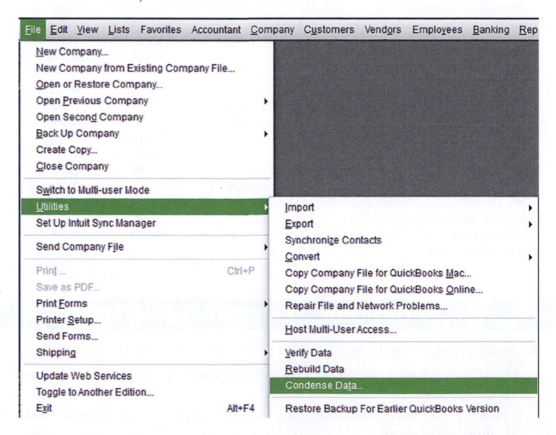

Click **Condense Data**. The following screen will appear:

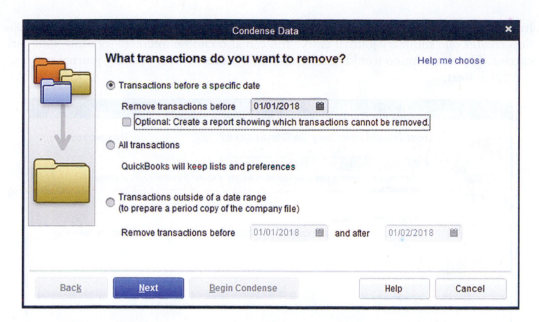

In this window, you can choose from the following options:

- Remove transactions before a specified date.
    - This would be the likely choice for companies that are looking to reduce files sizes. Most companies would leave two years' worth of transactions intact.

- Remove all transactions.
    - This option would leave basic data (lists, preferences, and company information intact) but would remove all transaction detail.

- Remove transactions outside of (before or after) a particular fiscal year.
    - This is known as making a **period copy** of a company file. Only transactions within the accounting period are retained.

Click **Next**.

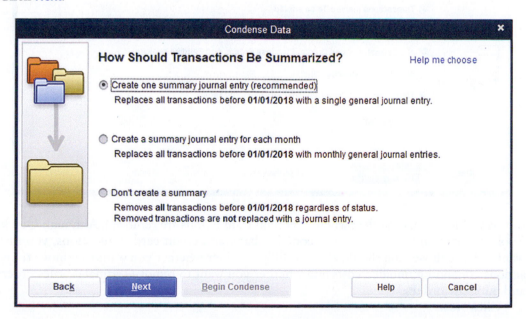

In this window, you can choose how transactions are summarized. The **recommended** option creates one summary journal entry. You can also choose to create monthly summary entries. The third option would remove all transactions without creating journal entries.

Click **Next**.

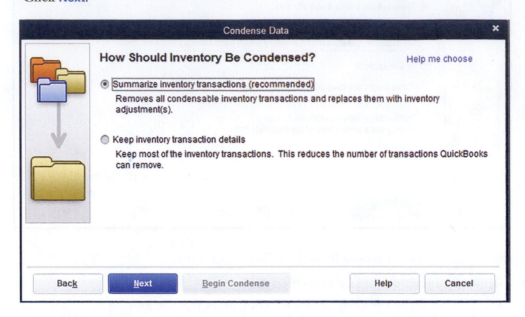

The **recommended** option to summarize inventory transactions would be the best option if file reduction is the primary goal.

Click **Next**.

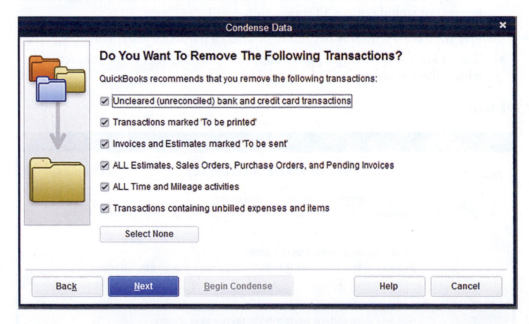

In this window, you can select whether certain transactions are removed. Although Quick-Books recommends removing unreconciled bank and credit card transactions, you may want to leave those. You should also carefully consider whether you want to remove transactions containing unbilled costs and whether you want to remove estimates, sales orders and purchase orders.

Click **Next**.

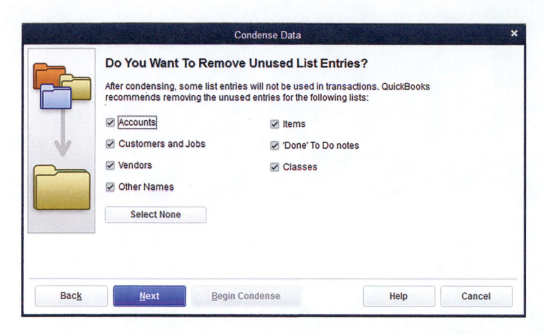

In this window, you can choose to remove customers, accounts, etc. that are not used in retained transactions. Removing names and accounts will reduce file sizes but if these names are needed to create transactions in the future, they would need to be re-established.

Click **next**.

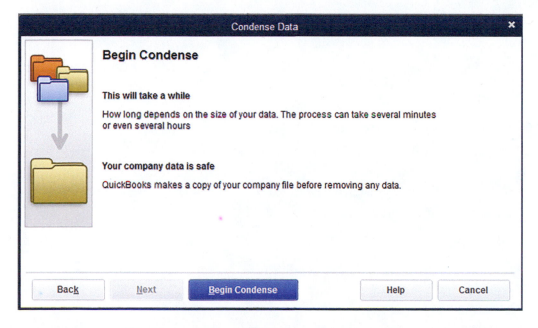

This is the final window before the condensing process begins. A message will appear when the process is complete. QuickBooks automatically makes a copy of the original file and will include the location of the copied file in the final message.

Intuit is very clear that condensing data should not be done unless all other options for improving performance have been tried. Although condensing data can positively affect the size of the file, there is no guarantee that the benefit will be substantial. Companies with inventory will usually experience the least benefit.

QuickBooks

Payroll, Project Costing, and Billing for Time

Employee-related functions (hiring, managing, paying, evaluating, terminating, etc.) are some of the most complex functions in business. They are also some of the most important. There aren't many businesses that can be successful over the long term if they don't have a strong employee base.

In accounting for payroll, the primary focus is on:

- Calculating, processing, and recording employee compensation.

- Recording, reporting, and remitting payroll taxes and employee benefits.

Those two processes may look straightforward but, as anyone who has worked in payroll can tell you, they can be very complex.

SECTION OVERVIEW

Chapter 8 covers basic payroll functions that would be used in all types of companies (service, merchandising, and manufacturing).

Chapter 9 covers job costing and billing for time. These topics are included in this section because the setup and processing of payroll is going to be different if project costing or billing for time is involved. Construction companies, law firms, accounting firms, architectural firms, and custom shops are just a few examples of the types of companies that need the ability to track employee time. They need this information in order to manage their business. In many cases, they also need this information for billing purposes.

BEFORE WE MOVE FORWARD

Most of you are familiar with payroll either through prior accounting classes or through your own work experience but the following review of terms and concepts might be helpful.

Compensation

- Employees are usually paid in the form of a salary (usually stated as an annual or monthly amount) or an hourly wage. They can also be paid bonuses, commissions, overtime, etc. The total amount earned by an employee during a pay period is called the employee's **gross pay**. The amount of the paycheck (gross pay less taxes and other withholdings) is called the employee's **net pay**.

- Employers normally pay employees on a set payroll schedule. The schedule can be monthly, semi-monthly, weekly, etc.

Payroll Taxes

- There are federal, state, and local payroll taxes. Some are the responsibility of the employer, some are the responsibility of the employee, and some are a shared responsibility of both employer and employee.

- Most payroll taxes are calculated as a percentage of a base amount. The percentage and the base will depend on the specific payroll tax.

- Federal taxes include:
  - Federal income (FIT)—employee tax.
  - FICA (Social Security and Medicare)—shared tax (both employer and employee pay) except for the additional Medicare tax on compensation over a set amount that is only paid by the employee.
  - Federal unemployment (FUTA)—employer tax.

- State taxes (for California as an example) include:
  - State income (SIT)—employee tax.
  - State unemployment (SUI)—employer tax.
  - Employment training (ETT)—employer tax.
  - State disability (SDI)—employee tax.

BEHIND THE SCENES In most states, employers are also required to maintain insurance (known as workers' compensation insurance) to cover medical expenses and lost wages for employees who suffer job-related injuries or illnesses. In some states, workers' compensation insurance is paid through state government programs. In others, the insurance coverage is purchased from private insurance carriers and would be entered and paid as a bill. In states that allow a company to be self-insured, a reserve would be accrued as a liability for potential claims.

Benefits

- Employers often provide benefits to employees. These might include:
  - Paid time off—might include sick, vacation, and family leave time.
  - Medical insurance plan—can be fully or partially paid by employer.
  - Retirement plan—can be fully or partially paid by employer.

8

Paying Employees

Objectives

After completing Chapter 8, you should be able to:

1. Turn on manual payroll processing.

2. Add and edit payroll items.

3. Add and edit salaried and hourly employees.

4. Create paychecks and payroll tax liability checks.

5. Create and modify payroll and payroll tax reports.

WHAT IS THE PAYROLL CYCLE?

The payroll cycle includes all the business activities related to managing a company's labor force (hiring, training, paying, evaluating, and terminating). The specific activities that affect the accounting records are:

- Hire employees and obtain their tax information.

- Track employee time if appropriate.

- Calculate compensation and withholdings for each employee for the pay period.

- Distribute paychecks to employees with information about current and year-to-date payroll information.

- Calculate employer taxes.

- Remit employee withholdings and employer taxes.

- File required tax reports with federal and state taxing authorities.

In a manual system, managing employees and processing payroll is very labor intensive. If any employees are paid on an hourly basis, employees must submit timesheets used in calculating compensation. Withholdings and deductions must be determined for each employee before paychecks can be prepared. Employer taxes must be calculated and tax forms must be completed. And, of course, payroll transactions must be journalized and entered into the general ledger. All of these functions are done in all types of companies (service, merchandising, and manufacturing).

In QuickBooks, various payroll services are available that calculate employee withholdings and employer taxes, create paychecks, and update the general ledger automatically. There are even software programs available from other vendors that allow for remote online entry of time by employees directly into QuickBooks.

PAYROLL PLANS AVAILABLE IN QUICKBOOKS

Federal and state payroll tax rates and wage thresholds change fairly regularly. In a small company with limited accounting staff, it can be difficult to stay current with those changes. Payroll **can** be calculated manually in QuickBooks, but, for a fee, users can subscribe to various payroll plans in QuickBooks. Depending on the plan selected, QuickBooks will:

- Allow the user to download tax rates and tables from federal and state taxing authorities. (Basic Plan)

- Automatically prepare federal and state payroll tax returns and electronically file W-2s at year-end. (Enhanced Plan)

- Automatically file returns and remit taxes to taxing authorities. (Full-Service Plan)

Direct deposit of employee paychecks is available in all of the plans.

The vast majority of users subscribe to one of the payroll plans. Withholding, remitting, and reporting payroll taxes correctly is a critical business function, and having accurate and up to date tax information is essential.

In this course, however, we will be processing payroll manually. You need to learn the procedures for processing payroll, and we can enter payroll taxes manually, without purchasing a payroll plan.

TURNING ON MANUAL PAYROLL PROCESSING

Intuit does **not** make it easy to process payroll manually. As you'll soon see, QuickBooks will ask you several times if you **really** want to choose that option.

Turning on manual payroll processing is done through the **Have a Question?** window. That window opens when you press the F1 function key with QuickBooks open.

The window looks something like this:

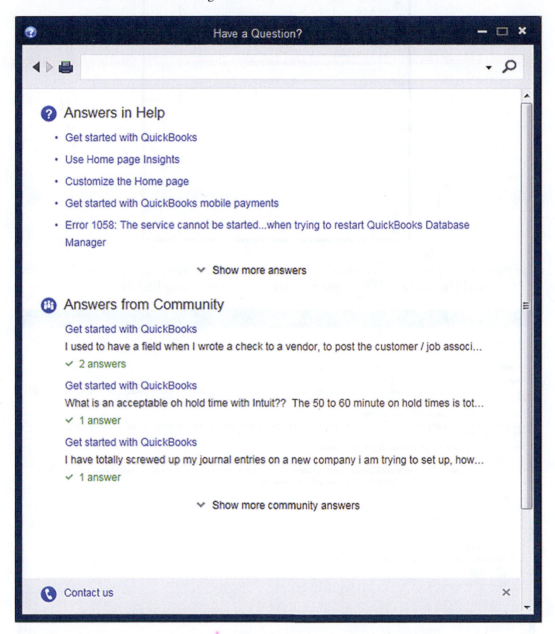

When the phrase "manual payroll" (or something similar to that) is entered in the search field at the top of the window, the topics displayed look something like this:

The topic—"Calculate payroll taxes manually (without a subscription to QuickBooks Payroll)"—should be selected. The topic narrative looks something like this:

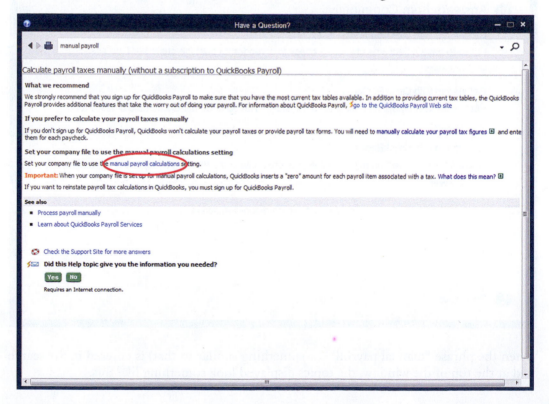

You must click on the "manual payroll calculations" link embedded in the **third** paragraph. The screen now looks something like this:

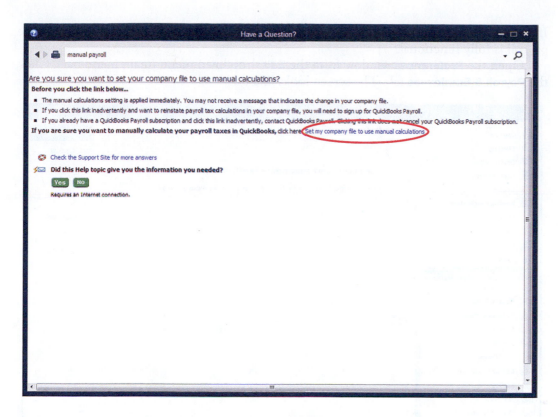

At the very bottom of the narrative, QuickBooks instructs you to click "Set my company file to use manual calculations."

After clicking the link, you get the following message, letting you know that the manual payroll processing is now available:

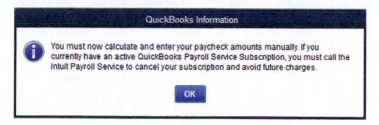

Setting up manual payroll processing for Sac City Accounting.

PRACTICE
EXERCISE

1. Click **Help** (main menu bar).

2. Click **QuickBooks Help**.

3. Enter "manual payroll" in the search field and click the magnifying glass in the top right corner of the window.

4. Click **Calculate payroll taxes manually (without a subscription to QuickBooks Payroll)**.

5. Click the **Manual Payroll Calculations** link in the **third** paragraph.

6. Click **Set my company file to use manual calculations** (bottom of the narrative).

7. Click **OK**. (You may have to close the **Help** window to see the **OK** button.)

If payroll was deactivated in a QuickBooks file, a few additional steps are necessary before payroll is fully functional.

Open the **Preferences** window from the **Edit** dropdown menu (main menu bar). Click the **Payroll & Employees** tab. The screen looks like this:

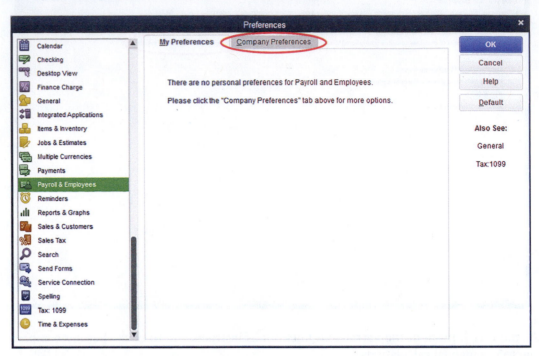

Click the **Company Preferences** tab. The screen looks like this:

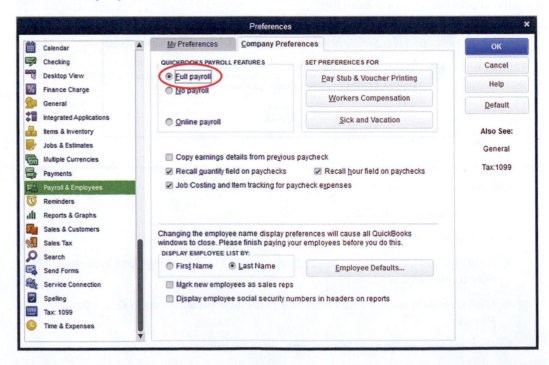

Selecting **Full payroll** will update the Home Page to include the basic payroll functions. Click **OK** to save the preference change.

HINT: Most companies display the employee list in alphabetic order by last name, so that should be changed in this screen. There are a number of defaults that can be set in this screen as well.

The preceding steps are not necessary in the Practice Exercises because payroll was already activated in your student data file for Sac City Accounting.

MANAGING PAYROLL ITEMS

The payroll process in QuickBooks uses **payroll items** in much the same way as the sales process in QuickBooks uses **items**.

In the sales process, **items** are used in the preparation of **invoices** and **sales receipts**. In the payroll process, **payroll items** are used in preparing timesheets and paychecks. If you want to include something on a timesheet or a paycheck, there **must** be a **payroll item** set up for it.

Payroll items track more details about wages and payroll taxes than a company would want to track in the general ledger (much like **items** track details about revenues). Each **payroll item** is associated with only one general ledger account. One general ledger account can have many **payroll items** linked to it.

The **Payroll item type** (just like **item type**) determines functionality in QuickBooks.

Setting up a **payroll item** is a bit more involved than setting up **items**, but the basic concept is the same. Certain information must be entered for each **payroll item** so that QuickBooks can properly track and manage the **payroll item**.

BEHIND THE SCENES QuickBooks has a **Payroll Setup** feature that can be accessed through the **Employees** menu (main menu bar). This guided walk-through allows a user to initially set up all of the **payroll items** and employee information at one time. We do not use that feature in this chapter so that you have the opportunity to learn how to add and modify **payroll items** and employees as needed. We cover the **Payroll Setup** feature in Chapter 12.

The **Payroll Item List** can be accessed through the **Lists** menu (main menu bar):

When open, the list looks something like this:

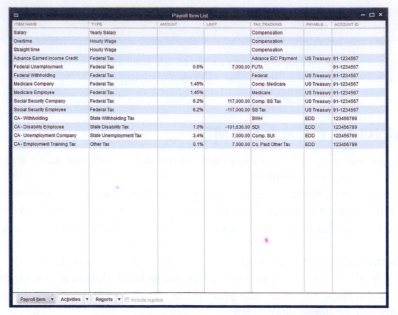

You can see that many **payroll items** are already listed. QuickBooks sets up basic compensation and tax **payroll items** automatically when the payroll feature is turned on. Some of these can be modified or even deleted. Certain **payroll items** (federal income and FICA taxes for example) **cannot** be deleted. Tax rates for Social Security and Medicare **cannot** be modified.

There are options on the **Payroll Item** button at the bottom left of the screen for adding or editing **payroll items**:

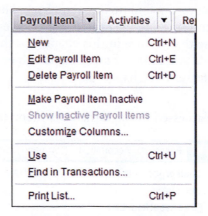

Selecting **New** gives you the following screen:

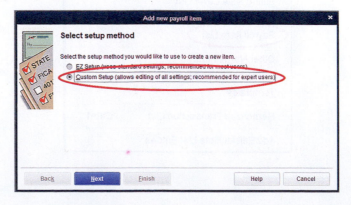

We are using the **Custom Setup** method in this course. (The **EZ Setup** option takes the user to the **payroll setup** feature described earlier.)

When you select **Custom Setup** and click **Next**, the screen looks like this:

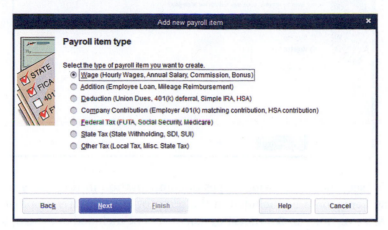

As you can see, there are a number of different **payroll item types**. In this chapter, we are adding **wage payroll items**.

If you want to add a new type of compensation, select **Wage** and click **Next**. The screen looks like this:

Companies might pay employees in the form of salaries, hourly wages, bonuses, commissions, etc. All of these forms of compensation can be handled through QuickBooks. We cover hourly wages and salaries in this chapter, but the basic procedures are the same for other types of compensation.

> **BEHIND THE SCENES** The **type** you select activates the QuickBooks functionality associated with that type. For example, an **hourly wage payroll item** prompts QuickBooks to calculate **gross pay** based on hours worked. An **annual salary payroll item** prompts QuickBooks to calculate gross pay based on the pay frequency. (For example, if the salaried employee is paid monthly, QuickBooks calculates gross monthly pay for an **annual salary payroll item** as 1/12 of the annual amount.)

Gross pay The amount an employee earns before any withholdings or deductions.

Hourly Wage Setup

If you select **Hourly Wage** and click **Next**, the screen looks like this:

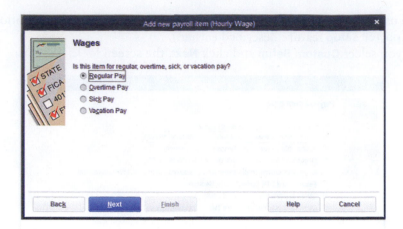

As you can see, there are various types of compensation in the **hourly wage** category. A **Regular Pay item** would be included in the setup of every hourly employees. If hourly employees work overtime, an **Overtime Pay item** would be included in the employee setup as well. A company would need to set up multiple **overtime pay items** if they have, for example, both time-and-a-half and double-time overtime pay rates.

A company would set up **sick pay** and **vacation pay** items if it is tracking paid time off through QuickBooks.

> **BEHIND THE SCENES** These are **types** of compensation, **not** pay rates. A company might have one **Regular Pay item** for hourly wages. That **payroll item** would be included in the employee record for every employee paid on an hourly basis. The actual hourly **rate** for the specific employee is linked to that **payroll item** in the employee setup, which is covered later in this chapter.

Setting Up Regular Pay Items

If **Regular Pay** is selected, the screen looks something like this after you click **Next**:

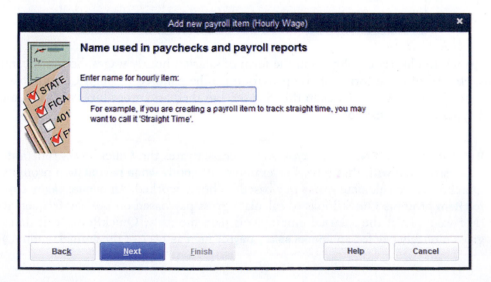

The **item name** entered in the preceding screen appears on paychecks. After the name is entered, clicking **Next** gives you the final screen:

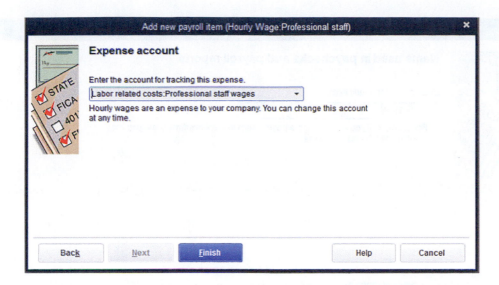

This screen allows the user to attach a general ledger account to the **payroll item**. All compensation paid to employees under that **payroll item** will be debited to the account indicated here. Remember, there can only be one account linked to each **payroll item**.

> **BEHIND THE SCENES** Because each **payroll item** can be linked to only one general ledger account, a company would need to set up multiple **regular pay** items if it wants hourly salaries tracked in multiple general ledger accounts. The same would be true if a company wanted to track overtime, sick, or vacation pay in various general ledger accounts.

Setting Up Overtime Pay Items

To set up overtime **payroll items**, **overtime pay** should be selected in the **Add new payroll item (Hourly Wage)** screen:

In the next screen, the name for the **payroll item** should be entered. The name should clearly identify the type of overtime pay:

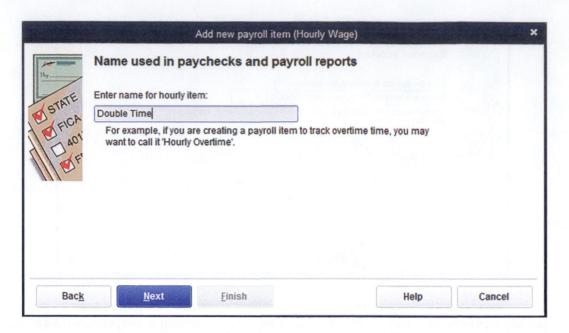

The method for calculating overtime is entered in the next screen. Time-and-a-half and double-time are common overtime rates, but you have the option of creating a custom calculation.

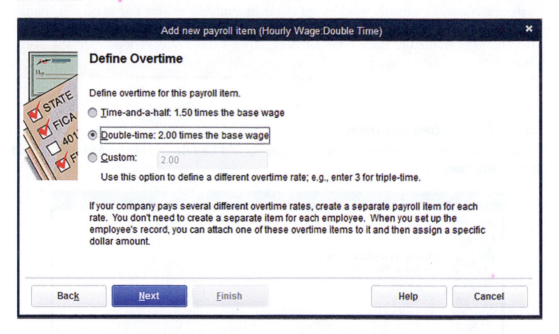

BEHIND THE SCENES All of the overtime calculations in QuickBooks are based on the straight-time (regular) hourly rate. For example, if an employee's normal rate is $10 but he or she works overtime at time-and-a-half, the pay rate would be $15 per hour ($10 × 1.5).

In the final screen, the general ledger account for posting overtime pay is entered:

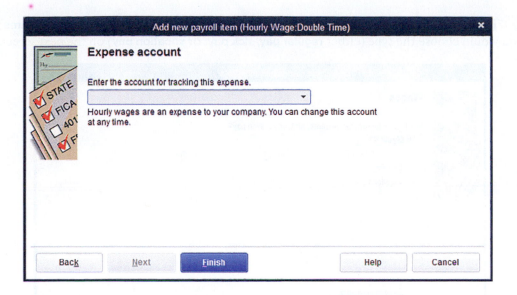

Annual Salary Setup

The process for adding a new salary **item** is very similar to the process for adding an hourly wage **item**.

New is selected on the **payroll item list** dropdown menu:

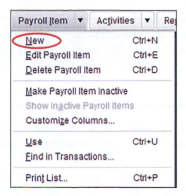

Custom Setup should be selected. On the next screen, **Wage** should be selected. The following screen appears next:

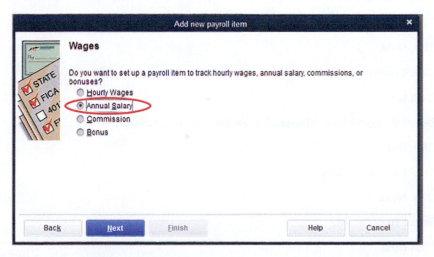

Annual Salary should be selected.

There are various types of **annual salary items** (similar to those for **hourly wage items**). You would choose the type (either **regular pay, sick pay,** or **vacation pay**) on the next screen:

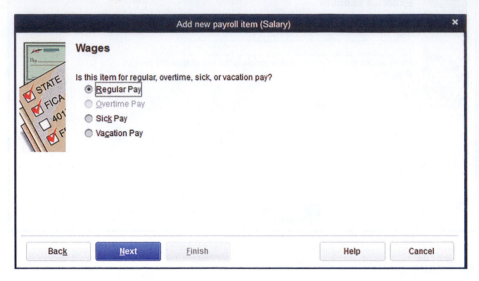

The **payroll item** name is entered on the third screen.

The general ledger account to be used for posting the salaries paid would be entered on the final screen.

> **HINT:** Remember, multiple **annual salary payroll items** would need to be set up if a company wants to track salaries in multiple general ledger accounts.

PRACTICE EXERCISE

Setting up new payroll items for Sac City Accounting Services.

(Sac City wants to set up a payroll item for salaried professional staff.)

1. Click **Lists**.

2. Click **Payroll Item List**.

3. Click **No** if you are prompted about payroll service information. [**TIP:** Click **No** whenever this prompt appears.]

4. Click **Payroll Item** (bottom left corner of screen).

5. Click **New**.

6. Click **Custom Setup**.

7. Click **Next**.

8. Select **Wage (Hourly, Wages, Annual Salary, Commission, Bonus)**.

9. Click **Next**.

10. Select **Annual Salary**.

11. Click **Next**.

12. Select **Regular Pay**.

13. Click **Next**.

(continued)

14. Enter "Professional Staff" as the name.

15. Click **Next**.

16. Select **Add New** as the **account**.

    a.   Select **Expense** as the **account type**.

    b.   Enter "Professional staff wages" as the **account name**.

    c.   Check **subaccount** and select **Labor related costs**.

    d.   Click **Save & Close**.

17. Click **Finish**.

18. Exit out of the **Payroll Item List**.

Editing Payroll Items

As noted previously, QuickBooks automatically sets up a number of critical **payroll items**. Of course, QuickBooks doesn't know how the company wants to report payroll expenses, so there's usually a significant amount of editing that must be done.

    Payroll items are accessed through the **Payroll Item List** on the **Lists** menu (main menu bar). The initial screen looks like this:

    A **payroll item** can be edited by highlighting it and selecting the **Edit Payroll Item** option on the **Payroll Item** dropdown menu at the bottom left corner of the screen.

    The subsequent screens will differ depending on the type of **payroll item** being edited. A **payroll item**'s name and associated general ledger account can be changed for **all payroll items**. There are limitations on other editing (rates and wage thresholds, for example) specific to the **payroll item** being modified.

Special Considerations: Federal And State Payroll Taxes

Payroll items for all of the federal and most state taxes are automatically set up by QuickBooks. For FICA taxes, the rates and wage thresholds are also automatically set up.

However, the following information may need to be edited for the various taxes:

- For all taxes:
    - Associated general ledger accounts.
    - The vendor name (name of agency to whom taxes will be remitted).
    - Identification of the types of wages subject to the tax.
        - It is particularly important to review these settings when new **wage**, **addition** or **deduction payroll items** are added.
- For FUTA taxes:
    - Tax rate.
- For all state taxes:
    - Tax rate.
    - Wage thresholds.

BEHIND THE SCENES For every tax **payroll item**, there can be only one associated liability account and, if applicable, one associated expense account. (Expense accounts would be needed only for payroll taxes paid, in full or in part, by the employer.) That can be a problem if companies want to report employer payroll tax expenses in multiple accounts. For example, let's say a company wants to track administrative labor costs separately from sales labor costs. The wages are easily separated. Two compensation **payroll items** are set up, and each is associated with its own general ledger account. There is a problem, however, if the company also wants to separate out, in the financial statements, the employer payroll tax expenses related to administrative wages from the employer tax expenses related to the sales wages. Why is this a problem? Because both administrative and sales wages are subject to Medicare tax, but the employer Medicare **payroll item (Medicare Company)** can only be associated with one expense account. All employer Medicare tax costs, regardless of type of compensation, would be automatically debited to the same account in QuickBooks. If separation of taxes were important, journal entries could be used.

QuickCheck
8-1

True or False? State income tax withholdings are expenses of the company. (Answer at end of chapter.)

PRACTICE
EXERCISE

Editing existing payroll items for Sac City Accounting Services.
(Sac City wants a separate payroll item for administrative salaries. The company also wants to set up overtime correctly for hourly employees and edit the agency name for the FUTA tax item. The company needs to edit the chart of accounts and various compensation items accordingly.)

1. Click on **Lists** (main menu bar) and select **Chart of Accounts**.
    a. Highlight **Salaries expense** (under **Labor related costs**).
    b. Click **Account** (bottom left corner).
    c. Select **Edit Account**.
    d. Change **account name** to "Administrative staff wages".

(continued)

   e.   Check **Subaccount** and select **Labor related costs**, if not already selected.

   f.   Click **Save & Close** and exit out of the **chart of accounts** window.

2. Click on **Lists** (main menu bar).

3. Click on **Payroll item list**.

   a.   Highlight **Salary**.

   b.   Click **Payroll Item** (bottom left corner of screen).

   c.   Click **Edit Payroll Item**.

      i.   Change name to "Administrative Staff."

      ii.   Click **Next**.

      iii.   Select **Administrative staff wages** as the **account** (subaccount of **Labor Related Costs**).

      iv.   Click **Finish**.

   d.   Highlight **Overtime** (on the **Payroll Item List** window).

   e.   Click **Payroll Item** (bottom left corner of screen).

   f.   Click **Edit Payroll Item**.

      i.   Leave name as is.

      ii.   Click **Next**.

      iii.   Click **Time and a half: 1.5 times the base wage** if not already selected.

      iv.   Click **Next**.

      v.   Change account to "Professional staff wages."

      vi.   Click **Finish**.

   g.   Highlight "Straight Time."

   h.   Click **Payroll Item** (bottom left corner of screen).

   i.   Click **Edit Payroll Item**.

      i.   Leave name as is.

      ii.   Click **Next**.

      iii.   Change account to "Professional Staff wages."

      iv.   Click **Finish**.

   j.   Highlight **Federal Unemployment**.

   k.   Click **Payroll Item** (bottom left corner of screen).

   l.   Click **Edit Payroll Item**.

      i.   Leave name as is.

      ii.   Click **Next**.

      iii.   Select **US Treasury** as **agency**.

      iv.   Leave the accounts as is.

      v.   Click **Next**.

      vi.   Click "0.6%" as the **rate**, if not already selected.

      vii.   Click **Next**.

      viii.   Make sure all of four Sac City compensation items are checked as subject to federal unemployment.

      ix.   Click **Finish** and exit out of Edit **payroll item** window.

MANAGING EMPLOYEES

Now that you've seen how much detail is needed for paying employees and handling payroll taxes, you might guess that employee records will need to include considerable information as well. You would be correct!

Employee master records are maintained in the **Employee Center** accessed through the **Home Page**:

The initial screen looks something like this when the **Employees** tab is selected:

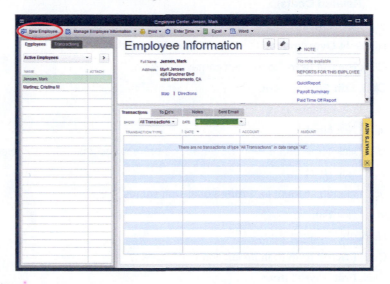

New Employee Setup

Employees can be added through the **New Employee** button (top left of **Employee Center** window). The setup screen looks like this:

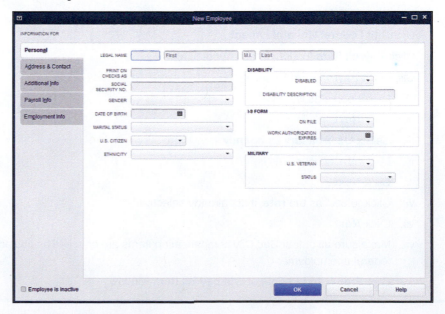

There are five tabs in the **New Employee** screen.

- **Personal**
  - The initial window just shown.
  - Used for entering general information about an employee.

- **Address & Contact**
  - Used for entering employee contact information.

- **Additional Info**
  - Used to enter an employee identification number (if used) and to set up custom fields.

- **Payroll Info**
  - Used primarily for entering compensation and tax information.

- **Employment Info**
  - Used primarily to enter employment dates.

We cover the **Payroll Info** and **Employment Info** tab in some detail. Entering information in the other tabs is very straightforward and is only covered through the Practice Exercise at the end of the section.

Payroll Info Tab

The **Payroll Info** tab screen looks like this:

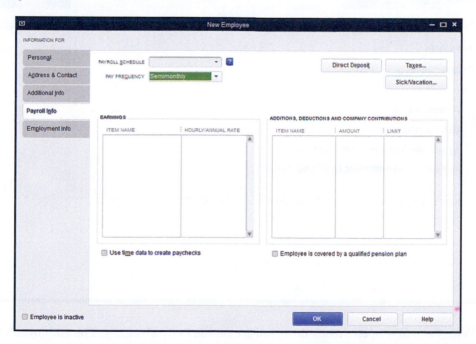

The first field, **Payroll Schedule**, is often used when a company has different payroll cycles for different employee groups or when it wants to run payroll in batches by employee group. When **payroll schedules** are used, QuickBooks automatically determines payroll processing dates, taking into account bank holidays and weekends, so that the company has employee paychecks ready on time. **Payroll schedules** are not used in this course.

How often the employee will be paid (monthly, semimonthly, etc.) is selected in the **Pay Frequency** field.

> **WARNING: All employees assigned to a particular *payroll schedule* must have the same pay frequency.**

The expected **payroll items** and pay rates for the employee are entered in the **Earnings** section of the screen. (These are defaults only. Both rates and compensation types can be changed when paychecks are created for the employee.)

The **Use time data to create paychecks** option (bottom left of the screen) allows the user to use the **timesheet** feature in QuickBooks. This option can be used for hourly or salaried employees.

The **Additions**, **Deductions and Company Contributions** section would be used to enter other **payroll items** that might apply to the specific employee. Bonuses, commissions, union dues, garnishments, and so forth would be included here. (Again, these are defaults. Changes can be made when paychecks are created.)

At the top right of the **New Employee** screen (**Payroll Info** tab), there are three buttons: **Direct Deposit**, **Taxes**, and **Sick/Vacation**.

Direct Deposit is only available to QuickBooks payroll plan subscribers.

Using QuickBooks to track paid time off (**Sick/Vacation**) is covered in the appendix to this chapter.

The **Taxes** screen looks something like this:

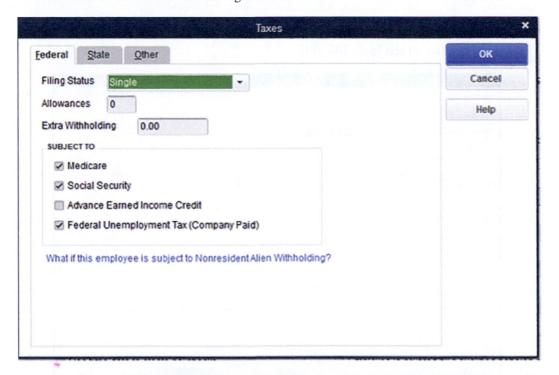

When you first open the window, you are on the **Federal** tax tab. The employee's filing status and allowances entered here would come from the W-4 completed by the employee. Most employees are subject to Medicare, Social Security and FUTA. There are situations, however, in which an employee would be exempt from one or more of those taxes.

The other two tabs in the **Taxes** window are **State** and **Other**. Different fields appear on the **State** and on the **Other** screen depending on the state in which the employee works.

The **State** screen looks something like this if the employee lives and works in California:

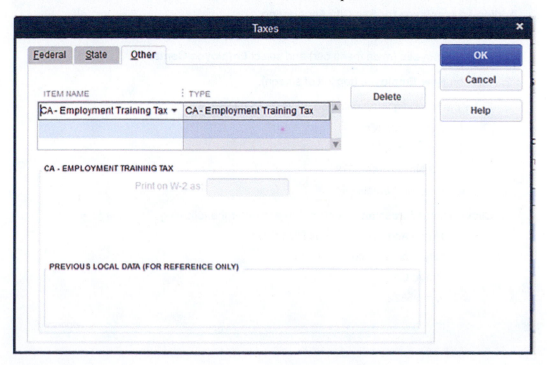

QuickBooks includes most state taxes. The **state worked** selected here should be the location of the specific employee's work location. (One company could have multiple state locations and would be subject to the payroll taxes for each of those states.) The **state subject to withholding** might differ from the **state worked** if the employee worked in one state but had his or her primary residence in another state. Most of the information entered here (filing status and allowances) comes from the state withholding form(s) completed by the employee.

The **Other** tab is used to enter other payroll taxes. Depending on the state selected on the **State** tab, the dropdown menu options change. The screen looks something like this, for California, after the correct tax is selected in the dropdown menu:

Employment Info tab

The **Employment Info** tab screen in the employee master record looks like this:

Hire, leave of absence, and termination dates are entered here. QuickBooks uses these dates to determine which employees should be paid during a particular pay period.

Information about the status of the employee (full- or part-time, supervisor, job title, department, etc.) can also be entered here.

PRACTICE EXERCISE

Adding an employee for Sac City Accounting.

(Sac City hires Mei Ling to work full-time as an administrative assistant.)

1. Click **Employees** (main menu bar) and select **Employee Center**.

2. Click on **New Employee** (top left of screen).

3. Enter the following information on the **Personal** tab.

    i.   First name: Mei

    ii. Last name: Ling

    iii. SS No: 123-44-5678

    iv. Gender: Female

4. Click on the **Address and Contact** tab and enter the following:

    v.   Home Address: 2121 Los Rios Drive

    vi.   City: Sacramento

    vii. State: CA

    viii. Zip: 95822

(continued)

---

5. Click on the **Payroll Info** tab.

   a. Select **Semimonthly** as the **pay frequency**.

   b. Select **Administrative staff** as the **item name** in the **Earnings** box. (Click in the **Earnings** box to get the dropdown menu.)

   c. Enter "40,000" as the **annual rate**.

   d. Click **Taxes** (top right of screen).

      i. On the **Federal** tab:

         1. Select **Single** as the **filing status**.

         2. Enter "1" in the **Allowances** field.

         3. **Medicare**, **Social Security**, and **Federal Unemployment Tax (Company Paid)** should be checked.

      ii. Click the **State** tab:

         1. Select **CA** for **State Worked**. (Both **SUI** and **SDI** should be checked.)

         2. Select **CA State Subject to Withholding**. (Select **Single** for **filing status** and enter "1" for **allowances**.)

      iii. Click the **Other** tab.

         1. Select **CA-Employment Training Tax** in the **Item Name** field.

         2. If the **Medicare Employee Additional Tax** item appears in the list, you can leave it. We do not use that **payroll item** for any of the employees but QuickBooks will occasionally add it automatically.

      iv. Click **OK**.

6. Click on the **Employment Info** tab.

   a. Enter "1/8/18" as the **hire date**.

7. Click **OK**.

   a. Click **Leave As Is** if prompted to enter sick and vacation leave information.

8. Exit the **Employee Center**.

Editing Employees

Changes can easily be made to employee records.

WARNING: Changes to compensation and taxes would be effective for the first pay period <u>after</u> the change is made.

Editing employees is done through the **Employee Center**. The initial screen looks something like this:

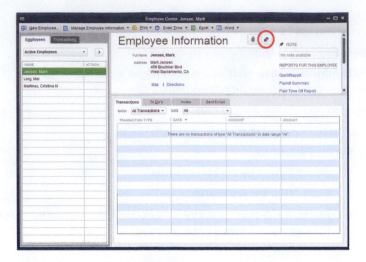

To edit an employee, the name is highlighted. The **edit** icon (the pencil) at the top right of the screen takes you to the highlighted employee's record. Information on all tabs (**Personal**, **Address & Contact**, **Additional Info**, **Payroll Info**, and **Employment Info**) can be modified.

PRACTICE EXERCISE

Edit employee records for Sac City Accounting.

(Sac City changes payroll information for Mark Jensen, full-time salaried staff accountant, and Cristina Martinez, part-time hourly staff accountant.)

1. Click **Employees** (main menu bar) and **select Employee Center**.

2. Highlight **Jensen, Mark**.
   a. Click the **edit** icon (the pencil at the top right of screen).
   b. Select the **Payroll Info** tab.
   c. In the **Earnings** box, change **Item Name** to "Professional Staff."
   d. Leave **hourly/annual rate** at $50,000 and **pay frequency** as **Semimonthly**.
   e. Click the **Employment Info** tab.
   f. Enter "1/8/18" as the **hire date**.
   g. Click **OK**.

3. Highlight **Martinez, Cristina**.
   a. Click the **edit** icon (the pencil at the top right of the screen).
   b. Click the **Payroll Info** tab.
   c. Change **hourly rate** to $25.
   d. Select **Overtime** as an additional **item name**.
      i. QuickBooks will automatically set the rate at $37.50 (time and a half).
   e. **Pay Frequency** should be **semimonthly**.
   f. Uncheck "Use time data to create paychecks" if necessary. (We cover using timesheets in Chapter 9.)
   g. Click the **Employment Info** tab.
   h. Click "1/8/18" as the **hire date**.
   i. Click **OK**.

4. Exit out of the **Employee Center**.

PROCESSING PAYROLL

Creating Paychecks

The payroll function in QuickBooks uses information from a number of sources within the company file. The sources are:

✓ Employee record (for pay rates).

✓ Timesheets, if applicable, (for hours worked).

✓ **Payroll item list** (for underlying journal entry accounts).

> **!** **WARNING:** One piece of advice before we continue: *Paychecks* and *payroll tax payments* are two transaction types that can be difficult to correct in QuickBooks. This is because the posting of a *paycheck* affects not only general ledger account balances, but also employee payroll subsidiary records. (QuickBooks maintains gross wages and employee tax withholding totals for each employee to facilitate preparation of payroll reports including year-end W-2s.) Try to be as accurate as possible when creating paychecks.

Paychecks are created through the **Pay Employees** button on the Home page:

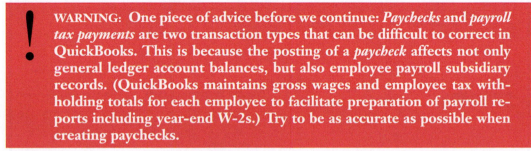

The screen looks something like this:

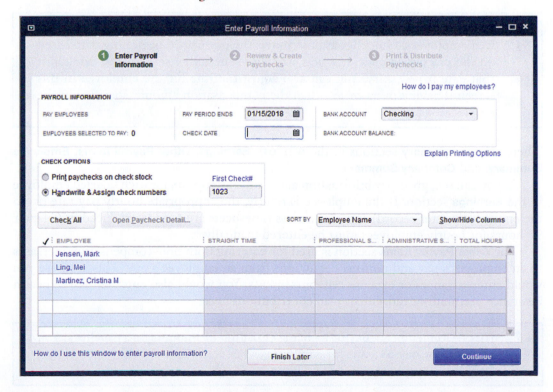

The **pay period ends** date, the **check date**, and the **bank account** to be charged must be entered.

Employees to be paid are selected by putting a checkmark in the field to the left of their name. (Companies can pay some or all employees in one session.)

To enter taxes manually, **Open Paycheck Detail** must be selected (middle left section of the screen) **before** clicking **Continue**. A **Preview Paycheck** screen will then appear for each employee selected, in alphabetic order. The **Preview Paycheck** screen looks something like this:

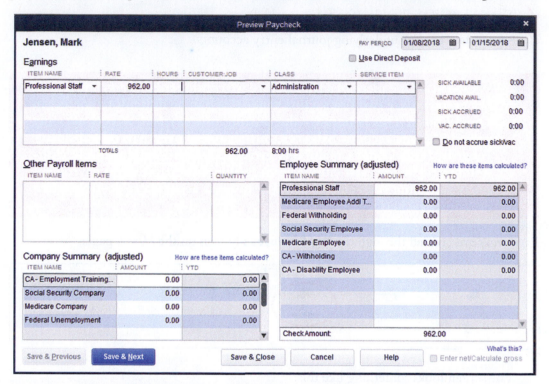

 HINT: Check to determine that the pay period indicated is correct. For salaried employees, QuickBooks determines the pay period beginning date based on the **pay period ends** date you entered in the initial screen. You can adjust that date if necessary. You can also adjust the **rate** for the employee in this screen if paying more or less than the compensation amount specified in the employee setup.

There are four primary sections in the window: **Earnings**, **Other Payroll Items**, **Employee Summary**, and **Company Summary**.

As you can see, gross pay information automatically appears for each salaried employee in the **Earnings** section. If the employee is hourly, the appropriate hourly pay rate (from the employee master record) appears. Unless timesheets are used (introduced in Chapter 9), hours for hourly employees must be entered manually.

The **Other Payroll Items** section is used for entering both non-compensation increases to an employee's pay and non-tax deductions from an employee's pay. This is where you would enter advances or expense reimbursements. You would also enter employee health insurance premium or retirement plan contributions here.

 HINT: Remember, a **payroll item** must exist for all amounts on a paycheck. You can add new **payroll items** for employees when in this window by selecting **Add New** in the appropriate field.

Employee tax withholdings are entered in the **Employee Summary** section. Employer payroll taxes are entered in the **Company Summary** section. (This is automatic if you subscribe to one of the payroll plans offered by Intuit.)

The screen looks like this for Mark Jensen after you complete step 6 of the following Practice Exercise:

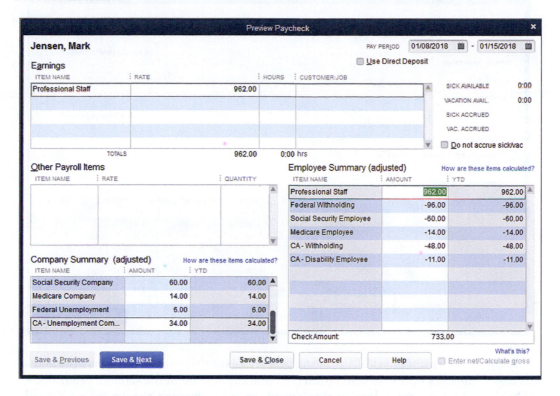

Clicking **Save & Next** takes you to the next employee selected for payment.

When all employee paycheck forms have been completed, the following window appears:

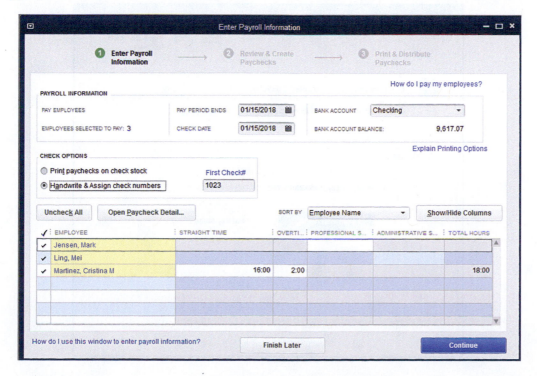

Paycheck Detail can be reopened and modified at this point, if needed. If no modifications are needed, **Continue** should be clicked.

The screen looks like this:

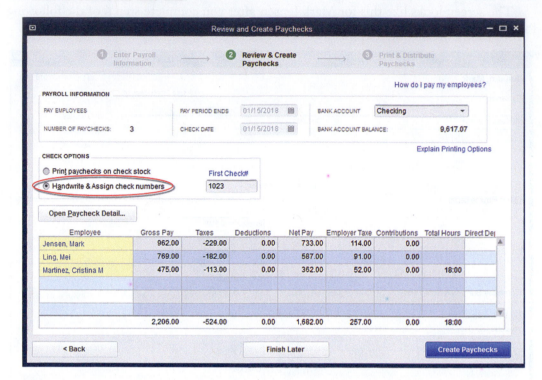

Because we are not physically printing paychecks for this course, the **handwrite and assign check numbers** option should be selected (middle section of the screen). (Your version of QuickBooks may have an **assign check numbers to handwritten checks** option instead.)

Once the user selects **Create Paychecks** (bottom right of the screen), the following screen appears:

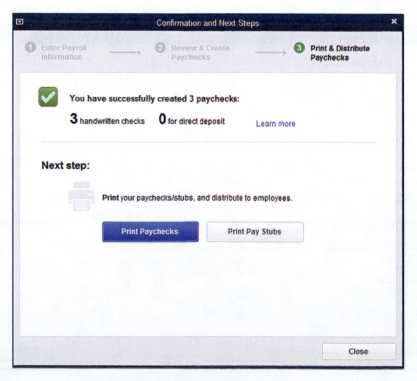

Note that **Pay stubs** can be printed in addition to paychecks. **Pay stubs** provide a summary of current and year to date payroll detail for employees.

> **BEHIND THE SCENES** Normally, employees must be provided with written detail of compensation amounts and tax withholdings. If a company does not include those amounts on the paycheck, a pay stub is a convenient alternative.

> What is the underlying journal entry for a **paycheck** transaction? (Answer at end of chapter.)

QuickCheck
8-2

PRACTICE
EXERCISE

Preparing paychecks for Sac City Accounting Services.
(Sac City pays employees on the last day of the pay period.)

1. Click **Pay Employees** (Home page).

2. Enter "1/15/18" as the **Pay Period Ends** date.

3. Enter "1/15/18" as the **Check Date** and Select **Checking** as the **bank account**.

4. Click the **Check All** button above the employee names.

5. Click **Open Paycheck Detail**.

6. For Mark Jensen:

   a. Make sure the pay period start date is 1/8/18.

   b. Change the rate to $962 in the **Earnings** section (pay for the one week ending 1/15).

   c. Enter employee taxes (bottom right section) as follows:

      i. Medicare Employee Addl Tax—0

         1. This line **may not appear** in your version of QuickBooks.

      ii. Federal Withholding—96

      iii. Social Security Employee—60

      iv. Medicare Employee—14

      v. CA–Withholding—48

      vi. CA–Disability—11

   d. Note: You do **not** need to enter employee taxes as negatives. QuickBooks will automatically deduct the tax amounts.

   e. Enter employer taxes in the **Company Summary** section as follows:

      i. CA–Employment Training Tax—1

      ii. Social Security Company—60

      iii. Medicare Company—14

      iv. Federal Unemployment—6

      v. CA–Unemployment Company—33

   f. Net check should total $733.

   g. Click **Save & Next**.

7. For Mei Ling:

   a. Make sure the pay period start date is 1/8/18.

   b. Change the rate to $769 in the **Earnings** section (pay for the one week ending 1/15).

(continued)

c. Enter employee taxes as follows:

     i.   Medicare Employee Addl Tax, if applicable—0

     ii.   Federal Withholding—77

     iii.   Social Security Employee—48

     iv.   Medicare Employee—11

     v.   CA–Withholding—38

     vi.   CA–Disability—8

d. Enter employer taxes in the **Company Summary** section as follows:

     i.   CA–Employment Training Tax—1

     ii.   Social Security Company—48

     iii.   Medicare Company—11

     iv.   Federal Unemployment—5

     v.   CA–Unemployment Company—26

e. Net check should total $587.

f. Click **Save & Next**.

8. For Cristina Martinez:

   a. Make sure the pay period start date is 1/9/17.

   b. In the **Earnings** section, select **Straight time** and enter "16" in the **Hours** column. Select **Overtime** and enter "2" in the **Hours** column.

     i.   Cristina worked 8 hours on Tuesday and 10 hours on Thursday. Total gross compensation should equal $475.

   c. Enter employee taxes as follows:

     i.   Medicare Employee Addl Tax, if applicable—0

     ii.   Federal Withholding—48

     iii.   Social Security Employee—29

     iv.   Medicare Employee—7

     v.   CA–Withholding—24

     vi.   CA–Disability—5

   d. Enter employer taxes in the **Company Summary** section as follows:

     i.   CA–Employment Training Tax—0

     ii.   Social Security Company—29

     iii.   Medicare Company—7

     iv.   Federal Unemployment—3

     v.   CA–Unemployment Company—13

   e. Net check should total $362.

   f. Click **Save & Close**.

9. Click **Continue**.

10. Click **Handwrite and assign check numbers** (or **Assign check numbers to handwritten checks**, if applicable).

11. Enter "1023" as the **First Check Number**.

12. Click **Create Paychecks**.

13. Click **Close**.

Editing Paychecks

Editing paychecks should only be done if a payroll error is found **before** the check is printed. If an error is found after the paycheck has been printed but before the check has been distributed to the employee, the **paycheck** should be voided and a new **paycheck** created. If an error is found **after** a paycheck has been distributed, the correction(s) should be made as part of a subsequent paycheck so that the employee payroll records are adjusted appropriately. Only **paycheck** and **liability adjustment** transaction types affect the employee's record, so corrections made by issuing a regular **check** to the employee (in the case of an underpayment) or by taking cash from an employee (in the case of an overpayment) would not adjust the employee records and should not be used. (Advanced users of QuickBooks can make certain adjustments to employer and employee tax records through a **liability adjustment** transaction, but that process is not covered in this course.)

To edit a **paycheck**, you must first open the **paycheck** form. **Paycheck** transactions can be found using the **Find** feature or through the **Employee Center**. If the **Employee Center** is used, **paychecks** issued to an employee are displayed when the employee name is highlighted and the appropriate dates are selected.

The **paycheck** screen looks something like this:

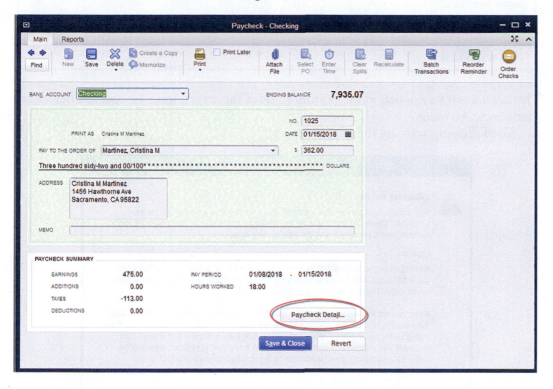

To edit the **paycheck**, click **Paycheck Detail**. The next screen looks something like this:

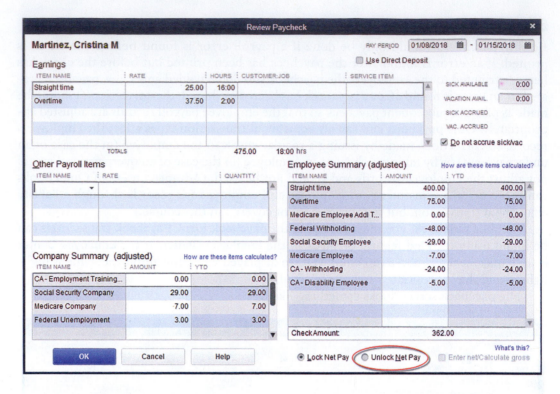

The **Unlock Net Pay** option at the bottom right of the screen must be checked before any changes can be made.

The following warning then appears:

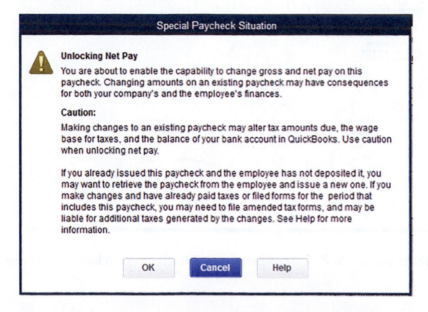

If **OK** is selected, the **paycheck** can be edited. After the **paycheck** is adjusted and the transaction is closed, QuickBooks will automatically lock the **paycheck**.

> **!** **WARNING: Editing a *paycheck* should only be done if the check hasn't been issued <u>or</u> if you're taking this class and made an error the first time through!**

PRACTICE EXERCISE

Editing a paycheck for Sac City Accounting.
(The state unemployment tax was calculated incorrectly for Cristina Martinez. The amount should have been $16. The paycheck has **not** been printed yet.)

1. Open the **Employee Center** (main menu bar).

2. Highlight **Cristina Martinez**.

3. Double-click the **paycheck** dated 1/15.

    a. You may have to change the **date** field in the middle tool bar to **All** to see that paycheck.

4. Click **Paycheck Detail**.

5. Click **Unlock Net Pay**.

6. Click **OK** at the warning.

7. Change **CA–Unemployment Company** to 16. (Last **payroll item** in the **Company Summary** section.)

8. Click **OK**.

9. Click **Yes** to save the changes.

10. Click **Save & Close**.

11. Exit out of the **Employee Center**.

PROCESSING AND REPORTING PAYROLL TAXES

Payroll taxes are generally remitted to the appropriate taxing authorities quarterly, monthly, or semiweekly, depending on the particular tax and the size of the payroll. (Companies with large payrolls remit certain taxes more frequently.)

Here's a brief summary of some of the reporting and remittance requirements of the various types of payroll taxes:

✓ Federal income tax withholding and FICA taxes:
  ○ Employee taxes withheld and employer taxes are remitted together.
  ○ Taxes are deposited quarterly, monthly, or semiweekly, depending on the size of the payroll.
  ○ Form 941 is used to report wages and taxes and is filed quarterly.

✓ Federal unemployment taxes:
  ○ Taxes must be deposited periodically, depending on the size of the payroll.
  ○ Form 940, filed annually, is used to report wages and taxes.

✓ State taxes:
  ○ Each state sets the filing requirements for state payroll taxes.
  ○ Generally, states with a personal income tax match the state deposit requirements to the federal deposit requirements for federal income taxes and FICA.
  ○ Quarterly filings are common for other types of state payroll taxes.

Remitting (Depositing) Payroll Taxes

The process for remitting payroll taxes is similar to the process for remitting sales taxes collected from customers (covered in Chapter 6). QuickBooks accumulates the payroll tax liabilities throughout the reporting period in the liability account designated in the setup of each tax **payroll item**. At the end of the reporting period, the amounts due, by taxing authority, are displayed in the **pay liabilities** window. If necessary, payroll liabilities can be adjusted after payroll liability checks (**payroll liability check** is the transaction type) are created.

> **!** **WARNING:** Like *sales tax payments, payroll liability checks* cannot be edited. They must be voided (or deleted) and reissued if an error is made.

Payroll tax liability checks are created through the **Pay Liabilities** option on the **Home Page**:

The initial screen looks something like this:

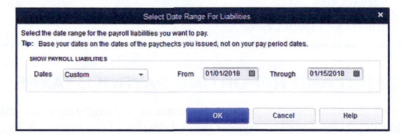

The reporting period entered would be based on the deposit requirements of the particular tax.

> **BEHIND THE SCENES** Payroll tax deposits are based on pay dates (paycheck dates), **not** pay period dates.

Clicking **OK** would take to a screen that looks like this:

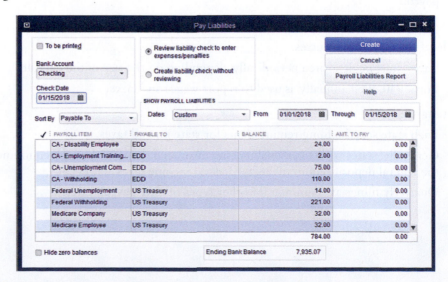

The **bank account** to be charged must be selected. The **check date** must also be entered. (The date entered should be the date of the **liability** check not the **paycheck** date.)

Tax agencies to be paid are then selected. (A company can pay some or all payroll taxes.)

 HINT: QuickBooks will include multiple payments to the same taxing authority on a single check.

BEHIND THE SCENES All federal tax deposits must be made by electronic funds transfer through the Electronic Federal Tax Payment System (EFTPS). Many states either require or allow companies to make deposits electronically. For the purposes of this course, we record the remittance of federal taxes as checks payable to the U.S. Treasury and the remittance of state withholdings as checks payable to Employment Development Department (the agency responsible for employment taxes in the state of California).

The option **Review liability check to enter expenses/penalties** can be selected if a company has penalties or interest to enter or if the user wants to review the checks before printing. A separate check will be issued for each taxing authority selected.

(continued)

PRACTICE
EXERCISE

Remitting payroll taxes for Sac City Accounting.
(Sac City decides to deposit federal income taxes, FICA taxes, and state employee taxes early.)

1. Click **Pay Liabilities** on the Home page.

2. Enter "1/1/18" through "1/15/18" as the dates and click **OK**.

3. Make sure the **To Be Printed** box is not checked.

4. Select **Checking** as the **bank account** and enter "1/15/18" as the **check date**.

5. Put a checkmark next to:

    a. **CA–Disability Employee**

    b. **CA–Withholding**

    c. **Federal Withholding**

    d. **Medicare Company**

    e. **Medicare Employee**

    f. **Social Security Company**

    g. **Social Security Employee**

6. **Amt. To Pay** should show as $693.

7. Click **Review liability check to enter expense/penalties** (top of window).

8. Click **Create**.

9. Enter check number 1026 for the check to EDD.

    a. You may need to de-select the **Print Later** box before you can add the check number.

    b. Amount should be $134.

10. Click the right arrow just above **Find** at the top left of the screen and enter check number 1027 for the check to the U.S. Treasury. (Agree to the transaction change if prompted.)

    a.   De-select the **Print Later** box if necessary.

    b.   Amount should be $559.

11. Click **Save & Close**.

Editing Payroll Tax Liabilities

Employer and employee payroll tax amounts can be adjusted in QuickBooks through **Liability Adjustment** transactions. Open the dropdown menu on the main menu bar, click **Payroll Taxes and Liabilities**, and select **Adjust Payroll Liabilities** to access the form. As noted earlier, we are not covering that process in this course.

Preparing Payroll Tax Forms

Federal and state payroll tax forms can be completed in QuickBooks if the user has subscribed to the **Enhanced** payroll plan. Local tax forms are included in the **Full Service** subscription payroll service.

Users without a payroll service subscription can complete the forms manually using information available in QuickBooks payroll reports.

PREPARING PAYROLL REPORTS

There are a variety of payroll reports that summarize compensation and payroll tax transactions. Some of the most commonly used reports include:

- Payroll Summary
  - Summary by employee of components of gross pay, **net pay**, and employer taxes for the selected period.
- Payroll Liability Balances
  - Shows unpaid payroll liability balances by type.
- Employee State Taxes Detail
  - Default report summarizes state taxes (employee and employer) by employee.
  - Can be modified to show all taxes (state and federal) by tax **payroll item**.

All payroll reports can be accessed through the **Employees & Payroll** option on the **Reports** menu (main menu bar).

Net pay The amount of an employee's paycheck, after subtracting withheld amounts.

PRACTICE EXERCISE

Preparing payroll reports for Sac City Accounting.

1. Click **Reports**.

2. Click **Employees & Payroll**.

3. Click **Payroll Summary**.

    a.   Change dates to 1/1 to 1/15/18.

(continued)

4. Exit out of window.

5. Click **Reports**.

6. Click **Employees & Payroll**.

7. Click **Employee State Taxes Detail**.

   a.   Change dates to 1/1 to 1/15/18.

   b.   On menu bar at top of screen,

       i.   Select "Payroll item detail" for **Total By**.

       ii.   Select "All Company" for **Payroll Item**.

   c.   Click **Refresh** if necessary.

   d.   The report now shows all employer taxes, totaled by type.

8. Exit out of report window.

False. Taxes withheld from employees are expenses to the employee, not the employer.

QuickCheck
8-1

	Wage expense (gross payroll)	XXX	
	Payroll tax expense (employer taxes)	XXX	
	Cash (net pay)		XXX
	Payroll taxes payable (employee + employer taxes)		XXX

QuickCheck
8-2

CHAPTER SHORTCUTS

Turn on manual payroll processing
1. Click Help
2. Click QuickBooks Help
3. Click the Search field
4. Enter Manual Payroll
5. Click Process payroll manually (without a subscription to QuickBooks Payroll)
6. On step 1, click link to Manual Payroll Calculations
7. Click Set my company file to use manual calculations

Add an employee
1. Click Employee Center
2. Click New Employee

Edit an employee
1. Click Employee Center
2. Highlight employee to change
3. Click Edit Employee (pencil icon)

Add payroll item
1. Click List/Payroll Item List
2. Click Payroll Item/New

Edit payroll item
1. Click List/Payroll Item List
2. Highlight item to change
3. Click Payroll Item/Edit Payroll Item

Pay an employee
1. Click Pay Employees on Home Page
2. Click Open Paycheck Detail to record taxes

Edit a paycheck

1. Find and open the paycheck to be edited
2. Click Paycheck Detail
3. Select Unlock Net Pay

Pay payroll liabilities

1. Click Pay liabilities on Home Page

CHAPTER REVIEW

Matching

Match the term or phrase (as used in QuickBooks) to its best definition.

1. Manual payroll
2. Personal
3. Payroll item list
4. Pay frequency

5. Paycheck
6. Payroll Info
7. Payroll schedule
8. Payroll liability check

_____   Transaction type used to record payment of employee and employer payroll taxes

_____   Transaction type used to record wage payments to employees

_____   Tool available to pay employees in specific cycles

_____   How often employee wages are paid

_____   Tab in employee setup where compensation rates and withholding allowances are entered

_____   Database of compensation and employee withholding types

_____   Method used to record employee paychecks without a payroll service subscription

_____   Tab in employee setup where name and Social Security number are entered

Multiple Choice

1. The social security number of new employees is entered in the _____ tab of the **new employee** window.
   a. Personal
   b. Additional Info
   c. Payroll Info
   d. Employment Info

2. Payroll items in QuickBooks include:
   a. compensation items only.
   b. payroll tax items only.
   c. compensation and payroll tax items only.
   d. all items that would increase or decrease an employee's paycheck.

3. Which of the following taxes are paid by both the employee and the employer?
   a. Federal withholding
   b. Federal unemployment
   c. FICA
   d. State withholding (if applicable)

4. Taxes withheld from employees are:
    a. remitted on or before the tax report due date, depending on the size of the employer.
    b. always remitted monthly.
    c. always remitted within three days of issuing paychecks.
    d. always remitted with the tax report.

5. Which of the following is not an expense of the employer?
    a. State unemployment
    b. Federal unemployment
    c. FICA
    d. All of the above are expenses of the employer.

ASSIGNMENTS

Background information from Chapter 5: You are one of three owners of Software 2 Go, a small retail store specializing in computer software. You have been in business for almost two years and have been fairly profitable both years. The business is a corporation with a 12/31 year-end.

The owners share business responsibilities.

- Rey Martinez runs retail operations at the shop and handles all merchandise purchasing.

- Elena Turgenev manages commercial sales.

- You handle all the accounting and administrative functions.

The company's primary commercial customers are professional service firms in Sacramento, although they also sell to a private tutoring center for children (Computer Fun Park). Credit terms for these customers are currently Net 30.

You also sell to walk-in customers. (You take cash/checks or credit cards.) Cash and checks are held in the safe and deposited once a week, on Fridays. Credit cards receipts are batched and transmitted to the merchant bank (Bank of Sutterville) every Friday. It generally takes one business day for the bank to process the receipts and deposit the funds in Software 2 Go's account. Bank of Sutterville charges a processing fee of 2% of the credit card total.

In November, the buyer for Komputer Kidz called Rey and asked about purchasing software from Software 2 Go. Komputer Kidz is a tutoring center specializing in children ages 6–12. Unlike Computer Fun Park, it will be reselling the software titles to its customers (actually Komputer Kidz will be selling to its customer's parents!). It means you'll have to increase your inventory levels for certain titles, but you're all very happy for the increase in sales volume!

Your current inventory includes financial, educational, graphic, and simulation software. All items are taxable (except, of course, any sales to resellers like Komputer Kidz).

You took out a loan from Bank of Sutterville when you first started the business. The balance at 11/30/17 is $6,673.00. The monthly payment (due on the 30th of each month) is $200 (including interest). The interest rate on the note is 5%.

You rent the shop for $1,500 per month under a five-year lease.

12/1/17

✓ Rey calls an owner's meeting. He explains that he'd like to hire a couple of employees to help him run the store. He's thinking of hiring a full-time person to handle the walk-in customers and a part-time person to work on the busier days of the week. He's convinced that sales would increase with better customer service.

Assignment 8A

Software 2 Go

✓ You and Elena agree with Rey's plan.

- The full-time person will be offered a $30,000 per year salary with insurance benefits provided after 60 days.
- The part-time person will be offered $14 per hour.
- Employees will be paid semimonthly.
- Software 2 Go doesn't currently have any kind of retirement plan but might consider that at a later date.

✓ Rey calls the local community college and talks with its Career Center, which agrees to post both positions on its job board.

12/8/17

✓ Rey interviews several people and, after checking their references, offers the full-time position to Richard Yang and the part-time position to Sharice Young. They both accept the offers and will be starting on December 18th. You will set them up as employees as soon as they complete the necessary tax forms.

✓ You realize you need to get payroll set up in QuickBooks. You first turn on manual payroll processing.

✓ You also edit the company's preferences to include **Full Payroll** functionality. [**TIP**: An employee section should now appear on the Home Page.]

✓ You set up an annual salary **payroll item** and an hourly **payroll item** using the **Custom Setup** option. You don't think there will be any overtime for Sharice, but you set up an overtime **payroll item** (time-and-a-half) just in case. (Overtime is paid on all hours over 8 in a single day.)

- Because you might be hiring additional employees in the future, you decide to use "Salary," "Hourly Pay," and "Overtime Pay" for the **payroll item** names.
- You decide to record all employee compensation (including overtime) in the Staff Wages account that's already been set up.

✓ Your review the tax withholding **payroll items** set up automatically by QuickBooks. You edit all federal taxes **payroll items** so that U.S. Treasury is the agency (**quick add** U.S. Treasury as a vendor) and Payroll Taxes Expense is the account used for employer tax expenses. You do not change the liability account, any of the tax rates, or any of the types of wages subject to tax.

✓ You set up the following California state taxes using the **Custom Setup** option (State Tax **item type**). You enter Employment Development Department (**quick add** Employment Development Department as a vendor) as the tax agency and 12345 as the number. You use Payroll Taxes Expense as the expense account (where appropriate) and Payroll Liabilities as the liability account. All compensation is subject to state payroll taxes.

- State Withholding.
- State Disability—Set rate as 1%.
- State Unemployment—Set rate as 3.4%.
- Other Taxes—You select CA–Employment Training Tax as the tax type; set 0.1% as the rate.

12/18/17

✓ Both Richard and Sharice come in to work today. Before they report to Rey, you have them complete all the necessary tax forms.

✓ Using the following information provided by Richard and Sharice, you set them up as new employees:

	Richard Yang	Sharice Young
SSN	123-45-6789	987-65-4321
Date of birth	11/18/86	12/31/86
Address	5406 First Ave Sacramento, CA 95822	5844 NE 75th St Sacramento, CA 95822
Pay frequency	Semimonthly	Semimonthly
Pay	$30,000 per year	$14 per hour
Filing status	Single	Single
Federal allowances	1	1
State allowances	1	1
Hire date	12/18/17	12/18/17

[**TIP:** Don't forget to add CA–Employment Training Tax on the **Other** taxes tab.]

✓ You decide not to track sick/vacation pay in QuickBooks, so you click **Leave As Is** if prompted.

12/31/17

✓ Rey lets you know that Sharice worked 4 hours each Thursday and Friday during the past two weeks (16 hours in total). She also worked 10 hours on December 18th organizing the stockroom. You're glad you went ahead and set up the overtime **payroll item**.

✓ You create payroll checks for both Richard and Sharice. The payroll period is 12/17-12/31. The first payroll check is #2484. Richard's net payroll check is $953.12. Sharice's net payroll check is $288.22.

	Richard	Sharice
Withholdings:		
Federal Withholding	125.00	37.80
Social Security	77.50	23.44
Medicare.	18.13	5.48
CA–Withholding	62.50	18.90
CA–Disability	13.75	4.16
Employer taxes:		
CA–Employment Training Tax	1.25	0.38
Social Security	77.50	23.44
Medicare.	18.13	5.48
Federal Unemployment	7.50	2.27
CA–Unemployment	42.50	12.85

✓ You remit the following December taxes:

- CA-Withholding
- CA-Disability Employee
- Federal Withholding
- Medicare (company and employee)
- Social Security (company and employee)
- The total amount remitted is $511.21. State taxes total $99.31 (check #2486). Federal taxes total $411.90 (check #2487).

Check numbers 12/31

Checking account balance. . . . $ 10,917.06
Net income—December . . . . . $ 11,193.67
Total assets. $114,487.55
Total liabilities . . . . $ 6,792.55

REPORTS TO CREATE FOR ASSIGNMENT 8A

All reports should be in portrait orientation; fit to one page wide.

- Journal (12/1–12/31)—include **Paycheck** and **Liability Check** transaction types only.
    - Remove **Trans #** and **Adj** columns.
- Payroll Summary report for December 2017.
- Payroll Item Listing (on the **Reports/Employees and Payroll** dropdown menu) including the following columns:
    - Payroll Item.
    - Type.
    - Amount.
    - Expense Account.
    - Liability Account.
    - Payable to.
- Payroll Liability Balances (dated 12/31/17). Total Only.

Assignment 8B

The Abacus Shop

Background information from Chapter 5: You are one of three owners of The Abacus Shop, a small retail store specializing in books and supplies for accountants. You have been in business for a few years, and although the operation has been profitable, you and the other owners would like to grow the business a bit this year. You have hired an outside accountant, Martin Schmidt, to help you develop a business plan. The business is a corporation with a 12/31 year-end.

The owners share business responsibilities.

- Marvena Smith runs retail operations at the shop and handles all merchandise purchasing.
- Brandon Nguyen manages sales to the accounting firms.
- You handle all the accounting and administrative functions.

The company's primary regular customers are accounting firms in Sacramento. Credit terms for these customers are 2%/10, Net 30.

You also sell to walk-in customers (cash/checks or credit cards only). Cash and checks are held in the safe and deposited once a week, on Fridays. Credit cards receipts are batched and transmitted to the merchant bank (Bank of Sutterville) every Friday. It generally takes one business day for the bank to process the receipts and deposit the funds in The Abacus Shop's account. Pocket Bank charges a fee of 2% of the credit card total.

In September, the buyer for Sactown College Bookstore called Marvena and asked about purchasing specialty textbooks from The Abacus Shop. The bookstore is understaffed and overcrowded and would like Abacus to handle some of the accounting course textbook orders. The margin will be smaller than normal for Abacus but the volume is good, so the three of you agree to accept the bookstore's order. The textbooks for spring semester arrived on 9/30.

Your current inventory includes financial analysis software, calculators, accounting books, desk lamps, high-quality stationary paper, and, of course, the textbooks. All items are taxable.

You took out a loan from Pocket Bank when you first started the business. The balance at 9/30/17 is $3,556.44. The monthly payment (due on the 30th of each month) is $129 (including interest). The interest rate on the note is 9%.

You rent the shop for $800 per month.

10/2/17

✓ Marvena calls an owner's meeting. She explains that she'd like to hire a couple of employees to help her run the store. She's thinking of hiring a full-time person to handle the walk-in customers and a part-time person to work on the busier days of the week. She's convinced that sales would increase with better customer service.

✓ You and Brandon agree with Marvena's plan.

- The full-time person will be offered a $36,000 per year salary with insurance benefits provided after 60 days.

- The part-time person will be offered $15 per hour.

- Employees will be paid semimonthly.

- The Abacus Shop doesn't currently have any kind of retirement plan but might consider that at a later date.

✓ Marvena calls the local community college and talks with its Career Center, which agrees to post both positions on its job board.

10/9/17

✓ Marvena interviews several people and, after checking their references, offers the full-time position to Zoe Hermosa and the part-time position to Anton Petrov. They both accept the offers and will be starting on October 17th. You will set them up as employees as soon as they complete the necessary tax forms.

✓ You realize you need to get payroll set up in QuickBooks. You first turn on manual payroll processing.

✓ You also edit the company's preferences to include **Full Payroll** functionality. You click **Last Name** so that the employee list will be listed alphabetically by last name. [**TIP**: An employee section should appear on the Home Page once you saved these preferences.]

✓ You set up an annual salary **payroll item** and an hourly **payroll item** using the **Custom Setup** option. You don't think there will be any overtime for Anton, but you set up an overtime **payroll item** (time-and-a-half) just in case. (Overtime is paid on all hours over 8 in a single day.)

- Because you might be hiring additional employees in the future, you decide to use "Salary," "Hourly Pay," and "Overtime Pay" for the **payroll item** names.

- You decide to record all employee compensation (including overtime) in the Staff Wages Expense account that's already been set up.

✓ Your review the tax withholding **payroll items** set up automatically by QuickBooks. You edit all federal taxes **payroll items** so that U.S. Treasury is the agency (**quick add** U.S. Treasury as a vendor) and Payroll Taxes Expense is the account used for employer tax expenses. You do not change the liability account, any of the tax rates, or any of the types of wages subject to tax.

✓ You set up the following California state taxes using the **Custom Setup** option (State Tax **item type**). You enter Employment Development Department (**quick add** Employment Development Department as a vendor) as the tax agency and 134679 as the number. You use Payroll Tax Expense as the expense account (where appropriate) and Payroll Liabilities as the liability account. All compensation is subject to state payroll taxes.

- State Withholding.

- State Disability—Set rate as 1%.

- State Unemployment—Set rate as 3.4%.

- Other Taxes—You select CA–Employment Training Tax as the tax type; set 0.1% as the rate.

10/17/17

✓ Both Zoe and Anton come in to work today. Before they report to Marvena, you have them complete all the necessary tax forms.

✓ Using the following information provided by Zoe and Anton, you set them up as new employees:

	Zoe Hermosa	Anton Petrov
SSN	123-45-6789	987-65-4321
Date of birth	12/31/86	11/18/86
Address	8221 Martyn Place Sacramento, CA 95822	4188 Simmons Way Sacramento, CA 95822
Pay frequency.	Semimonthly	Semimonthly
Pay	$36,000 per year	$15 per hour
Filing status	Single	Single
Federal allowances.	1	1
State allowances	1	1
Hire date.	10/17/17	10/17/17

[**TIP**: Don't forget to add CA–Employment Training Tax on the **Other** taxes tab.]

✓ You decide not to track sick/vacation pay in QuickBooks, so you click **Leave As Is** if prompted.

10/31/17

✓ Marvena lets you know that Anton worked three 4-hour shifts each week during the past two weeks (24 hours in total). He also worked 10 hours last Friday (the 27th) organizing the stockroom. You're glad you went ahead and set up the overtime **payroll item**.

✓ You create payroll checks for both Anton and Zoe. The payroll period is 10/17-10/31/17. The first payroll check is #1939. Zoe's net payroll check is $1,143.75. Anton's net payroll check is $400.31.

	Zoe	Anton
Withholdings:		
Federal Withholding	150.00	52.50
Social Security	93.00	32.55
Medicare.	21.75	7.61
CA–Withholding	75.00	26.25
CA–Disability	16.50	5.78
Employer taxes:		
CA–Employment Training Tax	1.50	0.53
Social Security	93.00	32.55
Medicare.	21.75	7.61
Federal Unemployment	9.00	3.15
CA–Unemployment	51.00	17.85

✓ You remit the following October taxes:

- CA-Withholding
- CA-Disability Employee
- Federal Withholding
- Medicare (company and employee)
- Social Security (company and employee)
- The total amount remitted is $635.85. State taxes total $123.53 (check #2486). Federal taxes total $512.32 (check #2487).

Check numbers 10/31

Checking account balance.... $20,836.80
Net income—October....... $38,402.61
Total assets................ $93,052.26
Total liabilities............ $ 5,497.52

REPORTS TO CREATE FOR ASSIGNMENT 8B

All reports should be in portrait orientation; fit to one page wide.

- Journal (10/1–10/31)—include **Paycheck** and **Payroll Liability Check** transaction types only.
    - Remove **Trans #** and **Adj** columns.
- Payroll Summary report for October 2017.
- Payroll Item Listing (on the **Reports/Employees and Payroll** dropdown menu) including the following columns:
    - Payroll Item.
    - Type.
    - Amount.
    - Expense Account.
    - Liability Account.
    - Payable to.
- Payroll Liability Balances (dated 10/31/17). Total Only.

APPENDIX 8A TRACKING EMPLOYEE SICK AND VACATION TIME

In QuickBooks, companies can:

- Track available leave time (sick and vacation) by employee, in hours.
- Record vacation and sick leave wages expense.

> **BEHIND THE SCENES** QuickBooks recognizes vacation and sick leave wage expenses, through the employee's **paycheck**, when the leave is taken. No journal entry is created for earned leave time.

To use the leave time tracking feature, **payroll items** must be set up, and employee records must include information related to how leave time is calculated.

SETTING UP PAYROLL ITEMS FOR LEAVE TIME

If a company has both hourly and salaried workers, four additional **payroll items** would need to be set up to track leave time.

- Sick pay (hourly workers).
- Vacation pay (hourly workers).
- Sick pay (salaried workers).
- Vacation pay (salaried workers).

The process is similar to the process for setting up other types of pay covered in Chapter 8. For example, to set up sick pay for hourly workers, click **Payroll Item List** on the **Item** dropdown menu (main menu bar):

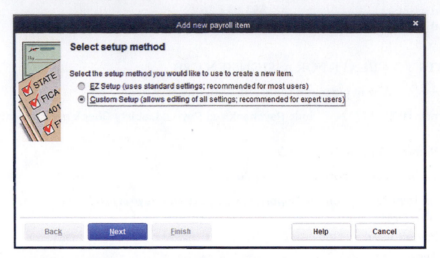

Select **Custom Setup** and click **Next**:

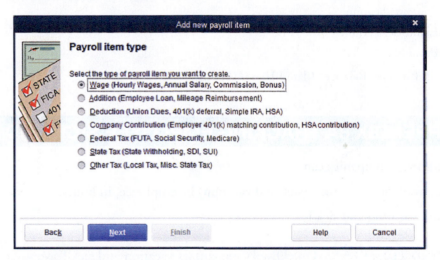

Select **Wage** and click **Next**. Select **Hourly** and click **Next**:

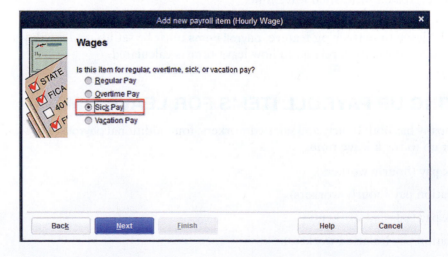

Select **Sick Pay**, click **Next**, and enter a name for the **payroll item**. You might use something like "Sick Hours" as the name.

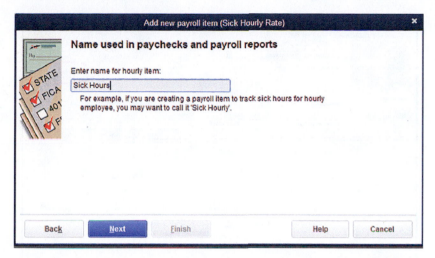

Click **Next**, choose the appropriate general ledger account, and click **Finish**.

> **BEHIND THE SCENES** Most companies either record vacation and sick pay in a leave time wages expense account or simply record it in their general administrative wages expense account.

SETTING UP SICK AND VACATION LEAVE IN EMPLOYEE RECORDS

The amount of leave time and the policy for using leave time must be set up for each employee in his or her employee record. This can be done when the employee record is first created (a new hire), or the record can be edited at a later date. In the following example, leave time is being set up as an edit to an existing employee's record.

The employee record is accessed through the **Employee Center**:

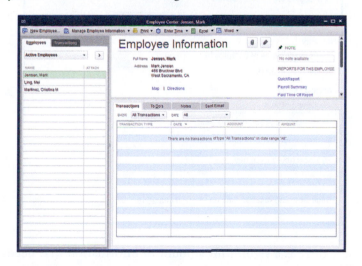

Highlight the employee name and click the **edit** icon (the pencil) in the top right corner of the window. The following window will open:

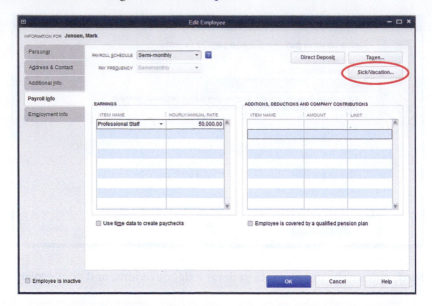

Policies for sick and vacation time are entered by clicking the **Sick/Vacation** link on the **Payroll Info** tab. The screen looks something like this:

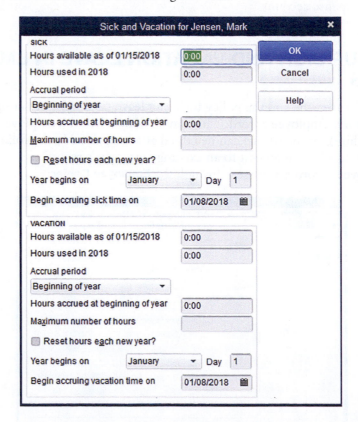

As you can see, there is a significant amount of information that needs to be entered in this screen.

- If leave tracking had already been set up, the **Hours Available** and **Hours Used** fields would have been automatically updated by QuickBooks.

- The policy for determining when leave time will be earned by the employee is set in the **accrual period** field. Both sick and vacation hours can be accrued at the beginning of the year, every paycheck, or based on the number of hours in each paycheck. The company policy is identified in the **Accrual period** dropdown for each type of pay (sick and vacation).

- The amount of leave time earned is entered next. If leave is earned at the beginning of the year, the annual amount would be entered in the **hours accrued at beginning of year** field. The window will change depending on the **accrual period** selected. For example, if leave time is accrued **every paycheck**, the window will include a field for **hours accrued per paycheck**.

- The **maximum number of hours** field is used if there's a policy limiting the total amount of leave time that can be carried over from year to year. If you want leave time to reset to zero when a new year begins, check the **reset hours each new year?** box.

The screen might look something like this for an employee who earns 40 hours of sick leave and 80 hours of vacation at the beginning of each calendar year. The company allows the employee 160 hours of vacation time that can be accrued. Sick leave is reset each year (no carryover):

RECORDING SICK AND VACATION LEAVE TAKEN

Leave time taken is recorded through the employee's **paycheck**. In the following example, Cristina Martinez, an hourly employee, worked 40 hours and took 4 hours of sick time during the pay period.

The following window opens when you click **Pay Employees** on the Home page:

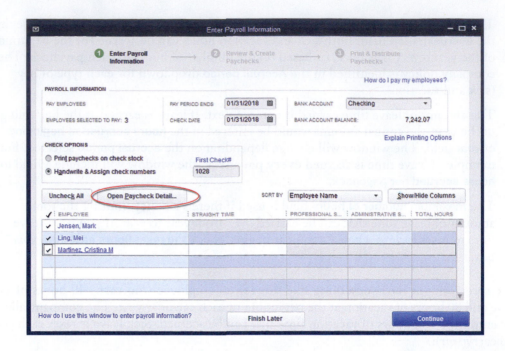

Employees to be paid must be selected. Click **Open Paycheck Detail** to enter sick or vacation leave.

Hours of regular time and leave time are entered on the **Preview Paycheck** screen. The screen would look something like this for Cristina:

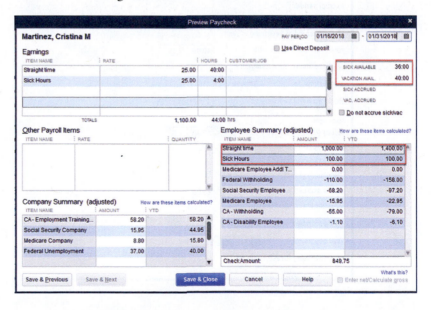

Cristina was given 40 hours of vacation and sick leave at the beginning of the year. Note that the number of sick hours available (top right corner of window) was automatically reduced by the 4 hours taken during the pay period.

LEAVE TIME REPORTING

A report showing used and available leave time by employee can be accessed by clicking **Employees & Payroll** on the **Reports** dropdown menu (main menu bar):

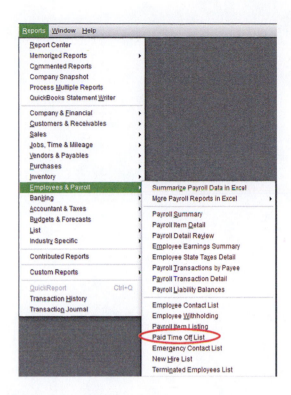

Click **Paid Time Off List**:

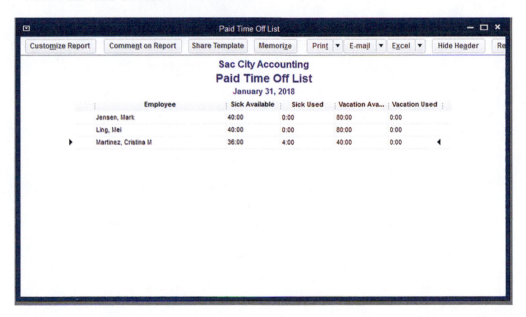

This report will always show current data. It can't be modified to show leave data for a prior period.

Project Costing and Billing for Time and Expenses

Objectives

After completing Chapter 9, you should be able to:

1. Set up jobs (project tracking) in QuickBooks.

2. Track billable and non-billable employee time by customer and by service using timesheets.

3. Process payroll checks using timesheet data.

4. Create invoices and sales receipts from tracked time.

5. Add billable expenses to invoices and sales receipts.

6. Prepare job reports.

In this chapter, we're going to cover tracking projects in QuickBooks and billing for time and expenses.

Many companies have employees and **don't** track specific projects or jobs. Retail stores, restaurants, banks, and gas stations are just a few examples. In a retail store, for example, managers generally don't track how much profit is made on a specific customer during the month. Instead, they might track how much gross profit is made on sales of a specific product or how much profit is made in a specific store. They may need to track which store an employee works in, but managers don't generally need to track how much time a specific employee spends helping a specific customer. The sections on project tracking in this chapter do not apply to those types of companies. (See Chapter 5 for reporting on profit by product and Chapter 10 for reporting on profit by department or location.)

However, there are many companies that **do** need to track costs and revenues by project (or **job** as called in QuickBooks).

For example, let's look at two construction companies. One bills its customers under "time-and-materials" contracts. The other bills its customers under "fixed-fee" contracts. The time-and-materials contractor is billing for labor and materials plus some kind of markup. Payroll records **must** include the hours for each customer, by project **and** by type of work if billing rates differ, because those hours will be used to invoice customers. If those hours are tracked in QuickBooks (which they can be), the invoicing process is more efficient.

The fixed-fee contractor generally bills a portion or percentage of the agreed upon price (the fixed fee) as the work progresses. The number of hours worked aren't needed to prepare the **invoice** or **sales receipt**. However, in order to evaluate project profitability, fixed-fee contractors need to be able to compare the revenue earned on a specific project to the specific costs (including labor costs) of that project. That information helps them evaluate the company's overall performance and the specific performance of project managers and improves their ability to bid on future projects.

There are two features available in QuickBooks for companies that work on projects that we do not work with in this course—estimating and progress invoicing. If you're interested in those features, talk with your instructor.

SETTING UP JOBS

Understanding a few basic concepts helps when working with **jobs** in QuickBooks:

- Multiple **jobs** can be tracked for a single customer.
  - QuickBooks also considers the customer itself a **job**, so you have to be careful when charging time or expenses. Once you set up **jobs** for a customer, all transactions should be charged to a specific **job**, not to the customer **name**.

- Multiple **jobs** for a customer **cannot** be billed on the same **invoice** or **sales receipt**. A separate **invoice** or **sales receipt** must be created for each **job**.

- When entering customer payments, QuickBooks displays all outstanding **invoices** for the customer on all **jobs** associated with the customer.

- All costs (labor, inventory, expenses) incurred on a **job** must be defined as **billable** **if** you intend to charge the customer for those costs on a future **invoice** or **sales receipt**. Costs are defined as **billable** on the transaction form (**bill**, **check** or **timesheet**, for example) by placing a checkmark in the **billable** column.

- Costs that are not defined as **billable** are included in all **job** reports but are not accessible when preparing **invoices** or **sales receipts**.

The process for setting up a **job** is very straightforward. **Jobs** are set up in the **Customer Center**:

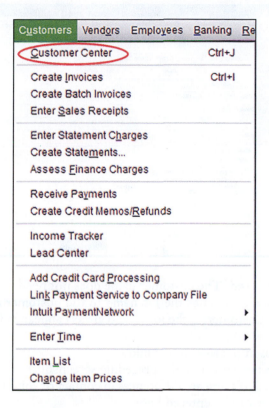

The **Customer Center** screen looks like this:

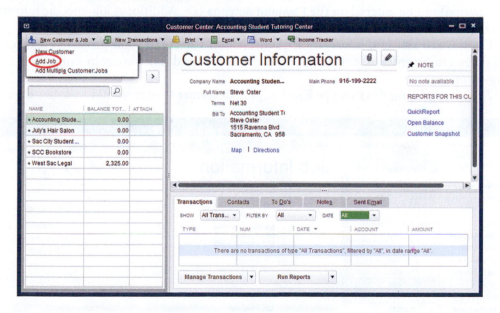

The customer name must be highlighted. The **Add Job** menu option on the **New Customer & Job** dropdown menu (top left of the screen) should be selected.

The **New Job** window looks like this:

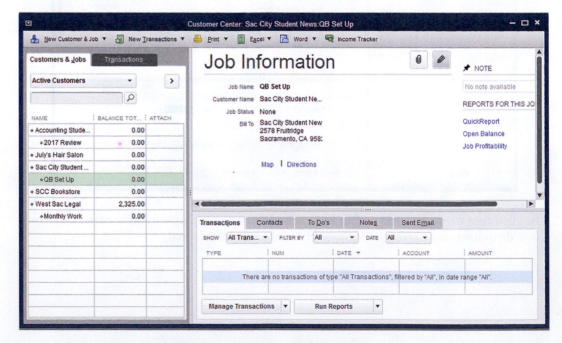

A **Job Name** must be entered. The customer name does not need to be included in the job name because QuickBooks attaches the **job name** to the **customer name**. For example, if Job 1 were created for Customer A, the job would always appear in QuickBooks reports as **Customer A:Job 1**.

There are four tabs in the **New Job** window.

In the **Address Info** tab (shown in the preceding screenshot), the customer information is automatically included. If there are differences in contact or shipping information related to the specific job, those can be entered here.

Job-specific information about payments (preferred payment method and credit card information) can be entered on the **Payment Settings** tab. Additional job-specific information can be entered on the **Additional Info** tab.

On the **Job Info** tab, information about the job's start date and projected and actual end dates can be entered. Information on this tab is used most often by companies with long-term contracts.

After completing the Practice Exercise, the **Customer Center** should look like this:

Adding jobs for Sac City Accounting.

(Accounting Student Tutoring Center needs a financial statement review and Sac City Student News wants some help setting up its new QuickBooks program. Sac City also decides to set up a separate job for tracking monthly bookkeeping work for West Sac Legal.)

1. Click **Customer Center** (main menu bar).

2. Highlight **Accounting Student Tutoring Center**.

3. Click **New Customer & Job** (top left corner of screen).

4. Select **Add Job**.

   a. Enter "2017 Review" as the **job name** and click **OK**.

5. Highlight **Sac City Student News**.

6. Click **New Customer & Job** (top left corner of screen).

7. Select **Add Job**.

   a. Enter "QB Set Up" as the **job name** and click **OK**.

8. Highlight **West Sac Legal**.

9. Click **New Customer & Job** (top left corner of screen).

10. Select **Add Job**.

    a. Enter "Monthly Work" as the **job name** and click **OK**.

11. Close **Customer Center**.

USING TIMESHEETS

The **timesheet** feature in QuickBooks is available to track hours worked by both hourly and salaried employees in a company. You can also use **timesheets** to track hours worked by non-employees (independent contractors, for example). **Timesheet** data can be used to do one or more of the following:

✔ Create a paycheck based on hours worked for hourly employees.

✔ Track paid time off for all employees.

✔ Track billable hours for invoicing customers (employees and non-employees).

✔ Track billable and non-billable hours for management purposes (employees and non-employees).

In this course, **timesheets** will only be used for employees.

Timesheets do not **have** to be used to pay employees. Compensation (including hours) can be entered directly during paycheck processing as you learned in Chapter 8. You can also attach wages to **jobs** during paycheck processing. Using **timesheets** just makes the process a bit easier.

Timesheets **do** have to be used if you intend to use employee hours for billing purposes.

If **timesheets** are used to create paychecks (almost always the case with hourly employees), time tracking must be set as a preference in the company file and the employee record must include that preference.

Turning On Time Tracking

Time tracking is turned on in the **Time & Expenses** tab of the **Preferences** screen. The **Preferences** screen is accessible through the **Edit** dropdown menu on the main menu bar:

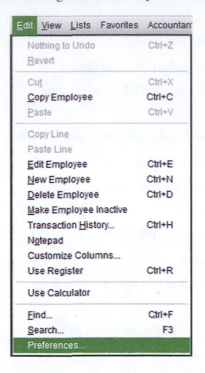

The **Company Preferences** tab of the **Time & Expenses** page looks like this:

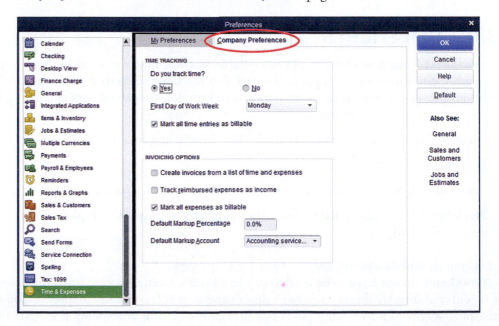

Yes should be selected in answer to the question **Do you track time?** at the top of the screen. The user can set the first day of the workweek here and select various default options.

Once time tracking is turned on for the company, specific employee records need to include that preference when appropriate. The **timesheet** option is turned on in the **Payroll Info** screen for each employee.

Open the **Employee Center**, highlight the employee, and click the **pencil icon**:

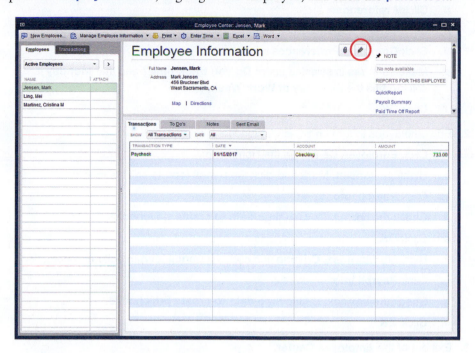

The **Payroll info** tab screen looks like this:

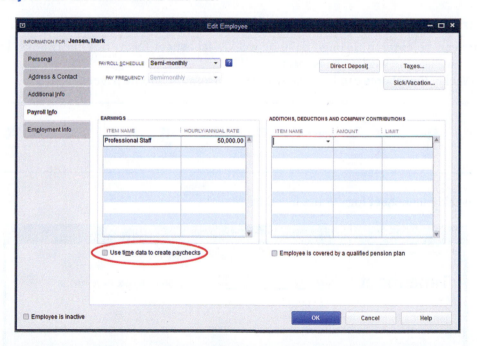

PRACTICE
EXERCISE

Setting up time tracking for Sac City Accounting.

(Sac City will be using timesheets to track time for Mark Jensen and Cristina Martinez. Timesheets will not be necessary for Mei Ling because she is a salaried employee and she will do administrative work, not working directly on Sac City clients.)

1. Turn on time tracking.

   a.   Click **Edit** (main menu bar).

(continued)

    b.   Click **Preferences**.

    c.   Click **Time & Expenses** (left column).

    d.   Click **Company Preferences** tab.

    e.   Make sure **Yes** is selected under **Do you track time?** and that **Monday** is selected as the **First Day of Work Week**.

    f.   Click **OK**.

2. Edit employees to turn on timesheet functionality

    a.   Click **Employee Center** on the Home page.

    b.   Highlight **Jensen, Mark** and click the **pencil icon** to edit his record.

    c.   Click **Payroll Info**.

    d.   Check the box next to **Use time data to create paychecks**.

    e.   Click **OK**.

    f.   Highlight **Martinez, Cristina** and click the **pencil icon** to edit her record.

    g.   Click **Payroll Info**.

    h.   Check the box next to **Use time data to create paychecks**.

    i.   Click **OK**.

3. Exit out of the **Employee Center**.

Entering Timesheet Data

Hours can be entered through daily or weekly **timesheet** forms in QuickBooks. In this course, we use the weekly **timesheets**.

    Weekly **timesheets** can be directly accessed from the Home page:

The weekly **timesheet** form looks like this:

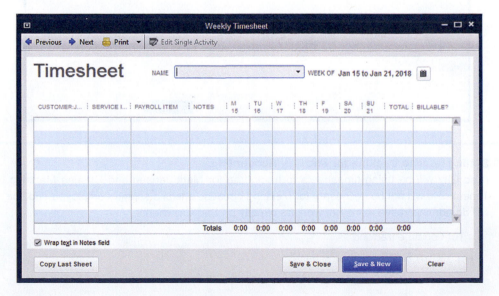

> **BEHIND THE SCENES** If timesheets are used for billing purposes only, the screen will change slightly. (The Payroll Item column will disappear.)

The name of the employee and the workweek are entered first.
Some of the fields in the timesheet are optional, some aren't.

- The Customer:Job field is optional. You must enter a job only if you want to bill the hours to a customer and/or you want to track wages by job.

- The Service Item field **must** be completed if you have entered a job.
  - The item selected will determine the income account credited from any invoice or sales receipt generated from the hours entered.

- The Payroll Item field **must** be completed if the timesheet is prepared for an employee.
  - The payroll item is used to differentiate between regular and overtime hours, sick and vacation hours, etc.

- The Billable? field should be checked only if the company intends to bill the customer for hours worked.

> **BEHIND THE SCENES** The **amount billed** to the client from timesheet data will be determined by the rate associated with the service item, not by the pay rate.

If an employee works on various jobs and/or has various pay rates, there will be multiple lines.

If the timesheet is for an hourly employee, the total hours entered must equal the total hours worked so that no additional entry is required when preparing paychecks.

If the timesheet is for a salaried employee and hours are entered for jobs, QuickBooks will allocate the wages charged to a specific job based on the ratio of job hours to total hours entered on the timesheet. For the most accurate management reports, hours entered for salaried employees should equal total hours worked **even if** not all hours are chargeable.

To enter employee hours not spent working on a particular project, the Customer:Job column is left blank. A company can set up service items for non-job hours if tracking of non-billable time is desired. Otherwise, the Service Item column can also be left blank.

PRACTICE
EXERCISE

Entering employee time for Sac City Accounting.

(During January, Mark Jensen and Cristina Martinez worked on the review of Accounting Student Tutoring Center's financials. Mark Jensen also worked with Sac City Student News on setting up QuickBooks. Cristina worked on the monthly bookkeeping for West Sac Legal. The hours for the financial statement review and the QuickBooks set up will be billed to the clients. West Sac Legal pays a flat rate of $1,000 per month, so actual hours will not be billed to the company.)

1. Click Employees (main menu bar).

2. Click Enter Time.

3. Click Use Weekly Timesheet.

(continued)

4. Select **Jensen, Mark** as the **name** and **Jan 15 to Jan 21, 2018** as the **Week Of**.

   a. Select **Accounting Student Tutoring Center:2017 Review** as the **Customer:Job**.

      i. Select **Staff Hours** as the **Service Item**.

      ii. Select **Professional staff** as the **Payroll Item**.

      iii. Enter "8" on Tuesday and Thursday. Enter "10" on Friday.

      iv. Check **Billable**.

   b. On the second line, select **Sac City Student News:QB Set Up as the Customer:Job**.

      i. Select **Software set up** as the **Service Item**.

      ii. Select **Professional staff** as the **Payroll Item**.

      iii. Enter "6" on Wednesday.

      iv. Check **Billable**.

   c. On the third line, leave the **Customer:Job** and **Service Item** fields blank. (Mark did some training Wednesday morning.)

      i. Select **Professional staff** as the **Payroll Item**.

      ii. Enter "2" on Wednesday.

      iii. Uncheck the **billable** box.

   d. Total hours for Mark should show as 34. Mark was paid through Monday (Jan 15) as part of Chapter 8.

   e. Click **Next** (top of the window).

5. **Jensen, Mark** should appear as the **Name**. The **Week Of** should start 1/22.

   a. Select "Professional Staff" as the **Payroll Item**.

      i. Enter "8" for Monday through Friday hours. (Mark was training and working on administrative projects all week.)

      ii. Uncheck the **Billable** box.

   b. Total hours should equal 40.

   c. Click **Next** (top of the window).

6. **Jensen, Mark** should appear as the **Name**. **The Week Of** should start 1/29.

   a. On the first line, select **Accounting Student Tutoring Center:2017 Review** as the **Customer:Job**.

      i. Select **Staff Hours** as the **Service Item**.

      ii. Select **Professional staff** as the **Payroll Item**.

      iii. Enter "8" on Monday and Wednesday.

      iv. Check **Billable**.

   b. On the second line, select "Professional Staff" as the **Payroll Item**.

      i. Enter "8" for Tuesday. (Mark was working on administrative projects.)

      ii. Uncheck the **Billable box**.

   c. Total hours should equal 24.

   d. Click **Save & New**.

7. Select **Martinez, Cristina M** as the **Name**.

(continued)

    a.   Select **Jan 15 to Jan 21** as the **Week Of**.

    b.   Select **Accounting Student Tutoring Center:2017 Review** as the **Customer:Job**.

        i.   Select **Staff Hours** as the **Service Item**.

        ii.   Select **Straight Time** as the **Payroll Item**.

        iii.   Enter "8" on Tuesday through Friday.

        iv.   Check **Billable** column.

    c.   On the second line, select **Accounting Student Tutoring Center:2017 Review** as the **Customer:Job**.

        i.   Select **Staff Hours** as the **Service Item**.

        ii.   Select **Overtime** as the **Payroll Item**. (Cristina is an hourly employee and receives overtime for any hours over 8 in a day. She worked 10 hours Friday on the 2017 review for Accounting Student Tutoring Center; 8 hours are entered as straight time, 2 hours as overtime.)

        iii.   Enter "2" on Friday.

        iv.   Check the **Billable** column.

    d.   On the third line, select **West Sac Legal:Monthly Work** as the **Customer Name**.

        i.   Select **Monthly** as the **Service Item**.

        ii.   Select **Straight Time** as the **Payroll Item**.

        iii.   Enter "8" on Saturday.

        iv.   Uncheck the **Billable** column. (West Sac Legal is billed a fixed monthly fee.)

        v.   Total hours for Cristina should show as 42.

    e.   Click **Save & Close**. (Sac City didn't have any work for Cristina for the rest of January.)

8. Exit out of the **Employee Center**.

PROCESSING PAYROLL USING TIMESHEET DATA

Creating Paychecks

The process of creating paychecks from timesheet data is identical to the process learned in Chapter 8. However, because payroll errors are more difficult to correct, it's important for users to check the data entered into the system before creating **paychecks**.

There are several tools that can be used. For example:

- Completed timesheets can be printed directly from any **Weekly Timesheet** window:

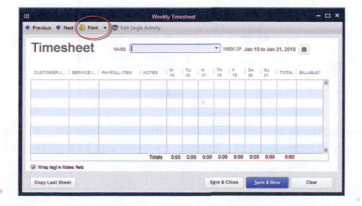

- Click the **Print** dropdown menu at the top of the **Weekly Timesheet** form and select **Print**. The following window opens:

- Enter the desired dates. Names of all employees with time for the period selected are displayed.

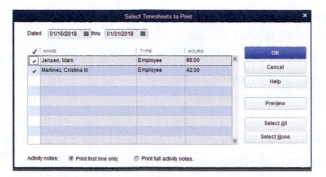

- You can print some or all **timesheets** from this screen.

- There are several reports detailing time available in the **Jobs, Time & Mileage** report category of the **Reports** dropdown menus:

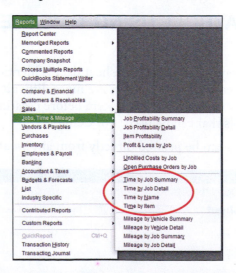

- The **Time by Name** report, which summarizes customer hours by employee, would look like this using the Practice Exercise you just completed:

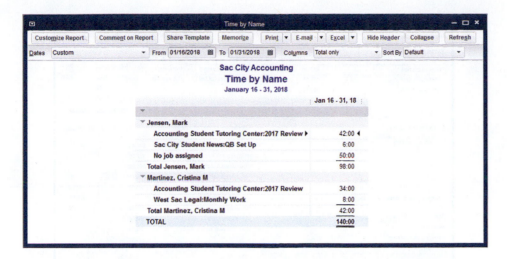

The **paycheck** process begins when **Pay Employees** is selected on the Home page. When the **pay period ends** date is entered, the following message appears if the company uses time data:

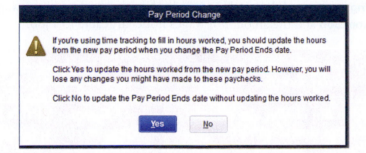

If **Yes** is clicked, QuickBooks automatically retrieves all hours, by employee, from the **timesheets** for the pay period. The screen looks something this this:

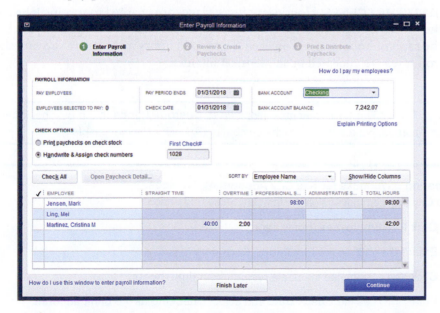

There is also, of course, much more detail available when timesheet data is used to prepare **paychecks**. The **Preview Paycheck** screen for Mark Jensen looks something like this after you complete step 7 of the following Practice Exercise.

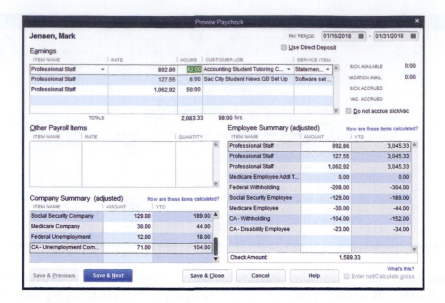

The **Earnings** section of the window now displays the amount of the wages chargeable to each **Customer:Job** and the amount of wages not chargeable to a job.

> **! WARNING:** *Hours* and *Customer:Job* names can be changed while creating a *paycheck*, and those changes are reflected in the costs charged to a particular project. However, changes in *Customer:Job* names made in this screen do not change the original timesheet. Because billable hours are pulled from timesheets when *invoices* and *sales receipts* are later created, the timesheet must be changed independently to get accurate billing information.

> **BEHIND THE SCENES** Hourly employee wages are charged to specific **jobs** based on the timesheet data. Salaried employee wages are allocated to specific **jobs** based on the ratio of hours worked on each **job** to total hours included on the timesheet. Payroll taxes are allocated in an identical manner.

QuickCheck 9-1

True or False? The dollar amounts allocated to **Customer:Jobs** in the paycheck are the dollar amounts that are billable to the customer. (Answer at end of chapter.)

PRACTICE EXERCISE

Preparing paychecks for Sac City Accounting Services.

(Sac City pays employees on the last day of the pay period.)

1. Click **Pay Employees** (Home page).

2. Enter "**1/31/18**" as the **Pay Period Ends** date.

3. Click **Yes** if prompted to update records from **timesheets**.

4. Enter "**1/31**" as the **Check Date** and select **Checking** as the **bank account**.

5. Click "Check All" (middle right of the screen).

6. Click **Open Paycheck Detail**.

(continued)

7. For Mark Jensen:
   a. Make sure the pay period start date is 1/16.
   b. Enter employee taxes as follows:
      i. Medicare Employee Addl Tax—0
         1. This line may not appear in your version of QuickBooks.
      ii. Federal Withholding—208
      iii. Social Security Employee—129
      iv. Medicare Employee—30
      v. CA–Withholding—104
      vi. CA–Disability—23
   c. Enter employer taxes as follows:
      i. CA–Employment Training Tax—2
      ii. Social Security Company—129
      iii. Medicare Company—30
      iv. Federal Unemployment—12
      v. CA–Unemployment Company—71
   d. Net check should total $1,589.33.
   e. Click **Save & Next**.

8. For Mei Ling:
   a. Make sure the pay period start date is 1/16.
   b. Enter employee taxes as follows:
      i. Medicare Employee Addl Tax—0
      ii. Federal Withholding—167
      iii. Social Security Employee—103
      iv. Medicare Employee—24
      v. CA–Withholding—83
      vi. CA–Disability—18
   c. Enter employer taxes as follows:
      i. CA–Employment Training Tax—2
      ii. Social Security Company—103
      iii. Medicare Company—24
      iv. Federal Unemployment—10
      v. CA–Unemployment Company—57
   d. Net check should total $1,271.67.
   e. Click **Save & Next**.

9. For Cristina Martinez:
   a. Make sure the pay period start date is 1/16.
   b. Enter employee taxes as follows:
      i. Medicare Employee Addl Tax—0
      ii. Federal Withholding—108

(continued)

      iii.   Social Security Employee—67

      iv.   Medicare Employee—16

      v.   CA–Withholding—54

      vi.   CA–Disability—12

    c.   Enter employer taxes as follows:

      i.   CA–Employment Training Tax—1

      ii.   Social Security Company—67

      iii.   Medicare Company—16

      iv.   Federal Unemployment—6

      v.   CA–Unemployment Company—37

    d.   Net check should total $818.00

    e.   Click **Save & Close**.

10. Click **Continue**.

11. Click **Handwrite and assign check numbers** (or **Assign check numbers to handwritten checks**, if applicable).

12. Enter "1028" as the **First Check Number**.

13. Click **Create Paychecks**.

14. Click **Close**.

BILLING FOR TIME AND COSTS

Identifying Billable Costs Other Than Labor

Many companies that work with projects (**jobs**) bill some or all of their direct expenses to their clients in addition to labor hours.

Expenses can be flagged as billable when **bills** or **checks** are created.

For example, to designate an expense (or an **item**) as **billable** in a **check**, the **Customer:Job name** is entered and the **billable** column is checked in the distribution section of the form on the **expenses** or **items** tab. The screen looks something like this when an expense is flagged as billable on a **check** form:

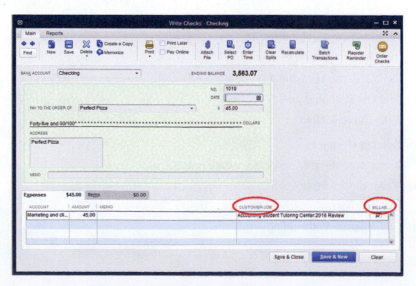

The same fields exist on **bill** forms.

Being able to flag an expense (or item) as billable when the **bill** or **check** is first entered is particularly useful to building contractors who often purchase materials for specific projects.

 HINT: A **Customer:Job** can be identified on a **purchase order** as well, but the cost can't be flagged as billable until the order is received.

Entering a billable cost for Sac City Accounting.
(On 1/20/18, Sac City staff work overtime on the Accounting Student Tutoring Center at the client's request. Pizza is purchased for dinner, and the partners decide to bill the client for the meal.)

1. Click **Write Check** on the Home page.

2. Enter "1019" as the check **no.**

3. Enter "1/20" as the **date**.

4. Enter "Perfect Pizza" as the **pay to the order of**. (**Quick Add** as a vendor.)

5. Enter "45" in the **$** field. (Definitely high quality pizza!)

6. Select **Meals and entertainment** in the **account** column on the **Expenses** tab.

7. Select **Accounting Student Tutoring Center:2017 Review** in the **Customer:Job** column.

8. Leave the checkmark in the **Billable?** column.

9. Click **Save & Close**.

Adding Billable Time And Expenses To A Sales Form

If there are pending **billable** costs for a specific customer, the following message will appear when an **invoice** or **sales receipt** is started for that customer:

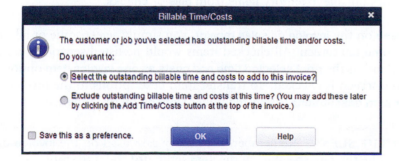

In order to include some or all of the time and expenses on the sales form, the **Select the outstanding billable time and costs to add to the invoice** option must be selected.

The next screen looks something like this:

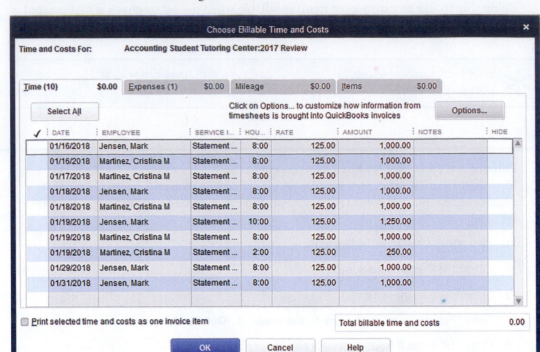

As you can see, there are a number of different tabs. Each tab represents a different type of **billable** cost:

- **Time**
  - Includes billable hours from **timesheets**.

- **Expenses**
  - Includes billable expenses from **bills** or **checks** or **journal entries**.

- **Mileage**
  - Includes billable mileage charges (not covered in this course).

- **Items**
  - Includes billable inventory **items** from **bills** or **checks**.

To include **time** on the **invoice** or **sales receipt**, you simply select some or all of the hours listed in the **Time** tab screen. All checked items would be listed separately on the **invoice** (**sales receipt**) unless the **print selected time and costs as one invoice item** option at the bottom left of the screen is checked. To transfer item descriptions to the invoice, make sure that **Transfer item descriptions** is selected under **Options** on the **Time** tab.

> **BEHIND THE SCENES** Remember, the hourly rate used on the **invoice** or **sales receipt** will be the rate specified in the **item** setup **not** the wage rate.

To include **expenses** on the **invoice** or **sales receipt**, you must select some or all of the **expenses** listed in the **Expenses** tab screen.

The screen looks something like this:

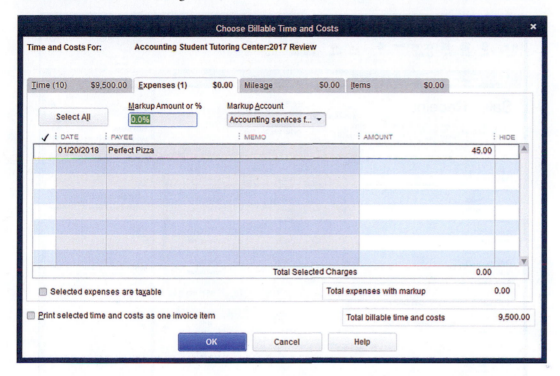

You can invoice the client for just the amount of the expense, or you can add a markup. The markup can be a flat amount or a percentage. If you add a markup, you must designate the account that will be credited for the markup amount.

> **BEHIND THE SCENES** The expense amount (not including the markup), by default, will be credited to the original expense account. That can be changed in **Time & Expenses** settings under **preferences**.

To include **items** on the **invoice** or **sales receipt**, you must select some or all of the **items** listed on the **Items** tab screen. The amount that will be charged to the customer is the amount indicated in the **item** setup. If no amount is entered in the **item** record, the customer is charged the **cost** of the **item**.

> **HINT:** There are other features in QuickBooks that can be used when billing customers for time and costs. These features are set in the **Time & Expenses** option of the **preferences** menu. For example, a preference can be set to bill all time and materials at cost plus a fixed markup percentage.

Once all billable time and costs are selected, the **invoice** or **sales receipt** form screen will appear.

A **Sales Receipt** looks something like this:

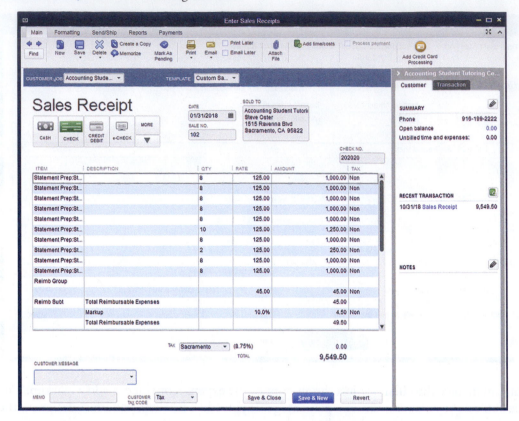

Additional **items** can be added or rates and **items** can be changed at this point. The **Add time/costs** link at the top of the screen will take you back to the **Choose Billable Time and Costs** screen. Clicking **revert** at the bottom right corner of the screen will clear the entries and allow you to start over.

Special attention should be paid to the **Tax** column of the sales form. Direct costs that are passed through to (billed to) customers are not subject to tax. However, markups on those costs may be subject to state sales tax.

> **BEHIND THE SCENES** Once **billable** time or costs have been added to an **invoice** or **sales receipt**, the "billable" status for those costs changes to "billed," and those hours or costs are no longer available to added to a sales form. This prevents companies for double-billing their customers. If the **invoice** or **sales receipt** is later deleted, that status does **not** automatically change back to "billable." To re-invoice time and other costs, the "billable" status must be reset (rechecked) in the original form (**timesheet**, **bill**, or **check**).

PRACTICE EXERCISE

Charging Sac City Accounting clients for time and costs.

(Sac City is worried about getting low on cash. It decides to ask for immediate payment from the Accounting Student Tutoring Center for the January hours worked and direct expenses incurred on the financial statement review. Sac City Student News is also paying all January charges by check.)

(continued)

1. Click **Create Sales Receipts** on the Home page.

2. Select **Accounting Student Tutoring Center:2017 Review** as the **Customer:Job**.

   a. Choose **Select the outstanding billable time and costs to add to this invoice?**.

   b. Click **OK**.

   c. Click "Select All" on the **Time** tab.

   d. Click the **Expenses** tab.

   e. Enter "10%" in the **Markup** field.

      i. You must add the % sign.

   f. Select **Financial Statement Reviews** as the **markup account**.

   g. Select **Perfect Pizza**.

   h. Click **OK**.

   i. Change the **date** to 1/31 and enter 102 as the **Sale No.**

   j. Click the **Check** icon and enter "202020" as the **Check No.**

   k. Total should be $9,549.50. (You can ignore any possible tax due on the markup.)

   l. Click **Save & New**.

3. Select **Sac City Student News:QB Setup** as the **Customer:Job**.

   a. Choose **Select the outstanding billable time and costs to add to this sales receipt?**.

   b. Click **OK**.

   c. Select Mark Jensen's hours.

   d. Click **OK**.

   e. The **sales receipt** date should be 1/31.

   f. Click the **Check** icon and enter "19993" as the **Check No.**

   g. Total should be $600.00.

   h. Click **Save & Close**.

4. Click **Record Deposits** on the Home page.

5. Click **Select All** and click **OK**.

6. Enter "1/31" as the **date**. (Deposit total should be $10,149.50.)

7. Click **Save & Close**.

PREPARING JOB REPORTS

There are a variety of reports that can be used to review and evaluate jobs. Two of the most commonly used reports are:

✓ Job Profitability Detail

   ○ Shows total revenues and costs, by **item**, for a specific job.

     ■ Reimbursed expenses show under a **No item** category.

✓ Profit & Loss by Job
  ○ Shows revenues and costs, by general ledger account, for the specified accounting period.
  ○ All transactions associated with a **job** would appear on this report.

All job reports can be accessed through the **Jobs, Time & Mileage** option on the **Reports** drop-down menu (main menu bar).

PRACTICE
EXERCISE

Preparing project reports for Sac City Accounting.

1. Click **Reports**.
2. Click **Jobs, Time & Mileage**.
3. Click **Job Profitability Detail**.
4. Select **Accounting Student Tutoring Center:2016 Review** as the **Customer:Job**.
5. Click **OK**.
6. Close report window
7. Click **Reports**.
8. Click **Jobs, Time & Mileage**.
9. Click **Profit & Loss by Job**.
10. Change dates to 1/1 to 1/31.
11. Resize the columns to make the report easier to read.
12. Close report window.

ANSWER TO
QuickCheck
9-1

False. The dollar amounts billable to customers are determined using the **service item** rates set in the **item list**. The amount billable to a customer would be the rate multiplied by the hours charged to the **job** on the timesheet.

CHAPTER SHORTCUTS

Add a Job
1. Click Customer Center
2. Highlight Customer
3. Click New Customer & Job/Add Job

Enter a timesheet
1. Click Home
2. Click dropdown menu next to Enter time
3. Click Use Weekly Timesheet

Charge customers for billable time and expenses
1. Click Create Invoices (or Sales Receipts) on Home page
2. Enter Customer:Job
3. Click Select the outstanding billable time and costs option
   a. Billable time and costs can also be accessed by clicking Add Time/Costs on the invoice or sales receipt

CHAPTER REVIEW

Matching

Match the term or phrase (as used in QuickBooks) to its best definition.

1. Job
2. Billable
3. Preview Paycheck
4. Time by Job Summary report
5. Payroll Info
6. Time by Name report
7. Job Info
8. Profit & Loss by Job report

_____ Report that displays revenue and expenses by job for a specified period of time

_____ Tab in employee record where option to use timesheets to create paychecks is selected

_____ Tab in customer job record where start and end dates for the job can be entered

_____ Identifiable project tracked for a specific customer

_____ Report that summarizes timesheet hours by job and service

_____ Report that summarizes timesheet hours by employee name and job

_____ Field in timesheet used to flag hours chargeable to a client

_____ Window used to review employee earnings and deductions before a paycheck is created

Multiple Choice

1. An engineering company enters into "fixed-fee" and "time-and-materials" contracts with its clients. The company:

   a. would have no reason for tracking labor hours for "fixed-fee" jobs.

   b. would have no reason for tracking labor hours for "time-and-materials" jobs.

   c. would normally track labor hours for both "fixed-fee" and "time-and-materials" jobs.

   d. must track hours for "time-and-materials" jobs but should never track hours for "fixed-fee" jobs.

2. A service item must be selected for timesheet entries:

   a. only if time will be billed to a client.

   b. only if the user tracks time by job but doesn't bill time to clients.

   c. if user tracks time by client (whether time is billed or not).

   d. None of the above. Timesheets never have to include service items.

3. The rates used to bill clients for employee hours are:

   a. found in the item list.

   b. found in the employee center.

   c. always set when the invoice or sales receipt is created.

   d. Found in either the item list or employee center, depending on preferences selected.

4. Which of the following statements is not true?

   a. Both expenses and items can be identified as billable as part of the entry of a vendor bill.

   b. Changes to hours and Customer:Job can be made in the preview paycheck screen.

   c. If changes are made to Customer:Job in the preview paycheck screen, the related timesheets will be automatically adjusted.

   d. Data entered into timesheets in QuickBooks should be carefully reviewed before paychecks are created.

5. The **Time by Name** report is found under _____ in the **Reports** dropdown menu.

   a. Accountant & Taxes
   b. Lists
   c. Jobs, Time & Mileage
   d. Company & Financial

ASSIGNMENTS

Assignment 9A

Champion Law

Background information: You have decided to open your own law firm, specializing in family and employment law. The business is a corporation with a 12/31 year-end. You contributed $100,000 in cash to start the business. You already have a few clients but won't start working on their cases until the office opens on 1/2/18.

You rented space (and prepaid the January rent) and purchased furniture and equipment in December 2017. You also prepaid the local newspaper for some ads to run in January newspapers and purchased two insurance policies (one for professional liability and one for general business).

You have decided to pay yourself a salary of $75,000 per year. You have one other employee (Nancy Svenborg). Nancy will be working as a paralegal and also performing some administrative duties. She will be paid $25 per hour. Timesheets are entered on the 15th and 31st. Payroll is paid semimonthly, also on the 15th and 31st.

You are a small operation, so you bill your clients twice a month, and your credit terms are Net 10. Remember: In QuickBooks, clients are called **customers**; cases (matters) are called **jobs**. The clients and matters you know you'll be working on are:

- Jordan & Jamie Childress—Adoption (Katie).
- Sam & Serena Johnson—Adoption (Terrence).
- Urban Settings—Employment contract for architects.
- Janice Williams—Wrongful termination.

You've already set up the listed clients in QuickBooks. You've set yourself and Nancy up as employees in QuickBooks as well. You have also set up frequently used vendors and most of the **payroll items** you think you'll need. Manual payroll processing has already been turned on.

You've set up **service items** for each of the professional services you expect to perform. Professional services will be billed on any hourly basis. You've also set up a **service item** for non-billable time. Non-billable time represents time spent on general company business (time not chargeable to a specific client).

You intend to bill your clients for any direct costs incurred on their behalf and so have also set up **items** for those costs (**other charge** items). You do not intend to mark up direct costs.

Other information:

- Professional liability insurance policy premium: $3,000; term: 1/1 to 6/30/18.
- General insurance policy premium: $600; term: 1/1 to 6/30/18.
- Monthly depreciation (straight-line) on computer equipment and copier: $93.
- Monthly depreciation (straight-line) on furniture: $30.

Before you start your assignment:

✓ Change the company name to Your Name Champion Law, Inc.

✓ Change "Student Name" to "Your Name" in the **Employee Center**. (Use your first and last names.)

✓ Familiarize yourself with the **item**, **payroll item**, and **chart of account** lists.

1/2/18

✓ You file the documents for the adoption cases at the courthouse. The fees (paid to the Superior Court of California) total $40. You pay with check #1009 ($20 for the Childress [Katie] adoption and $20 for the Johnson [Terrence] adoption).

- Remember, you will be charging your clients for all direct costs. If you're charging clients, the costs must be entered on the **items** tab. **Don't forget to charge the cost to the job**, not to the main customer name. [**TIP:** There is an **item** already set up for filing fees. Ignore the prompt about updating costs. There is no set amount for filing fees. You might want to turn off the message.]

✓ You receive the January bill for a legal library service. The company (Legal Eagle) provides you with unlimited online access to various legal research materials (including updates to laws and regulations) for a monthly fee of $800. The vendor bill number is 78922, and the terms are Net 15.

1/4/18

✓ You meet with a new client for an **initial consultation**. Unfortunately, she decides not to hire the firm. Because she won't be an ongoing client, you don't set her up as a **customer**. You do prepare a sales receipt (start with #101), using **Consultation Only** as the **Customer:Job**. The meeting lasted three hours. The total fee paid, in cash, is $225.

✓ You deposit the cash in the bank ($225 total).

1/5/18

✓ You receive two bills in the mail. The terms are Net 15 on both. You accept the change in payment terms.

- Horizon Phone, dated 1/5 for $185—#1229900 (January service).
- Sac Electric, dated 1/5 for $110—#7771119923 (January service).

✓ You enter timesheets for the first week. No one worked on January 1st.

- [**TIP:** Because you've already collected the fees for the **Consultation Only** client, you do not make the hours **billable**. You **do** include the hours on the timesheet though (using the appropriate **Customer:Job** name and **Service Item**) so that the labor cost shows up on the job reports. All other client hours are billable.]
- [**TIP:** You don't need a **Customer:Job** for administrative or non-billable time. You do, however, need to enter those hours in the timesheet so the wages are allocated properly. You'll only enter **service** and **payroll items** for those hours. Don't forget to unclick the **billable** box.]

Week of January 1–7		M	Tu	W	Th	F
You (33 total hours)						
Childress: Katie Adoption	Documents		2			
Childress: Katie Adoption	Meetings			2		
Childress: Katie Adoption	Research			3		
Johnson: Terrence Adoption	Documents		2			
Johnson: Terrence Adoption	Meetings				2	
Johnson: Terrence Adoption	Research				2	
Urban Settings: Associate Agree.	Documents			2		2
Consultation Only	Initial consultation				3	
	Non-billable		4	2	1	6
Nancy Svenborg (22 total hours)						
Urban Settings: Associate Agree.	Paralegal assistance				2	2
Childress: Katie Adoption	Paralegal assistance		2			
Johnson: Terrence Adoption	Paralegal assistance		2			
	Non-billable		2	4	4	4

1/9/18

✓ You decide to hire another attorney. You've known Frank Williams for years, and he has an excellent reputation as an attorney. He's been working in a large firm and wants to have a little less pressure. You and Nancy meet with him, and you both think he'd be a perfect fit. Frank accepts the job. Although he won't be starting for a few weeks, you have him fill out all the paperwork and get him set up in QuickBooks.

- His Social Security number is 225-12-8886.

- His address is 4242 Riverstone Blvd., Sacramento, CA 95822.

- Starting pay—Frank's starting salary will be $120,000. He is making more than you because he's not an owner of the firm. Frank will be paid semimonthly. (**Payroll Schedules** aren't used by the firm, so the field can be left blank.)

- He's salaried, but you choose the option to **use time data to create paychecks** so you can track labor costs by job.

- On his W-4, Frank enters a filing status of single with one allowance (use for both federal and state).

- In addition to federal and state withholding, Frank's wages are subject to the following taxes: federal (Medicare, Social Security, and FUTA), state (SUI and SDI), and other (CA Employment Training Tax).

- Hire date (start date)—1/16.

- You will not be setting up sick/vacation pay tracking.

✓ You celebrate by taking everyone out to dinner at Gourmet Platter. The meal cost $225. You charge it on the company credit card (Capital Two card) and record the charge in QuickBooks. (This is a labor-related expense.)

1/10/18

✓ You will be attending a workshop this week hosted by a company called Negotiating Skills, Inc. The workshop costs $385. You pay for it with the company credit card. NOTE: Continuing education is required for professionals like attorneys. It's a labor cost.

✓ You receive a bill (#111014) dated 1/10 from Wally Wright (a court reporter) for $275. The terms are "due on receipt." The charges (all billable) are for the Johnson (Terrence) adoption ($150) and the Childress (Katie) adoption ($125). You make sure you record it on the **item** tab.

✓ You get a call from Urban Settings. The company is pleased with the work you're doing and asks you to review its client contracts. You agree and set up a new **job** in QuickBooks. You call it "Contract Review."

✓ You have an appointment with LeAnne Diamond. She owns a company and wants you to help negotiate an upcoming union contract. You agree and set them up as a new client. Client information:

- Mega Manufacturing Company
  1234 Folsom Blvd
  Sacramento, CA 95822

- Phone: (916) 208-8944

- Terms: Net 10

✓ You add "Union contract" as a **job** to Mega Manufacturing.

✓ You pay all bills due on or before 2/1 (total of $4,970.00; five checks, #1011–#1015).

1/12/18

✓ You take Jordan and Jamie Childress to lunch at Tasty Bite ($85) and charge it on the company credit card. Taking clients to lunch is good for client relations, so you don't make the charge billable.

✓ You enter timesheets for the week. All client hours are billable.

Week of January 8–14		M	Tu	W	Th	F
You (45 total hours)						
Childress: Katie Adoption	Meetings	2				
Childress: Katie Adoption	Research	1				
Childress: Katie Adoption	Court					6
Johnson: Terrence Adoption	Meetings	2				
Johnson: Terrence Adoption	Research	2				
Mega Manu: Union Contract	Initial consultation		3			
Urban Settings: Contract Review	Research		5			2
	CPE			8	8	
	Non-billable	2	2			2
Nancy Svenborg (20 total hours)						
Urban Settings: Associate Agreement	Paralegal assistance	1				
Urban Settings: Contract Review	Paralegal assistance					1
Mega Manu: Union Contract	Paralegal assistance				3	
	Non-billable	4	3	4	1	3

1/15/18

✓ You enter time for 1/15.

Week of January 15–21	M	Tu	W	Th	F
You (8 total hours)					
Non-billable			8		
Nancy Svenborg (2 total hours)					
Non-billable			2		

✓ You prepare payroll checks for Nancy and yourself for the period 1/1 to 1/15.

> **HINT: Before you start creating paychecks,** compare your **Time by Name** and **Time by Job Summary** reports to the reports posted in the Student Materials section of the book's website: https://cambridgepub.com/book/quickbooks-2015. If you have hours or clients recorded incorrectly (and that's very easy to do) you won't be able to create accurate invoices.

• The first check number should be #1016.

> **HINT:** Because of differences in payroll calculations of salaried employees by different QuickBooks programs, you may get **slightly** different amounts (less than $0.05 difference) from the gross and net pay amounts shown HERE.

• Nancy's gross pay is $1,100.00; net pay is $838.75.

• Your gross pay is $3,124.99; net pay is $2,382.81.

	Nancy	You
Withholdings:		
Federal Withholding	110.00	312.50
Social Security	68.20	193.75
Medicare	15.95	45.31
CA–Withholding	55.00	156.25
CA–Disability	12.10	34.37
Employer taxes:		
CA–Employment Training Tax	1.10	3.12
Social Security	68.20	193.75
Medicare	15.95	45.31
Federal Unemployment	6.60	18.75
CA–Unemployment	37.40	106.25

✓ You prepare invoices for all clients covering the period 1/1 to 1/15 using the **intuit Professional Invoice** template. All invoices are dated 1/16 with terms of Net 10. Start with Invoice #1200.

- Uncheck **Print Later** if necessary.
- All direct billable costs are included on the **invoice**, at cost. [**TIP:** On the **Time** tab, make sure the **Transfer item descriptions** is selected under **Options**.]
- Invoice totals:
  - Childress (Katie Adoption), $3,795.
  - Johnson (Terrence Adoption), $2,020.
  - Mega Manufacturing (Union Contract), $450.
  - Urban Settings (Associate), $1,175.
  - Urban Settings (Contract Review), $1,300.

1/18/18

✓ Frank just started on Tuesday, and he already has his first client! He's representing a company that's being sued for false advertising. The plaintiffs are claiming that the company advertised a guaranteed 100% pass rate on the CPA exam. Frank knows this is going to be a tough case, but he's up for the challenge.

✓ You set up Frank's new client in QuickBooks:

- Exam Prep, Inc.

  4124 Illusions Way

  Sacramento, CA 95822
- 916-444-3452
- Terms: Net 10
- Job name: "CPA exam"

✓ Frank tells you that he will be using an outside firm for investigative work.

- You set up the new vendor:
- Silver Sleuths

  71 Tinpan Alley

  Sacramento, CA 95822
- Main Phone: (916) 322-8821
- Terms: Net 30
- You also set up a new **item** to track investigative costs that are billable to the client. [**TIP:** Frank doesn't do his own investigating, so this is not a **service item**. It's an **Other Charge** item. You use "Investigative Services" as the description for invoicing and make it a **sub-item** of **Client Costs**.]

> **HINT:** You need to check the **This item is used in assemblies or is a reimbursable charge** box so that you can properly record bills from the vendor. An account is already set up in QuickBooks for this type of direct client cost.

- ○ If and when investigative costs are charged to the client, you want the revenue to be recorded in the **Reimbursed expenses** income account.

✓ You decide to subscribe to *Time* magazine so you have some reading material available in your reception area. You pay the **annual** subscription fee of $48 (2/1/18–1/31/19) with the company credit card. Even though it's a small amount, you apply the matching principle when you record the charge.

✓ Nancy comes in to see you before she leaves the office. She loves her job, but because she isn't getting full-time work, she'd like to make a bit more per hour. You agree to raise Nancy's hourly rate to $30 an hour. That's a big increase, but she's been doing great work. You change the rate in QuickBooks. By default, it will be effective on her 1/31 paycheck.

1/19/18

✓ You enter timesheets for the week. All client hours are billable. You will be adding the hours for Tuesday through Friday.

Week of January 15–21		M	Tu	W	Th	F
You (33 hours added; 41 total hours)						
Johnson: Terrence Adoption	Court.		6			
Urban Settings: Contract Review	Research		2			
Mega Manu: Union Contract	Meetings.			6	6	9
	Non-billable.				2	2
Nancy Svenborg (27 hours added; 29 total hours)						
Mega Manu: Union Contract	Paralegal assistance			4	4	3
Urban Settings: Contract Review	Paralegal assistance		2			
Exam Prep: CPA Exam	Paralegal assistance					1
	Non-billable.		4	3	4	2
Frank Williams (32 total hours)						
Exam Prep: CPA Exam	Initial Consultation		3			
Exam Prep: CPA Exam	Research		2	5	5	5
Exam Prep: CPA Exam	Documents			3		
	Non-billable.		3		3	3

1/25/18

✓ You receive the following checks in the mail all dated 1/25:

- • Check #1888, from Childress in the amount of $3,795.

- • Check #8882, from Johnson in the amount of $2,020.

- • Check #915667 from Urban Settings (Associate) $1,175.

✓ You take the checks down to the bank and deposit them. (The total deposit is $6,990.)

✓ You record two bills you received in the mail.

- • Silver Sleuths billed you $1,800 on #1789 dated 1/25. The bill is for investigative work on the class action suit (Exam Prep). This is a billable **item**. Terms are Net 30.

- • Wally Wright (a court reporter) sent a bill for $150 related to the Johnson (Terrence) adoption. The terms are "due on receipt" and the reference number is #111082. The bill is dated 1/25. This is a billable **item**.

✓ You receive the credit card statement in the mail dated 1/25. All charges through 1/25 appear on the statement. The amount due is $743. You reconcile the account and pay the balance due (check #1018).

1/26/18

✓ Frank meets with Giuseppe Adams from Toys for Tots. His company is being sued because the wheels keep falling off of the toy bus they manufacture for preschoolers. You set them up as a new client in QuickBooks using "Wheels" as the **job** name.

- Toys for Tots, Inc.

  4900 Fernwood Lane

  Sacramento, CA 95822

- Main Phone: (916) 555-8989

- Terms: Net 10

✓ Wally Wright calls you about bill #111082 dated 1/25. He's going to be out of town for a while and is trying to collect from all his clients before he leaves. You pay him in full with check #1019 for $150.

✓ You enter timesheets for the week. All client hours are billable.

Week of January 22–28		M	Tu	W	Th	F
You (47 total hours)						
Mega Manu: Union Contract	Meetings	9		10	10	10
Urban Settings: Contract Review	Documents		2			
	Non-billable		6			
Nancy Svenborg (34 total hours)						
Mega Manu: Union Contract	Paralegal assistance	2	4	4		
Exam Prep: CPA Exam	Paralegal assistance	3	2	1	3	4
	Non-billable	2	2	2	2	3
Frank Williams (40 total hours)						
Exam Prep: CPA Exam	Research	5	3	4		
Exam Prep: CPA Exam	Meetings			2		3
Exam Prep: CPA Exam	Documents		2		3	
Toys for Tots: Wheels	Initial consultation					3
	Non-billable	3	3	2	5	2

1/31/18

✓ You and Frank do some strategic planning this week.

✓ You enter timesheets for 1/29–1/31.

Week of January 29-31		M	Tu	W	Th	F
You (24 total hours)						
	Non-billable	8	8	8		
Nancy Svenborg (20 total hours)						
	Non-billable	4	8	8		
Frank Williams (24 total hours)						
Exam Prep: CPA Exam	Research	3				
Exam Prep: CPA Exam	Documents	2				
	Non-billable	3	8	8		

✓ You prepare payroll checks for the period 1/16 to 1/31 (first check number is 1020). Don't forget to check your **Time by Name** and **Time by Job** reports **before** you create the paychecks.

- Nancy's gross pay is $2,430.00; net pay is $1,852.87.
- Your gross pay is $3,125.02; net pay is $2,382.83.
- Frank's gross pay is $5,000.00; net pay is $3,812.50

	Frank	Nancy	You
Withholdings:			
Federal Withholding	500.00	243.00	312.50
Social Security	310.00	150.66	193.75
Medicare	72.50	35.24	45.31
CA–Withholding	250.00	121.50	156.25
CA–Disability	55.00	26.73	34.38
Employer taxes:			
CA–Employment Training Tax	5.00	2.43	3.13
Social Security	310.00	150.66	193.75
Medicare	72.50	35.24	45.31
Federal Unemployment	30.00	14.58	18.75
CA–Unemployment	170.00	82.62	106.25

✓ You prepare invoices, dated 1/31, for all clients:

- Exam Prep, $11,425
- Mega Manufacturing, $10,575
- Urban Settings (Contract Review), $900
- Johnson, $1,950
- Toys for Tots, $225

✓ You remit the following payroll taxes to the appropriate agencies (the payroll period is 1/1 to 1/31. The check date is 1/31.):

- Federal withholding.
- FICA taxes (Social Security and Medicare).
- California withholding.
- California disability.
- There are two **payroll liability** checks (#1023, #1024), totaling $4,640.92, dated 1/31.

After month-end:

- You reconcile your checking account to the bank statement (see below).
- You record all necessary adjusting journal entries (all journal entries are dated 1/31).
  - Supplies—You have $120 worth of office supplies on hand at 1/31.

 HINT: Read through the information given in the background information listed on the first page of the assignment, and carefully look at the balance sheet. You've reconciled your cash account, so that should be okay. How about the other asset accounts? Does Accounts Receivable agree to the aging? Do the prepaid accounts represent amounts you've paid for services or items you haven't used yet? What about the liability accounts? Are you confident they're correct?

- You review your balance sheet and profit-and-loss statement. You rearrange the account order so that the statements look professional.

Check numbers 1/31

Checking account balance.	$ 73,401.32
Account receivable	$ 26,825.00
Total assets.	$111,421.32
Total liabilities	$ 2,405.98
Net income (January)	$ 9,015.34

> **!** **WARNING:** You may have differences (less than $0.05) in your checking account balance and net income check figures. This is due to differences in the calculation of gross salary for salaried employees. If necessary, change the ending balance on the bank statement to reconcile.

Central Valley Bank
212 Folsom Drive
Sacramento, CA 95822
(916) 343-4751

Champion Law
3835 Freeport Blvd
Sacramento, CA 95822
Account # 78459525—Checking Account   January 31, 2018

	CREDITS	CHARGES	BALANCE
Beginning Balance, January 1			$89,400.00
Deposit, 1/4	$ 225.00		89,625.00
Check 1006, 1/6		$ 600.00	89,025.00
Check 1005, 1/6		550.00	88,475.00
Check 1004, 1/6		250.00	88,225.00
Check 1009, 1/9		40.00	88,185.00
Check 1011, 1/12		185.00	88,000.00
Check 1014, 1/12		3,600.00	84,400.00
Check 1012, 1/13		800.00	83,600.00
Check 1013, 1/15		110.00	83,490.00
Check 1015, 1/15		275.00	83,215.00
Check 1016, 1/18		838.75	82,376.25
Check 1017, 1/18		2,382.81	79,993.44
Deposit, 1/25	6,990.00		86,983.44
Ending balance, January 31			**$86,983.44**

> **HINT:** Payroll checks are issued alphabetically so, depending on your name, the check numbers may differ slightly.

REPORTS TO CREATE FOR ASSIGNMENT 9A

All reports should be in portrait orientation; fit to one page wide (unless otherwise noted).

- Balance Sheet as of 1/31.
- Profit & Loss Summary for January.
- Payroll Summary for January.

- ■ Remove the hours and rate columns.
- ● Sales by Item Summary for January.
- ● Journal for January, in date order (Remove the **Trans #** and **Adj** columns).
  - ■ Make sure the account names are visible.
- ● Profit & Loss by Job for January.
  - ■ Try to narrow the column width as much as you can but make sure the job names are still readable.

Assignment 9B

Constructed with Style

You are the owner of a small construction company. Your specialties are residential kitchen and bathroom remodels. The business is a corporation with a 12/31 year-end. You are currently working out of a home office, but you have put a $1,400 security deposit on a new space. You expect to move in February.

It's January 1, 2018, and you just started using QuickBooks. You've entered all the account balances as of 12/31/17. You have set up frequently used vendors and most of the payroll items you think you'll need. Manual payroll processing is already turned on.

You are active in the business, and you pay yourself a salary. You have two employees: Monica Smith (a skilled electrician) and Henri Navarre (a skilled plumber). They are both paid hourly (with overtime for hours over 8 in a single day). Employees are paid **semimonthly**. You, Monica, and Henri are already set up as employees in the **Employee Center**.

You took December 2017 off so there were no jobs in process at 12/31 (and no accounts receivable or payable), but you do have contracts with two new clients, and you've already set those **jobs** up in QuickBooks. You are a small operation, so you bill your clients twice a month, and your credit terms are Net 10. The new customers are:

- ● Mark and Janice Perkins—Kitchen remodel.
- ● Janine Thomas—Bathroom remodel.

All of your contracts are time-and-materials contracts. (All direct costs are billed to the client.) You have entered the hourly rates for various types of labor charges. You do not charge a markup on the cost of materials. All sales are subject to sales tax.

You have set up all the **items** you currently need for your business. All materials are bought specifically for the projects, so you don't maintain any inventory of appliances, cabinets, etc. All material **items** are, therefore, set up as **non-inventory parts**, which allows you to bill for and track the specific materials costs of your jobs without using the perpetual tracking system tools. You bill your clients for **all** materials, labor, plans, and permits.

You do keep some small construction items on hand (nails, glue, etc.), but you generally do not maintain much of a supply, so you expense those costs to the "Job Supplies and Small Tools" account as they're purchased. You do **not** charge your clients for these costs.

You do keep some office supplies on hand. You record those in "Supplies on Hand" and adjust the balance at the end of the month.

Before you start your assignment:

- ● Change the company name to Your Name Constructed with Style.
- ● Change "Student Name" to **your** name in the **Employee Center** (use your first and last names).
- ● Familiarize yourself with the **item**, **payroll item**, and **chart of account** lists.

1/2/18

✓ You head down to the City of Sacramento to pick up some building permits. The total cost is $905, which you pay with check #1088. (You "Quick Add" the City of Sacramento as a vendor.) [**TIP:** You charge your clients for costs of plans and permits, so you need to record the charges as **items** and select the **Customer:Job**. If prompted about changing cost information for the **item**, answer "no." You might want to opt to turn off the message.]

- Fee for Perkins (Kitchen remodel), $655.
- Fee for Thomas (Bathroom remodel), $250.

✓ You need some electrical and plumbing supplies for the jobs. You stop by Contractor's Hardware and spend $485. You pay with check #1089. You expect to use all supplies in January. Remember: You do **not** charge clients for job supplies and small tools.

✓ You also stop by Office Mini and pick up some office supplies. Total cost is $185, and you pay with your credit card (World Wide Card). You're not sure how long the supplies will last, but it will probably be more than a few months.

- You will not be setting up an account with Office Mini, so you **Quick Add** them as a vendor.
- Add any necessary new accounts to your chart of accounts.

✓ When you return to the office, you see that the cabinetry for the Perkins Kitchen job (from Martinez Cabinets and Hardware) has arrived. The bill (#89998), dated 1/2, totals $10,820 with terms of Net 30. [**TIP:** Don't forget to charge the **item** (cabinetry) to the **job**. You must be on the **Items** tab of the **bill**.]

✓ You get your neighbor to drive one of your trucks to the gas station (Gus' Gasoline). You drive the other truck. You fill up both trucks for $150. You use your credit card. (Quick Add Gus' Gasoline as a vendor.)

1/3/18

✓ Brentley Appliances delivers the appliances for the Perkins Kitchen job. Their bill (#12-1011), dated 1/3, totals $2,500. Terms with Brantley are Net 15.

✓ You receive a reminder notice from your insurance company. You hurry up and write a check (#1090) to Contractor's Insurance Co. for $2,400. The policy period is 1/1 to 6/30.

1/4/18

✓ Flooring materials are delivered by Tuan's Flooring (with the bill) for both jobs. The total bill (#2784) was $2,600. The terms were Net 30. The bill was dated 1/4.

- Perkins Kitchen tile flooring, $2,050.
- Thomas Bathroom linoleum flooring, $550.

✓ You receive the cabinetry (with a bill) for the Thomas Bathroom from Martinez Cabinets. The total bill (#90046) for $2,985 is dated 1/4. Terms are Net 30. Included with the cabinetry are some miscellaneous installation supplies you ordered. None of the supplies are expected to last longer than the month. The supplies can't be directly traced to a specific job and are not billable. [**TIP:** Use the "**Expenses**" tab.]

- The cost of the Thomas Bathroom cabinets, $2,600.
- The cost of miscellaneous job supplies, $385.

✓ The sink for the Perkins Kitchen job also arrives. The bill (#78-789) from Folsom Fixtures for $152.00 is dated 1/4 with terms of Net 30. (NOTE: Sinks, tubs and toilets are considered "fixtures".)

1/5/18

✓ You enter timesheets for the week beginning January 1st. No one worked on Monday.

- All job hours are billable, so you enter a **service item** and a **Customer:Job** when entering those hours in addition to a **payroll item**. [**TIP:** You don't need a **job** or **service item** for your own administrative time. You do, however, need to enter the non-billable **administrative** hours in the timesheet so the wages are allocated properly. Rows for administrative hours only need to include a **payroll item**.

Week of January 1-7		M	Tu	W	Th	F
Henri Navarre (24 total hours)						
Perkins Kitchen	Demolition.		8			
Perkins Kitchen	Plumbing.				8	
Perkins Kitchen	Cabinet install.					8
Monica Smith (24 total hours)						
Perkins Kitchen	Demolition.		8	6		
Perkins Kitchen	Electrical.				6	4
You (30 total hours)						
Perkins Kitchen	Demolition.				6	4
Perkins Kitchen	Cabinet install.					8
Perkins Kitchen	General.			2	2	2
Administrative.			4		2	

1/10/18

✓ You get a call from Frank Wang. He and his wife Annie are looking for a contractor to build them a new deck, and he got your name from a former client. You haven't built decks before, but this is a great opportunity to expand your business. (You start looking for a good carpenter to hire right away.) You tell Frank that you'll be able to start the project during the week of the 22nd.

✓ You set the Wang family up as a new customer (terms of Net 10).

  • You use Wang for the **Customer Name**.

  • Annie & Frank Wang

    4678 NE 50th St

    Sacramento, CA 95822

  • Terms are Net 10

  • You add the deck job. [**TIP:** Set up and save the customer first. Then go back and add the job.]

✓ You also set up two new **items** for your new business:

  • You need a **service** item for labor (you might want to call it "Deck Labor"). You expect to charge $80 an hour (**Sales Price**) for the service (this service is subject to tax). You decide to record the labor income in the "Construction Income" account and the labor cost in the "Direct Costs–Labor" account. [**TIP:** You'll need to click "This service is used in assemblies or is performed by subcontractors or partners" in order to enter the cost of goods sold account for both **items**. Don't forget to complete all necessary fields, including the **subitem** field.]

  • You'll also need a **non-inventory part** item for the lumber materials (you might want to call it "Lumber"). You will be billing the customer for the cost, so you don't need to set a rate (price). You decide to record the income in the "Construction income" account and the cost in the "Direct Costs–Materials" account. [**TIP:** You'll need to click "This service is used in assemblies or is performed by subcontractors or partners" in order to enter the cost of goods sold account for both **items**. Don't forget to complete all necessary fields, including the **subitem** field.]

1/11/18

✓ The fixtures for the Thomas Bathroom are delivered by Folsom Fixtures. The bill (#78-999) totals $685. The bill is dated 1/11 with terms of Net 30.

1/12/18

✓ You interview a number of candidates for the carpenter job and decide to offer the job to Luis Garcia. He has more than 15 years of experience, and you've seen his work before. Luis accepts the job. Although he won't be starting until later in January, you have him fill out all the paperwork and get him set up in QuickBooks.

- On his W-4, Luis enters a filing status of single with one allowance (use for both federal and state).

- SS number: 522-21-6888

- Address: 3835 Pocket Road, Sacramento, CA 95822

- Straight-time rate—$30 per hour. Luis will be paid semimonthly like the other employees. Payroll schedules are not used by the company so you leave that field blank.

- You will be using time data to create his paychecks. Start date is 1/22.

- Besides federal and state withholding, Luis is subject the following taxes: federal (Medicare, Social Security, and FUTA), state (SUI and SDI), and other (CA Employment Training Tax).

- You will not be tracking sick/vacation hours.

✓ You want Luis to meet your other employees, so you take them all to dinner at Tasty Corner for the monthly staff meeting. The meal cost $125. You charge it on your credit card.

✓ You enter timesheets for the week. All job hours are billable.

Week of January 8-14		M	Tu	W	Th	F
Henri Navarre (26 total hours)						
Perkins Kitchen	Flooring install			8	2	
Perkins Kitchen	Other install		4			
Perkins Kitchen	Cabinet install.	8				
Thomas Bathroom	Demolition.		4			
Monica Smith (24 total hours)						
Perkins Kitchen	Other install				8	4
Thomas Bathroom	Demolition.			8		
Thomas Bathroom	Electrical.					4
You (40 total hours)						
Perkins Kitchen	Flooring install			4	4	
Perkins Kitchen	Cabinet Install.	8			2	8
Perkins Kitchen	General.	2		2	2	
Thomas Bathroom	Demolition.		6			
Administrative.			2			

1/15/18

✓ You also enter time for 1/15.

Week of January 15-21		M	Tu	W	Th	F
Henri Navarre (3 total hours)						
Perkins Kitchen	Other install	3				
Monica Smith (8 total hours)						
Perkins Kitchen	Other install	8				
You (10 total hours)						
Perkins Kitchen	General.	2				
Thomas Bathroom	Cabinet Install.	4				
Administrative.	4					

You prepare payroll checks for Henri, Monica, and yourself (two-week period ending January 15) dated 1/15/18.

> ✳ **HINT: Before you start creating paychecks,** compare your **Time by Name** and **Time by Job Summary** reports to the reports posted in the Student Materials section of the book's website: https://cambridgepub.com/book/quickbooks-2015. If you have hours or clients recorded incorrectly (and that's very easy to do), you won't be able to create accurate invoices.

- The first check number should be #1091.
- Monica's gross pay is $1,680.00; net pay is $1,281.00.
- Henri's gross pay is $1,590.00; net pay is $1,212.37.
- Your gross pay is $2,500.33; net pay is $1,906.51.

> ✳ **HINT:** Because of differences in payroll calculations of salaried employees by different QuickBooks programs, you may get **slightly** different amounts (less than $0.05 differences) from the gross and net pay amount shown here for your paycheck.

	You	Henri	Monica
Withholdings:			
Federal Withholding	250.03	159.00	168.00
Social Security	155.02	98.58	104.16
Medicare	36.25	23.06	24.36
CA–Withholding	125.02	79.50	84.00
CA–Disability	27.50	17.49	18.48
Employer taxes:			
CA–Employment Training Tax	2.50	1.59	1.68
Social Security	155.02	98.58	104.16
Medicare	36.25	23.06	24.36
Federal Unemployment	15.00	9.54	10.08
CA–Unemployment	85.01	54.06	57.12

1/16/18

 You prepare invoices for Perkins and Thomas. All invoices are dated 1/15 with terms of Net 10. Start with Invoice #1200 using the Intuit Professional Invoice template.

- All labor is billed at the standard rates. [**TIP:** On the **Time** tab, make sure the **Transfer item descriptions** is selected under **Options**.]
- All materials costs to date are included on the **invoice**.
- Invoice totals (**including tax**): Perkins, $30,252.97; Thomas, $6,297.99.

✓ You pick up the decking materials for the Wang Deck job at Tulio Lumber. You did business with them years ago, so they set up an account for you but you haven't entered them in QuickBooks yet. Total cost of the lumber needed for the deck was $1,500. Bill # is 8621.

- Tulio Lumber

  1444 Franklin Blvd

  Sacramento, CA 95822

- Terms: Net 30

✓ You fill up the trucks with gasoline at Gus' Gasoline. Total cost for both trucks is $180. You use your credit card.

1/18/18

✓ Monica and Henri stop by the office after work. Although they are grateful they have a job, they would like you to consider increasing their pay to $35 per hour because they've been working for you for a little over a year. You explain that an almost 17% raise is too high but you agree to give them a 5% raise, effective 1/16. You change both their pay rates to $31.50 per hour.

1/19/18

✓ You enter timesheets for the week. You will be adding the hours for Tuesday through Friday.

Week of January 15-21		M	Tu	W	Th	F
Henri Navarre (30 hours added; 33 total hours)						
Thomas Bathroom	Plumbing.		8			
Thomas Bathroom	Cabinet install.			8	8	
Thomas Bathroom	Other install					6
Monica Smith (15 hours added; 23 total hours)						
Thomas Bathroom	Electrical.		4	3		
Thomas Bathroom	Flooring install					8
You (32 hours added; 42 total hours)						
Thomas Bathroom	Plumbing.		4			
Thomas Bathroom	Cabinet install.			8	6	
Thomas Bathroom	Other install					4
Thomas Bathroom	General.		2	2		2
Administrative.					2	2

1/23/18

✓ You decide to place an ad in the Sacramento Journal advertising your additional deck services. You sign up for 2 ads, to be placed in the Sunday papers (**2/4** and **2/18**). The Journal faxes you a bill (#185-99) for the $400 rate ($200 per ad). The terms are Net 15.

1/24/18

✓ You receive the following checks in the mail:
   - Check #2299, dated 1/24, from Perkins in the amount of $30,252.97.
   - Check #1889, dated 1/24, from Thomas in the amount of $3,000.00. (This is a partial payment. Janine agrees to pay you the balance of $3,297.99 at the end of February.)

✓ You take the checks down to the bank and deposit them. (The total deposit is $33,252.97.)

✓ You come back to the office and prepare checks for all bills due on or before February 3rd.
   - Total amount paid is $19,057.00; 5 bills and 4 checks. First check number should be 1094.

1/26/18

✓ You enter timesheets for the week. All job hours are billable.
   - Monica took most of the week off.

Week of January 22-26		M	Tu	W	Th	F
Henri Navarre (18 total hours)						
Thomas Bathroom	Other install	8				
Wang Deck	Deck labor			4	4	2
Luis Garcia (20 total hours)						
Wang Deck	Deck labor			8	4	8

Week of January 22-26		M	Tu	W	Th	F
Monica Smith (3 total hours)						
Thomas Bathroom	Other install	3				
You (33 total hours)						
Thomas Bathroom	Other install	6				
Thomas Bathroom	General.	2				
Wang Deck	Deck labor			4	4	4
Wang Deck	General.				2	
Administrative	. . . .		2	6		3

1/31/18

✓ Most of your jobs wrapped up last Friday so you told Monica and Henri to take a few days off. You enter the timesheets for you and Luis.

Week of January 29-31		M	Tu	W	Th	F
Luis Garcia (8 total hours)						
Wang Deck	Deck labor	8				
You (26 total hours)						
Wang Deck	Deck labor	4				
Wang Deck	General.	3				
Administrative	. . . .	3	8	8		

✓ You prepare **paychecks** for the two-week payroll period ending 1/31. First check should be #1098. (Don't forget to check the **Time by Name** and **Time by Job** reports first.)

- Gross pay for Luis is $840.00; net pay is $640.50.
- Gross pay for Henri is $1,512.00; net pay is $1,152.91.
- Gross pay for Monica is $567.00; net pay is $432.34.
- Gross pay for you is $2,500.33; net pay is $1,906.51.

 HINT: Because of differences in payroll calculations of salaried employees by different QuickBooks programs, you may get **slightly** different amounts (less than $0.05 differences) from the gross and net pay amount shown here for your paycheck.

	Luis	You	Henri	Monica
Withholdings:				
Federal Withholding	84.00	250.03	151.20	56.70
Social Security	52.08	155.02	93.74	35.15
Medicare.	12.18	36.25	21.92	8.22
CA–Withholding	42.00	125.02	75.60	28.35
CA–Disability	9.24	27.50	16.63	6.24
Employer taxes:				
CA–Employment Training Tax	0.84	2.50	1.51	0.57
Social Security	52.08	155.02	93.74	35.15
Medicare.	12.18	36.25	21.92	8.22
Federal Unemployment	5.04	15.00	9.07	3.40
CA–Unemployment	28.56	85.01	51.41	19.28

✓ Frank Wang gives you a call. They love their new deck, and they want to pay you today because they're going out of town. Frank stops by the office, and you prepare a sales receipt (#1000) for him. He hands you a check (#1299) for the full amount ($6,809.80).

✓ You prepare an invoice for the Thomas Bathroom job ($8,307.53, including tax). All hours are billed at the standard rates.

✓ You deposit the check you received from Frank Wang.

✓ You remit the following payroll taxes to the appropriate agencies (the payroll period is 1/1 to 1/31). [**TIP:** There should be two **payroll liability** checks (#1102, and #1103) totaling $3,513.51.] You use 1/31 for the check date:

- Federal withholding.
- FICA taxes (Social security and Medicare).
- California withholding.
- California disability.

✓ You receive your credit card statement from World Wide Credit Card Co., dated 1/31. The balance due of $640.00 includes all charges through the statement date. You reconcile the account and enter a bill for payment later.

After month-end:

✓ You reconcile your bank account (see below).

✓ You record all necessary adjusting journal entries (all journal entries are dated 1/31).

- Supplies—You have $50 worth of office supplies on hand at 1/31.

> **HINT:** Read through the information given in the background information listed on the first page of the assignment, and carefully look at the balance sheet. You've reconciled your cash account, so that should be okay. How about the other asset accounts? Does Accounts Receivable agree to the aging? Do the prepaid accounts represent amounts you've paid for services or items you haven't used yet? What about the liability accounts? Are you confident they're correct?

- The company uses the straight-line method of depreciation. Depreciation expense is $945 per month for the trucks and construction equipment and $55 per month for office furniture and equipment.
  - ○ You set up a new account for depreciation expense on office equipment so you can report that expense as a subaccount of "Facilities Cost."

✓ You review your balance sheet and profit-and-loss statement. You rearrange the account order so that the statements look professional.

Check numbers 1/31/18

Checking account balance......	$28,670.12
Account receivable	$11,605.52
Total assets.................	$84,805.64
Total liabilities..............	$ 7,400.06
Net income (January)	$10,825.58

Central Bank
1335 K Street
Sacramento, CA 95822 (916) 232-5862

Constructed with Style
3835 Freeport Blvd
Sacramento, CA 95822
Account # 52578459—Checking Account   January 31, 2018

	CREDITS	CHARGES	BALANCE
Beginning Balance, January 1			$23,500.00
Check 1088, 1/6		$ 905.00	22,595.00
Check 1089, 1/7		485.00	22,110.00
Check 1090, 1/7		2,400.00	19,710.00
Check 1093, 1/17		1,281.00	18,429.00
Check 1092, 1/20		1,212.37	17,216.63
Check 1091, 1/20		1,906.51	15,310.12
Deposit, 1/24	$33,252.97		48,563.09
Deposit, 1/31	6,809.80		55,372.89
Ending balance, January 31			**$55,372.89**

 HINT: Payroll checks are issued alphabetically so, depending on your name, the payroll check numbers may differ slightly.

REPORTS TO CREATE FOR ASSIGNMENT 9B

All reports should be in portrait orientation unless otherwise noted; fit to one page wide.

- Journal—1/01 through 1/31 transactions only.
  - Put report in date order.
  - Columns should be Type, Date, Num, Name, Memo, Account, Debit, Credit.
  - Make sure the account name is visible.

- Payroll Summary for January.
  - Remove the hours and rate columns.

- Profit & Loss by Job for January. NOTE: Gross profit on this report will not equal gross profit on the profit and loss statement because your administrative labor was charged to "Direct Costs–Labor" but was not associated with a customer.

- Sales by Item Summary (January).
  - Remove the cost of goods sold data from the report.

- Balance Sheet as of 1/31.

- Profit & Loss Summary for January.

QuickBooks

SECTION FIVE
Beyond the Basics

Although recording transactions is a very important part of accounting, reporting accounting activity in a way that is useful to management is just as important.

In this section, a number of tools and features that can be very useful in managing a business are introduced and we discuss the set-up and conversion of companies in QuickBooks.

SECTION OVERVIEW

Chapter 10 covers segment reporting using classes and budgeting—two important management tools available in QuickBooks.

Chapter 11 covers creating reversing entries, memorizing custom reports, customizing forms, and exporting reports to Excel.

Chapter 12 covers setting up new companies in QuickBooks and converting existing companies to QuickBooks.

Chapter 13 gives you a brief introduction to QuickBooks Online Plus, Intuit's cloud computing accounting solution.

Management Tools

Objectives

After completing Chapter 10, you should be able to:

1. Turn on class tracking in QuickBooks.

2. Assign classes when recording transactions.

3. Set up budgets in QuickBooks.

4. Prepare reports by class.

5. Prepare budget and budget variance reports.

369

Accounting is a system in which an organization's economic events are identified, recorded, summarized, analyzed, and reported. From this system comes financial information that can be used by management, creditors, and investors to plan and evaluate.

In this course, we focus on **recording and reporting** transactions in an electronic environment, but it's also important to look at ways accounting software might be helpful in the planning and evaluation functions of an organization.

In this chapter, we cover a few of the tools in QuickBooks that can be used to provide useful information to management. There are a few others that are listed in Chapter 11, but for now we cover:

* Using **classes**.

* Preparing budgets.

TRACKING BY CLASS

One of the main advantages of computerized accounting systems is the incredible amount of detail that can effectively **and** efficiently be maintained. The use of **items** in QuickBooks is a good example of that. A company can easily track revenues and costs for every model of every product sold by a company and still have a one-page income statement!

Class is another tool in QuickBooks for tracking detail. A **class** represents a specific reporting **segment**. Examples of business segments include:

Segment A subdivision of an entity for which supplemental financial information is disclosed.

* Departments.

* Sales regions.

* Product lines.

If **class tracking** is used, every transaction (and, for the most part, every component of every transaction) can be linked to a **class**. Reports can then be prepared by segment.

Class tracking requires additional work. so it should only be used if an organization can be separated into segments **and** if there are meaningful differences between the segments that make them worth tracking.

As an example, let's look at two retail companies selling diamond rings. Company A has one store and one manager. Company B has five stores and five managers. Company A could set up a **class** for every type diamond ring they sell, but it can already get that information from **item** reports. It could also set up a class for every day of the week, but that probably wouldn't give management much meaningful information and would require **a lot** of allocation! Company A doesn't appear to have any meaningful segments.

Company B, on the other hand, might use **classes to** track sales and costs by store. Management could then use that information to evaluate the product mix at the various stores, to evaluate the performance of store managers, or to plan for new stores.

You have to be very careful when designing your system of **classes**. The most common mistake users make is to create **classes** that conflict. For instance, let's say you own a law firm with two locations (Sacramento and West Sacramento). Both offices handle criminal and civil cases. You want to track operations by location and by service, so it might seem logical to create four classes—Sacramento, West Sacramento, Criminal, and Civil.

When you enter the salary for the receptionist at the Sacramento office, it's easy to see that the appropriate **class** would be "Sacramento," but what **class** do you choose when you enter an **invoice** charging a client for civil work performed by the West Sacramento office? Remember, you want to track operations by both office and type of service, but you can only assign one class to each line item on the **invoice**. Obviously, this company couldn't track both types of segments (office and service) using four **classes**. The company would either need to choose a primary **class** (say, offices) and create two **subclasses** for each (criminal and law), or it might use **items** and/or accounts to track revenues and direct costs for both types of service and use **class** to track overall operations in each office.

So, here are two tips for using **class tracking**:

- Set up the **classes** based on the segments that provide the most useful information.
  - Segment information is useful if it can help a company evaluate or plan or if segment detail is necessary for reporting to regulatory authorities.
  - You can use **subclasses** for additional detail, but remember, the **subclass** must be directly related to the **class** and must not conflict with any other **subclasses**.
- Make sure **all** transactions can be and are assigned to a **class**.
  - Most companies set up a **class** specifically to track activities that don't fit in one of the identified business segments.
    - If, for example, a company set up a **class** for each product line, owners' salaries or corporate legal fees might be examples of transactions that would be linked to an "Other" or "Administration" **class**.

Using **classes** is not mandatory in QuickBooks. It is a **preference**.

Turning On Class Tracking

Setting up **class tracking** is done through **Preferences**, an option on the **Edit** dropdown menu:

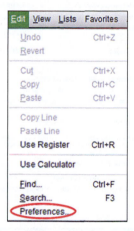

The **class tracking** tool selection is done in the **Accounting** option (first item in the far left column) screen. The **Company Preferences** tab screen for **Accounting** looks something like this:

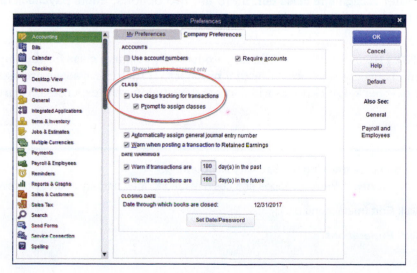

Use class tracking for transactions must be checked. If the Prompt to assign classes option is checked, the user gets a reminder message if a class isn't entered for a transaction. The reminders are especially useful when users first start using class tracking.

Once the preference for class tracking is set, fields will be available on all forms for designating the appropriate classification.

On most forms, a different class can be set for each line item. There are a few exceptions. When completing the purchase order form, one class is set for all items on the purchase order. However, class can easily be changed for specific items later, when the bill or item receipt is entered.

The QuickBooks default, on the paycheck form, is to associate the entire paycheck to one class. If you are using class to track by location and employees only work in one location, one class per paycheck is sufficient. However, if you're using class to track, for example, types of services (and a single employee performs various services), you need the option to assign a class to every wage distribution on a paycheck. That option is available by changing a preference.

Setting up class tracking by earnings item on paychecks is done on the Payroll & Employees page in the Preferences window. The Company Preferences tab screen looks something like this:

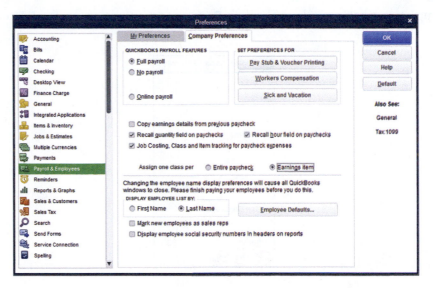

The Job Costing, Class and Item tracking for paycheck expenses option should already be checked. After Assign one class per, there are two options: Entire paycheck or Earnings item. You must check the Earnings item box.

> **BEHIND THE SCENES** QuickBooks automatically assigns a class for the employer payroll tax expenses associated with a paycheck. If multiple classes are used in a single paycheck, QuickBooks will allocate the employer tax expenses on a pro-rata basis.

PRACTICE EXERCISE

Turning on class tracking for Sac City Accounting.
(Sac City decides to track revenues and costs related to their primary sources of revenue.)

1. Click **Edit** (main menu bar).

2. Click **Preferences**.

(continued)

3. Set up **class tracking**.

    a.   Highlight the **Accounting** option in the leftmost column of the screen.

    b.   Click the **Company Preferences** tab.

    c.   Put a check in the box next to **Use class tracking for transactions**.

    d.   Put a check in the box next to **Prompt to assign classes**.

4. Set up **class tracking** for each wage item on a **paycheck**.

    a.   Highlight the **Payroll & Employees** option in the leftmost column of the **preferences** screen.

        i.   Click **Yes** at the prompt to save.

    b.   Click the **Company Preferences** tab.

    c.   Select the **Earnings item** option next to **Assign one class per** (middle of the screen).

    d.   Click **OK**.

Setting Up Classes

Once you've identified the segments you want to track, setting up the categories in Quick-Books is a simple process.

The **Class List** window is accessed through the **Lists** dropdown menu on the main menu bar:

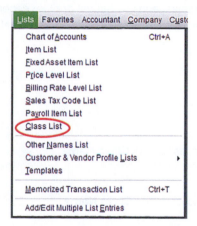

The window looks like this:

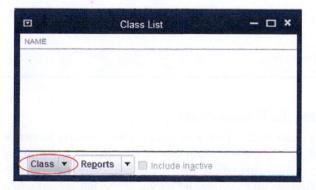

Classes are added (or edited) using the options on the **Class** dropdown menu (bottom left corner of the screen. If **New** is selected, the screen looks like this:

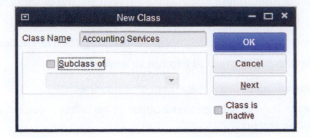

A name must be entered to identify the segment you wish to track. **Subclasses** are used when multiple class levels are needed.

 HINT: You can rearrange the order of the **classes** on the **Class List** using the diamond bullets to the left of the **class** name if you want **class** information to appear in a particular order on reports.

PRACTICE EXERCISE

Setting up a class list for Sac City Accounting.
(Sac City has decided to track operations by type of service. One class, labeled Accounting Services, will be used to report on bookkeeping and financial statement preparation services. A class labeled Consulting Services will be used to track all QuickBooks related services, including software sales, and any budget or other general consulting services provided to clients. A class labeled Administration will be used for all shared costs.)

1. Click **Lists** (main menu bar).

2. Click **Class List**.

3. Click **Class**.

4. Click **New**.

5. Enter "Accounting Services" as the **Class Name**.

6. Click **Next**.

7. Enter "Consulting Services" as the **Class Name**.

8. Click **Next**.

9. Enter "Administration" as the **Class Name** and click **OK**.

10. Click the diamond bullet next to **Administration** and move it below **Consulting Services**.

11. Exit out of the window.

Assigning Classes To Transactions

Assigning classes is done within forms (**invoices**, **bills**, **general journal entries**, **timesheets**, etc.). The **class** assigned to a transaction can be changed at any time by editing the form.

When **class tracking** is turned on, forms automatically include a column in which the **class** can be identified. As an example, let's look at the **bill** screen when **class tracking** has been set up:

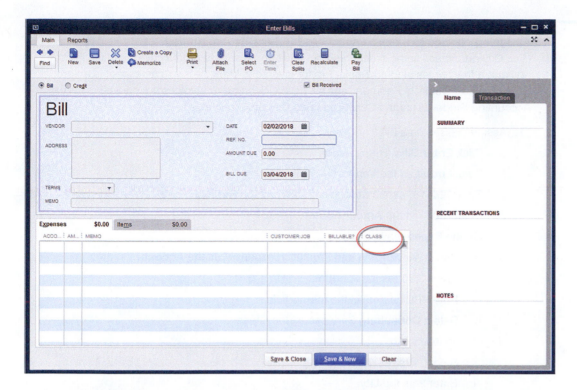

On a **timesheet**, the **class** column is added just to the left of the date columns:

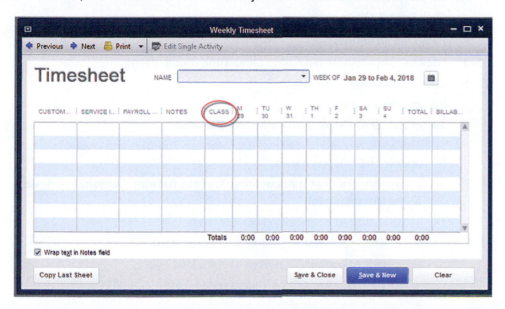

All the other forms used in QuickBooks are similarly changed (that is, a **class** column is added when the **class tracking** feature is turned on).

> **BEHIND THE SCENES** Although **class** can be assigned to transactions affecting balance sheet accounts, segment reporting is most commonly done for operating reports like profit and loss statements, wage summaries, sales summaries, etc. QuickBooks does not require that every transaction be linked to a **class**, so users may elect not to designate a class in distributions to asset, liability, or equity accounts.

Assigning classes to a few transactions for Sac City Accounting.

(Sac City purchases some brochures from Intuit [to be sent to prospective clients in February] and a few copies of QuickBooks Pro for inventory. Mark Jensen's timesheet is entered for the first two weeks of February, and his paycheck created. Invoices are created to bill the Accounting Student Tutoring Center and Sac City Student News.)

1. Assign classes on a bill:
   a. Click **Enter Bills** (Home page).
   b. Select **Intuit** as the **Vendor**.
   c. Enter "2/2/18" as the **date** and "25882" as the **Ref. No.**
   d. Enter "500" as the **Amount Due**.
   e. On the **Expenses** tab:
      i. Select "Advertising and Promotion expense" as the **Account**.
      ii. Enter "200" as the **Amount**.
      iii. Enter "Brochures" in the **memo** field.
      iv. Select **Consulting Services** as the **Class**.
   f. On the **Items** tab:
      i. Select "Pro" as the **Item**.
      ii. Enter 2 as the **Qty.**
      iii. Select "Consulting Services" as the **Class**.
   g. Click **Save & Close**.

2. Enter **classes** on **timesheets**.
   a. Click the drop-down menu next to **Enter Time** (Home page).
   b. Click **Use Weekly Timesheet**.
   c. Select **Jensen, Mark**.
   d. Select **Jan 29 to Feb 4, 2018** as the **Week Of**.
      i. The hours recorded in Chapter 9 for Monday, Tuesday, and Wednesday will appear on the first two lines.
      ii. On the third line, select **Accounting Student Tutoring Center:2017 Review** as the **Customer:Job**.
         1. Select **Staff hours** as the **service item**.
         2. Select **Professional Staff** as the **Payroll Item**.
         3. Select **Accounting Services** as the **Class**.
         4. Enter 8 hours (each) for Thursday and Friday.
         5. Make sure the **Billable** column is checked.
         6. Click **Next**.
            a. Click **Save Anyway** when prompted about the Monday through Wednesday hours not being assigned a class.
   e. **Week of Feb 5 to Feb 11** should appear (if not, enter date).
      i. On the first line, Select **Sac City Student News:QB Set up** as the **Customer:Job**.
         1. Select **Software Setup** as the **service item**.
         2. Select **Professional staff** as the **Payroll Item**.

(continued)

3.   Select **Consulting Services** as the **Class**.

4.   Enter 8 hours (each) for Monday through Friday.

5.   Make sure the **billable** column is checked.

6.   Hours should total 40.

7.   Click **Next**.

f.   **Week of Feb 12 to Feb 18** should appear (if not, enter date).

   i.   On the first line, select **Professional Staff** as the **Payroll Item**.

   ii.   Enter 8 hours (each) for Monday, Tuesday, and Wednesday.

   iii.   Unclick **Billable**.

   iv.   On the second line, select **Accounting Student Tutoring Center: 2017 Review** as the **Customer: Job**.

     1.   Select **Staff hours** as the **service item**.

     2.   Select **Professional Staff** as the **Payroll item**.

     3.   Select **Accounting Services** as the **Class**.

     4.   Enter 8 hours on Thursday.

     5.   Make sure the **Billable** column is checked.

   v.   Hours should total 32.

   vi.   Click **Save & Close**.

g.   Exit out of **timesheet** window.

3.   Create **paychecks** with **class** detail.

a.   Click **Pay Employees** (Home page).

b.   Enter "2/15" for **Pay Period Ends**.

   i.   Enter "yes" if prompted to update hours worked.

c.   Enter "2/15" for **Check Date** and select Checking for **Bank Account**.

d.   Select **Handwrite & Assign check numbers**. First check number should be 1031.

e.   Put a checkmark next to **Jensen, Mark**.

f.   Click **Open Paycheck Detail**.

g.   Enter the following:

   i.   Employee taxes:

     1.   Medicare Employee Addl Tax—0

     2.   Federal Withholding—208

     3.   Social Security Employee—129

     4.   Medicare Employee—30

     5.   CA-Withholding—104

     6.   CA-Disability Employee—23

   ii.   Employer taxes:

     1.   CA – Employment Training Tax—2

     2.   Social Security Company—129

     3.   Medicare Company—30

     4.   Federal Unemployment—12

(continued)

5.   CA – Unemployment Company—71

   iii.   Net check should be $1,589.33.

h.   Click **Save & Close**.

i.   Enter 1031 as the **First Check #**. Hint: Employer taxes should total $244.

j.   Click **Continue**.

k.   Click **Create Paycheck**.

l.   Click **Close**.

4. Assign Classes to an invoice.

a.   Click **Create Invoices** (Home page).

b.   Select **Accounting Student Tutoring Center: 2017 Review** as the **Customer: Job**.

   i.   Click **OK** at prompt to select outstanding billable time and costs.

   ii.   Click **Select All** on the **Time** tab.

   iii.   Click **Options** button and choose **transfer item descriptions**.

   iv.   Click **OK**.

   v.   Click **OK** again to close the **billable time and costs** window.

   vi.   **Invoice #** should be 1008. Date of 2/15. Balance due should be $3,000.

      1.   Note that the class **Accounting Services** appears for each line item (automatically updated from the **timesheet** entry).

      2.   Note that **Class** can be changed for each **item**. It can also be set for an entire **invoice** using the drop-down menu next to **Class** at the top of the window.

   vii.   Make sure **Print Later** and **Email Later** are not checked.

   viii.   Click **Save & New**.

c.   Select **Sac City Student News: QB Setup** as the **Customer: Job**.

   i.   Click **OK** at prompt to select outstanding billable time and costs.

   ii.   Click **Select All** on the **Time** tab.

   iii.   Click **OK**.

   iv.   **Class** should be **Consulting Services**.

   v.   Leave **date** as 2/15 and 1009 as the **Invoice #**.

   vi.   Total should be $4,000.

   vii.   Make sure **Print Later** and **Email Later** are not checked.

   viii.   Click **Save & Close**.

Reporting By Class

There are several reports that are frequently used to report segment information, but most reports can be filtered by **class**.

The **Profit & Loss by Class** report is probably the one most commonly used. This report can be accessed through the **Company & Financial** option on the **Reports** menu (main menu bar) by selecting **Profit & Loss by Class**. The report would look something like this:

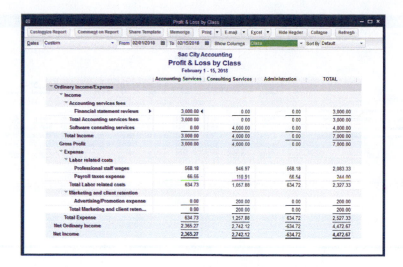

As you can see, there is a column for each **class**. If **subclasses** were set up, there would be a column for each **subclass** and a subtotal column for each primary **class**. If a transaction had not been classified, it would be included in a column labeled "Unclassified".

The **Sales by Item Summary** report can be modified to report sales by **class**. The report can be accessed through the **Sales** option on the **Reports** menu (main menu bar) by selecting **Sales by Item Summary**. The report must be modified (accessed by clicking **customize report**) to show **class** detail.

The modification screen looks like this with the dropdown menu open:

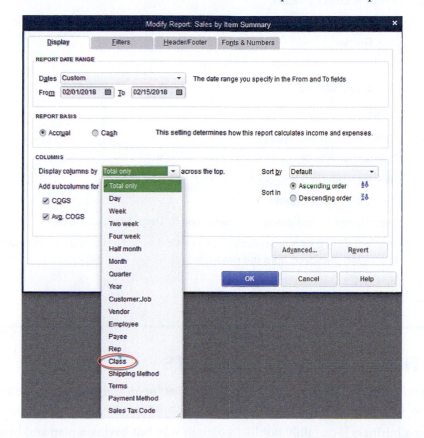

Selecting **Class** in the dropdown menu after **Display columns by** and deselecting the **subcolumn** boxes (for COGS detail) modifies the report to look something like this:

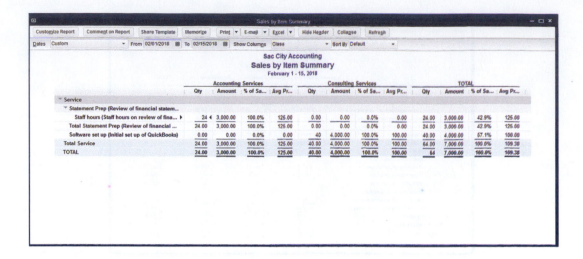

PRACTICE EXERCISE

Preparing reports by class for Sac City Accounting.
(Sac City needs a profit and loss statement by class and would like to see item detail by class.)

1. Click **Reports** (main menu bar).

2. Click **Company & Financial**.

3. Click **Profit & Loss by Class**.
   a. Change dates to 2/1 to 2/15.
   b. Click **Refresh**.
   c. Exit out of report window.

4. Click **Reports** (main menu bar).

5. Click **Sales**.

6. Click **Sales by Item Summary**.
   a. Change dates to 2/1 to 2/15.
   b. Click **Refresh** (or tab through).
   c. Click **Customize Report**.
   d. Select **Class** on the dropdown menu next to **Display columns by**.
   e. Deselect **COGS** as a subcolumn. (The related subcolumns will automatically be deselected [removed from the report].)
   f. Click **OK**.
   g. Exit out of report window.

CREATING AND USING BUDGETS

"The general who wins the battle makes many calculations in his temple before the battle is fought. The general who loses makes but few calculations beforehand."—*Sun Tzu*

Managing a business is certainly not like going to war, but having a plan and being able to evaluate actual results against that plan can definitely help a business succeed.

A financial plan for a business is commonly called a **budget**. In a simple budget, revenues and costs are generally estimated by month. Estimates might be based on:

- Past experience.
- Projections of sales growth (or contraction).
- Industry statistics.
- Combinations of the others.

There are a number of tools in QuickBooks for creating and using budgets.

Creating Budgets

You can create multiple budgets in QuickBooks. There are two basic types:

- Balance Sheet.
- Profit and Loss.

Profit and loss budgets can be prepared for a company overall, by **Customer:Job**, or by **class**. In this course, we cover creating a budget for a company overall.

All of the planning tools in QuickBooks are accessed through the **Planning & Budgeting** option on the **Company** menu (main menu bar).

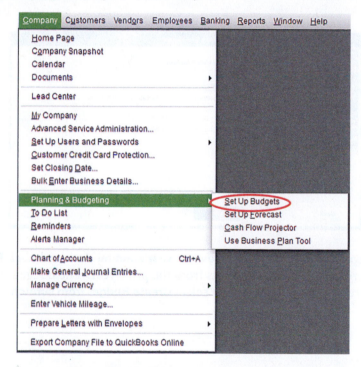

Selecting **Set up Budgets** from the menu takes you to this screen:

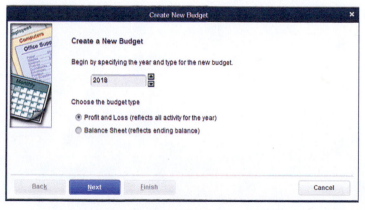

The year and type of budget must be selected. The next screen looks like this if you select **Profit and Loss (reflects all activity for the year)**:

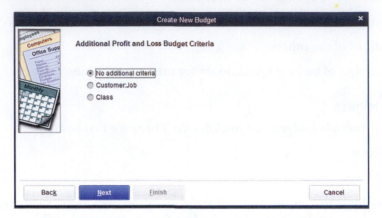

The level of budget detail is selected in this screen. Choosing **No additional criteria** allows you to create an overall revenue and expense budget for the company. The next screen looks like this:

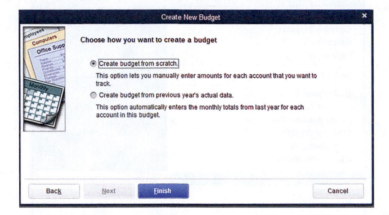

If you choose to **Create budget from previous year's actual data** and click **Finish**, a draft budget will be created using actual results from the prior year. The budget can be edited as needed. The screen looks like this if you select **Create Budget from scratch**:

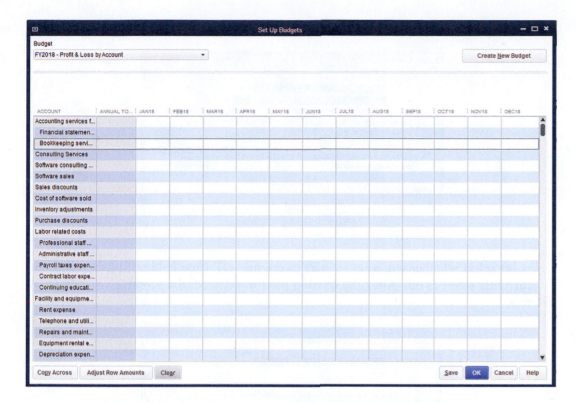

The accounts are listed in the same order as the **chart of accounts** (revenue and expense accounts only of course). (The **chart of accounts** for Sac City Accounting was reorganized a bit for the preceding screenshot.)

You can enter data in all or some of the cells. There are three basic ways that budget data can be entered. All three methods can be used when creating a single budget.

Manual Method Of Entering Budget Amounts

If the budget amounts for a particular account vary considerably from month to month, without any particular pattern, the user would need to manually enter amounts into the appropriate cells for each month.

Copy Across Method Of Entering Budget Amounts

If the monthly budget amounts are the same for consecutive months, the amount can be entered into a particular cell and then copied across the row.

An amount is entered in any cell. The **Copy Across** option is selected (bottom left corner of screen):

QuickBooks automatically copies that amount into every cell to the right.

Trend Method Of Entering Budget Amounts

If the monthly budget amounts increase or decrease by a set amount or percentage over the period, an amount is entered in any cell, and the **Adjust Row Amounts** option is selected:

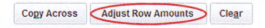

The following screen appears:

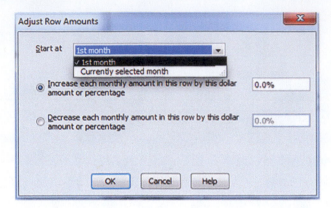

You must select whether you want to start in the first cell (first column) of the row or in the currently selected cell. After the starting point is selected, the screen changes to look like this:

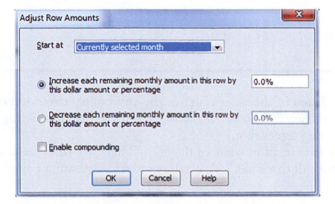

You must now select whether you want the amount entered to be increased or decreased in the remaining cells of the row and, if so, by how much. A set dollar amount or a percentage can be used.

!   WARNING: The % sign must be included in the field if a percentage change applies.

A compounding tool is also available. If you check **Enable compounding**, the amount in each cell is based on the cell that precedes it. It is higher (or lower) by the amount or percent entered. For example, if you select March as the "start" month, enter $100, and select a 10% increase, compounding enabled, then April will change to $110, May will change to $121, June will change to $133.10, and so on.

If you don't **Enable compounding**, then each cell (including the "start" cell) changes (from what it was previously) by the amount indicated. For example, let's say you select March as the "start" month and choose 10%, no compounding. If March had $100 in it, the new amount would be $110. If April already had $400 in it, the new amount would be $440. If May were blank, the new amount would be $0.

The final budget screen looks something like this after the Practice Exercise:

ACCOUNT	ANNUAL TO...	JAN18	FEB18	MAR18	APR18	MAY18	JUN18	JUL18	AUG18	SEP18	OCT18	NOV18	DEC18
Accounting services f...													
Financial statemen...	47,751.41	3,000.00	3,150.00	3,307.50	3,472.88	3,646.52	3,828.85	4,020.29	4,221.30	4,432.37	4,653.99	4,886.69	5,131.02
Bookkeeping servi...	45,000.00	1,000.00	1,500.00	2,000.00	2,500.00	3,000.00	3,500.00	4,000.00	4,500.00	5,000.00	5,500.00	6,000.00	6,500.00
Consulting Services													
Software consulting ...													
Software sales	30,000.00	2,000.00	2,000.00	2,000.00	2,000.00	2,000.00	2,000.00	3,000.00	3,000.00	3,000.00	3,000.00	3,000.00	3,000.00
Sales discounts													
Cost of software sold	15,000.00	1,000.00	1,000.00	1,000.00	1,000.00	1,000.00	1,000.00	1,500.00	1,500.00	1,500.00	1,500.00	1,500.00	1,500.00
Inventory adjustments													
Purchase discounts													
Labor related costs													
Professional staff ...	60,000.00	5,000.00	5,000.00	5,000.00	5,000.00	5,000.00	5,000.00	5,000.00	5,000.00	5,000.00	5,000.00	5,000.00	5,000.00
Administrative staff ...	36,000.00	3,000.00	3,000.00	3,000.00	3,000.00	3,000.00	3,000.00	3,000.00	3,000.00	3,000.00	3,000.00	3,000.00	3,000.00
Payroll taxes expen...	11,520.00	960.00	960.00	960.00	960.00	960.00	960.00	960.00	960.00	960.00	960.00	960.00	960.00
Contract labor expe...													
Continuing educati...													
Facility and equipme...													
Rent expense													
Telephone and utili...													
Repairs and maint...													
Equipment rental e...													
Depreciation expen...													

Setting up a budget for Sac City Accounting.

(Sac City decides to create a simple budget for 2018. Before it starts, Sac City rearranges its chart of accounts.)

1. Click **Lists** (main menu bar).

2. Click **Chart of Accounts**.

   a. In the **income** type accounts section:

      i.   Delete the **Returned Check Charges** account.

      ii. Move **Sales discounts** below **Software sales**.

      iii. Move **Bookkeeping Services** below **Financial Statement Reviews**, if necessary.

   b. In the **expense** type accounts section:

      i.   Delete the **Bank Service Charges** account below **Cost of software sold**.

      ii. Move **Inventory Adjustments** below **Cost of Software Sold**.

      iii. Move **Purchase discounts** below **Inventory Adjustments**.

      iv. Move **Contract labor** below **Payroll tax expense**.

      v.   Move **Miscellaneous Expense** below **Bank Service Charges** under **Other costs**.

3. Exit out of the **Charts of Accounts**.

4. Click **Company** (main menu bar).

5. Click **Planning & Budgeting**.

PRACTICE
EXERCISE

(continued)

6. Click **Set up Budgets**.

7. Select "2018."

8. Check **Profit and Loss**.

9. Click **Next**.

10. Click **No additional criteria**.

11. Click **Next**.

12. Click **Create budget from scratch**.

13. Click **Finish**.

14. Enter the following budget amounts in the "start" month (the start month will always be January for this exercise).

    a.   Financial Statement Reviews—$3,000

        i.   Click **Adjust Row Amounts**.

        ii.   Select **Start at currently selected month** in the **Start at** field.

        iii.   Enter "5%" in the **increase** box.

        iv.   Click **enable compounding**.

        v.   Click **OK**.

    b.   Bookkeeping Services—$1,000

        i.   Click **Adjust Row Amounts**.

        ii.   Select **Start at currently selected month** in the **Start at** field

        iii.   Enter "500" in the **increase** box.

        iv.   Click **Enable compounding**.

        v.   Click **OK**.

    c.   Software Sales—$2,000

        i.   Click **Copy Across**.

        ii.   Select the cell for July.

        iii.   Enter "3,000" and **Copy Across**.

    d.   Cost of software sold—$1,000

        i.   Click **Copy Across**.

        ii.   Click in July.

        iii.   Enter "1,500" and click **Copy Across**.

    e.   Professional staff wages—$5,000

        i.   Click **Copy Across**.

    f.   Administrative staff wages—$3,000

        i.   Click **Copy Across**.

    g.   Payroll taxes expense—$960

        i.   Click **Copy Across**.

15. Click **OK**.

Creating Budget Reports

There are a variety of budget reports in QuickBooks. All of them can be accessed through the **Budgets & Forecasts** option on the **Reports** menu (main menu bar).

- The **Budget Overview** report presents budget figures only.

- The **Budget vs. Actual** report presents actual and budget figures by month. The dollar difference (actual less budget) and the percentage relationship of actual to budget (actual divided by budget) are also displayed for each account.

 HINT: Accountants usually prefer to display negative numbers in parentheses. The displays can be changed on the **Fonts & Numbers** tab in the **Modify Report** window.

- The **Profit & Loss Budget Performance** report presents actual and budget figures for the period selected and for the year-to-date by account. The annual budget amounts are also listed.

CHAPTER SHORTCUTS

Set up Class Tracking
1. Click Edit (main menu bar)
2. Click Preferences
3. Select Accounting (left column)
4. Select Company Preferences tab
5. Check Use class tracking for transactions box

Enable class tracking per earnings item for payroll
1. Click Edit (main menu bar)
2. Click Preferences
3. Select Payroll & Employees (left column)
4. Select Company Preferences tab
5. Check Per earnings item

Create a budget
1. Click Company
2. Click Planning & Budgets
3. Click Set up Budgets

CHAPTER REVIEW

Matching

Match the term or phrase (as used in QuickBooks) to its best definition.

1. Compounding
2. Class
3. Budget vs. Actual report
4. Assign one class per earnings item
5. Budget
6. Budget Overview report
7. Subclass
8. Profit & Loss by Class report

_____ Report that displays revenue and expenses by class for a specified period of time

_____ Tool used in creating a budget that allows the user to base future budget amounts on past budget amounts in the same budget period

_____ Report that shows variances between actual and budgeted results for a period of time

_____ A primary segment of an organization

_____ Estimate of account balances for a period of time (or point in time)

_____ Preference allowing wages in a single paycheck to be tracked in more than one class

_____ A class within a class

_____ Report that shows budgeted account balances for a period of time

Multiple Choice

1. In QuickBooks, a **class** can be set up to track specific:
    a. departments in a company.
    b. sales regions in a company.
    c. services provided by a company.
    d. any of the above.

2. Which of the following statements is true?
    a. **Class tracking** is done automatically by QuickBooks.
    b. A **class** must be designated for every entry in a transaction.

    c. The **class(es)** for employer payroll taxes on a paycheck will follow the **class(es)** assigned to the salary(wages) in the paycheck.

    d. Only one **class** can be set per vendor **bill**.

3. Budgets can be created for:

    a. profit and loss in a fiscal year.

    b. a specific **job**.

    c. a specific **class**.

    d. any of the above.

4. When creating a budget, you enter $100 in January, click **adjust row amounts** and enter 5% in the **increase each monthly amount in this row** field. You check the **enable compounding** box. The amount that will appear in March is:

    a. $100.00.

    b. $105.00.

    c. $110.00.

    d. $110.25.

5. Which of the following QuickBooks reports compares actual amounts to budgeted amounts by month (in dollars and percent)?

    a. Budget Overview

    b. Budget vs. Actual

    c. Profit & Loss Budget Performance

ASSIGNMENTS

Background information from Chapter 9: You have decided to open your own law firm, specializing in family and employment law. The business is a corporation with a 12/31 year-end. You contributed $100,000 in cash to start the business. You already have a few clients but won't start working on their cases until the office opens on 1/2/18.

    You rented space (and prepaid the January rent) and purchased furniture and equipment in December 2017. You also prepaid the local newspaper for some ads to run in January newspapers and purchased two insurance policies (one for professional liability and one for general business).

    You have decided to pay yourself a salary of $75,000 per year. You have one other employee (Nancy Svenborg). Nancy will be working as a paralegal and also performing some administrative duties. She will be paid $25 per hour. Payroll is paid semimonthly, on the 15th and 31st.

    You are a small operation, so you bill your clients twice a month, and your credit terms are Net 10. Remember: In QuickBooks, clients are called **customers**; cases (matters) are called **jobs**. The clients and matters you know you'll be working on are:

- Jordan & Jamie Childress—Adoption (Katie).

- Sam & Serena Johnson—Adoption (Terrence).

- Urban Settings—Employment contract for architects.

- Janice Williams—Wrongful termination.

You've already set up the listed clients in QuickBooks. You've set yourself and Nancy up as employees in QuickBooks as well. You have also set up frequently used vendors and most of the payroll items you think you'll need. Manual payroll processing has already turned on.

Assignment 10A

Champion Law

You've set up service items for each of the professional services you expect to perform. Professional services will be billed on any hourly basis. You've also set up a service item for non-billable time. Non-billable time represents time spent on general company business (time not chargeable to a specific client).

You intend to bill your clients for any direct costs incurred on their behalf and so have also set up items for those costs (other charge items). You do not intend to mark up direct costs.

Other information:

- Professional liability insurance policy premium: $3,000; term: 1/1 to 6/30/18.

- General insurance policy premium: $600; term: 1/1 to 6/30/18.

- Monthly depreciation (straight-line) on computer equipment and copier: $93, with a 3-year life.

- Monthly depreciation (straight-line) on furniture: $30, with a 5-year life.

2/1/18

✓ You realize that you really need to have a few more management tools to run your business effectively.

✓ You want to be able to evaluate and compare the profitability of your major business lines using the **class** feature available in QuickBooks, so you turn on the **class** feature in **Preferences**.

- On the **Accounting** tab, you check **Use class tracking for transactions**.

- You also check the **prompt to assign classes** box so that you won't miss adding a class when you're entering transactions.

- On the **Payroll & Employees** tab, you elect to assign classes by earnings item.

✓ You look over your cases and determine that you have specialties. You set up a **class** for each specialty and a separate **class** for administrative costs as follows:

- Family Law (includes adoptions, divorces, etc.).

- Employment Law (includes union negotiations, employment contracts, etc.).

- Class-Action Lawsuits (includes cases like Toys for Tots and CPA Exam).

- Administration (includes all indirect job costs and administrative expenses).

- You delete the **Partner/Location classes** set up by QuickBooks. You won't be using those.

✓ You also decide you want to create a budget for 2018.

✓ You create a profit and loss budget for 2018 (no additional criteria) from scratch. Starting with January, unless otherwise noted, you use the following estimates:

- Legal services revenue

  ○ $30,000 for January; $60,000 per month for the rest of the year.

- Labor-related expenses

  ○ Attorney salaries—$12,000 for January; $17,000 per month for the rest of the year.

  ○ Paralegal wages—$4,000 per month.

  ○ Payroll tax expense—2,000 for January; $2,050 per month for the rest of the year.

  ○ Continuing education—$500 per month

  ○ Other staff expenses—$200 per month

- Facilities and equipment costs

  ○ Rent—$3,000 per month.

  ○ Telephone and utilities—$300 per month.

  ○ Repairs and maintenance—$400 in March, June, September, and December.

  ○ Depreciation—$125 per month through June, then $150 per month through December.

- Advertising and promotion
  - Advertising—$500 per month.
  - Client relations—$500 in January with a 2% increase per month for the rest of the year. [**TIP:** Don't forget to enable compounding.]
- Insurance and professional fees
  - Liability Insurance—$500 per month.
  - General business insurance—$100 per month.
  - Professional fees—$2,500 in April.
- Other operating expenses
  - Legal library—$800 per month.
  - Office supplies—$150 in January with a 3% increase per month for the rest of the year.
  - Dues and subscriptions—$10 per month.
- You don't set up a budget for direct costs (or for the related income account **Reimbursed expenses**). All direct costs are passed through to the client without markup, so the company wouldn't show any profit or loss on that activity.

2/2/18

✓ You forgot to pay the rent yesterday, and you get a call from your landlord. You bring the check (#1025) for February's rent ($3,000) to Professional Spaces' main office during your lunch hour. You forget to include the **class**, but QuickBooks reminds you when you try to **Save & Close**.

✓ You met with Andrew and Connie Nguyen yesterday. They want to adopt a baby girl named Lisa and need you to prepare the documents for them. You work on the documents in the morning and take them down to the courthouse (Superior Court) with the $20 filing fee (check #1026). [**TIP:** You need to add a client and then add a job to the client.]

- Remember, you charge your clients for all direct costs. Direct costs are entered as **items**. Adoptions are family law cases.
- Other information:
  - 2500 Green Street
    Sacramento, CA 95822
    (916) 534-4444
  - Terms: Net 10

✓ Frank files documents at the Superior Court of California for Exam Prep (CPA Exam lawsuit) and Toys for Tots (Wheels lawsuit). The fees total $120 (split equally between the two cases) and are paid with check #1027. These are class-action cases.

✓ You enter timesheets starting with Thursday 2/1.

- You'll be adding hours to the timesheet for the workweek beginning 1/29. You won't be adding **class** to the January hours that were entered previously.

Week of January 29 to Feb 4		Class	M	Tu	W	Th	F
You (18 new; 42 total hours)							
Mega Manu: Union Contract	Meetings.	EL					8
Nguyen: Lisa Adoption	Initial consultation.	FL				3	
Nguyen: Lisa Adoption	Documents	FL					2
	Non-billable.	A				5	
Nancy Svenborg (13 new; 33 total hours)							
Nguyen: Lisa Adoption	Paralegal assistance	FL					3
	Non-billable.	A				5	5

Frank Williams (16 new; 40 total hours)		Class	M	Tu	W	Th	F
Exam Prep: CPA Exam	Documents	CA				4	
Toys for Tots: Wheels	Documents	CA				4	
Toys for Tots: Wheels	Meetings	CA					6
	Non-billable	A					2

2/8/18

✓ You get a call from Janice Williams. You spoke to her in December before the firm had officially opened. She was fired from her job and wanted some information about filing a lawsuit against her former employer for wrongful termination. She needed some time to think about it but has now decided to proceed with the case. You tell her to come in today. She's already set up in QuickBooks.

✓ You receive checks in the mail as follows, all dated 2/8.

- Mega Manu—$11,025, #121867.
- Johnson—$1,950, #925.
- Urban Settings—$2,200, #33680.

✓ You deposit the checks in the bank ($15,175).

2/9/18

✓ You file documents in the Williams wrongful termination case at the Superior Court. The filing fees total $450, and you pay with check #1028. The fee is billable to Janice Williams.

✓ You receive a bill (#1998), dated 2/9, from Silver Sleuths for $700. The bill is for investigative work on the class-action suit against Toys for Tots (Wheels). This is billable to Frank's client. Terms are Net 30.

✓ You enter timesheets for the week:

Week of Feb 5 to Feb 11		Class	M	Tu	W	Th	F
You (40 hours)							
Mega Manu: Union Contract	Meetings	EL	8	8	4		5
Williams: Termination	Initial consultation	EL				2	
Williams: Termination	Research	EL				4	
Williams: Termination	Documents	EL					3
	Non-billable	A				4	2
Nancy Svenborg (24 hours)							
Toys for Tots: Wheels	Paralegal assistance	CA					3
Mega Manu: Union Contract	Paralegal assistance	EL	3	3	3		
	Non-billable	A	2	2	2	4	2
Frank Williams (41 hours)							
Exam Prep: CPA Exam	Meetings	CA				3	
Exam Prep: CPA Exam	Research	CA		6			4
Toys for Tots: Wheels	Meetings	CA	2		6		
Toys for Tots: Wheels	Research	CA				4	
	Non-billable	A	6	2	2	5	1

2/13/18

✓ You receive three bills in the mail, all dated 2/13.

- Horizon Phone—$210, #1234777 (February 1–28 service), Net 15
- Sac Electric—$95, #7771120023 (February 1–28 utility services), Net 15

- Legal Eagle—$800 (February access to the online legal library) #89942, Net 15. You use **Administration** as the **class**.

✓ You feel that the firm is doing well, but you want to make sure that you continue to have new clients coming in. You call Sactown News and get a special deal on advertising in the paper. For $600, the firm can get three large ads. You use the company credit card to pay Sactown News, and you record the charge using **Administration** as the **class**.

- The ads are set to appear on 2/18, 3/19, and 3/18, and 4/15 (the fee is $200 per ad).

✓ You ask Frank to go to Scissors Office Supplies to restock paper and other office supplies. He uses the company credit card and purchases supplies to have on hand totaling $378.00.

2/15/18

 You enter time for Monday through Thursday of this week so you can prepare paychecks for everyone.

Week of Feb 12 to Feb 18		Class	M	Tu	W	Th	F
You (35 hours)							
Mega Manu: Union Contract	Meetings.	EL	5				
Nguyen: Lisa Adoption	Meetings.	FL		3			
Nguyen: Lisa Adoption	Court.	FL			8	6	
Williams: Termination	Documents	EL	1				
Williams: Termination	Meetings.	EL		6			
	Non-billable.	EL	3			3	
Nancy Svenborg (22 hours)							
Toys for Tots: Wheels	Paralegal assistance	CA	3				
Williams: Termination	Paralegal assistance	EL		3			
Nguyen: Lisa Adoption	Paralegal assistance	FL			2	3	
Exam Prep: CPA Exam	Paralegal assistance	CL				2	
	Non-billable.	A	1	2	2	4	
Frank Williams (33 hours)							
Exam Prep: CPA Exam	Meetings.	CA	2				
Exam Prep: CPA Exam	Research	CA	4				
Exam Prep: CPA Exam	Documents.	CA			8	4	
Toys for Tots: Wheels	Research	CA	2				
Toys for Tots: Wheels	Documents	CA			8	4	
	Non-billable.	A	1				

✓ You prepare payroll checks for Nancy, Frank, and yourself for the period 2/1 to 2/15/18. The first check number should be #1029.

> ✱ **HINT:** Don't forget to compare your **Time by Name** and **Time by Job Summary** reports to the reports posted in the Student Materials section of the book's website, **https://www.cambridgepub.com/book/quickbooks-2015**, before you start creating paychecks. Add **class** to the **Time by Job Detail** by customizing the report.

- Nancy's gross pay is $1,770.00; net pay is $1,349.62.
- Frank's gross pay is $5,000.01; net pay is $3,812.51.
- Your gross pay is $3,125.00; net pay is $2,382.81.

> ✱ **HINT:** Remember, you may be off a few cents due to differences in QuickBooks programs.

	Frank	Nancy	You
Withholdings:			
Federal Withholding	500.00	177.00	312.50
Social Security	310.00	109.74	193.75
Medicare.	72.50	25.67	45.31
CA–Withholding	250.00	88.50	156.25
CA–Disability	55.00	19.47	34.37
Employer taxes:			
CA–Employment Training Tax	5.00	1.77	3.12
Social Security	310.00	109.74	193.75
Medicare.	72.50	25.67	45.31
Federal Unemployment	30.00	10.62	18.75
CA–Unemployment	170.00	60.18	106.25

✓ You prepare invoices for the following clients for the period 2/1 to 2/15/18. All invoices are dated 2/15 with terms of Net 10. (First invoice # should be 1210.) Use the Intuit Professional Invoice **template**.

- Invoice totals:

  ○ Exam Prep: CPA Exam—$6,610.

  ○ Mega Manufacturing: Union Contract—$6,375.

  ○ Nguyen: Lisa Adoption—$5,895.

  ○ Toys for Tots: Wheels—$7,560.

  ○ Williams: Termination—$3,225.

2/16/18

✓ You're anxious to see what kind of information you get from your new **class tracking** and budgeting tools. You make sure your balances are accurate for the first half of February before you prepare any reports.

- You look back at the adjusting entries you prepared in January. You know you'll need to make some similar entries. You take a good look at prepaid accounts and accumulated depreciation. You estimate that you have $400 of supplies on hand at 2/15. You ignore the *Time* subscription that started 2/1. The amount for 2/1 to 2/15 is $2, which is insignificant.

- You also look to make sure the **profit & loss** report shows only those expenses for the period 2/1 to 2/15. You realize that any full month charges for February that were expensed in full will need to be adjusted. (Assume 2/1 to 2/15 is one half of February.)

Check numbers 2/15
Checking account balance. . . $ 77,441.38
Account receivable . . . . $ 41,315.00
Total assets. $132,522.38
Total liabilities . . . . $ 8,701.70
Net income (2/1 to 2/15). . . . $ 14,805.34

REPORTS TO CREATE FOR ASSIGNMENT 10A

All reports should be in portrait orientation unless otherwise indicated; fit to one page wide.

- Budget Overview for 2018.

- Choose **Total Only** in the **Show Columns** dropdown menu (top of window).

- Journal for February 1 to February 15. (Remove the **Trans #** and **Adj** columns. Sort by Date.)

- Balance sheet as of 2/15.

- Profit & Loss by Class for 2/1 to 2/15.
- Budget vs. Actual for 1/1 to 2/15 (one and a half months).
  - Choose **Total Only** in the **Show Columns** dropdown menu (top of window).

Background information from Chapter 9: You are the owner of a small construction company. Your specialties are residential kitchen and bathroom remodels. The business is a corporation with a 12/31 year-end. You are currently working out of a home office, but you have put a $1,400 security deposit on a new space. You expect to move in February.

It's January 1, 2018, and you just started using QuickBooks. You've entered all the account balances as of 12/31/17. You have set up frequently used vendors and most of the payroll items you think you'll need. Manual payroll processing is already turned on.

You are active in the business, and you pay yourself a salary. You have two employees: Monica Smith (a skilled electrician) and Henri Navarre (a skilled plumber). They are both paid hourly (with overtime for hours over 8 in a single day). Employees are paid **semimonthly**. You, Monica, and Henri are already set up as employees in the Employee Center.

You took December 2017 off so there were no jobs in process at 12/31 (and no accounts receivable or payable), but you do have contracts with two new clients, and you've already set those jobs up in QuickBooks. You are a small operation, so you bill your clients twice a month, and your credit terms are Net 10. The new customers are:

- Mark and Janice Perkins—Kitchen remodel.
- Janine Thomas—Bathroom remodel.

All of your contracts are time-and-materials contracts. (All direct costs are billed to the client.) You have entered the hourly rates for various types of labor charges. You do not charge a markup on the cost of materials. All sales are subject to sales tax.

You have set up all the items you currently need for your business. All materials are bought specifically for the projects, so you don't maintain any inventory of appliances, cabinets, etc. All material items are, therefore, set up as non-inventory parts, which allows you to bill for and track the specific materials costs of your jobs without using the perpetual tracking system tools. You bill your clients for **all** materials, labor, plans, and permits.

You do keep some small construction items on hand (nails, glue, etc.), but you generally do not maintain much of a supply, so you expense those costs to the "Job supplies and small tools" account as they're purchased. You do **not** charge your clients for these costs.

You do keep some office supplies on hand. You record those in "Supplies on Hand" (an asset account) and adjust the balance at the end of the month.

2/1/18

✓ You realize that you really need to have a few more management tools to run your business effectively.

✓ You want to be able to evaluate and compare the profitability of your major business lines using the **class** feature available in QuickBooks, so you turn on the **class** feature in **Preferences** (on the **Edit** dropdown menu).

- On the **Accounting** tab, you check **Use class tracking for transactions**.
- You also check the **prompt to assign classes** box so that you won't miss adding a class when you're entering transactions.
- On the **Payroll & Employees** tab, you elect to assign classes by earnings item.

✓ You set up a **class** for each project type and a separate **class** for administrative costs as follows:

- Kitchens.
- Bathrooms.
- Decks.

Assignment 10B

Constructed with Style

- Other projects.
- Administration (this **class** includes all indirect job costs and administrative expenses).

✓ You also want to be able to compare your actual results to what you expected to earn in your business, so you create a profit and loss budget for 2018 (no additional criteria), starting with January, using the following estimates (you're starting from scratch):

- Construction income
  - $50,000 for January; $150,000 per month February through November.
  - You do not expect to have any revenue in December.
- Direct costs
  - Direct materials—$20,000 for January; $80,000 per month February through November.
  - Direct labor—$12,000 for January; $14,400 per month February through November.
  - Payroll taxes—$1,500 for January; $1,800 per month February through November .
  - You expect other direct costs to average $1,000 per month through November.
- Indirect job costs (You know you'll have some costs throughout the year, so you don't stop with November for indirect costs.)
  - Client relations—$300 per month.
  - Job supplies and small tools—$1,000 per month.
  - Gasoline—$400 in January. You expect gas prices to rise 1% per month. [**TIP:** Don't forget to enable compounding.]
  - Truck repairs and maintenance—$500 in March, June, September, and December.
  - Equipment repairs—$50 per month.
  - Depreciation—Equipment & Truck—$945 per month.
- Insurance & professional fees
  - Insurance—$400 per month.
  - Professional fees—$2,500 in April.
- Other labor costs
  - Staff meetings—$200 per month.
- Facilities cost
  - Rent—$1,400 per month starting in February.
  - Telephone and Utilities—$300 per month starting in February.
  - Depreciation—office—$55 per month starting in February.
- Other costs
  - Advertising—$100 per month.
  - Office supplies—$150 per month.

✓ Mark Perkins, one of your customers, called over the weekend. They've decided to redo their back deck. You call Henri and Luis and tell them to be at the Perkins home at 9:00 a.m. tomorrow.

 HINT: You need to set up a **job** for every project.

✓ You write a check (#1104) to your new landlord (Prime Properties, Inc.) for February's $1,400 rent. (Prime Properties' office is just down the street, so you don't bother setting up all the vendor information this time. You'll hand deliver the check to them.) Rent is an administrative expense.

✓ You finish moving in to the new space. You use the credit card to pay for the truck you rented from Burtz Rental. (You Quick Add Burtz as a vendor). The total cost was $189.00. You decide to set up an account called "Moving Expense" to track costs related to the move to the new facility. This isn't a recurring expense, so you pick the proper **account type** for non-recurring expenses.

✓ You had asked two of your nephews to help you move. They each worked for 16 hours. You write a check to "cash" for $480 and take it to the bank to withdraw the money. You give them each $240. You don't set them up as employees or as 1099 vendors because you won't be using them for other work this year.

✓ You pick up decking materials (lumber) for the Perkins deck at Tulio Lumber. Total cost of the materials needed for the deck is $6,000. Bill # is 8775. Terms are Net 30.

Remember: You charge your clients for all direct costs.

2/2/18

✓ Your client Janine Thomas calls at 5 a.m.! She needs some electrical work (rewiring) done as soon as possible. You let her know that Monica will be there by 8 a.m. You set up the **job** in QuickBooks.

✓ You drive over to Office Mini and use your credit card to purchase:

- Wastebaskets—$30.
- New calculator—$40.
- Copy paper—$80.

NOTE: You only capitalize items of furniture and equipment (like wastebaskets and calculators) that cost more than $50. You expect the case of paper to last you for several months.

✓ You stop by Contractor's Hardware. You pick up some specialty wiring for the Janine Thomas project ($150) and some other miscellaneous supplies ($500). Contractor's Hardware sets up an account for you with terms Net 10. The bill # is 21862.

- You decide to charge Janine Thomas for the specialty wire that's needed. You use **Miscellaneous** for the **item**.
- You expect to use all the other supplies in February on various jobs. You use Administration as the **class**.
- You receive check for $3,297.99, dated 2/2, from Janine Thomas (check #9966). Janine underpaid an invoice last month, so you apply this check to that balance.

✓ You enter timesheets starting with Thursday 2/1.

- You'll be adding hours to the timesheet for the workweek beginning 1/30. You don't need to add **class** to your January hours.

Week of January 29 to Feb 4		M	Tu	W	Th	F
Henri Navarre (8 hours)						
Perkins—Deck Job	Demolition.					8
Monica Smith (16 hours)						
Thomas—Rewiring job	Electrical.				8	8
Luis Garcia (8 new hours, 16 hours total)						
Perkins—Deck Job	Demolition.					8
You (16 new hours, 42 hours total)						
Perkins—Deck Job	General.				2	
Perkins—Deck Job	Deck Labor.					6
Thomas—Rewiring job	General.				2	2
Administrative.					4	

2/5/18

✓ You receive a call from Annie Wang. They want to hire you to remodel their kitchen. They need to have the job completed in time to host their daughter's wedding reception on February 28. This is a big remodel, but you are confident your crew can get the project completed on time. You expect to start demolition later this week.

✓ You head down to the City of Sacramento to pick up some building permits for the Wang family's kitchen remodel. The total cost is $680, which you pay with check #1106.

✓ You talk to Janine Thomas about the amount she still owes on the bathroom remodel. She agrees to make a $3,000 payment using her Visa card which you record.

✓ You deposit the $3,297.99 check received from Janine Thomas on February 2nd in the bank.

✓ You also "deposit" the $3,000 credit card payment. The bank charges you a 2% merchant fee, which you post to the bank service charge account. You consider merchant fees to be administrative costs.

✓ You remit the sales taxes you collected in January ($3,716.29) to the Board of Equalization (check # 1107).

2/7/18

✓ You stop at Gus' Gasoline and use your credit card to fill up both trucks. You wonder out loud if gasoline prices will ever be less than $1 a gallon. Your neighbor thinks you're pretty funny! (Your neighbor helped get both trucks to the station.) Total cost is $80.

2/8/18

✓ You spend the entire day picking up supplies for the Wang kitchen remodel. Luckily, the Wangs had already picked everything out with their designer, so you didn't have to wait for their review. You enter the following bills:

- Folsom Fixtures—$595, #79-500, dated 2/8, Net 30.
- Brentley's Appliances—$8,200, #12-458, dated 2/8, Net 15.
- Martinez Cabinets—$42,865, #95562, dated 2/8, Net 30.
  - These are super deluxe cabinets.
- Tuan's Flooring—$8,982.75, #2888, dated 2/8.

2/9/18

✓ You notice that the flooring materials bill is a bit higher than you expected. You call Tuan Nguyen and ask him about the pricing. He apologizes and explains that his new bookkeeper made an error. Tuan's Flooring faxes you a credit memo (CM2888), dated 2/9, for the $528.30 overcharge. [**TIP:** You must make the credit memo entry "billable" so that the correction is passed through to the customer.]

✓ You enter timesheets for the week. All job hours are billable.

February 5–11		M	Tu	W	Th	F
Henri Navarre (20 hours)						
Perkins—Deck Job	Deck Labor	4				
Wang Kitchen	Demolition				8	
Wang Kitchen	Plumbing					8
Monica Smith (24 hours)						
Thomas—Rewiring	Electrical	8				
Wang Kitchen	Demolition				8	
Wang Kitchen	Electrical					8

Luis Garcia (24 hours)						
Perkins—Deck Job	Deck Labor	8				
Wang Kitchen	Demolition			8		
Wang Kitchen	Cabinets				8	
You (40 hours)						
Perkins—Deck Job	Deck Labor	5				
Wang Kitchen	General		2	8	2	2
Wang Kitchen	Demolition				4	
Wang Kitchen	Plumbing					4
Thomas—Rewiring job	General		2			
Administrative		3	4		2	2

2/14/18

✓ You receive a bill in the mail from the City of Sacramento for utilities for 2/1 to 2/28. The total bill (#020206) is $485, Net 15.

✓ You also realize you forgot to pay the phone bill from Big Bell Phone Co. You use your credit card to pay the $200 bill for the period 2/1 to 2/28. You **quick add** Big Bell as a vendor.

✓ You pay all bills due on or before 2/15.

- You're paying five bills for a total of $3,875.
- You spilled a cup of coffee and ruined checks #1108 and #1109, so you start with check # 1110.

✓ On your way to the Wang's home, your truck overheats. You keep the truck going long enough to get the appliances to the jobsite, but you have to call Gus' Gasoline and have them come out to replace the radiator. They charge you $350 for parts and labor. You pay with your credit card.

2/15/18

✓ You enter time for Monday through Thursday of this week so you can prepare paychecks for everyone.

February 12–18		M	Tu	W	Th	F
Henri Navarre (24 hours)						
Wang Kitchen	Plumbing	8	8			
Wang Kitchen	Other install			4	4	
Monica Smith (24 hours)						
Wang Kitchen	Cabinets			4		
Wang Kitchen	Electrical	8	4	4	4	
Luis Garcia (24 hours)						
Wang Kitchen	Cabinets	8		8		
Wang Kitchen	Flooring				8	
You (32 hours)						
Wang Kitchen	General	2	6	2		
Wang Kitchen	Plumbing	2				
Wang Kitchen	Cabinets			4		
Wang Kitchen	Flooring				5	
Administrative		4	2	2	3	

✓ You prepare payroll checks for the pay period 2/1 to 2/15.

HINT: Don't forget to compare your **Time by Name** and **Time by Job Summary** reports to the reports posted in the Student Materials section of the book's website, https://www.cambridgepub.com/book/quickbooks-2015, **before** you start creating paychecks. Add **class** to the **Time by Job Detail** by customizing the report.

- Start with check #1116.
- Henri's gross pay is $1,638.00; net pay is $1,248.97.
- Luis' gross pay is $1,680.00; net pay is $1,281.00.
- Monica's gross pay is $2,016; net pay is $1,537.20.
- Your gross pay is $2,500.33; net pay is $1,906.51.

 HINT: Because of differences in payroll calculations of salaried employees by different QuickBooks programs, you may get slightly different amounts (less than $0.05 differences) from the gross and net pay amounts shown here.

	Luis	You	Henri	Monica
Withholdings:				
Federal Withholding	168.00	250.03	163.80	201.60
Social Security	104.16	155.02	101.56	124.99
Medicare	24.36	36.25	23.75	29.23
CA–Withholding	84.00	125.02	81.90	100.80
CA–Disability	18.48	27.50	18.02	22.18
Employer taxes:				
CA–Employment Training Tax	1.68	2.50	1.64	2.02
Social Security	104.16	155.02	101.56	124.99
Medicare	24.36	36.25	23.75	29.23
Federal Unemployment	10.08	15.00	9.83	12.10
CA–Unemployment	57.12	85.01	55.69	68.54

✓ You prepare invoices for your customers. All labor is billed at the standard rate. All invoices are dated 2/15 with terms of Net 10.

- First invoice should be #1203: Perkins Deck $9,697.50; Thomas Rewiring $3,135.53; Wang Kitchen $80,095.37.

2/16/18

✓ You're anxious to see what kind of information you get from your new **class tracking** and budgeting tools. You make sure your balances are accurate for the first half of February before you prepare any reports.

- You look back at the adjusting entries you prepared in January. You know you'll need to make some similar entries. You take a good look at prepaid accounts and accumulated depreciation. You estimate that you have $80 of office supplies on hand at 2/15. You don't have any job supplies on hand. You'll have to get down to Contractor's Hardware later today.

- You also look to make sure the **profit & loss** report shows only those expenses for the period 2/1 to 2/15. You realize that any full month charges for February that were expensed in full will need to be adjusted. (Assume 2/1 to 2/15 is one half of February.)

Check numbers 2/15

Checking account	$ 18,783.14
Account receivable	$ 98,235.93
Total assets.	$161,721.57
Accounts payable.	$ 66,599.45
Total liabilities	$ 77,492.35
Total equity	$ 84,229.22
Net income (2/1 to 2/15).	$ 6,823.64

REPORTS TO CREATE FOR ASSIGNMENT 10B

All reports should be in portrait orientation unless otherwise indicated; fit to one page wide.

- Budget Overview for 2018.

- Choose **Total Only** in the **Show Columns** dropdown menu (top of window).

- Journal for February 1 to February 15. (Remove the **Trans #** and **Adj** columns. Sort by Date.)

- Balance sheet as of 2/15.

- Profit & Loss by Class for 2/1 to 2/15.

- Budget vs. Actual for 1/1 to 2/15 (one and a half months).
  - Choose **Total Only** in the **Show Columns** dropdown menu (top of window).

11

Additional Tools

Objectives

After completing Chapter 11, you should be able to:

1. Create reversing entries.

2. Memorize transactions.

3. Memorize reports.

4. Process multiple reports.

5. Customize forms.

6. Export reports to Excel.

In this chapter, we cover a few additional tools in QuickBooks that can be very useful in practice.

There are no Practice Exercises included in this chapter. Follow along with the instructions to learn how the tools are used in QuickBooks.

REVERSING ENTRIES

By now, it's probably clear that accountants typically make a lot of adjusting journal entries when financial statements are prepared!

Many (if not most) of the adjusting entries are made to properly recognize (or defer) revenues or expenses for the reporting period. These adjusting entries must be made because physical transactions (sending out invoices to customers, receiving bills from vendors, preparing paychecks for employees) don't always occur in the same month that the related activities should be recognized in the financial statements. To use QuickBooks effectively and efficiently, however, the accountant wants to enter transactions using the appropriate QuickBooks **forms** (**invoices**, **bills**, **paychecks**, etc.). If the accountant isn't careful, the same transaction can inadvertently be recorded twice—once through an adjusting entry and once through a standard entry (form).

For example, many companies receive bills from vendors in the month **after** costs were incurred. The bill from the company's attorney for work performed in January might be received (and dated) in February. The accountant would need to accrue those expenses in January using an adjusting journal entry so that the profit and loss statement for January includes all expenses incurred in January. The accountant would also want to enter the vendor invoice (through the **enter bill** form) using the date on the attorney's bill so that the accounts payable subsidiary ledger agrees with the attorney's records and so that the **bill** can be paid through the **pay bills** screen. If the accountant distributes the bill to the same expense that was used in January, the attorney fees are now reported in **two** months. (They were recorded in January through the adjusting journal entry and in February through the **bill**.) The accountant would now need to make an additional journal entry in February to offset the February charge. Depending on the number of transactions in a company, remembering to adjust for those duplications can be difficult.

Reversing entries in QuickBooks is a tool for minimizing the possibility of duplicate transactions not being cleared. When an adjusting entry is dated the month **before** the standard entry (form) is recorded, the accountant can flag the journal entry as a **reversing entry**. QuickBooks will then automatically create a new entry (dated the first day of the subsequent month) to completely reverse the original entry. That way, when the appropriate form is created, it will not result in a double recognition of the same transaction. **Reversing entries** are very easy to create.

As an example, let's say a company knew it would be receiving a $1,000 bill from its attorney for February services but hadn't received it yet. The expense needs to be recognized in February so the company would make an adjusting entry that might look like this:

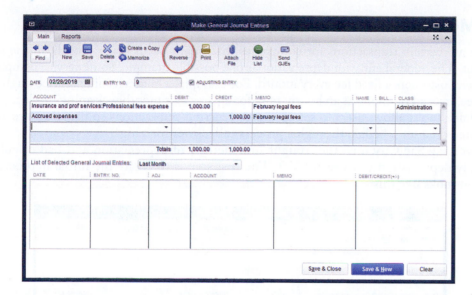

To create the automatic reversal of the entry in the following month, the **Reverse** icon on the menu bar at the top of the **journal** form is clicked.

QuickBooks will first prompt you to save the initial adjusting entry. QuickBooks then automatically creates a new entry dated the first of the subsequent month (March). In our example, it looks like this:

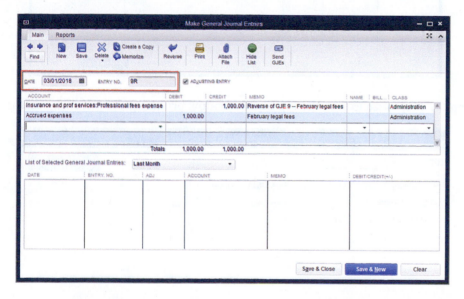

When the actual bill from the attorney is received and entered during the next month, the debit amount from the **bill** (DR Expense CR Accounts payable) will be offset by the credit amount from the reversing entry just shown. The expense is now properly reported in February's profit and loss statement only, although the **bill** is dated in March.

 WARNING: Once created, *reversing entries* are not linked to the original entry. Deleting or modifying the original entry will not change the reversing entry.

MEMORIZING TRANSACTIONS

There are certain transactions for companies that might occur every month, in the same amount. The general entry for depreciation is one possible example. Some service companies bill their customers a fixed fee every month. For example, a housecleaning service might bill a set fee, instead of billing at an hourly rate, for a particular monthly cleaning service.

QuickBooks allows users to set up these recurring transactions so that they are easily recreated on a set schedule through a process called **memorizing**.

Let's say Sac City used the straight-line method of depreciation and had calculated monthly depreciation expense at $379. The first step is to create the initial depreciation entry. It looks like this:

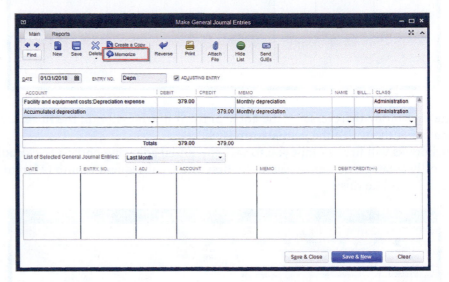

Clicking the **Memorize** icon at the top of the window brings up the following dialog box:

There are a number of options in this window:

- Transactions can be set for automatic entry (**Automate Transaction Entry**) or can be included on the **Reminders List**. (The user would then have the option of not recording the entry in a particular period.)

- The frequency of the entry is set in **How Often**.

- The date of the next entry is identified in the **Next Date** field. (This would be the first entry **after** the one the user is creating.)

- The user can specify how far into the future the transaction should be entered by specifying a **Number Remaining**.

A **memorized transaction** for Sac City Accounting might be set up something like this:

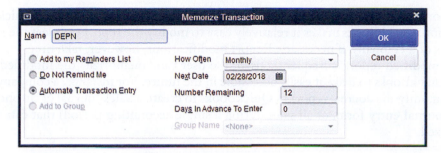

A **memorized transaction** list can be accessed through the **Lists** dropdown menu on the main menu bar:

The **memorized transaction** list looks like this for Sac City Accounting:

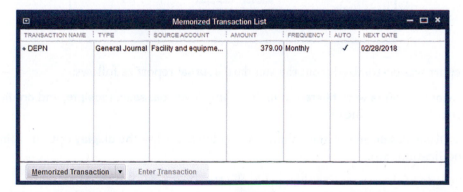

Memorized transactions can be edited and deleted in this window. It is also possible to create groups of **memorized transactions**. For example, a company might group all **memorized invoices** in one group and all **memorized** adjusting journal entries in another.

 WARNING: *Memorized* transactions can be very useful, but they must be monitored, especially if they are set up as automatic entries.

MEMORIZING REPORTS

The reports most commonly used by companies are automatically included in QuickBooks. In addition, QuickBooks makes it relatively easy to modify the reports to meet the particular needs of a company, if necessary. Report modifications, however, take time.

If a modified report is frequently used, the user can "memorize" the modified report within QuickBooks to make it easily accessible in the future. For instance, a company might want to modify the **Journal** report in QuickBooks to create a Sales Journal (a chronological list, in journal entry form, of all sales during a single accounting period) that can then be memorized.

Memorizing A Report

A customized report is created by the user. If Sac City Accounting created a Sales Journal in January, it might look something like this:

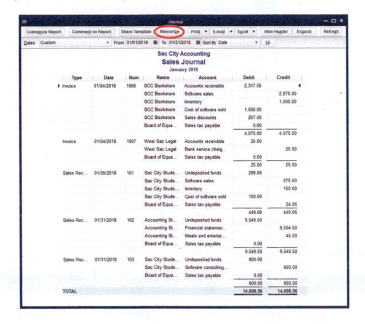

This report was customized from the standard **Journal** report as follows:

- **Transaction types** were **filtered** to include only **invoices**, **sales receipts**, and **credit memos** (**Filter** modification tab).

- The **Trans #**, **Adj**, and **Memo** columns were deleted using the **display** options (**Display** modification tab).

- The title of the report was changed in the **Header/Footer** modification tab.

Once the customized report is created, the report is memorized by clicking the **Memorize** button on the tool bar at the top of the report.

In the next screen, the user can change the name of the memorized report and save it in a **Memorized Report Group**:

WARNING: A memorized report retains the original report date(s) (that is, the report will not automatically update to the current date(s) when the report is later accessed). The user simply needs to change the dates and click *refresh* to update the data.

Creating A Memorized Report Group

QuickBooks automatically sets up a number of **memorized report groups**: accountant, banking, company, customers, employees, and vendors. These **groups** include only the most commonly used reports. (Remember: The full list of available reports can be accessed through the **Reports** menu on the main menu bar.) Users can also create additional memorized report groups.

To create a custom **memorized report group**, select **Memorized Reports** on the **Reports** menu. Select **Memorized Report List**. The screen looks like this:

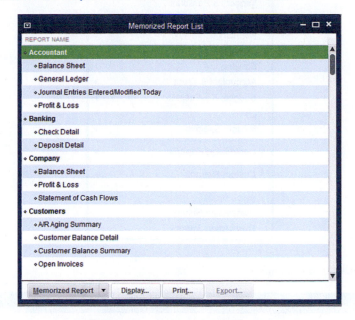

Select **New Group** from the **Memorized Reports** menu at the bottom left of the screen, and enter a descriptive name for the group. The screen might look something like this:

Separate **memorized report groups** are especially useful for companies that have multiple users accessing QuickBooks.

PROCESSING MULTIPLE REPORTS

There are certain reports that are most likely going to be accessed every month. The financial statement group is one example. Inventory reports are another example. Instead of opening each report separately, reports can be grouped and processed (displayed, printed, or emailed) together in QuickBooks.

To process a group of reports, **Process Multiple Reports** is selected in the **Reports** drop-down menu on the main menu bar:

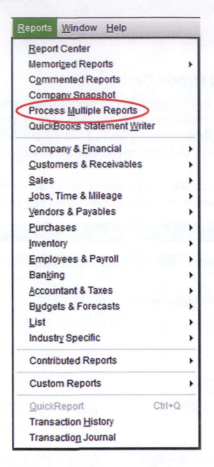

The window looks like this:

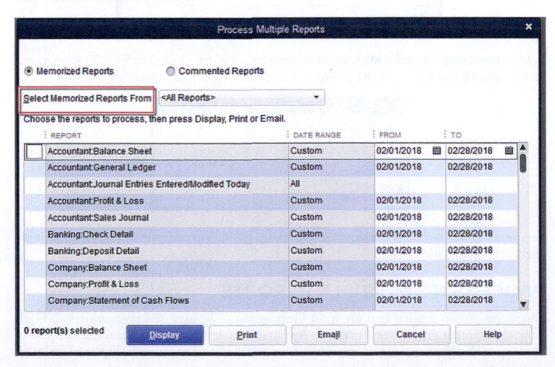

The user can select from **memorized reports** or **commented reports**. If **memorized reports** is selected, a particular report group can be identified. If **Accountant** was selected in the dropdown menu after **Select Memorized Reports from**, the screen looks like this:

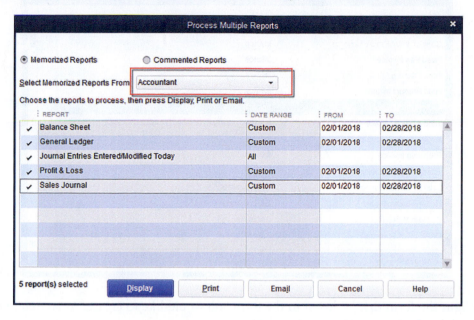

The report dates can be changed in this screen if necessary.

CUSTOMIZING FORMS

QuickBooks has designed the basic forms needed in a business (invoices, credit memos, sales receipts, etc.). Most likely, however, a company will want to customize these forms by adding the company logo, changing descriptions, or adding or deleting information included in the form. Companies can even have multiple customized forms of the same type. We're only limited by our imagination!

To customize a form, you must first start with a form of the correct transaction type. Remember: Each **transaction type** has specific default accounts and functionality. A customized form would need to be associated with those same features. The available forms can be accessed through the **Templates** option on the **Lists** menu (main menu bar):

The list looks something like this:

Highlight the form that is closest to the form you would like to create. As an example, we use the **Intuit Professional Invoice** template.

Create a copy of the highlighted **form** by selecting **Duplicate** from the **Templates** dropdown menu at the bottom left of the **list** screen.

> **! WARNING: QuickBooks will not allow you to delete or directly modify predefined forms, so you must start with a copy. Predefined forms can, however, be made *inactive*.**

The following screen appears:

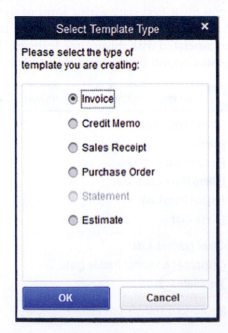

Select the correct form type and click **OK**. QuickBooks then automatically creates a copy of the form (a new template), which is added to the template list

Highlight the copy just created (on the **Templates** list screen), and select **Edit Template** from the **Templates** menu at the bottom left of the screen. The following screen appears:

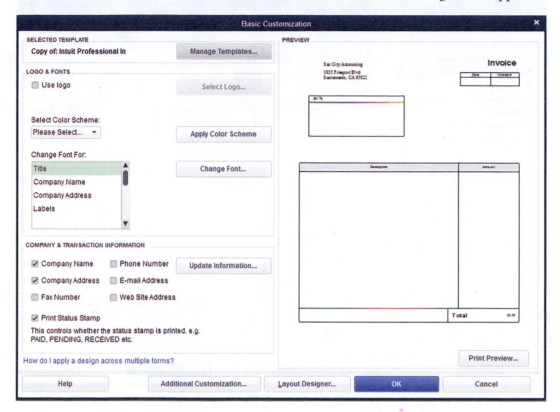

As you can see, there are quite a few tabs and tools available. On the initial (**Basic Customization**) screen, you can add logos, change colors, and change basic company information that will print on the form. On the **Additional Customization** screen, you can change the fields that appear on the printed form and on the screen form used in data entry. (The screen form is the form that would appear to the user creating the transaction.) On the **Layout Designer** screen, you can reposition fields.

Let's change a few items, using some of the tools, to give you a feel for the process.

Template Changes On The Initial (Basic Customization) Screen

To add a logo to the form, check the **Use Logo** box at the top left of the **Basic Customization** screen.

Click the **Select Logo** button on the next screen, and select (from your computer file) the image you want to use. QuickBooks will automatically resize the image to fit in a square space.

The logo appears to the left of the company name something like this:

Sac City Accounting

3835 Freeport Blvd
Sacramento, CA 95822

To change the name of the new form, click on the **Manage Templates** button at the top of the **Basic Customization** screen, and enter a new form name at the top of the screen and click **OK**. It might look something like this:

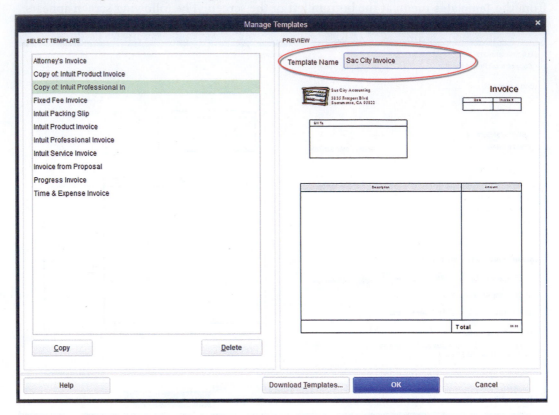

Template Changes On The Additional Customization Screen

The **additional customization** screen has five tabs:

On all of the tabs other than the **Print** tab, the user is able to change options that are visible on the screen when a transaction is created and/or on the printed form.

On the **header** tab, the user can select (or deselect) the primary fields that will appear in the top (header) section of both the screen and printed forms. The fields could include date, reference number, terms, addresses, etc.

On the **Columns** tab, the user can select (or deselect) the fields that will appear in the body of both the screen and printed forms. The fields could include quantities, descriptions, rates, etc. On the **Columns** tab, the user can also change the order of the fields on the form.

The left side of the **Header** tab screen might look like this if you added some fields in the new template.

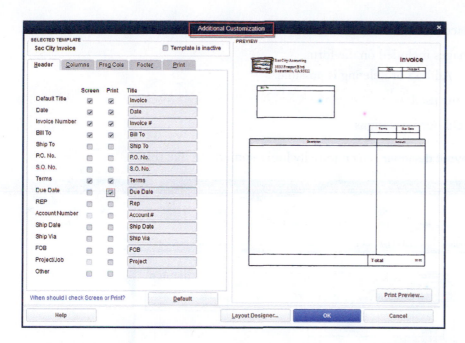

The **Preview** (right side of the screen) changes whenever you add or delete fields. When the order of fields is changed, the form would need to be saved before the change would appear.

The **Prog Cols** tab has elections for companies doing progress invoicing.

On the **Footer** tab, the user can select (or deselect) the fields that will appear at the bottom of both the screen and printed forms. These might include messages, balances due, etc.

On the **Print** tab, the user can set various printer settings and other options.

You can select or deselect many of the fields appearing on the form being modified—but not all of them. The fields that can't be modified are grayed out. In the **Screen** columns, you want to make sure that all the necessary fields are visible to the user entering transactions. In the **Print** column, you want to make sure that the form contains all necessary information for the recipient (usually the customer or the vendor).

Whenever you select or deselect a field, you get a message similar to this (unless you turn the message off!):

The message is simply warning you that you might need to reposition fields in the layout designer now that you've made a change. A variation of the message appears when a change creates overlapping fields.

Template Changes In The Layout Designer Screen

In the **layout designer** screen, text boxes can be added to the form and fill colors can be added to the fields on the form.

In addition, changes can be made to the:

- Data fields included on the form.
  - Adding or deleting is possible.

- Placement of fields on the form.
- Images included on the form.
  - Adding or deleting is possible.
- Fonts used.
- Field border designs.

The **layout designer** screen initially looks something like this:

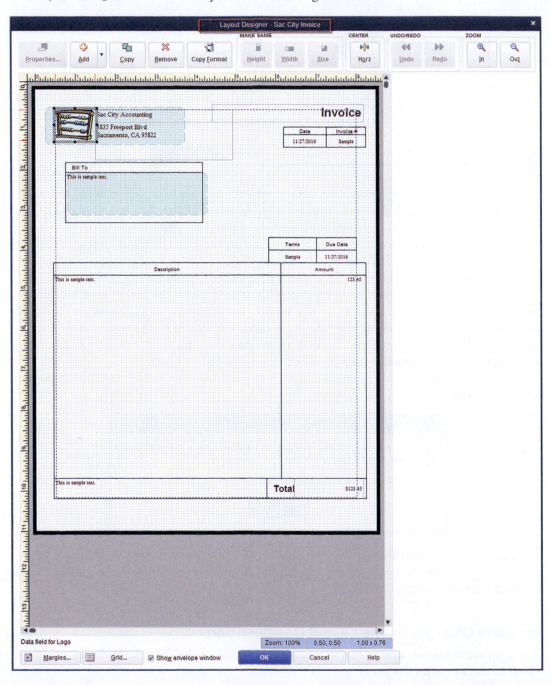

Each field within the form can be moved by using the tools at the top of the screen, by using the arrow keys on your computer keyboard, or by clicking and dragging the field.

To move the **Due Date** field to line up with the right edge of the invoice, click inside the field and drag to the right until the field is properly positioned. Do the same with the **Terms** field and the **Sample** fields directly below. **Sample** fields include information specific to a particular transaction. Fields like **Terms** or **Due Date** are header boxes.

Borders of fields can also be changed on a form.

To add a thicker border to the company name field, click inside the **company name** field on the **Layout Designer** screen, and select **Properties** from the tool bar at the top of the screen. Click the **Border** tab. The next screen looks something like this:

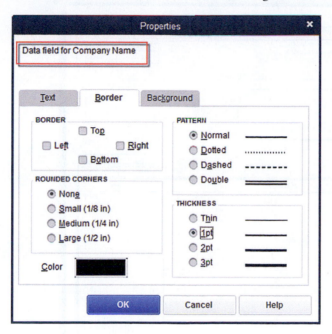

Check **2pt** under the **Thickness** section at the bottom right of the screen. Make sure the top, bottom, left, and right borders are checked. Click **OK**.

To add rounded corners to the customer address field, click inside the sample text box under the bill to field on the **Layout Designer** screen, and select **Properties** from the tool bar at the top of the screen. Click the **Border** tab. The next screen will look like this:

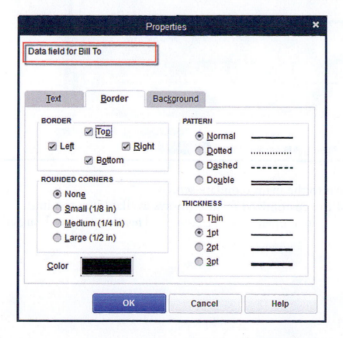

Check **Large** under the **Rounded Corners** section at the bottom left of the screen and **2pt** under the **Thickness** section. Click **OK.**

The final design layout might look something like this:

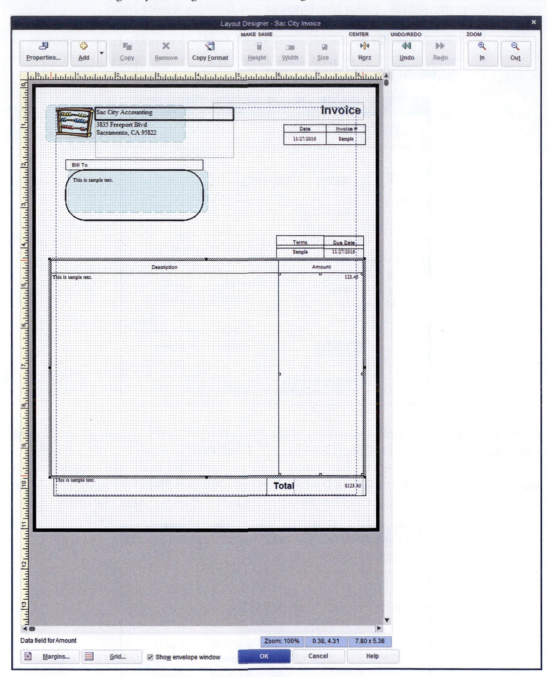

Click **OK** to return to the main template screen.

A preview of the customized form is always available on the initial (**Basic Customization**) screen for editing templates. The customized **invoice** prepared earlier looks something like this:

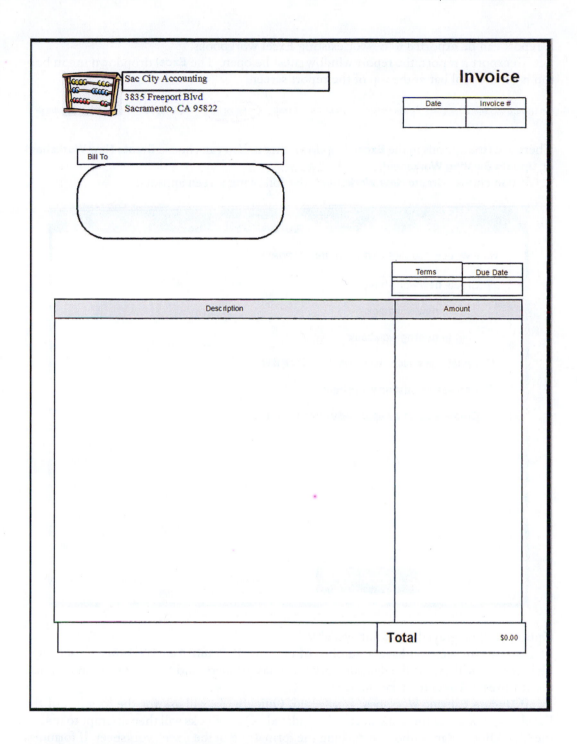

EXPORTING REPORTS TO EXCEL

QuickBooks reports can be exported to Excel. There are a number of reasons that a user might use this tool:

- The report format cannot be modified sufficiently in QuickBooks to meet the needs of the users.

- A user might want to create a report that includes QuickBooks data with data maintained elsewhere.

- A user might want to use Excel analysis tools on QuickBooks data.

A report can be exported to new or existing Excel workbooks.

To export a report, the report window must be open. The **Excel** dropdown menu button is on the tool bar at the top of the report screen:

There are two options in the **Excel** dropdown menu. You can choose **Create New Worksheet** or **Update Existing Worksheet**.

If you choose **Create New Worksheet**, the following screen appears:

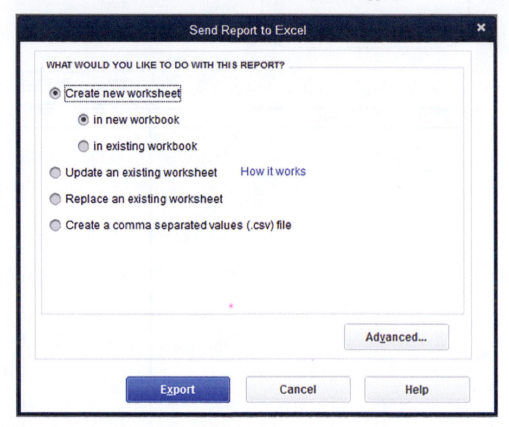

Options will be grayed out if not available.

As you can see, you have a number of options. If **Create New Worksheet** is selected, QuickBooks will export the data and any formulas, headers, and footers. You can then use the features in Excel to make changes.

If **Update Existing Worksheet** is selected, QuickBooks will ask for the location of the Excel workbook and the worksheet to be updated. QuickBooks will then attempt to update the QuickBooks data without disturbing the formatting of the Excel worksheet. If formulas had been added to the worksheet, those calculations would be updated as well. If **Replace Existing Worksheet** is selected, any formatting or calculation formulas on the former worksheet would be erased.

HINT: To use the export function effectively, companies often create a work-book in Excel with multiple worksheets. One of the worksheets would contain the QuickBooks data. The other worksheet(s) would reference the Quick-Books data to create various reports or make various calculations. When the QuickBooks data worksheet is replaced, any sheets with cells referencing the QuickBooks data worksheet will be updated automatically.

This process can be complicated by dissimilarities between the data currently being ex-ported and data that had been exported previously. QuickBooks will report any complica-tions so that the user can opt out of the update process.

There are various formatting options available on the **Advanced** tab in the initial screen. The **advanced** options screen looks like this:

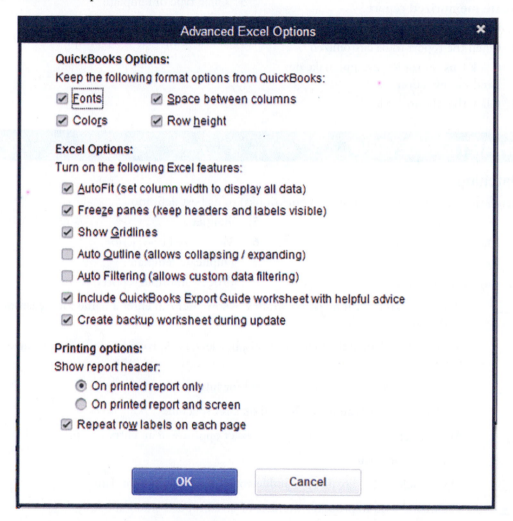

Many of the options offered on this tab can also be changed within Excel.

CHAPTER SHORTCUTS

Create a reversing entry

1. Click Company (main menu bar)
2. Click Make General Journal Entries
3. Create initial entry
4. Click Reverse icon

Memorize a transaction

1. Create a transaction
2. Click the Memorize icon

Create memorized report

1. Click Reports
2. Open the report to be customized
3. Click Customize Report and make desired modifications
4. Click the Memorize icon

Process multiple reports

1. Click Reports
2. Click Process Multiple Reports

Customize a form

1. Click Lists
2. Click Templates
3. Highlight form to be customized
4. Click Templates/Duplicate
5. Click type of template
6. Highlight copied form
7. Click Templates/Edit Template

CHAPTER REVIEW

Matching

Match the term or phrase (as used in QuickBooks) to its best definition.

1. Memorized report
2. Manage templates
3. Reversing entry
4. Layout designer
5. Template
6. Memorized transaction
7. Duplicate template
8. Process multiple reports

_____   Button in Basic Customization window where user can enter a name for a customized form

_____   Tool used to change the field locations, borders, backgrounds, etc., on customized forms

_____   Customized report that has been saved for future use

_____   A transaction that can be duplicated on a set schedule

_____   An entry created by a user that is the exact opposite of an entry in a prior period

_____   A transaction form

_____   Option selected to create an editable copy of an existing template

_____   Command used to process a number of saved reports simultaneously

Multiple Choice

1. The list of memorized transactions is found under _____.
   a. Company
   b. Reports
   c. Accountant
   d. Lists

2. Which of the following statements is true?
    a. There can be multiple versions of a **sales receipt** in a single company file.
    b. There is only version of a **sales receipt** in QuickBooks.
    c. There can be multiple versions of a **sales receipt** in a QuickBooks program, but a single company file can only access one version.

3. QuickBooks generated (predefined, not custom) templates:
    a. can be edited.
    b. can be duplicated.
    c. can be deleted.
    d. can be any of the above.

4. On March 10, a user customizes a Time by Job Detail report for the two weeks ended February 28 and memorizes the report. On April 15, the user opens the memorized report. The data displayed in the report will be for the two weeks ended:
    a. February 28.
    b. March 10.
    c. March 31.
    d. April 15.

5. The list of memorized reports is found under _____.
    a. Company
    b. Reports
    c. Accountant
    d. Lists

ASSIGNMENTS

Background information from Chapter 9: You have decided to open your own law firm, specializing in family and employment law. The business is a corporation with a 12/31 year-end. You contributed $100,000 in cash to start the business. You already have a few clients but won't start working on their cases until the office opens on 1/2/18.

You rented space (and prepaid the January rent) and purchased furniture and equipment in December 2017. You also prepaid the local newspaper for some ads to run in January newspapers and purchased two insurance policies (one for professional liability and one for general business).

You have decided to pay yourself a salary of $75,000 per year. You have one other employee (Nancy Svenborg). Nancy will be working as a paralegal and also performing some administrative duties. She will be paid $25 per hour. Timesheets are entered on the 15th and 31st. Payroll is paid semimonthly, also on the 15th and 31st.

You are a small operation, so you bill your clients twice a month, and your credit terms are Net 10. Remember: In QuickBooks, clients are called **customers**; cases (matters) are called **jobs**. The clients and matters you know you'll be working on are:

- Jordan & Jamie Childress—Adoption (Katie).
- Sam & Serena Johnson—Adoption (Terrence).
- Urban Settings—Employment contract for architects.
- Janice Williams—Wrongful termination.

Assignment 11A

Champion Law

You've already set up the listed clients in QuickBooks. You've set yourself and Nancy up as employees in QuickBooks as well. You have also set up frequently used vendors and most of the payroll items you think you'll need. Manual payroll processing has already turned on.

You've set up service items for each of the professional services you expect to perform. Professional services will be billed on any hourly basis. You've also set up a service item for non-billable time. Non-billable time represents time spent on general company business (time not chargeable to a specific client).

You intend to bill your clients for any direct costs incurred on their behalf and so have also set up items for those costs (other charge items). You do not intend to mark up direct costs.

Other information:

- Professional liability insurance policy premium: $3,000; term: 1/1 to 6/30/18.

- General insurance policy premium: $600; term: 1/1 to 6/30/18.

- Monthly depreciation (straight line) on computer equipment and copier: $93 with a 3-year life.

- Monthly depreciation (straight line) on furniture: $30 with a 5-year life.

✓ You would like your invoices to look more professional, so you create a customized **invoice**.

- You use the Intuit Professional template as the starting point.
- You name your invoice "Champion Law Invoice."
- You add a logo to the form appropriate to a law firm.
  - An easy way to find free logos is to go to <u>www.bing.com.</u>
  - Click **images**.
  - Type in a search term or phrase.
  - When the images appear, click **License** and select "**Free to modify, share, and use.**"
  - Save your choice to your computer.
- You change the font on at least one field on the **Basic Customization** tab.
- You change the title of at least one **Header** or **Columns** field.
  - Hint: Use the **Additional Customization** tab.
- You include the Terms on the printed invoice.
- You also include the date of service on the invoice in the far left column.
- You change the border on at least one field.

✓ You also decide to create a special report. You want a report that shows billable time by service provided (document preparation, research, etc.) for the period 2/1 to 2/15. You want to see the hours, rate, class, and amount, but you're not interested in seeing the date of the service or the client name or any other details.

- You give the report a name. You also change **Fonts & Numbers** in a way that you think makes the report most readable.
- You save the report in the **Accountant** memorized report group.

REPORTS TO CREATE FOR ASSIGNMENT 11A

All reports should be in portrait orientation; fit to one page wide (unless otherwise noted).

- Invoice for Exam Prep dated 2/15 using customized invoice.

- Memorized report for the period 2/1 to 2/15.

- Memorized report list. [**TIP**: To print the list, open the **Memorized Report List** window, and select **Print List** on the dropdown menu in the bottom left corner.]

Background information from Chapter 9: You are the owner of a small construction company. Your specialties are residential kitchen and bathroom remodels. The business is a corporation with a 12/31 year-end. You are currently working out of a home office, but you have put a $1,400 security deposit on a new space. You expect to move in February.

It's January 1, 2018, and you just started using QuickBooks. You've entered all the account balances as of 12/31/17. You have set up frequently used vendors and most of the payroll items you think you'll need. Manual payroll processing is already turned on.

You are active in the business, and you pay yourself a salary. You have two employees: Monica Smith (a skilled electrician) and Henri Navarre (a skilled plumber). They are both paid hourly (with overtime for hours over 8 in a single day). Employees are paid **semimonthly**. You, Monica, and Henri are already set up as employees in the **Employee Center**.

You took December 2017 off so there were no jobs in process at 12/31 (and no accounts receivable or payable), but you do have contracts with two new clients, and you've already set those **jobs** up in QuickBooks. You are a small operation, so you bill your clients twice a month, and your credit terms are Net 10. The new customers are:

* Mark and Janice Perkins—Kitchen remodel.

* Janine Thomas—Bathroom remodel.

All of your contracts are time-and-materials contracts. (All direct costs are billed to the client.) You have entered the hourly rates for various types of labor charges. You do not charge a markup on the cost of materials. All sales are subject to sales tax.

You have set up all the **items** you currently need for your business. All materials are bought specifically for the projects, so you don't maintain any inventory of appliances, cabinets, etc. All material **items** are, therefore, set up as **non-inventory parts**, which allows you to bill for and track the specific materials costs of your jobs without using the perpetual tracking system tools. You bill your clients for ALL materials, labor, plans, and permits.

You do keep some small construction items on hand (nails, glue, etc.), but you generally do not maintain much of a supply, so you expense those costs to the "Job supplies and small tools" account as they're purchased. You do **not** charge your clients for these costs.

You do keep some office supplies on hand. You record those in "Supplies on Hand" and adjust the balance at the end of the month.

✓ You would like your invoices to look more unique, so you create a customized **invoice**.

* You use the Intuit Service template as the starting point.

* You name your customized template Constructed with Style Invoice.

* You add a logo to the form appropriate to a construction company.

  ○ An easy way to find free logos is to go to www.bing.com.

  ○ Click **images**.

  ○ Type in a search term or phrase.

  ○ When the images appear, click **License** and select **"Free to modify, share, and use."**

  ○ Save your choice to your computer.

* You change the font on at least one field on the **Basic Customization** tab.

* You change the title of at least one **Header** or **Columns** field.

  ○ Hint: Use the **Additional Customization** tab.

* You also include the date of the work, description, hours, rate, and amount in the body of the invoice.

* You don't need a field for P.O.

* You change the border on at least one field.

✓ You also decide to create a special report. You want a report that shows billable time by service provided (demolition, electrical, plumbing, etc.) for the period 2/1 to 2/15. You want to see the hours, rate, class, and amount, but you're not interested in seeing the date of the service or the client name or any other details.

- You give the report a name. You also change **Fonts & Numbers** in a way that you think makes the report most readable.
- You save the report in the **Accountant** memorized report group.

REPORTS TO CREATE FOR ASSIGNMENT 11B

All reports should be in portrait orientation; fit to one page wide (unless otherwise noted).

- Invoice for Janine Thomas dated 2/15 using customized invoice.

- Memorized report for the period 2/1 to 2/15.

- Memorized report list. [**TIP**: To print the list, open the **Memorized Report List** window, and select **Print List** on the dropdown menu in the bottom left corner.]

APPENDIX 11A USING CUSTOM FIELDS

As you know, QuickBooks is a very popular program. One reason for its popularity is its flexibility. We've covered customizing features, reports, and templates. QuickBooks also allows users to create custom fields for tracking data for customers, vendors, employees, or **items**. Being able to extract information about customers, sales, etc., is a powerful tool for a business.

The process for creating custom fields is straightforward. Let's say Sac City Accounting wanted more information about its customers. It wanted to track the client's industry and wanted to know the client's fiscal year-end.

There's already a **customer type** field that could be used for the industry. Sac City decides to set up four **customer types**: Professional Firms, Education, Nonprofits, and Other.

To set up **customer types**, click **Lists** (main menu bar) and select **Customer & Vendor Profile Lists**:

Click **Customer Type List. Customer types** are added or edited in the following screen by selecting **New** or **Edit Customer Type** on the **Customer Type** dropdown menu. The new types are added through the following screen like this:

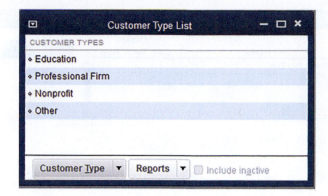

Customer types are added to customer records on the **Additional Info** tab of the customer record located in the **Customer Center**:

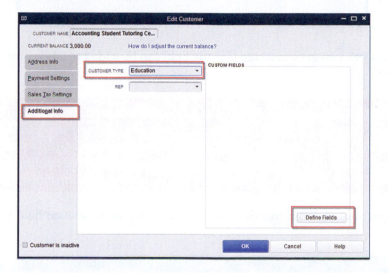

Custom fields for customers can also be added in this screen. Click **Define Fields**. The screen looks like this:

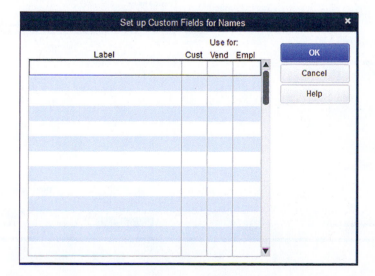

The new field name is entered in the **Label** column. The custom field can be associated with customers, vendors, and/or employees. The set up for tracking fiscal year end looks like this:

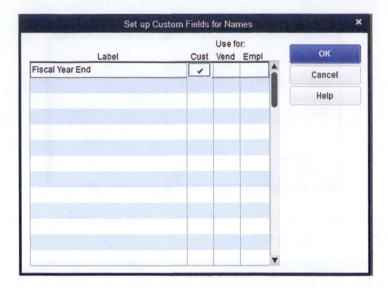

After you click **OK**, you get a message that the field can be added to any customer templates you've created.

> **!** **WARNING: Custom fields do not automatically update past transactions. If past data was needed, the custom field would need to be added to the form template (screen only is fine), and past transactions would need to be manually updated. Because *customer types* are predefined fields in QuickBooks, this is not necessary when adding new *customer types*.**

The **Additional Info** tab looks like this for a customer in the **Education** field with a June 30 year-end:

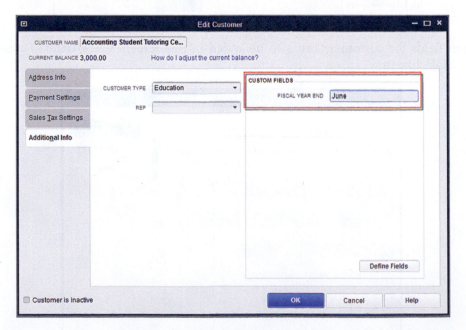

Reports can be filtered using the new fields. A report of all sales (1/1 to 2/15) for Education clients with June 30 year-ends might look like this:

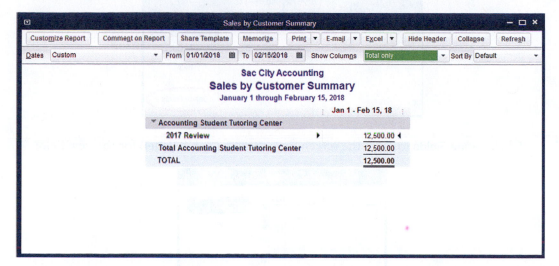

Custom fields can be added to templates.

The process for setting up custom fields for vendors and employees is similar to the process for customers. Custom fields are entered on the **Additional Info** tabs of the vendor or employee record.

To add a custom field to an **item**, click **Lists** (main menu bar) and select **item list**. The screen to add a new **service item** looks like this:

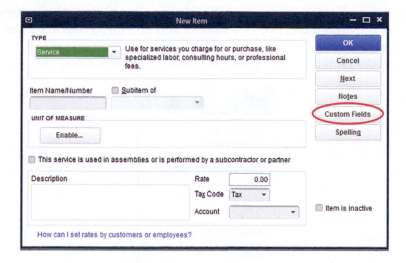

The following message appears the first time a custom field is created for **items**:

Click **OK**. The next screen looks like this:

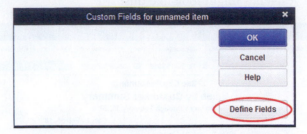

Click **Define Fields** to open the screen for entering a name (**label**) for the new field:

Placing a checkmark in the **Use** column activates the field.

APPENDIX 11B USING THE REPORT CENTER

Throughout this book, individual reports have been accessed through the **Reports** drop-down menu on the main menu bar. QuickBooks also provides a **Report Center** where additional tools are available.

The **Report Center** is initially accessed through the **Reports** drop down menu.

The **Report Center** window looks like this:

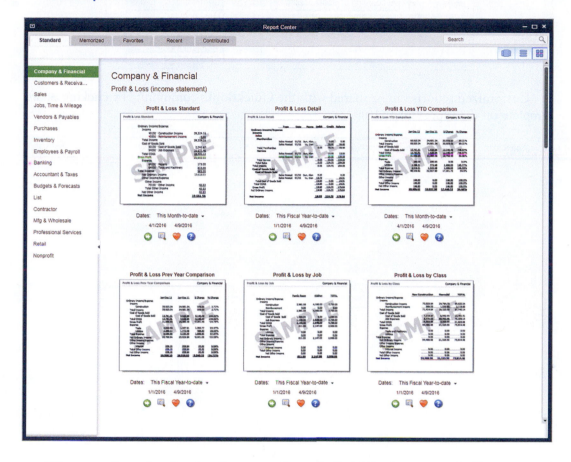

There are five tabs. On the **Standard** tab, each QuickBooks automatically generated report is listed (by category). A sample is provided that allows the user to quickly view the basic contents of the report. In addition, under each report are various icons.

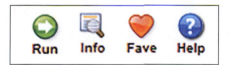

Information about the contents of the report is accessible by clicking either the **Info** or **Help** icons.

Clicking **Run** displays the full report that can then be customized as appropriate. Clicking **Fave** automatically includes the report on the **Favorites** tab of the **Report Center**.

The **Memorized** tab includes those reports that have been memorized by the user as well as some of the most commonly used QuickBooks reports.

Reports that have recently been viewed by the user are visible on the **Recent** tab of the **Report Center**.

The **Report Center** also includes reports that have been prepared by other QuickBooks users. These are visible on the **Contributed** tab. The user must be connected to the Internet to view these reports. Reports on this tab can be filtered by industry. To see only those reports created by other users, select **Community created** on the **SORT BY** dropdown menu.

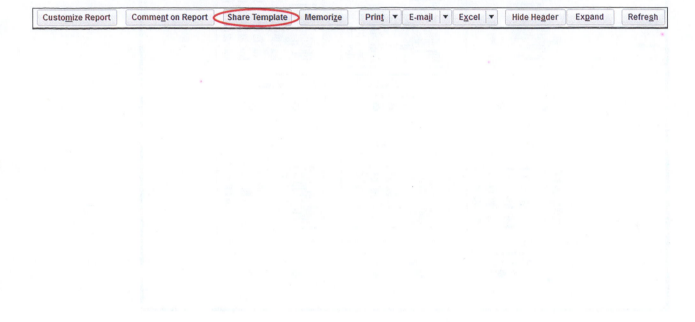

Customized reports can be shared with the QuickBooks community by clicking **Share Template** on the report menu bar.

Setting Up a Company in QuickBooks

Objectives

After completing Chapter 12, you should be able to:

1. Set up a new company in QuickBooks Pro.

2. Convert an existing company to QuickBooks Pro.

New company files can be created in QuickBooks for:

- Newly formed companies.
- Existing companies that are converting from a manual system (or other accounting software system) to QuickBooks.

In either case, obtaining a clear understanding of business operations and the organization's informational needs is the best place to start. Some questions you might ask your client or yourself (if you're the owner or the accountant) include:

- Does the company currently sell or anticipate selling products, services, or both?
  - If products are currently being sold:
    - Does the company manufacture the products?
    - Is a product inventory maintained, or are products purchased to order?
    - Are products sold to consumers, to distributors, or to both?
  - Is the company responsible for collecting sales taxes from customers?
- Are there significant business segments within the company currently or expected in the future?
- Does the company have employees?
- Does the company have specific reporting needs (internal or external) currently, or does it expect to have such needs in the future?

There is a reason that "anticipated" operations are part of some of the questions. If you understand the direction of the company, you can design a system that will accommodate expected changes. For example, let's say you're opening a barbershop. You have some great ideas and expect that you will be able to open several more shops within the next year. When you have multiple shops, you're going to want to track operations by shop. If you set up **class tracking** at the beginning, you'll easily be able to add locations and then report operations by all locations in the future.

If this is an existing company, management will need to decide the conversion date (start date). Although you can start recording transactions at any point in time, it is important to understand the implications of selecting various dates. For example, all payroll reporting is based on calendar quarters or calendar years, so companies often convert data as of the first day of a calendar quarter or calendar year. (QuickBooks does have tools for entering past payroll information, but the process can be cumbersome.)

Another consideration is the availability of transaction detail. Having detail readily available within the accounting system for all transactions occurring in an accounting period can be critical for operating efficiently. Many companies use the beginning of the fiscal year as the start date. At the very least, a company would want to convert data as of the beginning of a calendar month.

SETTING UP A NEW COMPANY FILE

To start the process of setting up a new company file, you can select the **New** option on the **File** menu (main menu bar), or you can select the **Create a new company** option in the **No Company Open** screen. (That's the screen that shows up when you first open QuickBooks in class.) Either way, the initial screen in the process looks like this:

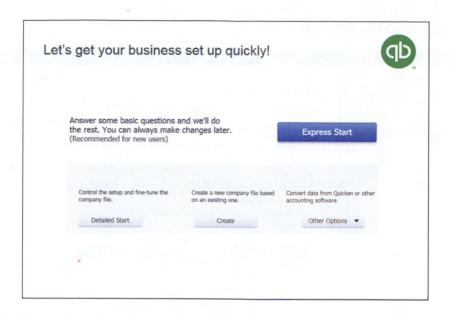

QuickBooks provides four options for setting up a company file:

- You can do an **Express Start** (most useful for users with minimal accounting knowledge).

- You can do a **Detailed Start** that takes you through an interview process.

- You can **Create** a new company using templates from an existing company.

- You can convert data from several popular software programs (**Other Options**).

We only cover the **Detailed Start** option in this course. If you choose the **Detailed Start** option, you go through an **Easy Step Interview** process to set up your company:

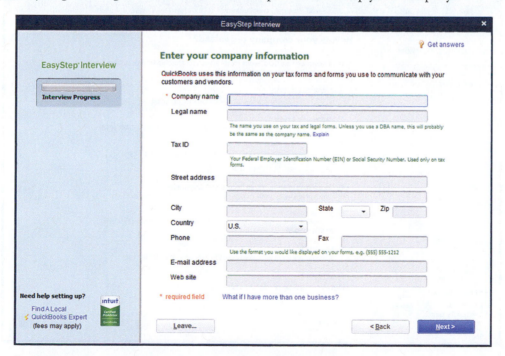

In this first screen, the Company Name **must** be entered. Additional information (like address and phone number) can be added now or later.

The next screen looks like this:

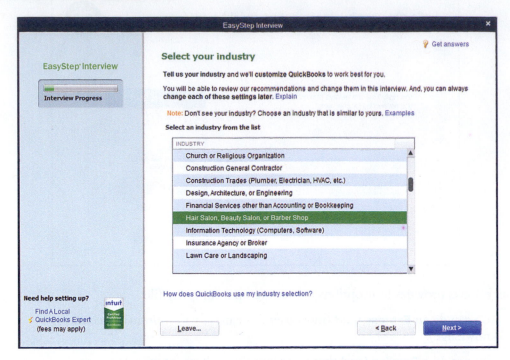

Your choice of industry simply determines options and suggestions that QuickBooks will present during the remainder of the interview. You can accept or reject their options and suggestions. You can also add or edit options and data after your company file is set up. To follow this example, select **Design**, **Architecture**, or **Engineering**.

The next screen looks like this:

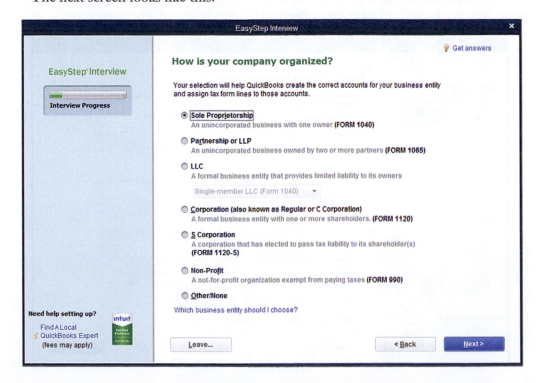

In this screen, you must enter the legal form under which the company is organized.

> **BEHIND THE SCENES** QuickBooks uses this information for setting up certain accounts (for example, equity accounts). This information is also used to map accounts in QuickBooks to the appropriate lines on federal income tax forms. Using QuickBooks for preparing income tax forms is not covered in this class.

The next screen looks like this:

The **first** month of your **fiscal year** **must** be selected. For example, if the company has a June 30 year-end, "July" would be selected here. QuickBooks uses this date to close revenue and expense accounts at year-end.

Fiscal year The annual accounting period used by a business.

The next screen looks like this:

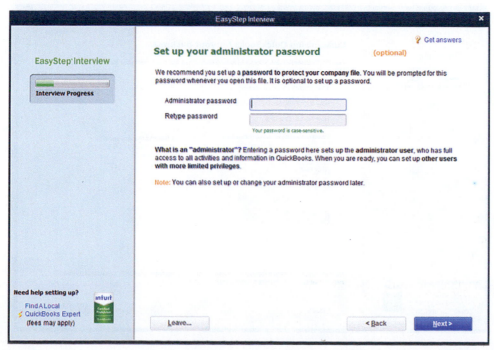

Passwords are now required in QuickBooks. They are part of a strong internal control system, particularly in company with multiple QuickBooks users. See Section Three for additional information on setting up users and passwords.)

The next screen looks like this:

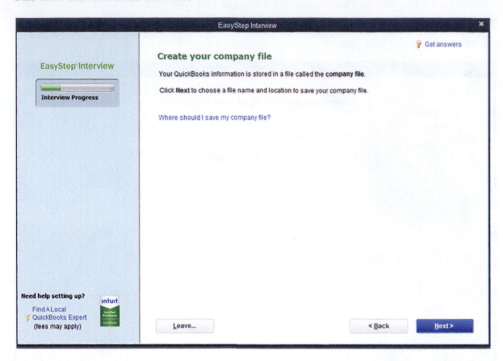

This is just an informational screen, letting you know that QuickBooks is ready to create a .QBW file.

If you choose to proceed, you must browse for the location to store your new working file. A company might store its working file on a network server. Once you've identified the location for your .QBW file, your file will be created and saved to that location.

The next screen looks like this:

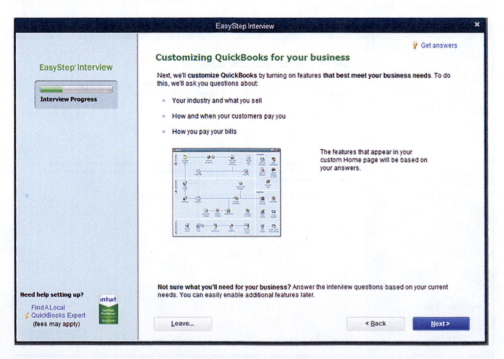

You are now ready to start setting preferences and entering data.

In a series of screens, QuickBooks offers options and suggestions based on the industry you indicated, but again, you are free to accept or reject the recommendations. In the screen series, you are asked to indicate, in this order:

- Whether you sell services, products, or both.

- Whether you charge sales tax.

- Whether you use estimates.

- Whether you track customer orders (sales orders).

- Whether you use statements.

- Whether you create invoices.

- Whether you do progress invoicing (invoice customers for a portion of a fixed fee).

- Whether you want to track vendor bills (accounts payable).

- Whether you need to track inventory.

- Whether you need to track time.

- Whether you have employees and/or use contract labor.

After this series of questions has been answered, many of the basic preferences have been turned on (or off). You can, of course, make changes later.

The next screen looks like this:

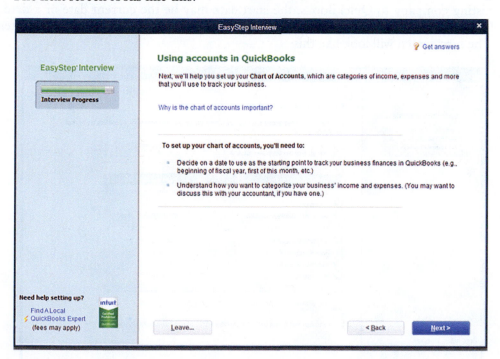

This screen provides some basic information about designing a chart of accounts and includes a link to additional help.

The next screen looks like this:

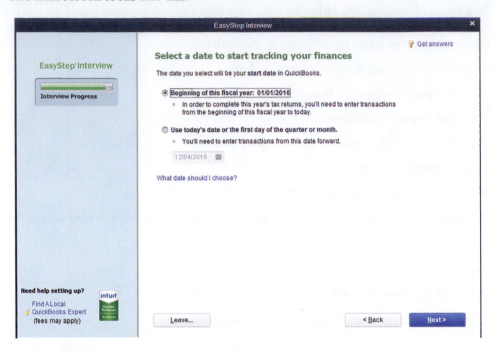

You must indicate the **start date** for entering transactions. If you are setting up a new company, the start date will normally be the first day of operations. If you are converting an existing company to QuickBooks, the start date may be the current date or a date in the future or the past. Beginning account balances (as of the start date) are entered later.

The next screen will look like this:

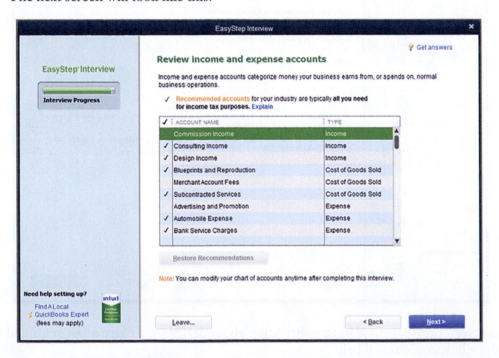

The accounts listed depend on the industry you selected earlier in the interview process. You can check (or uncheck) the accounts displayed, but you can't add new accounts. You can, of course, add them later.

The next screen looks like this:

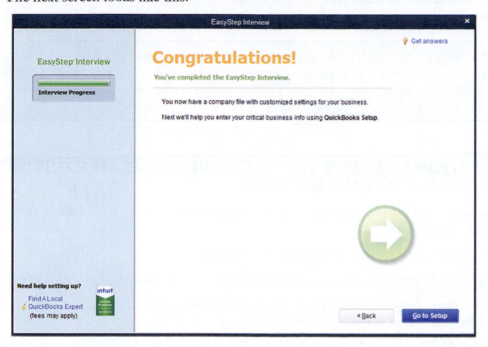

This screen marks the end of the **Easy Step Interview**. If you were setting up a new company, you would most likely close the **Easy Step Interview** at this point by exiting out of the window. If you were converting a company, you would have additional information to enter. We cover that process in the next section of this chapter.

For a new company, **items** and **payroll items** still need to be created. Entering **items** is most efficiently done using the **Add/Edit Multiple List Entries** process covered in the next section of this chapter. If payroll has been turned on, QuickBooks automatically created default **payroll items** for compensation types and for federal and state taxes. These defaults should be reviewed and changes to rates, associated accounts, agency name, identifying number, etc., should be made as necessary. A payroll setup process is covered later in this chapter.

For the setup of either new or existing companies, it is helpful to review the available **preferences** before moving forward. As you know, **preferences** are accessed through the **preferences** option on the **Edit** menu (main menu bar). The screen looks like this:

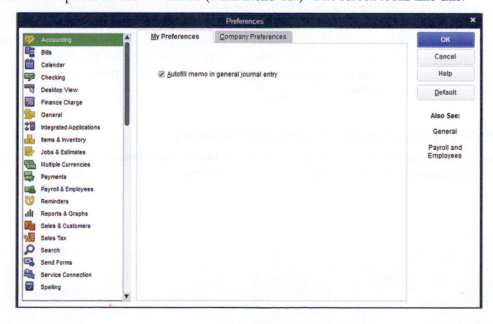

The **Company Preferences** tabs for each section should be reviewed and options changed as necessary.

 HINT: Although we have set a number of **preferences** as part of this course, there are many others that we haven't covered. If you're going to use Quick-Books in the future, try to find some time to explore all the available options in the various **preference** screens.

ADDITIONAL STEPS WHEN CONVERTING AN EXISTING COMPANY TO QUICKBOOKS

Companies that have been operating for any length of time have a considerable amount of data to contend with:

- Customer and vendor addresses, credit terms, etc.

- Customer and vendor account balances as of the date of conversion.

- Inventory records (price, associated income accounts, quantities on hand and inventory values as of the date of conversion, etc.).

- Employee addresses, wage rates, withholding allowances, etc. (prior payroll data for the calendar year, if necessary).

- General ledger account balances as of the date of conversion.

One option for entering additional data for customers, vendors, and **items** is to use Quick-Books' **Quick Start** tool. The tool can be accessed by choosing the **Continue** option on the final screen of the **Easy Step Interview** (see the **Congratulations** screen displayed earlier). The **Quick Start** tool allows you to quickly enter basic information about all customers through one screen. Additional screens are available for entering very basic information about all vendors and all **items**. More detailed information has to be added later through the **edit** process.

Another option is to enter each customer, vendor, and **item** separately using the **Centers** and **Lists** menu options for adding new records. This allows you to enter all detailed information right away, but the process is fairly time consuming.

A final option is to use the **Add/Edit Multiple List Entries** option on the **Lists** menu (main menu bar). This tool is similar to **Quick Start** in that multiple customers, vendors, or **items** can be entered at the same time. The difference is that this option allows you to enter more detailed information for each record right away. We use that tool setting up existing customers, vendors, and **items**.

Entering Information About Existing Customers

To enter multiple customers, select the **Add/Edit Multiple List Entries** option on the **Lists** menu (main menu bar). The initial screen looks like this:

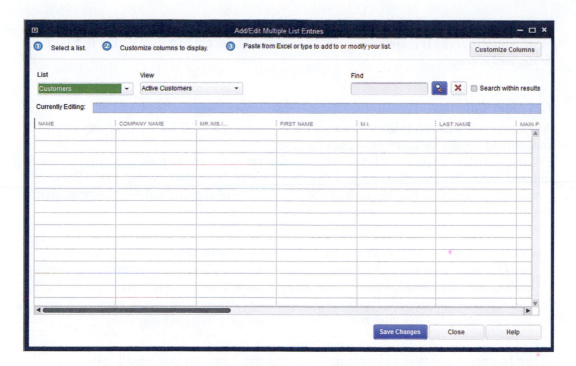

This window can be used for entering customers, vendors, or **items**. Clicking the drop-down menu under **List** allows you to select the proper list. As you can see, the initial screen defaults to customers.

The **type** of information that is entered in this screen for customers can be customized using the **Customize Columns** tool (top right of the screen). The customization screen looks like this:

The screen includes all available fields. Fields can be added by highlighting a field in the far left column and clicking the **Add** button. Highlighting a field in the far right column and clicking **Remove** removes the field from the screen. The order of the fields can be adjusted by highlighting a field in the far right column and using the **Move Up** or **Move Down** buttons.

 HINT: When entering customers, the **Name** column corresponds to the **Customer Name** in the customer record (the customer identifier). The **Company Name** is the name used in mailing addresses on printed forms.

When entering most addresses, use **Bill To 1** for the street address and **Bill To 2** for City, State, and Zip code. If there's a unit number, enter that in **Bill To 2** and use **Bill To 3** for City, State, and Zip code.

Customer Balances

A customer may have a balance due as of the conversion date. That balance may consist of one unpaid invoice or multiple unpaid invoices.

If the balance consists of one invoice, the amount and date of the invoice **can** be entered here (**Customer Balance** and **Opening Balance as of Date** fields). QuickBooks automatically creates an **invoice**. It does not include any of the original detail (**items**, partial payments, etc.). The original **invoice** number can be added later.

> **BEHIND THE SCENES** The underlying entry for **invoices** automatically created by QuickBooks is a debit to accounts receivable and a credit to an **income** account called **Uncategorized Income**. Additional entries are probably required to transfer revenues to the proper account. If the invoice represents the sale of a product, no entry is recorded to either the inventory or cost of goods sold accounts.

If the balance consists of multiple invoices, the **total** amount due on all invoices can be entered here. However, only one date can be chosen.

> **BEHIND THE SCENES** Combining invoices can create problems when applying payments and when communicating with customers because the detail will not be available.

As the **preferred alternative**, each unpaid invoice should be recreated in the new company (with the **invoice** template) using the original detail (date, number, terms, **item**, etc.). This creates a more accurate record.

> **BEHIND THE SCENES** Special care must be given when the invoice recreated includes **inventory part items**. QuickBooks will credit the inventory account (and debit cost of goods sold) when the **invoice** is saved. Opening balances of **Item** quantities and values would have to be adjusted accordingly to accommodate this.

A message confirming the number of customers entered or highlighting any records with improperly entered data is displayed when the **Save Changes** option at bottom right of screen is selected.

Entering Information About Existing Vendors

To enter multiple vendors, select the **Add/Edit Multiple List Entries** option on the **Lists** menu (main menu bar), and use the dropdown menu to select the **Vendor** list. The initial screen looks like this:

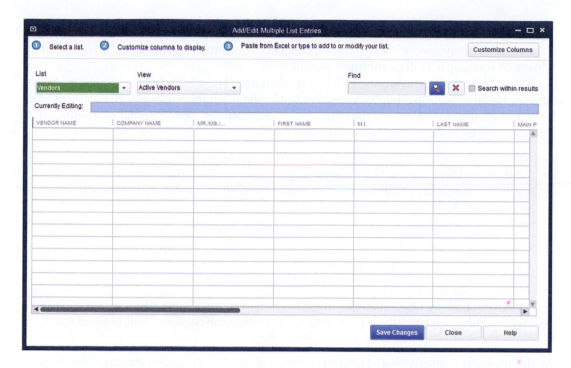

The type of information that can be entered can be customized using the **Customize** tool (top right of the screen). The customization screen looks like this:

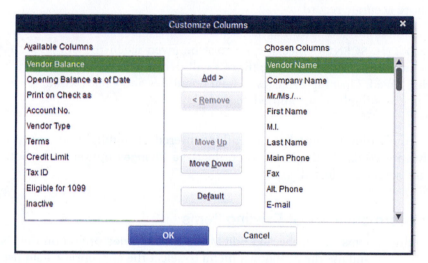

The screen includes all available fields. Fields can be added to the far right column or removed from the far right columns using the **Add** and **Remove** buttons in the middle of the screen. The order of the fields in the far right column can be adjusted using the **Move Up** and **Move Down** buttons.

HINT: When entering most vendor addresses, use **Address 1** for the street address and **Address 2** for City, State, and Zip code. If there's a unit number, enter that in **Address 2** and use **Address 3** for City, State, and Zip code.

Vendor Balances

The company may owe money to the vendor as of the conversion date. That balance may consist of one unpaid bill or multiple unpaid bills.

If the balance consists of one bill, the amount and date of the bill can be entered here (**Vendor Balance** and **Opening Balance as of Date** fields). QuickBooks automatically creates a **bill**. It does not include any of the original detail (**expenses, items,** partial payments, etc.). The original **bill** number can be added later.

> **BEHIND THE SCENES** The underlying entry is a debit to an **expense** account called **Uncategorized Expenses** and a credit to accounts payable. Additional entries would need to be made to properly categorize the entries.

If the balance consists of multiple bills, the **total** amount of all unpaid bills can be entered here. However, only one date can be chosen.

> **BEHIND THE SCENES** Combining bills can create problems when making payments and when communicating with vendors because no detail will be available.

As the **preferred alternative**, each unpaid vendor invoice should be recreated in the new company (as a **bill**) using the original detail (date, number, terms, **expense, item,** etc.). The underlying entry is a debit to the expense (or asset) and a credit to accounts payable. This creates a more accurate record.

> **BEHIND THE SCENES** Special care must be given when the bill recreated includes **inventory part items**. QuickBooks will debit the inventory account when the **bill** is saved. Opening balances of **Item** quantities and values would have to be adjusted accordingly to accommodate this.

A message confirming the number of vendors entered or highlighting any records with improperly entered data is displayed when the **Save Changes** option at the bottom right corner of the screen is selected.

Entering Information About Existing Items

To enter multiple **items**, select the **Add/Edit Multiple List Entries** option on the **Lists** menu (Main Menu Bar), and use the dropdown menu to select the appropriate **Item** list.

There are four different screens for entering **items**: one for **service items**, one for **inventory part items**, one for **non-inventory part items**, and one for **inventory assemblies**. All of them are accessed through the **List** dropdown menu at the top left of the screen. Other **item** types (**discount, subtotal, other charge, tax,** etc.) cannot be entered using this tool.

If you selected a specific industry in the original setup, QuickBooks automatically creates some possible **items**. These can be deleted or changed.

The **service item** screen looks something like this:

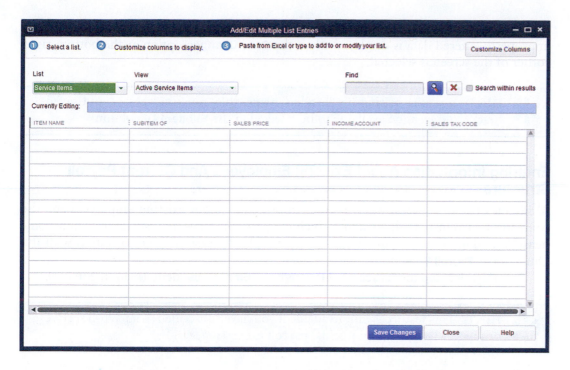

The type of information that can be entered can be customized using the **Customize** tool (top right of the screen). For example, the customization screen for adding multiple **inventory part items** looks like this:

For **inventory part items**, the quantity and value of inventory on hand can be entered here using the **Qty On Hand** and **Total Value** field options.

> **BEHIND THE SCENES** QuickBooks automatically creates an **inventory adjustment** for the quantity and value. The underlying entry is to debit the inventory account associated with the **item** and credit an **equity** account called **Opening Balance Equity**. **Opening Balance Equity** should be cleared out to retained earnings (if the company is a **corporation**) or an owner's capital account (if the company is structured as a **sole proprietorship** or as a **partnership**) when the company set up is complete.

QuickBooks automatically uses the actual entry date (not the **As Of** date) for the **inventory adjustment**. If the amounts are not being entered on the actual conversion date, the **inventory adjustment** form automatically created by QuickBooks should be edited later and the date changed to the conversion date.

Corporation A legal entity created under the laws of a state or the federal government. The owners of a corporation receive shares of stock as evidence of their ownership interest in the company.

Sole proprietorship A form of business organization in which one person owns the business.

Partnership A voluntary association of two or more persons for the purpose of conducting a business.

A message confirming the number of items entered or highlighting any records with improperly entered data is displayed when the **Save Changes** option at the bottom right corner of the screen is selected.

 HINT: If you're setting up "header" **items**, they must be created and saved first. They are then available to be selected in the **Subitem Of** column.

Entering Information About Existing Employees And Current Payroll Structure

Although there are several ways to enter information about existing employees and the company's current payroll structure (including payroll taxes, pay structures, non-compensation additions and deductions, etc.), probably the easiest place to start is with the QuickBooks **Payroll Setup** tool.

The **Payroll Setup** tool is accessed through the **Employees** menu (main menu bar).

 HINT: This feature is only available if you have subscribed to a payroll service or if you have turned on manual payroll processing.

The initial screen looks like this:

The screen provides you with information about the setup process and includes a link to a checklist that can be used to determine that all required information is available. The checklist is extensive and well worth the time to review.

 HINT: You can leave and come back to the setup at any time.

On the left side of the screen is the "table of contents" for **payroll setup**. The setup tool is divided into four sections (not including the "Introduction" and "Finishing Up" sections).

When you click **Continue**, the next screen looks like this:

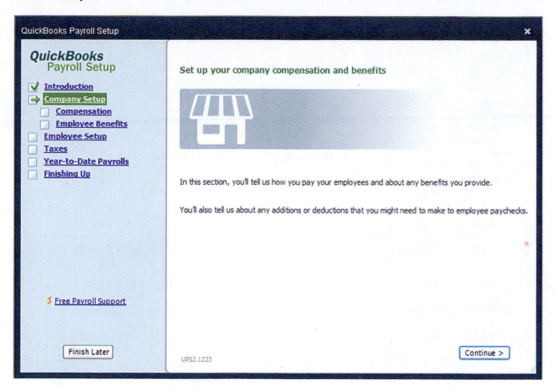

This screen introduces the first section (called **Company Setup**).

Compensation types, various other additions and deductions, paid time off, and insurance and health benefits offered by the company are covered in **company setup** section.

The next screen displays compensation **payroll item** options. The screen looks like this:

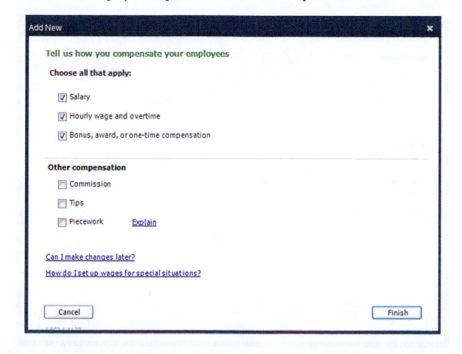

In this screen, you can choose the types of compensation you currently use. Remember you can always add items later. Depending on which compensation items you select, the next screen looks something like this:

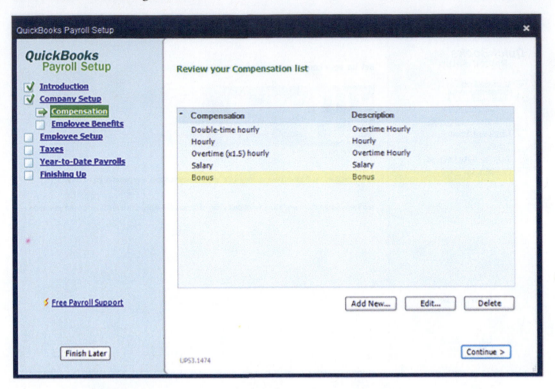

As you can see, QuickBooks has now set up various **payroll items**. You can add, edit, or delete **payroll items** in this screen.

As an example, the screen for editing an hourly compensation **item** looks something like this:

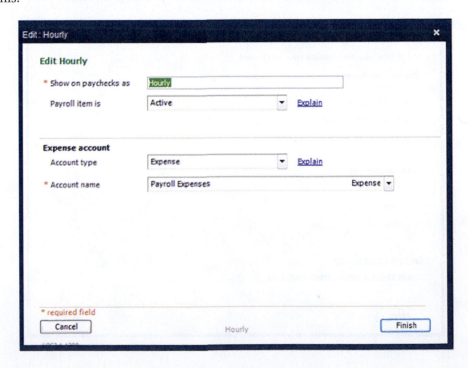

You can change the **account type** and the **account name** (account that should be debited for gross pay when a payroll check is prepared). Once you have completed the compensation section of the setup, the following screen appears:

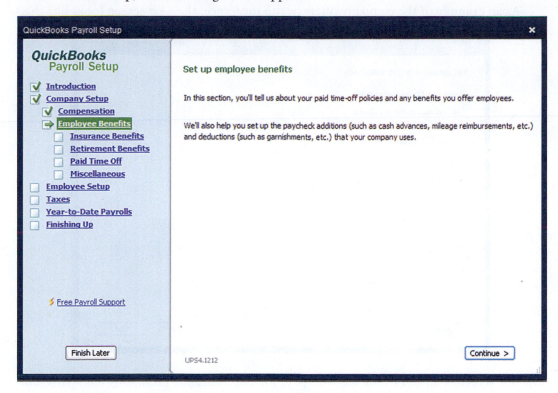

This is an informational screen that introduces the subsequent series of screens. The next screen looks like this:

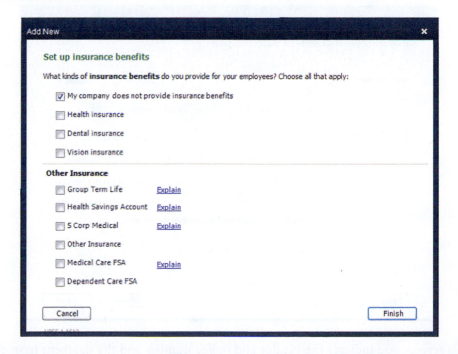

As you can see, you're now in the **Add New** screen for setting up insurance benefits. If the company offers no insurance benefits, you simply indicate that here (check **My company does not provide insurance benefits**).

If the company does offer insurance benefits, the types of insurance offered should be marked. You must then answer an additional series of questions for each type of insurance offered.

As an example, if the company offers health insurance, the next screen looks like this:

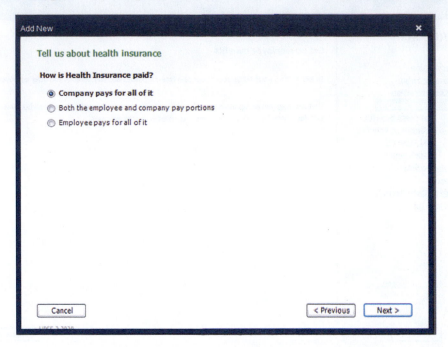

On this screen, you must indicate who pays for the insurance premiums (company, employee, or both). If you indicated that the company pays for the premiums, the next screen looks like this:

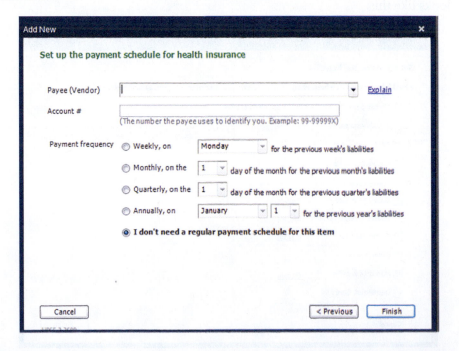

On this screen, you indicate the vendor and policy number and the payment frequency.

If other insurance benefits are offered, there will be additional screens asking additional questions. When all insurance information has been complete, the next screen looks like this:

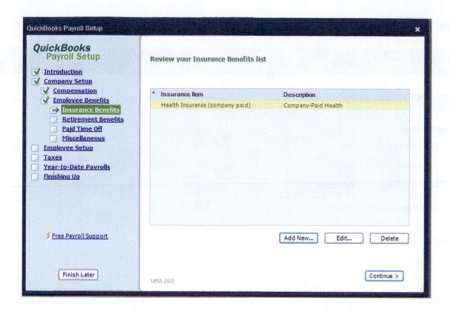

This is a **review** screen. If you entered insurance benefits, the associated **payroll items** would be displayed on this screen, and you would have the option of editing or deleting those items.

The same format is followed for other types of benefits. The **Add New** screen appears first (if there are no default **payroll items** set up by QuickBooks). Common benefits are listed. Additional screens appear depending on the type of benefit selected. The **Review** screen appears last.

Other types of benefits are entered in this order (after insurance benefits):

- Retirement benefits.

- Paid time off.

- Miscellaneous (other additions and deductions).
    - The miscellaneous items aren't always "benefits." For example, **payroll items** for union dues, garnishments, expense reimbursements, etc., are entered in this section.

The second section of the **payroll setup** is called the **Employee Setup** section. The first screen in this section looks like this:

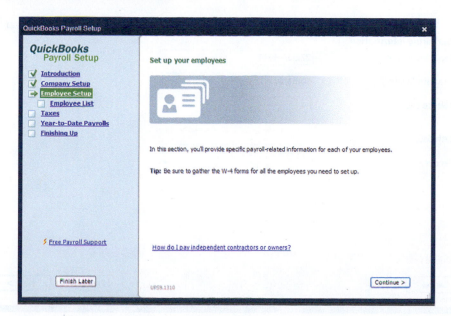

This is an information screen. The next screen looks like this:

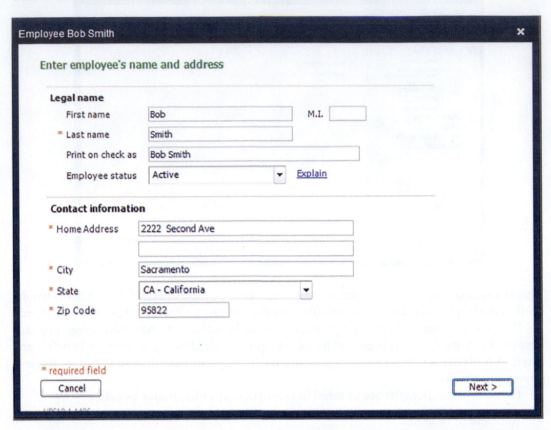

In this screen, the employee's name and address are entered. The next screen looks like this:

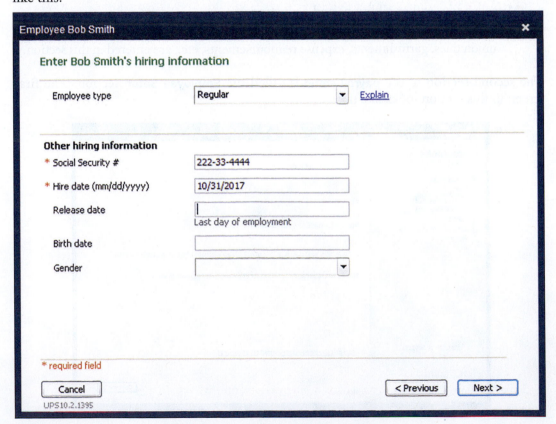

In this screen, the employee's Social Security number and hire date must be entered. The next screen looks like this:

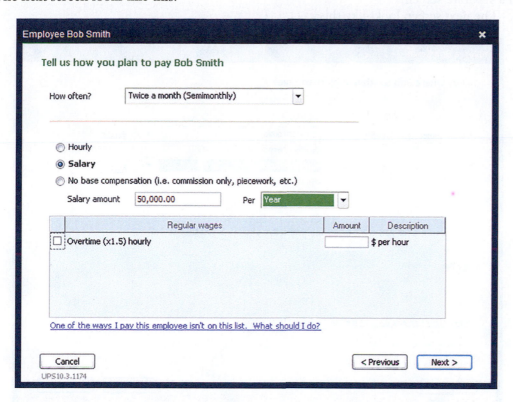

The employee's compensation is entered in this screen. The next screen looks like this:

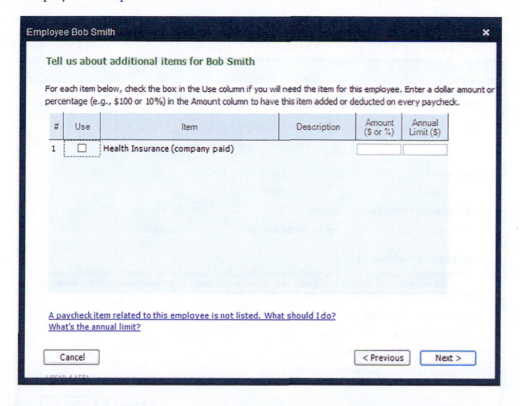

Information related to benefits and deductions are entered through this screen.

If the employee elects direct deposit of his or her paychecks, that information is input on a separate screen.

The next screen looks like this:

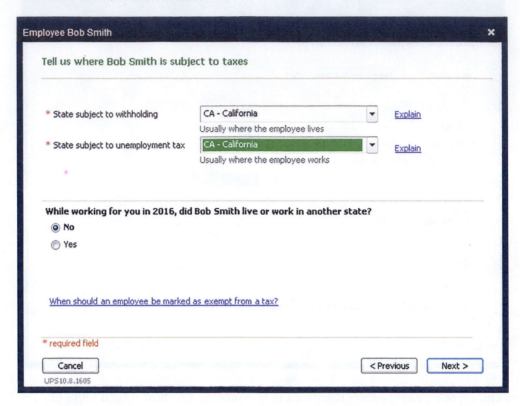

Information about employee state work locations is entered here. The next screen looks like this:

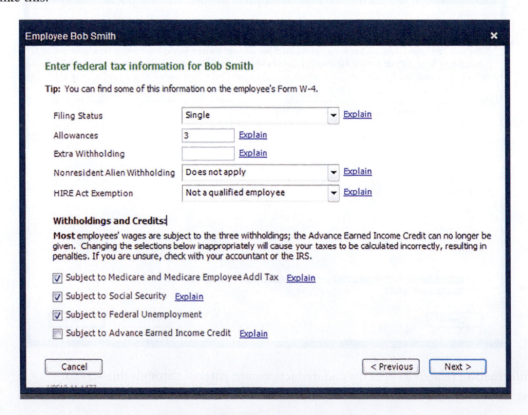

Information from the employee's W-4 is entered here. The next screen looks like this:

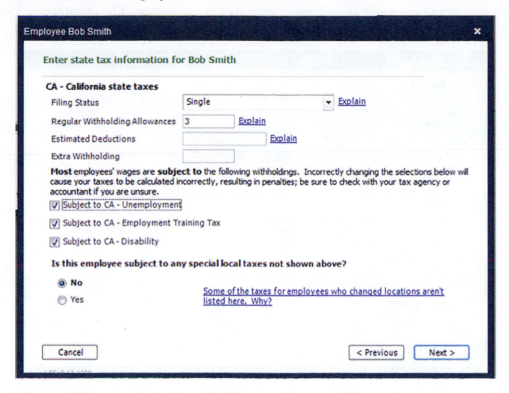

Information about state filing status and withholdings must be entered here.

Other screens will appear if there is additional state information that must be tracked for employees.

The final employee screen is an employee **review** screen. Employees can be added, edited, or deleted through this screen. The **Summary** link (bottom right corner of screen) allows you to print a report summarizing the employee record.

The review screen looks like this:

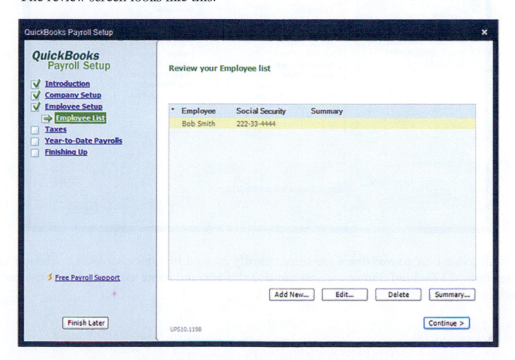

This third section of the **payroll setup** is called the **Taxes** section. All **payroll items** related to employee and employer payroll taxes are entered in this section. The initial screen looks like this:

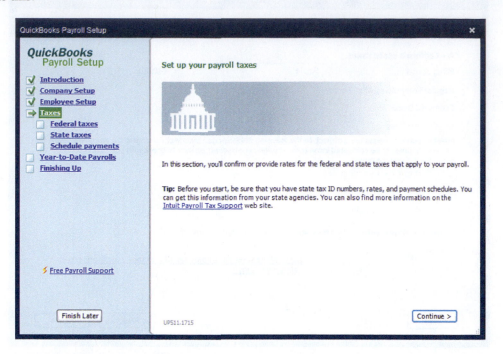

The next screen looks like this:

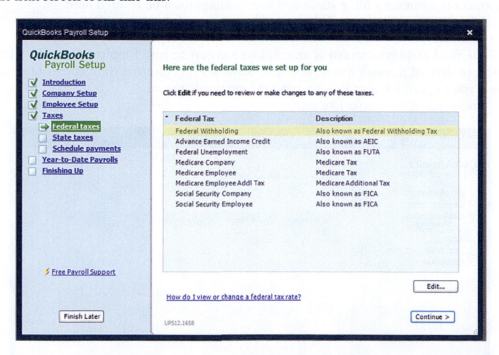

All federal tax **payroll items** are automatically created by QuickBooks. The default tax rates cannot be edited. However, you can edit the **account name** associated with the taxes and the description.

The next screen looks like this:

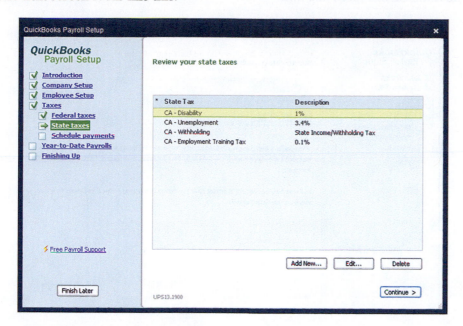

State **payroll tax items** are also automatically created by QuickBooks. The associated **account names** and descriptions can be edited.

In the next series of screens, information about tax authorities and payment schedules for federal and state taxes are entered. Rates can be entered for state taxes. State tax identification numbers can also be entered.

When all taxes are entered, the following screen appears:

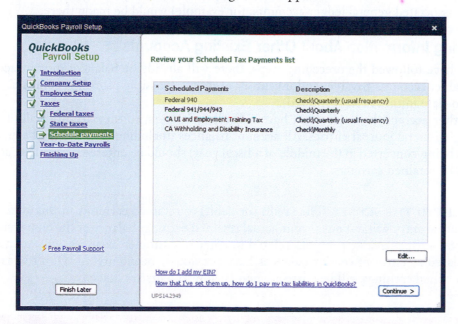

QuickBooks indicates any taxes (state or federal) with missing or incorrect information. The taxes with errors can be edited from this screen. Changes (like entering EIN numbers) can also be made by editing the **payroll item** in the **payroll item list**.

The fourth section of the **payroll setup** is called the **Year-To-Date Payrolls** section.

The initial screen looks like this:

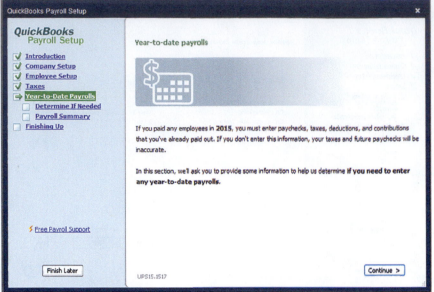

This is an informational screen.

If a company elects to enter year-to-date information, each employee's pay and company tax deposits are entered through a series of screens. Year-to-date information is entered by calendar quarter. We do not cover entering year-to-date payroll entry in this course.

When the **payroll setup** is complete, be sure and review the **payroll item list** (accessed through the **Lists** menu in the main menu bar). Any necessary changes to default **payroll items** (associated general ledger accounts, for example) would be made there.

Entering Information About Other Existing Accounts

If you have followed the preceding steps, there will already be balances in your accounts receivable, accounts payable, and inventory accounts (possibly payroll accounts as well if year-to-date information is entered).

Other account balances don't have subsidiary ledgers, so they are normally entered through general journal entries. All account balances (including revenues and expenses if data is being converted in the middle of a fiscal year) should be entered. The offset account would be retained earnings.

BEHIND THE SCENES The credit (or debit) to retained earnings in this general journal entry will **not** equal your actual retained earnings balance at the conversion date. That's because revenues related to entry of customer balances and expenses related to entry of vendor balances have previously been entered. Don't worry! Retained earnings will be correct when all adjustments are made.

! **WARNING:** There are special considerations when entering opening balances for bank accounts. To effectively use the bank reconciliation tool in QuickBooks, the <u>bank balance</u> at the conversion date—not the book balance—should be entered in the general journal entry. Any outstanding checks and/or deposits in transit should be entered as separate transactions. All necessary data is then available when the first bank reconciliation is prepared.

The general journal entry to record these remaining account balances should be made **after** customers, vendors, and items have been set up.

Summary Of Steps When Setting Up A Quickbooks File For An Existing Company

Although there are many methods used to convert existing companies to QuickBooks, here are the steps I've taken with my clients:

1. Obtain a trial balance, a detailed list of accounts receivable, and a detailed list of accounts payable as of the conversion date from the existing recordkeeping system.

2. Obtain the bank reconciliation prepared as of the conversion date.
   a. Companies should convert on the last day of a month so that the bank reconciliation is accurate.

3. Make sure the company takes a physical count of inventory on the conversion date.
   a. This is "best practice." If that isn't possible, make sure the company has a list of quantities and values for all items on hand as of the date of conversion.

4. Create the working (.QBW) file without entering any balances.

5. Set up the Chart of Accounts.

6. Set up customers, vendors, and items using the Add/Edit Multiple List Entries **without including any balances**.

7. Create bills (original dates, distributions, etc.) for all unpaid vendor accounts as of the conversion date.
   a. This allows the company to easily communicate with vendors and pay vendor bills going forward.

8. Create checks (original dates, distributions, etc.) for all checks outstanding as of the conversion date.
   a. This allows the company to easily reconcile the bank accounts going forward.

9. Create invoices (original dates, items, etc.) for all customer accounts uncollected as of the conversion date.
   a. You will receive messages about the lack of inventory on hand. Keep going. You will adjust inventory later.
   b. This allows the company to easily communicate with customers and process customer payments going forward.

10. Create deposits (original dates, amounts) for all deposits in transit as of the conversion date.
    a. This allows the company to easily reconcile the bank accounts going forward.

11. Create an inventory adjustment entry, matching the quantities and values of all items to the quantities and values of inventory items as of the conversion date.
    a. Use the conversion date as the entry date.
    b. You can use cost of goods sold for the credit account. You will correct that account later.

12. Print a trial balance from QuickBooks as of the conversion date.

   a. Trial balances are accessed through the **Accountant & Taxes** option of the **Reports** menu (main menu bar).

13. Compare the QuickBooks trial balance to the ending trial balance from the prior record-keeping system.

   a. Accounts receivable, accounts payable , and inventory accounts should all match. If there are differences, errors were made when entering open **invoices**, unpaid **bills**, and/or when making the **inventory adjustment** entry. These must be corrected before moving forward.

   b. For all bank accounts, the difference between the QuickBooks balance and the balance in from the prior recordkeeping system should equal the **bank balance** at the conversion date. If it doesn't, there's an error in the entry of outstanding checks and deposits in transit. The error should be resolved before moving forward.

14. Create a final general journal entry to record any remaining account balances. The entry for each account should equal the balance in the prior system less the balance already recorded in QuickBooks. The bank balances at the conversion date should be entered for any bank accounts as part of the final journal entry.

   a. Remember, there should be no entries needed for A/R, A/P, or Inventory accounts.

   b. When you **Save & Close** the entry, you will get a warning message about posting to Retained Earnings. Because this is the setup of a new company, the entry to retained earnings is appropriate and the warning can be ignored.

15. After the final entry is completed, the balance sheet and profit and loss statement as of the conversion date should be compared to the financial statements from the prior system. Any differences must be resolved.

You have now successfully converted a company to QuickBooks!

Setting up a company as a new company or an existing company on QuickBooks is not difficult, but there are certainly more than a few steps!

As mentioned at the beginning of the chapter, the most important aspect of the setup is the initial design of the file structure you want to use. Knowing what types of transactions a company might have and what types of information might be needed are the keys to a successful setup. That being said, QuickBooks is very forgiving and very flexible. As the company grows, changes can and will need to be made to the structure to accommodate new activities and new reporting needs.

CHAPTER SHORTCUTS

Create a new company file (two options)

1. Option 1
   a. Click Create a new company in the No Company Open window
2. Option 2
   a. Click File (main menu bar)
   b. Click New Company

Create Lists for Customers, Vendors, and Items (batch entry)

1. Click Lists (main menu bar)
2. Click Add/Edit Multiple List Entries

3. Select List to be created
4. Click Customize Columns to add or delete fields to be completed

Setup payroll items and employee records (batch entry)

1. Click Employees (main menu bar)
2. Click Payroll Setup

CHAPTER REVIEW

Matching

Match the term or phrase (as used in QuickBooks) to its best definition.

1. Easy Step Interview
2. Preferences
3. Opening Balance Equity
4. Detailed Start
5. Start date
6. Uncategorized income
7. Express Start
8. Fiscal year

_____ Annual accounting period

_____ Default account credited when customer account balances are entered through the Multiple List Entries window

_____ Conversion date for transferring an existing company's records

_____ Limited setup company file creation option

_____ Default account credited when inventory values are entered through the Multiple List Entries window

_____ Features available and processing rules established in company file

_____ Extensive setup company file creation option

_____ Process used in Detailed Start method of creating a company file

Multiple Choice

1. Which of the following statements is not true?
   a. As part of the **Easy Step Interview**, the user enters the first month of the fiscal year.
   b. The conversion date is always the first day of the fiscal year.
   c. The **Easy Step Interview** process is part of a **Detailed Start**.
   d. Users with minimal accounting knowledge can use the **Express Start** method to set up a new company.

2. When amounts owed to vendors at the conversion date are entered through **Add/Edit Multiple List Entries**, the underlying journal entry will include a debit to:
   a. Opening Balance Equity.
   b. uncategorized income.
   c. accounts payable.
   d. uncategorized expenses.

3. When inventory is set up through **Add/Edit Multiple List Entries**, the resulting journal entry is dated:
   a. using the actual entry date.
   b. using the as of date entered in the setup.
   c. using the start date.
   d. using the date of the first day of the most recent fiscal year.

4. Which of the following statements is true?

   a. All accounts to be used by the company must be selected as part of the **Easy Step Interview** process.

   b. **Item** quantities entered through **Add/Edit Multiple List Entries** can't be edited later.

   c. Although contact information (address and phone number) can be added later, the Company Name must be entered on the first screen of the **Easy Step Interview**.

   d. The new .QBW file is created immediately after the first screen (company information) is completed in the **Easy Step Interview**.

5. **Add/Edit Multiple List Entries** can be used for all of the following lists except:

   a. service items.

   b. chart of accounts.

   c. inventory items.

   d. vendors.

ASSIGNMENTS

Assignment 12A

Bella Beagles

You've decided to open a dog grooming business. You've always loved beagles and you've seen plenty of them at the local dog park, so you decide to specialize in that breed, although you will accept all breeds as customers! You've got two good-sized spare rooms in your basement with outside entry. One of the rooms contains a big, laundry-sized tub, so you think it will be pretty easy to get set up.

You decide to use QuickBooks for your accounting. You haven't had any transactions yet, but you want to get the company file set up.

Here's what you know:

- The name of your company will be "Bella Beagles."

- Your address is 32 Waggle Lane, Sacramento, CA 95822.

- You will be organized as a sole proprietorship and your fiscal year will begin in January.
  - You're starting your business on 1/1/18.

- You expect to sell goods (taxable) and services (nontaxable). They should be organized in a way that makes them easy to access.
  - Grooming services:
    - Wash & Dry—$20.
    - Ear Cleaning—$10.
    - Nail Clipping—$20.
    - Teeth Brushing—$10.
  - Retail products (you will be tracking inventory in QuickBooks):
    - Flea collar—$15 (expected cost—$10).
    - Flea comb—$5 (expected cost—$2).

- Tax rate is 8%—Agency is Board of Equalization, 3565 Green Street, Sacramento, CA 95822. Terms are Net 15.

- Although most of your customers will pay at time of service, you do have two veterinarian services that have agreed to try your service. You will bill them monthly with terms of Net 15.
  - Dr. Dee's Vet Care
    2106 Pampered Lane
    Sacramento, CA 95822
  - Midtown Pet Care
    301 K Street
    Sacramento, CA 95822

- You will be buying your supplies from:
  - Pet Ready Supplies
    1515 Retriever Lane
    Seattle, WA 98107
  - Terms: Net 30

- You do not expect to have any employees.

- You will need to purchase some furniture, some equipment, and some supplies.

- You will also need to apply for a business license at the City of Sacramento.

- You are going to get a company credit card to use as needed. The card (CityCard) will be with City Bank of Sacramento (321 Main St, Sacramento, CA 95822). Terms are Net 15.

- You're also going to purchase a van so that you can transport dogs to and from customer locations.

- You won't have any rent because you're working from home, but you will have a separate phone line installed for Bella's.

REPORTS TO CREATE FOR ASSIGNMENT 12A

All reports should be in portrait orientation unless otherwise noted; fit to one page wide.

- Account listing
  - Include columns for **Account** and **Type** only. Make sure the account names are fully visible. [**TIP**: You should include all accounts that you think will be needed given the preceding information. Make sure you organize the accounts so that your future financial statements will look professional.]

- Item listing (**landscape orientation**)
  - Include columns for **Item**, **Description**, **Type**, **Asset Account**, **Cost**, **Account**, **Price**, **Sales Tax Code**, **Preferred Vendor** only.

- Customer contact list
  - Include columns for **Customer**, **Bill To**, **Sales Tax Code**, **Tax Item**, and **Terms** only.

- Vendor contact list
  - Include columns for **Vendor**, **Bill from**, and **Terms** only.

Assignment 12B

Chewy's

You can't believe how fast your catering business is growing. It's time to get more serious about your accounting system. (You've been keeping track of everything in your notebook!) You decide to go with QuickBooks.

You're going to convert your accounting records as of 1/1/18.

Here's how your business is currently set up:

- You're organized as a sole proprietorship.
  - Fiscal year begins in January.
  - Tax ID # is 111-11-2222.
  - Your address is 3835 Freeport Blvd., Sacramento, CA 95822.

- You have no employees.

- You have a number of different catered meal options:
  - Casual Lunch ($15/person).
  - Elegant Lunch ($25/person).
  - Picnic at Home ($10/person).
  - Dinner Extraordinaire ($60/person).
  - Family Dinner ($25/person).
  - Romantic Dining ($40/person).

- You purchase all of your ingredients for your catering jobs on the day before the event. You leave anything left over (maybe a half jar of peanut butter or one too many apples!) with the customer.

- You use your customer's dinnerware and serving ware for the events. You do have cookware of your own that you prefer to use.

- You have a van that you use for the business. You owed $18,900 in principal to the bank as of 12/31. (Interest was paid through 12/31 before year-end.) Your bank is City Bank of Sacramento (321 Main St, Sacramento, CA 95822). [**TIP**: You show the entire balance as a long-term liability. You'll adjust that at the end of the year if necessary.]

- Now that you will be using QuickBooks, you will be purchasing a computer and printer for the business.

- You do all the cooking at the customer's home, so you don't need a facility. (If there's something you need to prepare in advance, you simply make it at home.) You do have a separate phone for Chewy's business, though.

- You want to track your profit on the basic event types (Lunch, Dinner, Other).

- All catering charges are taxable. The rate is 8 % and the agency is Board of Equalization, 3565 Green Street, Sacramento, CA 95822. Terms are Net 15.

- You bill for services on the day of the event. The bill is due upon receipt.
  - You do have one customer, an old friend, who, as of 1/1, hasn't paid you for several events in December.
    - Jeannie Williams
      2982 Skyline Blvd
      Sacramento, CA 95822
  - Her unpaid bills (terms Net 15) were:
    - 12/15—invoice #412, Romantic Dining for 2; $86.40 including tax.
    - 12/22—invoice #415, Dinner Extraordinaire for 10; $648.00 including tax.

- You hadn't paid your phone bill for December as of 1/1. The total due (on invoice #1216, dated 12/29) was $74.96.
  - Sacramento Phone Co
    6245 L Street
    Sacramento, CA 95822
  - Net 30

- You have a credit card (CityCard) with City Bank of Sacramento. Terms are Net 15.

- You use your credit card to purchase almost everything you use, so you don't have many vendors to keep track of. You paid your credit card bill on 12/27. You only had two charges after that. Both of them were for a "thank you" lunch you gave for some of your best customers.
  - Kringle's Bakery: $125.00 on 12/28.
  - Splendid Coffee: $22.45 on 12/29.

- Here's your bank reconciliation as of 12/31:

Chewy's Bank Reconciliation—12/31		
Balance per bank		$5,546.75
Deposits in transit		0.00
Outstanding checks:		
#4722—12/26	$114.00	
#4725—12/27	285.00	399.00
Balance per book		$5,147.75

Ck 4722 was made out to WorkSmart Office for purchase of office supplies.
Ck 4725 was made out to Knifty Knives for some new cooking equipment.

- Here's your trial balance as of 1/1:

 HINT: This is tricky. Make sure you look at what's already recorded in the general ledger from the preceding transactions before you start making your journal entry.

Chewy's Trial Balance—As of 1/1		
	DEBIT	**CREDIT**
Cash.	$5,147.75	
Accounts receivable.	734.40	
Supplies on hand	186.00	
Prepaid insurance.	400.00	
Van.	21,000.00	
Cookware	3,685.00	
Accumulated depreciation		$4,880.00
Accounts payable.		74.96
Sales tax payable.		54.40
CityCard payable		147.45
LT note payable		18,900.00
Owner's equity		7,096.34
	$31,153.15	**$31,153.15**

REPORTS TO CREATE FOR ASSIGNMENT 12B

All reports should be in portrait orientation unless otherwise noted; fit to one page wide

- Account listing
  - Include columns for **Account** and **Type** only. Make sure the account names are fully visible. [**TIP**: You should include all accounts that you think will be needed given the preceding information. Make sure you organize the accounts so that your future financial statements will look professional.]

- Item listing
  - Include columns for **Item**, **Description**, **Type**, **Account**, **Price**, and **Sales Tax Code**.

- Customer contact list
  - Include columns for **Customer**, **First Name**, **Last Name**, **Bill To**, **Sales Tax Code**, **Tax Item**, and **Terms** only.

- Vendor contact list
  - Include columns for **Vendor**, **Bill from**, and **Terms** only.

- Open Invoices as of 1/1/18 (one of the **Customers & Receivables** reports)
  - Include columns for **Type**, **Date**, **Num**, **Terms**, **Due Date**, and **Open Balance** only.

- Check Detail (12/1 to 12/31/17) (one of the **Banking** reports)
  - Include columns for **Type**, **Num**, **Date**, **Name**, and **Paid Amount** only.

- Balance Sheet as of 1/1/18.

QuickBooks Online

After completing Chapter 13, you should:

1. Have a basic understanding of the differences between Quick-Books Online and QuickBooks Desktop.

2. Be familiar with the basic structure of QuickBooks Online.

Objectives

Writing about QuickBooks Online is a little like trying to throw a dart at a moving target. By the time the chapter is written, the software has changed! So fair warning: The information and screenshots in this chapter are based on QuickBooks Online Plus as it existed at the beginning of 2016.

Of course, continuous change is one of the benefits of QuickBooks Online. Corrections can be made and new features can be added without users needing to download and install a new release. Given the popularity of cloud computing, Intuit is choosing to put a great deal of energy into developing its online accounting software products, and that benefits all users.

There are currently four primary versions of QuickBooks Online.

Version	Basic Features	Number of Users Allowed
Self-Employed	Can track income and expenses. Can download transactions from bank and credit card accounts.	1
Simple Start	Has all the features of Self-Employed plus the user can create estimates and invoices.	1
Essentials	Has all the features of Simple Start plus the user can enter and pay vendor bills. More extensive reports are available.	3
Plus	Has all the features of Essentials plus the user can track inventory, track employee hours, use classes, and create budgets. More extensive reporting.	5

Payroll is an add-on feature available to users of Simple Start, Essentials, and Online. There is also a QuickBooks Online Accountant version that includes additional features for those users who are working with multiple clients.

QuickBooks Online is a subscription service. Users pay a monthly fee based on the version of QuickBooks being used.

COMPARISON OF QUICKBOOKS ONLINE PLUS TO QUICKBOOKS PREMIER

There are a number of similarities between QuickBooks Online Plus and QuickBooks Premier. Both use **lists** and **transaction types**. **Account types** exist in QuickBooks Online, although they're referred to as **category types**. Budgeting is possible in both as is segment reporting (using **classes**). **Lists** and reports can be customized. Access to various areas can be limited by user. Transactions and reports can be memorized in both systems.

There are differences, however. Here are some features in QuickBooks Online Plus that aren't available in QuickBooks Premier:

- Remote access.
  - You can log in to your company file from any computer, anywhere.

- Location tracking.
  - In addition to using classes to track segments, **locations** can be set up. For example, let's say you own an architecture firm with three main specialties: commercial remodel, new residential, and residential remodel. You have offices in New York, Los Angeles, and Chicago. You could use **classes** to track by type of business and **location** to track by office.

- Automatic upgrades.
- Easy import of bank and credit card transactions.
  - Bank transactions can be downloaded into QuickBooks Premier using .iff files, but not as efficiently.
- First in, first out (FIFO) inventory valuation.
  - QuickBooks Premier uses an average cost.

Here are some features in QuickBooks Premier that aren't available in QuickBooks Online:

- Ability to adjust inventory values as well as quantities.
  - QuickBooks Online will allow for adjustment of quantities, but the valuation is automatic.
- Ability to run more than one company with the same product.
  - Although you can have more than one company in QuickBooks Online, a separate subscription fee is required for each one.
- Sales orders.
- Assembled inventory items.
  - QuickBooks Premier can be used by light manufacturing companies.
    - QuickBooks Online does have a **Bundle** item type that allows you to group products and services that are normally sold together.
- Manual payroll processing.
  - Without a payroll subscription, payroll can only be entered through journal entries in QuickBooks Online.
- More robust **Find** feature.
  - In QuickBooks Online, the search filter combinations are limited.
- Local backups.
  - Although company files in QuickBooks Online are, of course, backed up by Intuit, a user doesn't have automatic access to them. There is a "local copy" feature available. The downloaded file is stored as an .xml or .qbxml file, but these files cannot be easily imported back into QuickBooks Online.

There are other differences but these are some of the more significant. In general, there are far more features available in the desktop versions than there are in the online versions. There are more reports and more options. Although the term **preference** isn't used in QuickBooks, there are some options available as **settings**. There are just far fewer of them.

> **BEHIND THE SCENES** For those of you who are interested, here's the security process for QuickBooks Online:
> 1. Any data added or edited is written to two hard drives automatically.
> 2. Data is periodically copied to a third-party hard drive.
> 3. Data is backed up to tape each night.

A BRIEF LOOK AT QUICKBOOKS ONLINE

The Home page of QuickBooks Online looks something like this for Sac City Accounting Services:

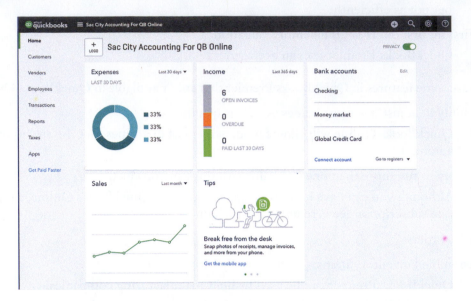

This area is probably most like the main menu bar in Premier.

- Clicking **Account and Settings** allows you to change options (similar to **preferences**).

- You can set user controls by clicking **Manager Users**.

- Templates can be modified in **Custom Form Styles**.

- **Lists** (**chart of accounts**, **product and services**, etc.) can be accessed from this screen.

- Tools such as reconciling and budgeting can also be accessed here.

- One of the more interesting links is **QuickBooks Labs**. Clicking the link opens a screen showing experimental plug-ins available. Users can see demos or even turn on the plug-ins. Options listed here are often incorporated into the product if user response is positive.

The icon bar on the left side of the Home page functions much like the icon bar in Premier:

If **Customers** is clicked, the following screen appears:

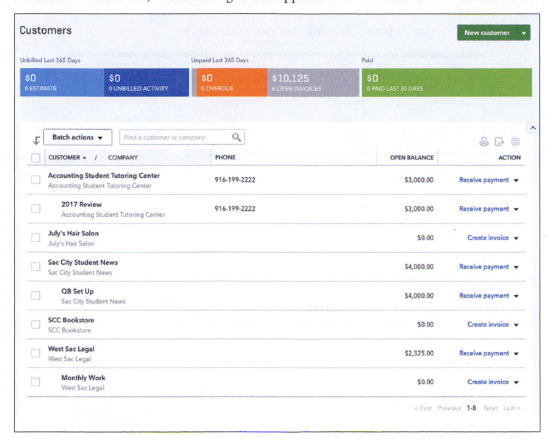

Similar to a **Customer Center**, customers can be added or edited here. Clicking a specific customer allows you to see transaction detail and enter new transactions. Similar screens are available for vendors and employees.

In the top right corner of the screen are four useful links.

Clicking the **magnifying glass** opens a search screen. Clicking the **?** opens a Help window.

Clicking the **gear** opens the following screen:

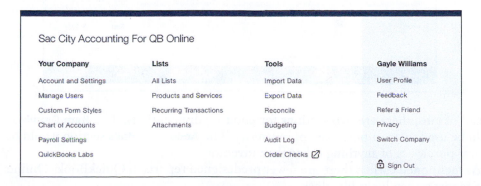

Here you can manage the chart of accounts and the product list and you can access various management tools.

Clicking the + icon opens following the following screen:

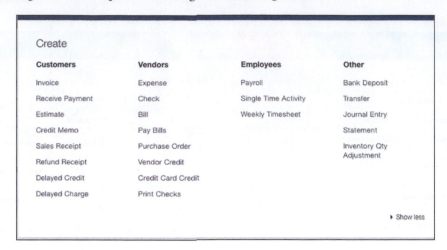

Here you can easily open the form necessary to enter a transaction.

The forms in QuickBooks Online are similar to those in Premier. For example, the **bill** form looks like this:

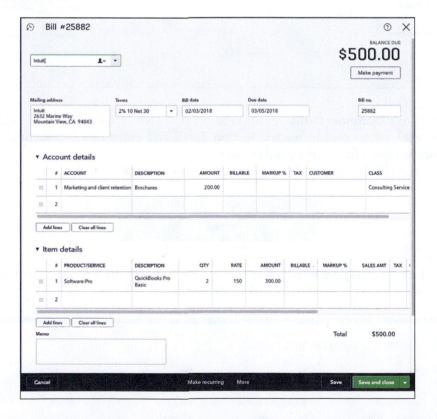

Instead of tabs, there are two sections for entering distributions. The **Item Details** section would be used to enter purchases of inventory. The **Account Details** section would be used to enter purchases of anything other than inventory.

As mentioned earlier, there are fewer predesigned reports in QuickBooks Online. The main report screen looks like this:

There are, of course, a number of different reports available in each category. Reports can be modified and memorized.

This gives you a very brief introduction to QuickBooks Online. Remember this: If you understand accounting principles, you can successfully use any accounting software application. New systems just take some practice and a willingness to search out what you need.

Optional Extra Credit Assignments

Extra Credit Assignments are available in myBusinessCourse (MBC).

OPPORTUNITY 1: LANGUAGE TUTORING SERVICES

You recently earned your degree in Linguistics, and you are having trouble finding a job. After considering all your alternatives, you decide to open your own business. You offer tutoring sessions for individuals wanting to learn a new language. You also sell language learning software programs for use at home. You keep a reasonable quantity of software programs on hand at all times.

You offer tutoring sessions, personally, in two different languages—French and Chinese. You also hire one employee, Felicia Kahlo, who tutors in two languages (Spanish and Russian).

Individuals are able to purchase individual sessions ($25 per session) or packages of 30 sessions ($650). Each session lasts one hour. All tutoring takes place in an office space you're renting from Econo Space at a cost of $300 per month.

You sell the language software programs for $200 each. Each of the four languages offered for tutoring has a separate software program. You purchase the software programs from a company called Learning Resources, Inc. They sell the programs to you for $125 each. The Sacramento sales tax rate is 8.75%.

Most customers pay at time of purchase (that is, at the end of a tutoring session or when software is purchased), but you sell on account as well. One of your customers, CIA Preparatory Academy, paid you in advance on December 29th for sessions to be held in January 2018.

Additional information:

1. You organized the company as a sole proprietorship. Your year-end is 12/31. You started business on 12/1/17.

2. You use class tracking (one class for each language and one for administration).

3. On 12/1/2017:

   a. You contributed $5,000 (cash) to start your new company.

   b. You paid your December rent plus a security deposit of $500 with check #101. (You signed a five-year lease agreement. The security deposit is refundable at the end of the lease period.)

477

    c. You paid the premium for a six-month insurance policy. Policy period was 12/1/17 to 5/31/18.

You ask a friend of yours to handle the accounting for you. She did the best she could, but she hasn't had any accounting training. When you look at the statements for December, you discover that she had made seven accounting errors.

To Do:

Find and correct the seven errors.

 HINT: Read the information above carefully. Look carefully at the Balance Sheet, the Profit and Loss Statement, and the Profit and Loss by Class Statement.

NOTE: There are no errors in transaction amounts. The errors are in timing (when the revenue or expense was recognized), entry (debit/credit issues), or presentation (including account classification).

Reports To CREATE For Extra Credit:

- Corrected balance sheet as of 12/31/17.
- Corrected profit and loss statement for December by class.

OPPORTUNITY 2: SAFE AT HOME

When you were in college, you earned some extra money housesitting for some of your friends' parents. It was a great way to get some quiet time for studying and earn some money for tuition and books at the same time. After you graduated, you realized that you wanted to start your own business. You needed an idea that didn't take a lot of up-front cash but could be expanded into a bigger operation. You knew that there was a demand for housesitting services. You also knew that there was a ready supply of college students and others who were looking for occasional jobs. The only thing missing was the go-between. With your experience, you were confident that you could match the homeowner who didn't want to leave an empty house with the person looking for some extra money. Your new company, Safe At Home, was born.

    You work out of a small office you're renting downtown for $400 per month on a two-year lease. You purchased a computer and some furniture.

    Your clients pay you a fee for connecting them with a housesitter. They, not you, pay the person who housesits for them. The client fees are $10 per night or $60 per week. There is a $2 per night ($10 per week) surcharge if pet care will be required. You bill your clients when they sign up for the service, and 50% of the fee is due before the service begins. The balance of the fee is due two days after the service ends. You offer a full refund for early returns.

    Additional information:

1. You organized the company as a sole proprietorship. Your year-end is 12/31. You started business on 12/1/17.
2. You use class tracking (two classes—Housesitting and Administrative).
3. You contributed $5,000 (cash) to start your new company.

4. You purchased the computer and furniture on 11/1/17 but didn't place it in service until 12/1/17.

   a. You paid $2,700 for the computer. You expect it to last three years with no salvage value.

   b. You paid $600 for the furniture. You expect that to last five years with no salvage value.

5. On 12/1/2017:

   a. You paid your landlord $1,200 ($400 refundable security deposit plus first and last month's rent).

   b. You paid the premium for a six-month insurance policy. Policy period was 12/1/17 to 5/31/18.

   c. You paid $25 to place an ad in the December 8th newspaper.

6. All of your December clients (except Martin and Rebecca Loan) returned home by 12/31/17. (Service dates are included on invoices.)

7. On 12/31/17, you had $30 worth of office supplies on hand.

You asked your brother to record the transactions for you in QuickBooks. He did the best he could, but he hasn't had any accounting training. When you look over the statements for December, you discover that he had made eight accounting errors.

To Do:

Find and correct the eight errors.

 HINT: Read the preceding information carefully. Look carefully at the Balance Sheet, the Profit and Loss Statement, and the Profit and Loss by Class Statement.).

NOTE: All eight errors are in timing (when the revenue or expense was recognized), entry (debit/credit issues), or presentation (including classification of account). There are no errors in the transaction amounts.

Reports To CREATE For Extra Credit:

- Corrected balance sheet as of 12/31/17.

- Corrected profit and loss statement for December by class.

Is Computerized Accounting Really the Same as Manual Accounting?

Before we compare computerized and manual accounting, let's briefly review the basics of accounting.

Accounting is an information system. The primary purposes of the system are:

- To identify and record accounting transactions.

- To analyze, summarize, and report information about business activities.

Accounting equation An expression of the equivalency of the economic resources and the claims upon those resources of a business, often stated as Assets = Liabilities + Stockholders' Equity.

We identify accounting transactions by considering the impact, if any, of an economic event on the **accounting equation**. If any of the elements in the equation (assets, liabilities, or equity) change as the result of the event, it's an accounting transaction and must be recorded.

> **BEHIND THE SCENES** **Assets** are resources with future benefit that the entity owns or has a right to. **Liabilities** are obligations of the entity payable with money, product, or service. **Equity** represents owner claims on the assets of the entity. Equity includes owner investments in the company plus any undistributed earnings. The components of earnings are **revenues** (amounts earned for the sale of a product or performance of a service) and **expenses** (costs incurred to generate revenues).

Journal entries An entry of accounting information into a journal.

Debits An entry on the left side (or in the debit column) of an account.

Credits An entry on the right side (or in the credit column) of an account.

We record accounting transactions using the double-entry bookkeeping system. Accounting transactions are expressed as **journal entries**. Each journal entry includes the date of the transaction, the names of the accounts to be debited and credited, and the amounts. Every journal entry must balance (the sum of the debit amounts must equal the sum of the credit amounts) so that the accounting equation stays in balance. **Debits** increase the asset, expense, and dividend accounts (credits decrease those accounts). **Credits** increase liability, equity, and revenue accounts (debits decrease those accounts).

Journal entries are recorded in (posted to) the appropriate accounts. All the accounts and the all activity in all the accounts are collectively known as the general ledger. Accounts are often depicted like this (referred to as T-accounts):

481

Account Name

Debit	Credit

Accrual basis of accounting
Accounting method whereby sales revenue is recorded when earned and realized and expenses are recorded in the period in which they help to generate the sales revenue.

Cash basis of accounting
Accounting method whereby sales revenue is recorded when cash is received from operating activities and expenses are recorded when cash payments related to operating activities are made.

To understand when and how journal entries are made, you need to know the method of accounting being used by the entity. The two primary methods are the **accrual basis of accounting** and the **cash basis of accounting**.

There are a few basic accounting principles that are fundamental to understanding when to record revenue and expenses under the accrual method of accounting. These are part of the body of generally accepted accounting principles (GAAP) that guide accountants.

- Revenue recognition principle—Revenue should be recognized when the earnings process is complete and collectibility of the revenue is reasonably certain.

- Expense recognition (matching) principle—Expenses should be recognized in the same period as the related revenue. In other words, expenses incurred to generate revenue should be recognized with the revenue generated.

Under the cash basis of accounting, revenue is recognized when collected and expenses are recognized when paid. The cash basis of accounting is not allowed under GAAP, but cash-based reports can provide useful information to management, so some companies prepare both accrual and cash basis reports.

The primary way we summarize and report information about business activities is through the preparation of four basic financial statements. These statements are issued at the end of an accounting period (generally a month, quarter, or year).

- The **balance sheet** presents the financial condition of the entity as a point in time.
  - All asset, liability, and equity accounts appear on the balance sheet.
  - The balance sheet is also known as the statement of financial position.

- The **income statement** presents the operating results of the entity for a period of time.
  - All revenue and expense accounts appear on the income statement.
  - The income statement is also known as the profit and loss statement or statement of operations.

- The **statement of cash flows** presents the cash inflows and outflows over a period of time.
  - The cash flows are grouped into three categories: operating activities, investing activities, and financing activities.

- The **statement of stockholders' (or owner's) equity** presents the change in equity during a period of time.
  - The changes would include any additional investments from owners, any distributions to owners, and operating earnings (or losses) during the period.

ACCRUAL AND CASH BASIS ACCOUNTING IN QUICKBOOKS

Most companies use the accrual basis of accounting. However, records can be maintained on a cash basis in QuickBooks. All revenues would be recorded as **sales receipts** when collected. All expenses would be recorded using **cash**.

You can also choose to use the accrual basis for recording transactions in QuickBooks but prepare reports under the cash basis. To automatically display all reports using the cash basis, the user can change the default in the **Reports & Graphs** tab of the **Preferences** screen from Accrual to Cash. To change a single open report, the user must click **Modify Report** and select **Cash** as the **Report Basis** on the **Display** tab.

There are some issues with converting accrual reports to cash basis reports. For example, QuickBooks does not adjust balance sheet accounts like prepaid expenses or supplies on hand when converting from accrual to cash. Depreciation and bad debt expense are also included on reports converted to the cash basis in QuickBooks. These issues result in inaccurate reports.

One solution is to create the cash basis reports in QuickBooks, export them to Excel, and then make any additional adjustments necessary to fully convert from accrual to cash.

COMPARISON OF COMPUTERIZED AND MANUAL ACCOUNTING SYSTEMS

As stated in Chapter 1, a computerized accounting system is **fundamentally** the same as a manual accounting system. If that's true, we should be able to find the same journal entries, journals, general ledger accounts (T-accounts), and trial balances in QuickBooks that you would find in a manual system, right? They might look a little different but they should be there.

Journal Entries

As you've learned, QuickBooks creates a journal entry for almost every **form** completed by the user. Let's take a look at the entry underlying check #1010, dated 12/1.

✓ Find check #1010 to see the **form** you used to enter the transaction.

    ○ Use CTRL F and filter by **Number** (1010) on the **Advanced** tab to find the check. (Put 1010 in the first field under **Number**.)

✓ Click **Go To** to open the form. The screen looks like this:

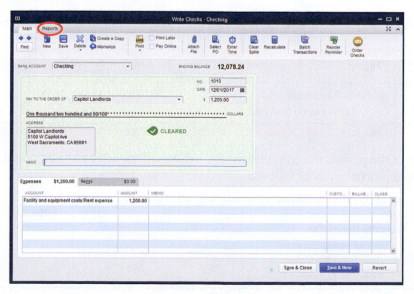

✓ Click the **Reports** tab at the top of the **Write Checks** window.

✓ Click **Transaction Journal**. The report looks like this:

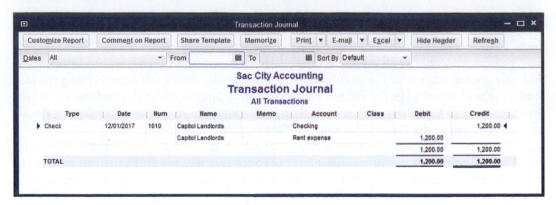

This is the journal entry that was created when you entered the payment of rent with check #1010.

Journals

In manual systems, separate journals (sometimes called special journals) are maintained for different types of transactions (sales, purchases, etc.). This simply makes it easier for the user when entering transactions. Special journals are used so that transactions for the period (usually a month) can be posted in summary (instead of in detail) to the general ledger. In QuickBooks, each transaction (in detail) is automatically posted to the general ledger, so special journals aren't needed to simplify posting.

As an example, the Sales Journal might look something like this in a manual system:

Date	Customer	Invoice #	Cash (DR)	A/R (DR)	Bookkeeping Services (CR)	Consulting Services (CR)	F/S Reviews (CR)
12/5	July's Hair Salon.........	103		320.00	320.00		
12/21	Sac City Student News....	100	3,200.00				3,200.00
12/29	West Sac Legal	104		1,500.00	1,000.00	500.00	
	TOTALS		3,200.00	1,820.00	1,320.00	500.00	3,200.00

Each transaction is recorded, in full, on a separate line instead of in journal entry form.

BEHIND THE SCENES In journal entry form, the first line (invoice #103) would be:

	Accounts Receivable	320.00	
	Bookkeeping Services		320.00

At the end of the period, the columns are totaled and all the sales transactions are recorded in one single journal entry as follows:

	Cash	3,200.00	
	Accounts Receivable	1,820.00	
	Bookkeeping Services		1,320.00
	Consulting Services		500.00
	Financial Statement Reviews		3,200.00

> **BEHIND THE SCENES** Most companies using manual systems record cash sales in the Cash Receipts Journal, not the Sales Journal. Cash sales are included in the preceding Sales Journal simply for purposes of illustration.

Although QuickBooks doesn't automatically create special journal reports, a user can create a similar report fairly easily. These reports can be memorized so they can be easily accessed every month. (Memorizing reports is covered in Chapter 11.)

✓ On the main menu bar, click **Reports/Custom Reports/Transaction Detail**.

✓ In the **Modify Report** window (**Display** tab), make the following changes:
  ○ Change the dates to 12/1/17 to 12/31/17.
  ○ In the **Columns** box only check **Type**, **Date**, **Num**, **Name**, **Debit**, and **Credit**.
  ○ Select **Account List** in the **Total by** dropdown menu.

✓ On the **Filters** tab of the **Modify Report** window, select **Transaction Type** in the left-most box.
  ○ Using the dropdown menu under **Transaction Type**, select **Multiple Transaction Types**.
  ○ Select **Invoice** and **Sales Receipt** and click **OK**.

✓ On the **Header/Footer** tab of the **Modify Report** window, change the default description in the **Report Title** field to Sales Journal and click **OK**.

Your report looks something like this:

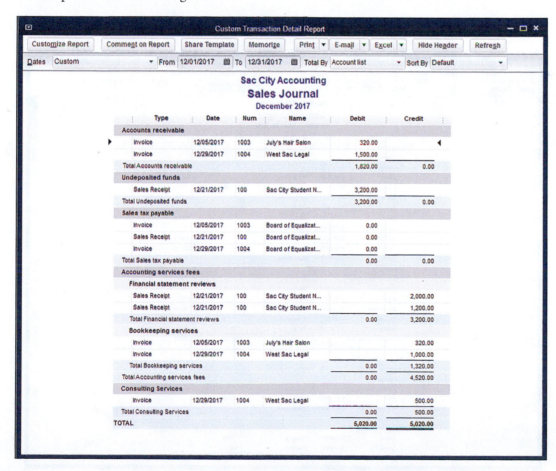

There are a few differences between the two journals. In the QuickBooks Sales Journal:

- The accounts are listed in rows instead of columns.

- The Undeposited Funds account (not Cash) is referenced. This is because the entry to record the cash was created when the **sales receipt** form was created, not when the **deposit** form was completed.

There is also an extra account listed on the QuickBooks report: Sales Tax Payable. That account is listed because Sac City Accounting was set up (by the author) to include taxable sales transactions. (Taxable sales of merchandise is covered in Chapter 5.) This account would not appear on the report if Sac City Accounting were strictly a service company.

As you can see, the formatting might be slightly different, but the information provided is the same in both journals (Date, Customer name, Invoice #, and the debit and credit amounts).

General Ledger and T-Accounts

There is, of course, a general ledger in QuickBooks. You can easily create a report to see the individual activity in a specific account in QuickBooks. It doesn't look exactly like a T-account, but it is close.

✓ On the main menu bar, click **Reports/Accountant & Taxes/General Ledger**.

✓ Change the dates to 12/1/17 to 12/31/17.

✓ Click **Customize Report**.

✓ In the **Columns** box, only check **Type**, **Date**, **Debit**, **Credit**, and **Balance**.

The first part of the report looks something like this:

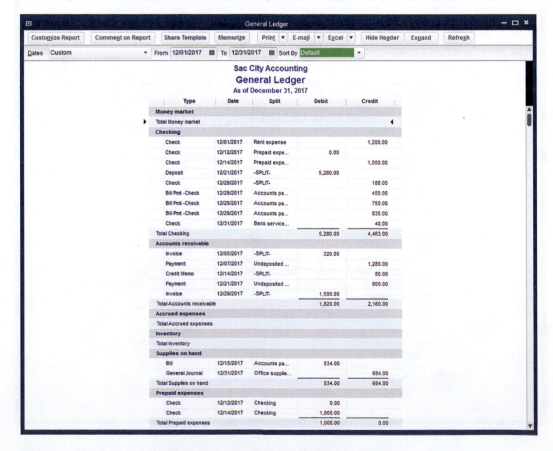

As you can see, the balances of the T-accounts are shown in a separate column in QuickBooks instead of at the bottom of each T-account. It's a slightly different format than the T-accounts you're familiar with from your financial accounting courses, but the information is the same.

If you want to create a report showing the activity for one account only, it's best to create a custom report. (If you filter the **general ledger** report for a specific account, all the accounts will still be listed. Only the account selected will show activity, however. It makes for an odd-looking report!)

✓ Click **Reports/Custom Reports/Transaction Detail** from the main menu bar.

✓ On the **Display** tab of the **Modify Report** window:

  ○ Change the dates to 12/1/17 to 12/31/17.

  ○ Select only **Date**, **Debit**, **Credit**, and **Balance** in the **Columns** box.

✓ On the **Filters** tab, select **Account** in the **Filter** box.

✓ Select **Bookkeeping services** in the **Account** dropdown box.

✓ On the **Header/Footer** tab, change the **Report Title to Bookkeeping Services Revenue**.

✓ Click **OK**.

The report looks something like this:

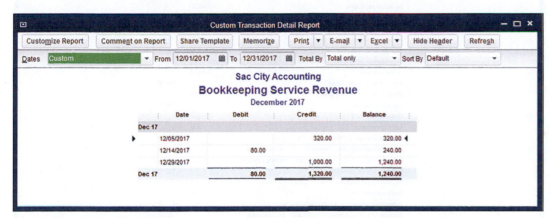

Trial Balances

A trial balance is a report listing all the accounts and their balances at a point in time. In a manual system, trial balances are prepared for two primary reasons:

* To make sure the debits equal the credits in the general ledger.

* To use as a worksheet for preparing the financial statements.

In a computerized system like QuickBooks, users don't need a trial balance for those reasons. Why? First, the program will not allow the user to create an unbalanced entry. (Unless, of course, the system malfunctions!) Second, QuickBooks prepares the financial statements automatically.

Trial balance reports are available in QuickBooks, however, and can be useful for other reasons.

A simple trial balance is created as follows:

✓ Click **Reports** on the main menu bar.

✓ Click **Accountant & Taxes**.

✓ Click **Trial Balance**.

✓ Change the date to 1/1/17 to 12/31/17.

> **BEHIND THE SCENES** It's really only the ending date that determines the amounts on a trial balance report. If you enter 12/31/17 in both the **From** and **To** fields, you will get the same amounts as you get entering 1/1/17 in the **From** field and 12/31/17 in the **To** field. Remember, a trial balance shows us the account balances at a **point in time** (not a period of time). However, entering a specific period of time allows you to see all the transactions that occurred during the identified period when an account balance is double-clicked.

The report looks something like this:

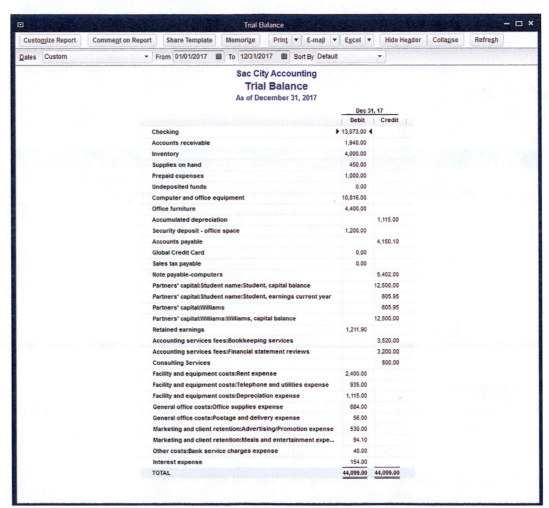

QuickBooks includes all accounts in a **Trial Balance** report that have had activity during the fiscal year, even if the balance is $0 at the report date. The nice thing about that feature is that the user can double-click on an account with a zero ending balance and see the activity for the period.

BEHIND THE SCENES In the preceding report, Retained Earnings shows a $1,211.90 debit balance, and the two partner equity accounts for current year earnings show a combined credit balance of $1,211.90. That's because of an entry made as part of the Practice Exercises to allocate the earnings to the partners. Without that entry, retained earnings would have a zero balance, as would the two current year earnings accounts for the partners.

In Chapter 4, we covered closing an accounting period. The day after year-end, QuickBooks automatically zeros out the revenue and expense account balances, removes the **Net Income** line from the balance sheet, and adds the net income (or loss) amount for the period to the appropriate equity account. A post-closing trial balance report can then be prepared.

✓ Change the date of the report created above to 1/1/18.

The report looks something like this:

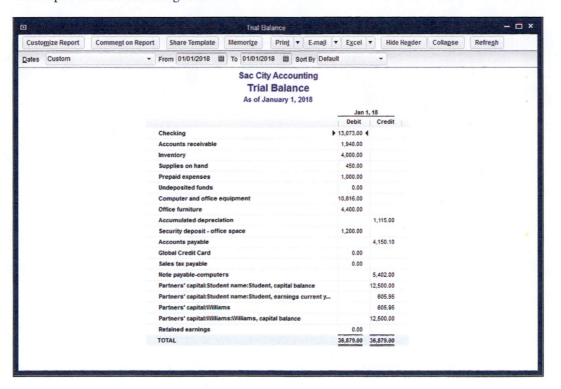

APPENDIX

B

How Do I?

HOW DO I? (GENERAL)

Manage Company Files

Create a new working file (.qbw file) from a backup file (.qbb) (Chapter 1)

1. Open QuickBooks Pro.
2. Click File/Open or Restore Company.
3. Click Restore a backup copy/Next.
4. Browse for location on server where backup is located.
5. Click Open.
6. Click Next.
7. Browse for location on USB where you want file created/Save.
8. Click OK.

Open a company working file (Chapter 1)

1. Open QuickBooks Pro.
2. Click File/Open or Restore Company.
3. Click Open a Company File/Next.
4. Browse for file on USB drive and double-click.

Back up a company file (Chapter 1)

1. Click File/Create Backup.
2. Click Local backup/Next.
3. Browse for location on USB where you want file saved/Next.
   a. Check Date and time stamp to clearly identify your backup files.
   b. Check Complete verification.
4. If you are saving to the USB containing your .qbw file, you will get a warning message. Click Use this Location.

5. Click Save it now/Next.

6. Check location and change name if desired.

Restore a backup file to an existing working file (Chapter 1)

1. Open the company file that you wish to override with the backup.

2. Click File/Open or Restore Company.

3. Click Restore a backup copy/Next.

4. Click Local Backup/Next.

5. Browse for location of backup file.

6. Click Open.

7. Click Next.

8. Click Continue.

9. Enter "YES".

Verify data (Chapter 7)

1. Click File/Utilities.

2. Click Verify Data.

Customize My Company File

Change the company name (Chapter 1)

1. Click Company/Company Information.

Change Icon Bar (Chapter 1)

1. Click View/Customize Icon Bar.

See what windows I have open (Chapter 1)

1. Click View/Open Window List.

Change preferences (Chapters 1, 9, 12)

1. Click Edit/Preferences.

Turn on manual payroll processing (Chapter 8)

1. Click Help.

2. Click QuickBooks Help.

3. Click the Search field.

4. Enter Manual Payroll.

5. Click Process payroll manually (without a subscription to QuickBooks Payroll).

6. On Step 1, click link to Manual Payroll Calculations.

7. Click Set my company file to use manual calculations.

Create budget (Chapter 10)

1. Click Company/Planning & Budgets.

2. Click Set up Budgets.

HOW DO I? (MANAGE LISTS)

Manage Chart Of Accounts

Add an account (Chapter 1)

1. Click Lists/Chart of Accounts.

2. Click Account/New.

Edit an account (Chapter 1)
1. Click Lists/Chart of Accounts.
2. Highlight account to change.
3. Click Account/Edit Account.

Delete an account (Chapter 1)
1. Click Lists/Chart of Accounts.
2. Highlight account to delete.
3. Click Account/Delete Account.

Make an account inactive (Chapter 7)
1. Click Lists/Chart of Accounts.
2. Highlight account.
3. Click Account/Make account inactive.

Merge two accounts (Chapter 7)
1. Click Lists/Chart of Accounts.
2. Highlight one of the accounts.
3. Click Account/Edit Account.
4. Change name so that it is identical to the name of the other account.

Manage Customer Records

Add a customer (Chapter 2)
1. Click Customer Center.
2. Click New Customer & Job/New Customer.

Edit a customer (Chapter 2)
1. Click Customer Center.
2. Highlight customer name.
3. Click Edit Customer.

Delete a customer (Chapter 2)
1. Click Customer Center.
2. Highlight customer name.
3. Right click/Delete Customer:Job.

Add a Job (Chapter 9)
1. Click Customer Center.
2. Highlight Customer.
3. Click New Customer & Job/Add Job.

Manage Vendor Records

Add a vendor (Chapter 3)
1. Click Vendor Center.
2. Click New Vendor.

Edit a vendor (Chapter 3)
1. Click Vendor Center.
2. Highlight Vendor.
3. Click Edit Vendor.

Delete a vendor (Chapter 3)

1. Click Vendor Center.
2. Highlight Vendor.
3. Right-click/Delete Vendor.

Set up 1099 vendor tracking for independent contractors (Chapter 3)

1. Click Edit/Preferences.
2. Select Tax:1099.
3. Click Company Preferences.
4. Check Yes.
5. Click dropdown menu for Box 7 and select general ledger account(s) used in recording payments to independent contractors.

Manage Employee Records

Add an employee (Chapter 8)

1. Click Employee Center.
2. Click New Employee.

Edit an employee (Chapter 8)

1. Click Employee Center.
2. Highlight employee to change.
3. Click Edit Employee.

Manage Item Records

Add item (Chapters 2 and 5)

1. Click List/Item List.
2. Click Item/New.

Edit item (Chapters 2 and 5)

1. Click List/Item List.
2. Highlight item to change.
3. Click Item/Edit item.

Delete item (Chapter 2)

1. Click List/Item List.
2. Highlight item to delete.
3. Click Item/Delete item.

Manage Payroll Item Records

Add payroll item (Chapter 8)

1. Click List/Payroll Item List.
2. Click Payroll Item/New.

Edit payroll item (Chapter 8)

1. Click List/Payroll Item List.
2. Highlight item to change.
3. Click Payroll Item/Edit Payroll Item.

HOW DO I? (RECORD TRANSACTIONS)

Record Sales Activity

Record cash sale (Chapter 2)

1. Click Home.
2. Click Create Sales Receipts.
   a. If Create Sales Receipts icon is not displayed:
      i. Click Edit/Preferences.
      ii. Select Desktop View.
      iii. Click Company Preferences.
      iv. Click Sales Receipts.

Record sale on account (Chapter 2)

1. Click Home.
2. Click Create Invoices.

Record customer credit memo (Chapter 2)

1. Click Home.
2. Click Refunds & Credits.

Record customer payments on account balances (Chapter 2)

1. Click Home.
2. Click Receive Payments.

Charge customers for billable time and expenses (Chapter 9)

1. Click Create Invoices (or Sales Receipts) on Home page.
2. Enter Customer:Job.
3. Click Select the outstanding billable time and costs option.
   a. Billable time and costs can also be accessed by clicking Add Time/Costs on the invoice or sales receipt.

Record Purchase Activity

Record vendor bill (Chapter 3)

1. Click Home.
2. Click Enter Bills.

Record vendor credit (Chapter 3)

1. Click Home.
2. Click Enter Bills.
3. Click Credit (top of page).

Record credit card purchase (Chapter 3)

1. Click Banking/Enter Credit Card Charges.

Record checks (not including payroll checks or checks written to record payment of bills previously recorded in QuickBooks) (Chapter 3)

1. Click Home.
2. Click Write Checks.

Record payment of vendor account balance (Chapter 3)

1. Click Home.
2. Click Pay Bills.

Record purchase order (Chapter 6)

1. Click Home.
2. Click Purchase Orders.

Receive inventory without a bill (Chapter 6)

1. Click Home.
2. Click dropdown menu next to Receive Inventory.
3. Click Receive Inventory Without Bill.

Receive inventory with the bill (Chapter 6)

1. Click Home.
2. Click dropdown menu next to Receive Inventory.
3. Click Receive Inventory With Bill.

Record bill received after inventory receipt has been recorded (Chapter 6)

1. Click Home.
2. Click Enter Bills Against Inventory.

Record payment of sales tax (Chapter 7)

1. Click Vendors.
2. Click Sales Tax.
3. Click Pay Sales Tax.

Record Payroll Activity

Enter a timesheet (Chapter 9)

1. Click Home.
2. Click dropdown menu next to Enter time.
3. Click Use Weekly Timesheet.

Pay an employee (Chapter 8)

1. Click Home.
2. Click Pay Employees.
3. Click Open Paycheck Detail to record taxes.

Pay payroll liabilities (Chapter 8)

1. Click Home.
2. Click Pay liabilities.

Record Bank And End Of Period Activity

Record deposits (Chapter 2)

1. Click Home.
2. Click Record Deposits.

Void checks (Chapter 3)

1. Open check to be voided.
   a. Click Edit/Find.
   b. Enter check number, payee, date or amount.
   c. Highlight check.
   d. Click Go To.
2. Click Edit/Void Check.

Record bank transfer (Chapter 7)

1. Click Banking/Transfer Funds.

Reconcile an account (Chapter 4)

1. Click Home.
2. Click Reconcile.

Record adjusting journal entries (Chapter 4)

1. Click Company.
2. Click Make General Journal Entries.

Adjust inventory quantities (Chapter 7)

1. Click Vendors/Inventory activities.
2. Click Adjust Quantity/Value on Hand.

Account and Transaction Types Used in QuickBooks Pro

ACCOUNT TYPES				
Bank	Accounts payable	Equity	Income	Cost of goods sold
Accounts receivable	Credit card		Other income	Expense
Other current asset	Other current liability			Other expense
Fixed asset	Long term liability			
Other asset				

TRANSACTION TYPES	DESCRIPTION
Bill	Bill received from vendor for purchase on account
Bill CCard	Payment on vendor balance using credit card
Bill Credit	Credit received from vendor
Bill Payment	Payment on vendor balance by cash or check
Build Assembly	Manufacture of unit(s)
CCard Refund	Refund to customer who paid with credit card
CCard Credit	Credit from vendor on credit card purchase
Check	Direct payment (not including payroll checks, payments on vendor balances, payments of payroll, or sales taxes)
Credit Card	Purchase using credit card
Credit Memo	Credit given to customer (cash or credit sales)
Deposit	Bank deposit
Estimate	Estimate of fees
Inventory Adjustment	Adjustment to inventory (quantity and/or value)
Invoice	Credit sale
Item Receipt	Receipt of inventory without bill
Journal	General journal entry
Liability Adjustment	Adjustment to payroll liability
Paycheck	Employee payroll check
Payment	Customer payment on account balance
Payroll Liability Check	Payment of payroll tax and employee withholdings
Purchase Order	Order to vendor
Sales Order	Order from customer
Sales Receipt	Cash sale
Sales Tax Payment	Remittance of state sales taxes
Statement Charge	Direct charge to customer account balance
Transfer	Transfers between cash accounts
YTD Adjustment	Adjustment of payroll items

Common Options Available on Various Form Toolbars

← and →: These options allow you to scroll through transactions of a similar type.

Save: Allows you to save the current transaction without closing the **form** or save the **form** as a PDF file.

✖: Allows you to delete the **form**.

Memorize: Allows you to memorize the **form**.

Print: Allows you to print the **form**.

Email: Allows you to email the **form**. **Forms** can be batched for sending by email.

Send/Ship tab: Allows you to arrange for shipping and to prepare shipping documents (FedEx or UPS).

Transaction History (on **Reports** tab): Allows you to look for transactions related to the current open **form.**

Transaction Journal (on **Reports** tab): Allows you to see the journal entry underlying the **form**.

Save & Close: Allows you to save the current **form** and exit.

Save & New: Allows you to save the current **form** and open a new **form** of the same type.

Clear: Allows you to "erase" all the data entered on the **form**. This would only be used in the initial creation of the **form**.

Revert: Allows you to return to the original saved **form**. This is only available when you open a saved **form**, make changes, and want to undo those changes. This would not be available if you had already saved the new version.

Additional Features

In this course, we covered the basic features in QuickBooks. There are many other features that you might consider exploring on your own. Here are some of the more commonly used features not covered in this textbook:

ADDITIONAL FEATURES RELATED TO THE SALES CYCLE

✓ Use sales estimates.

✓ Use sales orders.

✓ Prepare pick lists and packing slips.

✓ Assess finance charges on customer balances.

✓ Set customer credit limits.

✓ Set price levels.

✓ Set billing rate levels.

ADDITIONAL FEATURES RELATED TO THE PURCHASE CYCLE

✓ Track and bill for mileage.

✓ File 1096 and 1099 forms.

✓ Use **assembly items** in manufacturing companies.

APPENDIX F

What if I Have a Mac at Home?

This textbook covers the Windows version of QuickBooks. The trial version of Quick-Books that's included with the book is Windows based and the student data files provided to you for completing the practice exercises and the assignments are Windows based. So what do you do if you only have access to a Mac?

Here are some alternatives:

- You can create a virtual machine on your Mac where you can install Windows. Once the virtual machine is set up, you can download your trial version of QuickBooks using the directions in Chapter 1.

  - Two popular virtual machine programs for Mac are Parallels and VMware Fusion. You will need to purchase both a virtual machine program and a Windows license.

- You can purchase QuickBooks for Mac. You will then need to covert data so that it's accessible in the Mac program. To convert the data:

  - Create an initial .QBW file using a PC. (Your instructor should be able to direct you to school computers that could be used for this purpose.)

  - Choose **File** > **Utilities** > **Copy Company File for QuickBooks Mac**.

    ○ A Mac.QBB (backup) file will automatically be created. This should be saved to a USB drive.

  - In QuickBooks for Mac (on your Apple computer), choose **File** > **Open Company**.

  - Select the Mac backup on your USB and click **Open**.

  - Click **OK** when asked about restoring a QuickBooks for Windows file.

  - Enter a name for the restored file and click **Save**.

505

If you choose to use QuickBooks for Mac (the second alternative), be aware that there are differences between the Mac and Windows versions of QuickBooks. Some of the more important differences related to this course are:

- Manual payroll processing is not currently available in QuickBooks for Mac. You would need to work with your instructor on how to complete the assignments in Chapters 8-10.

- Certain data will not be converted. You would need to manually add or modify the data in QuickBooks for Mac for:
    - Open purchase orders
    - Customized forms

Although the basic look of the two programs is similar, there will be differences in how certain windows look and how certain transactions are entered. There is a QuickBooks for Mac 2016 User's Guide available at http://www.qblittlesquare.com/wp-content/uploads/2015/09/QBM-Users-Guide-150923-opt.pdf that is quite comprehensive and should help you navigate the program.

Glossary

A

Account A record of the additions, deductions, and balances of individual assets, liabilities, stockholders' equity, dividends, revenues, and expenses.

Accounting equation An expression of the equivalency of the economic resources and the claims upon those resources of a business, often stated as Assets = Liabilities + Stockholders' Equity.

Accounting period The time period, usually one year or less, to which periodic accounting reports are related.

Accounting The process of measuring the economic activity of a business in money terms and communicating those financial results to interested parties. The purpose of accounting is to provide financial information that is useful in economic decision making.

Accounting transaction An economic event that requires accounting recognition; an event that affects any of the elements of the accounting equation—assets, liabilities, or stockholders' equity.

Accounts receivable A current asset that is created by a sale of merchandise or the provision of a service on a credit basis. It represents the amount owed the seller by a customer.

Accrual basis of accounting Accounting procedures whereby sales revenue is recorded when earned and realized and expenses are recorded in the period in which they help to generate the sales revenue.

Accruals Adjustments that reflect revenues earned but not received or recorded and expenses incurred but not paid or recorded.

Allowance for doubtful accounts A contra-asset account with a normal credit balance shown on the balance sheet as a deduction from accounts receivable to reflect the expected uncollectible amount of accounts receivable.

Allowance method An accounting procedure whereby the amount of bad debts expense is estimated and recorded in the period in which the related credit sales occur.

B

Bad debt expense The expense stemming from the inability of a business to collect an amount previously recorded as receivable. It is normally classified as a selling or administrative expense.

Balance sheet A financial statement showing a business's assets, liabilities, and stockholders' equity as of a specific date.

C

Cash basis of accounting Accounting procedures whereby sales revenue is recorded when cash is received from operating activities and expenses are recorded when cash payments related to operating activities are made.

Classified balance sheet A balance sheet in which items are classified into subgroups to facilitate financial analysis and management decision making.

Closing process A step in the accounting cycle in which the balances of all temporary accounts are transferred to the Retained Earnings account, leaving the temporary accounts with zero balances.

Contra account An account with the opposite normal balance as other accounts of the same type..

Corporation A legal entity created under the laws of a state or the federal government. The owners of a corporation receive shares of stock as evidence of their ownership interest in the company.

Credit (entry) An entry on the right side (or in the credit column) of an account.

Credit memo A document prepared by a seller to inform the purchaser the seller has reduced the amount owed by the purchaser due to a return or an allowance.

D

Debit (entry) An entry on the left side (or in the debit column) of an account.

Direct write-off method An accounting procedure whereby the amount of bad debts expense is not recorded until specific uncollectible customer accounts are identified.

Double-entry accounting A method of accounting that results in the recording of equal amounts of debits and credits.

F

First-in, first-out (FIFO) method An inventory costing method that assumes that the oldest (earliest purchased) goods are sold first.

Fiscal year The annual accounting period used by a business.

Fraud Any act by the management or employees of a business involving an intentional deception for personal gain.

G

General ledger A grouping of all of a business's accounts that are used to prepare the basic financial statements.

Gross pay The amount an employee earns before any withholdings or deductions.

I

Income statement A financial statement reporting a business's sales revenue and expenses for a given period of time.

Internal controls The measures undertaken by a company to ensure the reliability of its accounting data, protect its assets from theft or unauthorized use, insure that employees follow the company's policies and procedures, and evaluate the performance of employees, departments, divisions, and the company as a whole.

J

Journal A tabular record in which business transactions are analyzed in debit and credit terms and recorded in chronological order.

Journal entry An entry of accounting information into a journal.

L

Last-in, first-out (LIFO) method An inventory costing method that assumes that the newest (most recently purchased) goods are sold first.

Lower of cost or market (LCM) A measurement method that, when applied to inventory, provides for ending inventory to be valued on the balance sheet at the lower of its acquisition cost or current replacement cost.

M

Materiality An accounting guideline that states that insignificant data that would not affect a financial statement user's decisions may be recorded in the most expedient manner.

Multiplestep income statement An income statement in which one or more intermediate performance measures, such as gross profit on sales, are derived before the continuing income is reported.

N

Net pay The amount of an employee's paycheck, after subtracting withheld amounts.

Normal balance The side (debit or credit) on which increases to the account are recorded.

P

Partnership A voluntary association of two or more persons for the purpose of conducting a business.

Periodic inventory A system that records inventory purchase transactions; the Inventory account and the cost of goods sold account are not updated until the end of the period when a physical count of the inventory is taken.

Perpetual inventory A system that records the cost of merchandise inventory in the Inventory account at the time of purchase and updates the Inventory account for subsequent purchases and sales of merchandise as they occur.

R

Reorder point The minimum level of inventory on hand that can safely meet demand until a new inventory order is received.

S

Sale on account A sale of merchandise or the provision of a service made on a credit basis.

Segment A subdivision of an entity for which supplemental financial information is disclosed.

Sole proprietorship A form of business organization in which one person owns the business.

Specific identification method An inventory costing method involving the physical identification of goods sold and goods remaining and costing these amounts at their actual costs.

Statement of cash flows A financial statement showing a firm's cash inflows and cash outflows for a specific period, classified into operating, investing, and financing activity categories.

Statement of stockholders' equity A financial statement presenting information regarding the events that cause a change in stockholders' equity during a period. The statement presents the beginning balance, additions to, deductions from, and the ending balance of stockholders' equity for the period.

Stock Inventory on hand.

Subsidiary ledger A ledger that provides detailed information about an account balance.

T

Trial balance A list of the account titles in the general ledger, their respective debit or credit balances, and the totals of the debit and credit balances.

W

Weighted average cost method An inventory costing method that calculates an average unit purchase cost, weighted by the number of units purchased at each price, and uses that weighted-average unit cost to determine the cost of goods sold for all sales.

INDEX

F

G

H

Q

R

S

T

W

Y

NOTES

NOTES

NOTES

NOTES